A Guide to 75 Tests for Special Education

Carolyn Compton, Ph.D.
Educational Director
Children's Health Council
Palo Alto, California

Fearon Education
a division of
David S. Lake Publishers
Belmont, California

Contributing Authors

Karen Travis
M.A., C.C.C., Speech and Language Pathologist and Bilingual Consultant

Joan Bisagno
M.S., Learning Disability Specialist

Polly Bredt
M.A., C.C.C., Speech and Language Pathologist

Barbara Fourt
OTR, Registered Occupational Therapist

Senior development editor: Janet Joers
Designer: McQuiston & Daughter
Cover designer: McQuiston & Daughter
Production editor: Kimberly Pesavento

Copyright © 1984 by David S. Lake Publishers, 19 Davis Drive, Belmont, California 94002. All rights reserved. No part of this book may be reproduced by any means, transmitted, or translated into a machine language without written permission from the publisher.

ISBN-0-8224-3583-7
Library of Congress Catalog Card Number: 83-62086
Printed in the United States of America.
1.9 8 7 6 5 4 3

Contents

LIST OF FIGURES v-vi
PREFACE vii-viii
ACKNOWLEDGMENTS ix-x
INTRODUCTION 1

Purposes of Testing 1
Screening 1
Diagnostic Testing 2
Program Planning 2
Evaluation 2
Abuses and Misuses of Tests 2
Types of Tests 3
Formal and Informal Tests 3
Individual and Group Tests 3
Diagnostic and Achievement Tests 3
Criterion-Referenced Tests 4
The Diagnostic Battery 4
Academic Skill Areas 4
Learning Processes and Modalities 4
Time and Personnel Available 5
Test Selection 6
Educational Relevance 6
Standardization, Validity, and Reliability 6
Design and Format 7
Appropriateness of Content 7
Time and Money 7
Inservice Training 8
Special Issues in Testing 8
The Use of Grade-Level Scores 8
Evaluating Progress 8
Testing the Student with Reading Problems 10
Measuring Reading Comprehension 11
Determining Instructional Level 12
The Diagnostic Report 12
Communicating Test Results to Parents 13
The Test Reviews 14

PART I: SKILL AREA TESTS 15

CHAPTER ONE: ACADEMIC TESTS 17
Achievement Tests 18
Wide Range Achievement Test 19
Peabody Individual Achievement Test 22
Basic Achievement Skills Individual Screener 26
Brigance Diagnostic Inventories 29
Reading Tests 33
Gray Oral Reading Tests 34
Gilmore Oral Reading Test 36
Spache Diagnostic Reading Scales 39
Durrell Analysis of Reading Difficulty 42
Gates-McKillop-Horowitz Reading Diagnostic Tests 46
McCarthy Individualized Diagnostic Reading Inventory 49
Woodcock Reading Mastery Tests 53
Gates-MacGinitie Silent Reading Tests 56
Test of Reading Comprehension 59
Spelling and Written Language Tests 62
Larsen-Hammill Test of Written Spelling 63
Diagnostic Achievement Test in Spelling 66
Diagnostic Analysis of Reading Errors 69
Diagnostic Spelling Potential Test 71
Myklebust Picture Story Language Test 73
Test of Written Language 77
Mathematics Tests 80
KeyMath Diagnostic Arithmetic Test 81
Enright™ Diagnostic Inventory of Basic Arithmetic Skills 86

CHAPTER TWO: PERCEPTION AND MEMORY TESTS 91
Comprehensive Tests 92
Detroit Tests of Learning Aptitude 93
Slingerland Screening Tests for Identifying Children with Specific Language Disability 102
Malcomesius Specific Language Disability Test 106
Auditory Tests 109
Wepman Auditory Discrimination Test 110
Goldman-Fristoe-Woodcock Test of Auditory Discrimination 112
Lindamood Auditory Conceptualization Test 114
Visual and Visual-Motor Tests 117
Marianne Frostig Developmental Test of Visual Perception 118
Motor-Free Visual Perception Test 125

The Bender Visual Motor Gestalt Test   130
Beery-Buktenica Developmental Test of Visual-Motor Integration   134

CHAPTER THREE: SPEECH AND LANGUAGE TESTS   139

Illinois Test of Psycholinguistic Abilities   141
Clinical Evaluation of Language Functions   148
Peabody Picture Vocabulary Test—Revised   155
Assessment of Children's Language Comprehension   157
Test for Auditory Comprehension of Language   159
Boehm Test of Basic Concepts   162
Token Test for Children   165
Northwestern Syntax Screening Test   167
Sequenced Inventory of Communication Development   169
Developmental Sentence Scoring   172
Environmental Language Inventory   176
Multilevel Informal Language Inventory   180
Expressive One-Word Picture Vocabulary Test   182
The Word Test   184
Test of Language Development   187
Test of Adolescent Language   191

CHAPTER FOUR: BILINGUAL (SPANISH-ENGLISH) LANGUAGE TESTS   195

Screening Test of Spanish Grammar   196
Prueba Illinois de Habilidades Psicolinguísticas   198
Ber-Sil Spanish Test   203
Dos Amigos Verbal Language Scales   205
Del Rio Language Screening Test   207
Bilingual Syntax Measure   209
Language Assessment Scales   212
Woodcock Language Proficiency Battery—Spanish   215

CHAPTER FIVE: GROSS MOTOR TESTS   219

Bruininks-Oseretsky Test of Motor Proficiency   220
Southern California Sensory Integration Tests   223

PART II: PRESCHOOL AND KINDERGARTEN TESTS   231

Denver Developmental Screening Test   233
Brigance Diagnostic Inventory of Early Development   237
Miller Assessment for Preschoolers   241
The Meeting Street School Screening Test   244
Basic School Skills Inventory   248
Preschool Language Scale   251
Kraner Preschool Math Inventory   254
Slingerland Pre-Reading Screening Procedures   257

PART III: GENERAL INTELLIGENCE TESTS AND DEVELOPMENTAL SCALES   263

Wechsler Intelligence Scale for Children—Revised   265
Stanford-Binet Intelligence Scale   276
Slosson Intelligence Test for Children and Adults   279
Leiter International Performance Scale and the Arthur Adaptation   282
Coloured Progressive Matrices   286
McCarthy Scales of Children's Abilities   290
Woodcock-Johnson Psycho-Educational Battery   293
Kaufman Assessment Battery for Children   300
System of Multicultural Pluristic Assessment   303
Goodenough-Harris Drawing Test   311

APPENDIX A: A GUIDE TO SPECIFIC TESTS FOR ASSESSING ACADEMIC SKILL AREAS   315
APPENDIX B: PROCESS-MODALITY CHART   318
APPENDIX C: EDUCATIONAL EVALUATION REPORT, SAMPLES 1 AND 2   320
APPENDIX D: A COMPARISON OF READING TESTS   324
APPENDIX E: THREE TESTS FOR ASSESSING ARTICULATION   325
APPENDIX F: A LIST OF TESTS THAT HAVE SPANISH TRANSLATIONS   328
APPENDIX G: A LIST OF TESTS APPROPRIATE FOR PRESCHOOL CHILDREN   329
GLOSSARY OF TESTING TERMS   330
REFERENCES   336
INDEX   339

List of Figures

Figure 1. PIAT Mathematics   23
Figure 2. PIAT Mathematics   23
Figure 3. PIAT Reading Recognition   23
Figure 4. PIAT Reading Comprehension   24
Figure 5. PIAT Spelling   24
Figure 6. PIAT Spelling   24
Figure 7. BASIS Mathematics Cluster   27
Figure 8. Brigance Inventories Examiner's Page for Initial Clusters Visually   30
Figure 9. Brigance Inventories Initial Clusters Visually   31
Figure 10. IDRI Reading Proficiency Levels   51
Figure 11. Woodcock Test Manual, Page 37   54
Figure 12. Gates-MacGinitie Vocabulary, Primary A, Form 1   57
Figure 13. Gates-MacGinitie Vocabulary, Survey D, Form 1   57
Figure 14. Gates-MacGinitie Comprehension, Primary A, Form 1   57
Figure 15. Gates-MacGinitie Comprehension, Primary C, Form 1   58
Figure 16. Gates-MacGinitie Comprehension, Survey D, Form 1   58
Figure 17. DATS Individualized Evaluation Form   67
Figure 18. TOWL Stimulus Picture   78
Figure 19. KeyMath Diagnostic Profile   84
Figure 20. Enright™ Skill Placement Test, Addition of Whole Numbers   87
Figure 21. Enright™ Examiner's Page for Addition of Whole Numbers   88
Figure 22. Enright™ Skill Test A-12   89
Figure 23. Enright™ Examiner's Page for Skill Test A-12   90
Figure 24. Detroit Tests   94
Figure 25. Detroit Pictorial Absurdities, Test 1   94
Figure 26. Detroit Pictorial Opposites, Test 3   96
Figure 27. Detroit Motor Speed and Precision, Test 5   97
Figure 28. Detroit Visual Attention Span for Objects, Test 9   98
Figure 29. Detroit Memory for Designs, Test 12   99
Figure 30. Detroit Visual Attention Span for Letters, Test 16   100

Figure 31. Detroit Disarranged Pictures, Test 17   100
Figure 32. Detroit Oral Directions, Test 18   101
Figure 33. DTVP Eye-Motor Coordination   119
Figure 34. DTVP Figure Ground   120
Figure 35. DTVP Constancy of Shape   121
Figure 36. DTVP Position in Space   122
Figure 37. DTVP Spatial Relations   123
Figure 38. MVPT, Section 1, Item 6   126
Figure 39. MVPT, Section 2, Item 12   127
Figure 40. MVPT, Section 3, Item 15   128
Figure 41. MVPT, Section 4, Item 29   129
Figure 42. MVPT, Section 5, Item 34   129
Figure 43. Bender, Plate I   131
Figure 44. Bender Error Types   132
Figure 45. VMI, Items 1, 2, 3   135
Figure 46. VMI, Items 10, 11, 12   136
Figure 47. VMI, Items 22, 23, 24   137
Figure 48. ITPA Summary Sheet   142
Figure 49. ITPA Profile Sheet   143
Figure 50. CELF Summary of Scores   150
Figure 51. TACL, Item 28   160
Figure 52. TACL, Item 63   161
Figure 53. Boehm Test, Form A, Item 4   163
Figure 54. ELI Recording Form   178
Figure 55. TOAL Three-Dimensional Model   192
Figure 56. TOAL Subtest Profile   193
Figure 57. SITPA Summary of Abilities   199
Figure 58. BSM Categories of Language Dominance   211
Figure 59. SCSIT Profile   230
Figure 60. DDST Scoring Sheet   235
Figure 61. Brigance Diagnostic Inventory of Early Development   238
Figure 62. Brigance Diagnostic Inventory of Early Development, Developmental Record Book   239
Figure 63. Slingerland Pre-Reading Screening Procedures, Procedure 1, Visual Perception   258
Figure 64. Slingerland Pre-Reading Screening Procedures, Procedure 2, Visual Perception   258
Figure 65. Slingerland Pre-Reading Screening Procedures, Procedure 3, Visual Perception and Memory   258
Figure 66. Slingerland Pre-Reading Screening Procedures, Procedure 4, Near-Point Copying   259

Figure 67. Slingerland Pre-Reading Screening Procedures, Procedure 5, Auditory-Visual Perception   259
Figure 68. Slingerland Pre-Reading Screening Procedures, Procedure 6, Letter Recognition   259
Figure 69. Slingerland Pre-Reading Screening Procedures, Procedure 7, Visual-Kinesthetic Memory   259
Figure 70. Slingerland Pre-Reading Screening Procedures, Procedure 8, Auditory Perception with Comprehension   260
Figure 71. Slingerland Pre-Reading Screening Procedures, Procedure 9, Far-Point Copying   260
Figure 72. Slingerland Pre-Reading Screening Procedures, Procedure 10, Auditory Discrimination   261
Figure 73. Slingerland Pre-Reading Screening Procedures, Procedure 11, Auditory-Visual-Kinesthetic Integration   261
Figure 74. Slingerland Pre-Reading Screening Procedures, Procedure 12, Auditory-Visual Association   261
Figure 75. WISC-R Picture Completion   272
Figure 76. WISC-R Picture Arrangement   272
Figure 77. WISC-R Block Design   273
Figure 78. WISC-R Object Assembly   273
Figure 79. WISC-R Coding A   273
Figure 80. WISC-R Coding B   273
Figure 81. WISC-R Mazes   273
Figure 82. WISC-R Record Form   273
Figure 83. WISC-R Profile   274
Figure 84. Leiter Scale Card Holder   283
Figure 85. Leiter Scale Number Discrimination   284
Figure 86. Leiter Scale Analogous Progression   284
Figure 87. Leiter Scale Block Design   284
Figure 88. CPM, Item 5, Set A   287
Figure 89. CPM, Item 12, Set A   288
Figure 90. WJPEB Selective Testing Procedure   296
Figure 91. WJPEB Spatial Relations   296
Figure 92. WJPEB Visual-Auditory Learning   296
Figure 93. WJPEB Analysis-Synthesis   297
Figure 94. WJPEB Concept Formation   297
Figure 95. K-ABC Face Recognition   301
Figure 96. K-ABC Face Recognition   302
Figure 97. K-ABC Gestalt Closure   302
Figure 98. SOMPA Profile Folder   308

Preface

An earlier version of this book, *A Guide to 65 Tests for Special Education*, reviewed educational testing in relation to the rapidly expanding field of learning disabilities. It quickly became clear that new tests were appearing on the market at a rapid pace and that a new edition was needed. As tests were selected for *75 Tests*, several new trends in testing became evident.

The first trend is a strong, renewed interest in formal, standardized tests. While many professors, researchers, and teachers may prefer informal testing techniques that allow more task analysis and curriculum orientation, there is increasing emphasis on the statistical properties of educational tests—their sampling procedures, reliability, and validity. Eligibility criteria for learning-disability programs require the documenting of a significant discrepancy between ability and achievement on standardized tests. Most of the new tests included in this volume are standardized, norm-referenced instruments.

A second trend is the development of fewer new tests assessing psychological processes or modality strengths. Psychological process testing and modality assessment are more likely to be found in tests of general intellectual ability. Consequently, no additions have been made to the perception and memory chapter, while several academic tests have been added.

A third trend is the use of more cost-effective means of test administration and scoring. More group tests are being published, and subtests for group testing are being added to formerly individual tests. More paraprofessionals may be used as test administrators. Several tests now allow computer scoring and analysis for more efficient processing of test scores.

The last evident trend is the combining of the aptitude and the achievement measures in the same instrument. In this way, these measures are standardized on the same population, permitting direct comparison of scores.

A Guide to 75 Tests for Special Education, as did its predecessor, has three functions: (1) to enable the teacher to understand and interpret students' test results based on knowledge of the test's format and limitations; (2) to help the teacher, psychologist, or administrator plan a testing program by providing basic information about the tests available in each major skill area; and (3) to provide a means for improved communication among teachers, diagnosticians, and parents about the purposes, procedures, and results of testing.

This book is intended to be a resource for teachers and diagnosticians who need to interpret reports on children completed by other examiners. The 75 tests are grouped according to skills assessed. Information is given to allow professionals in the field of education to find out what each test measures, how the test measures it, and what test scores mean.

For professionals planning a testing program in special education, *75 Tests* can be used as a selection guide. Tests have been selected because of their wide usage; enough information is given about each to enable professionals to review several tests in each skill area and determine which is the most useful and appropriate in a particular setting. However, *75 Tests* is not intended to provide all the information needed to administer the test; that can be obtained only from the examiner's manual and from practice and experience. Rather, this guide is intended to be an introduction to the tests, familiarizing teachers with the tests' formats, strengths, and limitations. Each test review includes the test's salient characteristics, such as what materials are included and what skills are assessed, which are important considerations in planning a testing program.

The third function of *75 Tests* is to improve communication among the people giving the tests, the people using the test results, and the parents of the students taking the tests. A glossary of testing terms is provided to increase knowledge of test terminology and to provide some clearer ways to explain test results to anyone who is inexperienced in educational testing.

Following an overview of assessment procedures in the introduction, the test reviews are organized into three parts. Part I contains the skill area tests, specifically, tests dealing with academic achievement and ability, perception and memory, speech and language, bilingual functioning, and gross motor skills. Part II reviews preschool and kindergarten tests, focusing on assessment tools for the child from birth to 6 years old. In Part III, general intelligence tests and developmental scales are reviewed. The ordering of the tests within each chapter is explained in the opening pages for that chapter.

This is a book written by clinicians. In addition to Karen Travis, who authored the chapter on bilingual (Spanish-English) tests and contributed several test reviews to the speech and language tests chapter, three other persons made significant contributions: Joan Bisagno, M.S., Learning Disability Specialist; Polly Bredt, M.A., C.C.C., Speech and Language Pathologist; and Barbara Fourt, OTR, Registered Occupational Therapist. We all work as diagnosticians at the Children's Health Council, a private, multidisciplinary clinic in Palo Alto, California, serving children of all ages who have mild to severe learning, language, and emotional disorders. All of the tests reviewed have been used in our clinic, and the strengths and limitations described for each test are those we have experienced in daily clinical practice.

Two areas of testing have been purposefully omitted. Personality assessment requires skills and training that are different from the kind most educational diagnosticians have acquired. Similarly, prevocational and vocational assessment, though extremely important, is a field of its own outside the scope of this book.

We hope that *A Guide to 75 Tests for Special Education* will provide you with guidelines to improve your test selection, usage, and interpretation and that it will help you as you go about the business of educational assessment.

Acknowledgments

Grateful acknowledgment is made to the following authors and publishers for their permission to reprint copyrighted sample test materials and illustrative matter.

LLOYD M. DUNN and FREDERICK C. MARKWARDT, JR., for Figure 4, from *Peabody Individual Achievement Test*. Circle Pines, Minn.: American Guidance Service, Inc. 1970.

THE PSYCHOLOGICAL CORPORATION, for Figure 7, from the standardization edition of *Basic Achievement Skills Individual Screener*. New York: The Psychological Corporation, 1982. Reproduced by special permission. All rights reserved.

ALBERT H. BRIGANCE, for Figures 8 and 9, from *Brigance Diagnostic Inventories*. Woburn, Mass.: Curriculum Associates, Inc., 1976. By permission of the author and publisher.

WILLIAM G. MCCARTHY, for Figure 10, from *McCarthy Individualized Diagnostic Reading Inventory*. Cambridge, Mass.: Educators Publishing Service, Inc., 1976.

RICHARD W. WOODCOCK, for Figure 11, from *Woodcock Reading Mastery Tests*. Circle Pines, Minn.: American Guidance Service, Inc., 1973.

A. I. GATES and W. H. MACGINITIE, for Figures 12–16. Reprinted, by permission of the publisher, from *Gates-MacGinitie Silent Reading Tests*. New York: Teachers College Press, ©1965 by Teachers College, Columbia University.

WILLIAM WITTENBERG, for Figure 17, from *Diagnostic Achievement Test in Spelling*. Baldwin, N.Y.: Barnell Loft, Ltd., 1980.

HELMER R. MYKLEBUST, for the photograph on page 74, from *Development and Disorders of Written Language* vol. 1. New York: Grune & Stratton, Inc., 1965. By permission of the author and publisher.

DONALD D. HAMMILL and STEPHEN C. LARSEN, for Figure 18, from *Test of Written Language*. Austin, Tex.: Pro-Ed, 1983.

A. CONNOLLY, W. NACHTMAN, and E. M. PRITCHETT, for Figure 19, from *KeyMath Diagnostic Arithmetic Test*. Circle Pines, Minn.: American Guidance Service, Inc., 1971, 1976.

CURRICULUM ASSOCIATES, INC., for Figures 20–23, from *Enright™ Diagnostic Inventory of Basic Arithmetic Skills*. North Billerica, Mass.: Curriculum Associates, Inc., ©1983. Reproduced by permission.

H. J. BAKER and B. LELAND, for Figures 24–32 from *Detroit Tests of Learning Aptitude*. Copyright © 1958, 1959, 1967 by The Bobbs-Merrill Co., Inc. Reprinted with permission.

M. FROSTIG, for Figures 33–37, from *Marianne Frostig Developmental Test of Visual Perception*. Palo Alto, Calif.: Consulting Psychologists Press, Inc., 1966.

RONALD P. COLARUSSO and DONALD D. HAMMILL, for Figures 38–42 from *Motor-Free Visual Perception Test*. Novato, Calif.: Academic Therapy Publications, 1972. By permission of the authors and publisher.

LAURETTA BENDER, for Figure 43, from *A Visual Motor Gestalt Test and Its Clinical Use*. Research Monograph no. 3, American Orthopsychiatric Association, Inc., New York, 1938. By permission of the author and publisher.

KEITH E. BEERY and NORMAN A. BUKTENICA, for Figures 45–47, from *Beery-Buktenica Developmental Test of Visual-Motor Integration*. Copyright © 1967 by Keith E. Beery and Norman E. Buktenica. Used by permission of Follett Publishing Company, Chicago.

SAMUEL A. KIRK, JEAN J. MCCARTHY, and WINIFRED D. KIRK, for Figures 48 and 49, from *Illinois Test of Psycholinguistic Abilities*. Copyright © 1968 by the Board of Trustees of the University of Illinois. University of Illinois Press, Urbana.

ELEANOR M. SEMEL-MINTZ and ELISABETH H. WIIG, for Figure 50, from *Clinical Evaluation of Language Functions*. Columbus, Ohio: Charles E. Merrill Publishing Company, 1980.

ELIZABETH CARROW, for Figures 51 and 52, from *Test for Auditory Comprehension of Language*. Copyright © 1973, by Elizabeth Carrow. Austin, Tex.: Learning Concepts, Inc., rev. 1977.

ANN E. BOEHM, for Figure 53. Reproduced from *Boehm Test of Basic Concepts* by permission. Copyright © 1969 by The Psychological Corporation, New York, N.Y. All rights reserved.

JAMES D. MACDONALD, for Figure 54, from *Environmental Language Inventory*. Columbus, Ohio: Charles E. Merrill Publishing Company, 1978.

DONALD D. HAMILL, VIRGINIA L. BROWN, STEPHEN C. LARSEN, and J. LEE WEIDERHOLT, for Figures 55 and 56, from *Test of Adolescent Language*. Austin, Tex.: Pro-Ed, 1980.

ALDINE VON ISSER and WINIFRED KIRK, for Figure 57, from *Preba Illinois de Habilidades Psicolinguísticas*. Tucson, Ariz.: University of Arizona, 1980.

HARCOURT BRACE JOVANOVICH, INC., for Figure 58, from *Bilingual Syntax Measure*. New York: Harcourt Brace Jovanovich, Inc., 1978. Reproduced by special permission. All rights reserved.

A. JEAN AYRES, for the blank form used for Figure 59, from *Southern California Sensory Integration Tests*. Los Angeles: Western Psychological Services, 1972.

WILLIAM K. FRANKENBURG and JOSIAH B. DODDS, for Figure 60, from *Denver Developmental Screening Test*. Copyright ©1969 by William K. Frankenburg and Josiah B. Dodds. Denver: Ladoca Project and Publishing Foundation, Inc., 1970.

ALBERT H. BRIGANCE, for Figures 61 and 62, from *Brigance Diagnostic Inventory of Early Development*. North Billerica, Mass.: Curriculum Associates, Inc., 1978. By permission of the author and publisher.

BETH SLINGERLAND, for Figures 63–74 (blank forms only for Figures 69 and 71), from *Slingerland Pre-Reading Screening Procedures*. Cambridge, Mass.: Educators Publishing Service, Inc., 1977.

D. WECHSLER, for the blank forms used for Figures 82 and 83. Reproduced from *Wechsler Intelligence Scale for Children—Revised,* by permission. Copyright © 1974 by The Psychological Corporation, New York, N.Y. All rights reserved.

J. C. RAVEN, for Figures 88 and 89, from *Coloured Progressive Matrices*. London: H. K. Lewis & Co., Ltd., 1956.

RICHARD W. WOODCOCK and M. BONNER JOHNSON, for Figures 90–94, from *Woodcock-Johnson Psycho-Educational Battery*. Hingham, Mass.: Teaching Resources Corporation, 1977.

AMERICAN GUIDANCE SERVICE, for Figures 95–97, from *Kaufman Assessment Battery for Children,* © 1983 by Alan S. Kaufman and Nadeen L. Kaufman. Reprinted by permission of American Guidance Service, Circle Pines, Minn.

THE PSYCHOLOGICAL CORPORATION, for Figure 98, from *System of Multicultural Pluristic Assessment*. New York: The Psychological Corporation, 1977. Reproduced by special permission. All rights reserved.

Introduction

Educational assessment, in its broadest sense, is the gathering of information about a student's performance in school. When the student's school performance is deemed inadequate, educational diagnosis is used to investigate and define the student's particular pattern of academic strengths and skill deficiencies and to translate them into an individualized program. The diagnostician uses many tools—observation, interview, diagnostic teaching, and testing. Testing, then, is just one part of educational assessment, a part that has recently received much applause and much criticism.

This book reviews the instruments of educational testing, and their uses and misuses, within the total process of educational assessment for students in academic difficulty because of learning disabilities and related problems.

PURPOSES OF TESTING

The general purpose of educational testing is to answer educationally relevant questions about a student. Broadly, these questions to be answered are:
- What is the student's current functioning level in basic skills?
- What are the student's specific skill deficiencies, if any?
- What are the student's strengths?
- What and how shall the student be taught?
- How well is the student progressing?

The general school testing program attempts to answer these questions through group achievement tests given periodically throughout the grades. Such tests as the Iowa Test of Basic Skills (Lindquist and Hieronymus 1956), the California Achievement Tests (Tiegs and Clark 1970), and the Sequential Tests of Basic Skills (1958) all give teachers and parents important information about students' progress from year to year and their academic relationship to other students at the same age and grade level.

But questions about an individual student's specific strengths and weaknesses are not easily answered by group achievement tests. Particularly for students with difficulties in academic areas, individual testing is essential to discover the pattern of strengths and weaknesses, which in turn leads to an individual instructional program. Educational tests for students in academic difficulty have four main functions: screening, diagnosis, program planning, and evaluation.

Screening

The first phase of the diagnostic process is screening. A test or series of tests is given to a group of students who have something in common—age, grade level, or signs of a special problem, such as deficient fine motor coordination or poor reading performance. The results from screening tests provide a first look at a group of students to determine temporary groupings or to identify students in need of further testing. Kindergarten screening, for example, is popular in many districts as a means of determining which children may have difficulty in first grade. The goal of any screening program is to identify students in need of further individual diagnostic testing. The essence of screening is its quickness; therefore, test items must be carefully selected to measure critical skills.

Because most students who are screened do not receive further testing, we must take care to ensure that the screening procedures will identify properly those students in need of further evaluation. False positives, students identified as having disabilities when they do not, and false negatives, students with difficulty who slip through the screening process, are both serious problems. False positives can be corrected by referrals for individual testing, but false negatives do not get that opportunity.

Diagnostic Testing

In contrast to screening, diagnostic testing is usually a lengthy individual process. A battery of tests assesses the student's functioning not only in basic academic skills but also in processes believed to be essential for all learning—perception, memory, concept development, visual-motor skills, language development, and expressive skills. These tests assess the primary modalities used in the learning process—auditory, visual, and kinesthetic or motor. Some attention is given to a possible cause for the academic problems, but much more attention is given to a description of their type and degree of severity. The result of diagnostic testing is usually a placement decision. Students are admitted to special programs, excluded from special programs, retained, placed in private schools, or referred for medical and psychological services on the basis of diagnostic testing. Thus it must be carried out thoughtfully by experienced professionals who understand the importance of careful diagnostic decisions.

Program Planning

Following the in-depth diagnostic process and the placement decision, program planning begins. The process of designing an instructional program for an individual student based on the results of diagnostic tests is called the *diagnostic-remedial process,* or *diagnostic-prescriptive teaching.* Salvia and Ysseldyke (1978) describe two different diagnostic-prescriptive teaching models: the ability-training model and the task-analysis model. Each of these models has its advocates and its critics.

In the *ability-training model,* the primary concern is the assessment of such learning processes as perception, memory, visual-motor skills, and concept development. The remedial program is designed to improve these abilities or to teach the student to compensate for deficiencies.

The *task-analysis model* attempts to identify skill deficiencies by breaking down a complex academic task (such as word recognition) into its many subparts; the parts that the student has not mastered are analyzed. The remedial program is then designed to teach the student those subskills.

Program planning is usually done by the remedial teacher. In order to plan appropriate remedial programs, the remedial teacher needs information on the student's learning abilities and academic skill deficiencies.

Evaluation

The final function of educational testing is evaluation. It is of two major types: evaluation of individual pupil progress and program evaluation. Measuring pupil progress includes pre- and posttesting on formal and informal tests, daily charting of performance on specific tasks, and observing student performance in the classroom. Program evaluation attempts to measure the progress of groups of students participating in special remedial programs as compared with similar students not receiving specialized assistance. Standardized tests and rating scales are usually used for this purpose.

Testing, in the best of situations, is a time-consuming, expensive process. Is it worth it? This is the critical question that must be asked of every person involved in planning and implementing a testing program. If the educational questions presented earlier are posed carefully, then educational testing (as a part of the total assessment process) becomes not only helpful but also essential in program planning and instruction.

ABUSES AND MISUSES OF TESTS

Many of the criticisms of educational tests are legitimate; in many instances tests have been abused and misused. One problem area in educational testing is the confusion of terms. As mentioned earlier, *assessment* is the total process of gathering information about a student's performance in school; *diagnosis* is one part of that process, and the diagnostician uses *testing* as one tool. Basing educational decisions on test results alone, without using the other tools of the diagnostician—observation, interview, and diagnostic teaching—is a misuse of tests. Viewing diagnosis as a once-only process rather than a continuous procedure is also a common error.

Anastasiow (1973, p. 349) describes four other consistent abuses of tests:

• Generalizing the interpretation of test scores to groups not represented in the norming sample

• Overinterpreting scores, say by focusing on a five-point gain in IQ score when five points is not statistically significant

• Teaching the answers to test questions in the belief that an improved test score alone will demonstrate pupil progress

• Violating students' confidentiality and privacy by revealing test scores to persons not directly involved with the educational program

Wallace and Larsen (1978, p. 22) add one other abuse to the list:

• Overgeneralizing the findings of a test, either by making decisions about an individual student based on performance on a group test or labeling students on the basis of single test scores

Salvia and Ysseldyke, in *Assessment in Special and*

Remedial Education (1978), discuss the misuses of tests extensively. They divide testing errors into three types: (1) the wrong test, (2) the wrong interpretation, and (3) "dumb" mistakes. A test may be wrong if it is technically inadequate, that is, invalid or unreliable. A test may be wrong if it is used for the wrong purpose, such as using the Reading subtest of the Wide Range Achievement Test as if it were a measure of total reading. A test may be wrong when it is used with the wrong child—a child whose characteristics differ greatly from the norming sample.

The wrong interpretation of test scores, according to Salvia and Ysseldyke, is easily done. Two common errors are inferring causation from a student's test behavior and assigning a student to a group of students with similar test behavior on the basis of that test behavior alone. A good test can elicit performance that will define a student's skill deficiencies—but not the cause of them. Also, a student whose test performance is similar to that of retarded children is not necessarily retarded.

"Dumb" mistakes described by Salvia and Ysseldyke include such things as equating IQ scores on different tests and clerical errors in scoring. Another "dumb" mistake is repeating the same test too frequently.

Testing is simply one diagnostic tool. When tests are part of a well-designed assessment procedure, planned and implemented by sensitive professionals, they provide important information about a student. But tests selected, administered, and interpreted incorrectly are worse than useless. They lead to incorrect and inappropriate placements and programs for children.

TYPES OF TESTS

There are many types of tests. To plan an appropriate testing program, one must understand the essential characteristics of each type.

Formal and Informal Tests

Formal tests are more appropriately called *standardized tests*. They may be group or individual tests. They have standardized procedures for administration, timing, and scoring. They are normed on a representative sample of students and provide age or grade-level scores, standard scores, or percentiles that allow the educator to compare a student with other students of the same age and grade. Once the standardized procedure has been altered, the norms are no longer valid, and legitimate comparisons cannot be made. Another term for formal or standardized tests is *norm-referenced tests*.

Informal testing does not produce normed scores. Informal tests are structured observations that appraise the student's performance without reference to other students. Informal tests are usually administered individually. Because there are no norms, the teacher can modify the test format, the timing, and the administration procedures to allow the student the best opportunity to demonstrate his or her skills. Test items can be selected to best reflect the curriculum being taught. Because the tests are not normed, interpretation of the results is very dependent on the skills of the examiner.

Individual and Group Tests

Some tests are designed to be administered individually, while others may be given to groups of students. Group tests save administration time and student time. They are appropriate instruments for assessing achievement in such skill areas as reading comprehension and math computation. They also measure student behaviors, such as the ability to follow group instruction or to work independently, persistence, and pacing. Often, learning-disabled and other special education students are exempted from group tests; as a result, their repertoires of group test-taking strategies are not developed.

Individual tests generally allow the student more opportunity to demonstrate skills. The examiner can establish rapport with the student and provide breaks to decrease anxiety or fatigue. The examiner also has more opportunity to clarify instructions and to encourage the student lacking in confidence. If presented skillfully, the tests can hold the student's interest and elicit cooperation without deviating from standardized procedures. For these reasons, individual tests are usually recommended for the diagnosis of learning disabilities and other academic problems.

Diagnostic and Achievement Tests

Diagnostic and achievement tests can be either standardized or informal, group or individual. Diagnostic tests are designed to determine whether a student has a specific learning disability and, if so, in what skill area or learning process it occurs. Some diagnostic tests, such as the Gates-McKillop-Horowitz Reading Diagnostic Tests, measure one specific academic skill area in depth. Others, such as the Marianne Frostig Developmental Test of Visual Perception, attempt to assess several subskills of an important learning process, such as visual perception. In diagnostic testing, observations of how the student does the task and the types of errors made are as important as the score. For this reason, individual diagnostic tests are usually more valuable than group tests in determining which students may have learning disabilities and in planning their instruction.

Achievement tests are designed to measure the student's present functioning level in basic academic skills. Items are selected to represent typical curriculum materials at specific grade levels. For example, a spelling test would include a graded list of words to be dictated by the examiner and written by the student. The score would reflect the student's present functioning level in spelling and suggest the instructional level. Evaluation of the student's error pattern on an achievement test is possible but not as easy as on a diagnostic test designed for that purpose. Achievement tests are often group tests, usually standardized and norm-referenced. They reflect curriculum content in a single area such as mathematics or in multiple areas such as reading, mathematics, and spelling.

Criterion-Referenced Tests
Relative newcomers to the field of testing, criterion-referenced tests (CRTs) were designed by educators who were dissatisfied with norm-referenced, standardized achievement tests. Standardized tests determine a student's rank in comparison to others of the same age or grade but do not assess how much or what the student knows. CRTs tell what the student is able to do and allow the educator to judge the student as an individual in relation to a set of skills in an academic area. The items either are arranged developmentally or follow the order of a specific curriculum.

The score on a CRT can be expressed as a ratio:

$$\frac{\text{Number of skills learned}}{\text{Number of skills required}} = \text{Score in percent}$$

For example, if Susan has mastered 190 words out of a 200-word spelling list, her score would be 190/200, or 95 percent (Smith, Smith, and Brink 1977, p. 2). The score on a CRT can also be translated into a statement of the student's expected performance. On the Woodcock Reading Mastery Tests, the relative mastery score permits such statements as "David can be expected to perform with 53 percent accuracy on tasks in word comprehension at a seventh-grade level." Some tests, such as the Woodcock Reading Mastery Tests, are both norm-referenced and criterion-referenced, yielding grade-level and percentile scores as well as ratios and percentages.

Criterion-referenced testing carefully identifies the specific skills mastered by a student. Because the test items have been arranged in developmental order, it is easy to see which skills must be mastered next, and they become the teaching objectives. CRTs, then, lead directly to individual instructional planning. Increasing numbers of commercial curriculum materials are including CRTs that assess the specific skills taught in that curriculum.

THE DIAGNOSTIC BATTERY
A major group of students for whom educational assessment is needed are those in academic difficulty because of suspected learning disabilities. The task of the diagnostician is to determine whether the student's academic problems are related to specific learning disabilities and, if so, what the nature and the degree of the disabilities are. From this information, a specific instructional program may be designed.

In designing a diagnostic testing battery for a student with suspected learning disabilities, the diagnostician must take into consideration three factors: academic skill areas, learning processes and modalities, and the time and personnel available for testing.

Academic Skill Areas
If time and personnel are not an issue, what academic skill areas should be assessed in a complete educational evaluation? Table 1 serves as a guide to the major academic skill areas and their subgroups. In Appendix A, the tests reviewed in this book are matched with the academic skill areas listed in Table 1.

Each of these major areas could be further broken down into multiple subskills. Testing could go on forever, and sometimes from the point of view of the parents, the student, and the teacher who referred the student, it seems as though it does. Fortunately, the constraints of time and personnel force some decisions about what areas should be assessed. Such decisions should be made by considering the following factors:

- *The concerns of the teacher or the parent in the referral or testing request.* If a student is referred because of difficulties in reading and spelling but exhibits superior math skills, the diagnostician may do a quick math screening but focus the evaluation in the areas of reading, writing, and spelling.
- *The age and grade of the student.* If the student is in first or second grade, the reading evaluation will focus on phonic skills, sight-word recognition, and oral reading rather than advanced word analysis skills or silent reading comprehension.
- *Relevance of the area to classroom performance.* Oral spelling and oral math are often omitted because of their low frequency as classroom tasks. Similarly, written expression, an essential skill, should always be included.

Learning Processes and Modalities
The second factor to consider in designing the diagnostic testing battery is the basic psychological processes and the primary sensory modalities in which they occur. Table 2 provides an outline for assessing the basic psychological processes in the three modalities, or sensory channels, most commonly used in classroom learning. Appendix B fills in the chart with the names of the tests reviewed in this book that are appropriate for assessment in each area.

The assessment of psychological processes and sensory modalities has been repeatedly criticized on several counts:

- Terms such as "memory," "attention," and "perception" are used differently in different test instruments (Ceci, Ringstorm, and Lea 1981).

Table 1. Academic Skill Areas

Reading

Decoding
  Phonic skills
  Sight-word recognition
  Oral paragraph reading
Comprehension
  Oral reading
  Silent reading
  Listening
  Comprehension in specific content areas

Writing

Penmanship
  Manuscript
  Cursive
Written Expression
  Fluency
  Syntax
  Mechanics
  Content

Spelling

Written
  Phonic words
  Irregular words
Recognition of Sight Words
Oral

Arithmetic

Concepts
Computation
  Addition
  Subtraction
  Multiplication
  Division
Word Problems
  Oral
  Written

Oral Language

Receptive
  Vocabulary
  Listening comprehension
Expressive
  Articulation
  Morphology
  Syntax
  Semantics
  Pragmatics

• The instruments used in process and modality testing have questionable validity and reliability (Arter and Jenkins 1978).

• There is little evidence that the specific programming information yielded by these instruments is related to academic growth (Myers and Hammill 1976; Arter and Jenkins 1978).

Despite these criticisms, the assessment of psychological processes and sensory modality continues to be a key component of the educational assessment of a student suspected of learning disabilities. State law in California requires that the assessment of students to determine eligibility for special education programs, first, must show a significant discrepancy between intellectual ability and achievement, and second, must demonstrate that the discrepancy is "directly related to a disorder in one or more of the basic psychological processes which include: attention, visual and auditory processing, sensory-motor skills, and cognitive abilities including expression, conceptualization, and association." (State of California 1982)

Again, the learning processes selected for assessment should be based on the individual student's needs. If the teacher reports that the student has great difficulty following oral classroom instructions and giving oral reports, tests that assess auditory reception, auditory memory, and verbal expression will be selected. If the academic testing reveals confusion between words such as *boy* and *day* or *came* and *come*, tests in the area of visual perception would have high priority. Selecting to answer specific educational questions is more appropriate than administering a standard battery to all students; the latter frequently results in excessive testing (Wallace and Larsen 1978, p. 71).

Process and modality tests are simply one part of the assessment process; they are neither perfect nor useless. But they often provide information about the tasks a student can do well—a part of the diagnostic process too often omitted.

Time and Personnel Available

The practicalities of time and personnel clearly affect the selection of tests in the diagnostic battery. Two hours of individual educational testing is generally considered a minimum amount of time for a basic educational evaluation; three to four hours would be more usual. Students with major learning disabilities, students who work slowly, or students who need frequent breaks and much encouragement often need several short testing sessions. Overtesting should be avoided; not only is it time-consuming, but it rarely leads to significantly more educationally relevant information.

Educational assessment is frequently done by a diagnostic team. The psychologist usually administers general intelligence tests and often tests of visual-motor development. The language therapist assesses receptive and expressive language skills, articulation, and auditory

Table 2. Process-Modality Chart

Modality	Process				
	Reception (initial receiving of information)	**Perception** (initial organizing of information)	**Association** (relating new information to other information)	**Memory** (short-term, sequential memory)	**Expression** (output)
Auditory (primary stimuli are auditory)					**Verbal expression**
Visual (primary stimuli are visual)					**Written expression**
Tactile/Kinesthetic (primary stimuli accompanied by motoric input)					**Motoric expression other than written or verbal**

processing. The educational diagnostician tests academic performance and related learning processes. A perceptual-motor specialist examines gross and fine motor skills. When the educational diagnostician is a one-person team, the test battery must include a broader range of tests, particularly in the areas of concept development, language, and motor skills.

TEST SELECTION

Most educators have little trouble identifying the academic areas or learning processes to be tested. The chief problem is choosing the specific tests to be used. Too often, tests are ordered rather than selected. Test selection should be based on the following criteria:

- Does the test answer the educational question being asked?
- Is the standardization sample appropriate for the student being tested?
- Is the test valid?
- Is the test reliable?
- Are the design and format appropriate for the student being tested?
- Is the content or skill area being measured appropriate for the age and grade of the student?
- Is the test economical in terms of time and money?

Educational Relevance

The most important question to ask in selecting a test is, What type of educational information do I need? Clearly, some tests should be given to every student, whereas other tests should be used only in highly specific situations. Screening tests should be quick and include items carefully selected to measure critical skills. Diagnostic tests must be thoughtful and yield information upon which placement decisions can be made and individualized program plans formulated. Tests used to measure pupil progress must be sensitive to the curriculum being taught. Random selection of tests without careful consideration of the type of educational information the tests will yield often results in overtesting or in trying to force a set of test scores to answer questions they were not intended to answer. The following examples illustrate this point.

Sycamore School District decided to give all students in their intermediate grades The Bender Visual Motor Gestalt Test. They designed group administration procedures and carried out the testing. Later, they realized the norms went only to the age of 9 years and were based on individual administration.

Maple School District decided to give a group standardized math test to all elementary-level students in the learning disability program in October and May to measure pupil progress in math. The test measured standard computation skills, but the curriculum being used was an experimental, "new math" approach. Few students showed progress in math between October and May. Teachers had to spend spring parent conferences explaining that Johnny actually had made progress despite his test scores.

Standardization, Validity, and Reliability

Once the purposes of testing have been defined and specific educational questions have been posed, test selection should be based on the standardization sample, the validity, and the reliability of the tests available.

The composition of the standardization sample of a standardized test is an important factor. The test author selects a population of students to whom he or she administers the new test. The performance of this group of students becomes the "norm." It is the author's responsibility to describe that population of students in depth—by age level, sex, racial background, socioeconomic level, intelligence level, and so forth. Examiners must learn to look for and pay attention to the composition of the norming sample to determine if that sample included students of the type being tested. Many standardization samples do not include minority groups or students with the same type of handicapping conditions as those to whom the test is typically given. Making judgments about a student's performance on a test with an inappropriate norming population is not a valid decision-making process and is one of the misuses of tests (Anastasiow 1973).

Validity is a primary consideration in test selection. Does the test measure the skill area well? There are many types of validity.

- *Content validity* considers whether the skills being measured are critical to the academic task and whether the test reflects the curriculum.
- *Concurrent validity* asks if the test correlates well with other accepted criteria of performance in that subject or skill area.
- *Predictive validity* asks how well the scores correlate with some criterion for future success. Predictive validity is of particular importance for screening instruments.
- *Construct validity* questions the theory and assumptions under which the test was constructed.
- *Discriminate validity* considers whether each of the subtests does, in fact, measure a separate, distinct skill.

Consideration of test validity is of critical importance in all test selection. For some tests, studies of validity are readily available in the examiner's manual; for others, library research is necessary; for some, no evidence of validity is offered.

Reliability is the third important criterion for test selection. The consistency with which a test measures what it measures is a critical variable. Many factors influence a student's score on a test. Some of them are within the student—attention, motivation, physical condition, anxiety, and so forth. The good diagnostician takes these factors into account when interpreting test scores. But other factors affecting reliability are part of the test itself—the length of the test, the clarity of instructions, the objectivity of the scoring, and others. The diagnostician must also learn to study the reliability data on a test and to select the most reliable test that yields the needed educational information. Reliable answers to educational questions not asked are of little value, but unreliable answers to critical educational questions can cause placement and instructional errors.

Design and Format
The design and format of a test should also be considered in selection. Students with learning disabilities and other academic problems need tests that are simple in design, are clearly printed, and have easy-to-understand instructions. Whether a test is timed or untimed should also be considered. Sometimes it is important to know how rapidly a student can perform a given task. Reading, for example, is not a usable tool until it becomes fluent. Speed is also a critical variable in measuring writing ability. When speed is a factor, a timed test that will yield a score based on both accuracy and speed should be selected. Just as often, we need to know how much a student can do in a skill area when no time constraints are imposed. Untimed tests, or power tests, allow students to continue working until they reach a ceiling or complete the tests. When students are first learning a skill, untimed tests are usually more appropriate.

Careful consideration should be given to the type of response required by the tests; the format of a test should not penalize a particular type of student. Students with learning disabilities frequently have a short attention span, little motivation for school tasks, great anxiety about testing, and difficulty following directions. These characteristics frequently result in an impulsive style of test taking. Tests with multiple-choice or yes-or-no responses often lead to impulsive guessing with little monitoring of answers and are therefore often less appropriate with these students. Other tests place a high demand on auditory memory. Because auditory memory is frequently a weak area for students with learning disabilities, selection of a test that does not focus on this skill will yield more meaningful results.

Appropriateness of Content
Another factor in test selection is the appropriateness of the test content for the age and grade level of the student. Perceptual tests are much more appropriate at the primary grade levels, when perceptual skills are normally developing. Only the most impaired secondary students will demonstrate difficulties on perceptual tests. Bright students will have developed compensation techniques; their continued perceptual problems will be seen more clearly through error analysis of academic tasks. Oral reading tests are also more appropriate for primary and intermediate students. During those grades, oral reading is an important classroom skill. As the student gets older, oral reading tests give information about word recognition skills but may not yield accurate information about silent reading comprehension of content material—the more essential classroom task.

Time and Money
Economics must also be considered in test selection. Students with academic problems are often tested

extensively during the identification, diagnostic, and placement phases and then again to measure progress. Group tests save time in administration and scoring and may appropriately be used in screening and in some types of progress evaluations. But generally, students with academic difficulties benefit more from individual or small group tests. Consumable tests (those in which the student writes on the test booklet rather than an answer sheet), although more expensive, are much easier for the student with learning problems, are more reliable, and provide more diagnostic information for the teacher. To save time, the examiner should use the most valid and reliable tests available, because if the examiner has confidence in the diagnostic information, "backup" tests may not have to be administered. Some tests, such as the Brigance Diagnostic Inventories or the KeyMath Diagnostic Arithmetic Test, take longer to administer and score but yield information that translates more directly into instructional programming. Others, such as the Wide Range Achievement Test, are quick to administer and score but need considerable time and expertise to translate into individual programs. A testing program that gains maximum information from minimum student time is essential. Teachers must have time to teach and students need time to learn—not just to be tested.

Inservice Training

Test selection should involve the full team of administrators, diagnosticians, and teachers. Available tests should be reviewed, and their standardization population, validity, and reliability should be studied. But careful test selection will be of little value unless it is followed by inservice training in administration and scoring procedures, test interpretation, and explanation of results to parents. Professionals involved in testing who do not take part in inservice training often use tests without critiquing their value. Inservice training sessions should serve as an ongoing evaluation of each test being given and its usefulness in providing answers to specific educational questions.

SPECIAL ISSUES IN TESTING
The Use of Grade-Level Scores

The type of test score most frequently reported by educational diagnosticians is the grade-level, or grade-equivalent, score. Even when percentiles and standard scores are provided in the test manual, many educational reports include only the grade scores. The reason for this is the easy communicability of the grade score; students, parents, and teachers all feel they understand its meaning. Despite repeated criticism of this procedure by experts in test construction, the practice has continued. The time has come to stop. Two sources support this point:

Because the continued use of grade norms is professionally indefensible, the Board of Directors of the International Reading Association in 1980 has asked (1) that examiners abandon the practice of reporting and interpreting test performance in grade equivalents, and (2) that test authors and publishers eliminate such norms from tests. (Brown, Hammill, and Wiederholt 1978)

Does anyone know how an assassination of the grade ratings could be accomplished? Perhaps a national hanging in effigy, a funeral, and a period of suitable mourning? Then a burial to put grade ratings to rest in honor beside their parent, the old Binet mental age constructs. (Brill 1979)

Brill's statement is taken from a speech given to school psychologists in San Diego in 1979 and later published as a technical report entitled *The Uses and Misuses of the WRAT*. He goes on to say that grade ratings give people—including professionals—false ideas of how learning takes place. Grade ratings should not be reported arithmetically as an indication of learning, because they represent the average scores of students in the sampling population at that grade level. Several other points about grade scores are important to keep in mind:

- They are not an equal-interval scale; the difference between grade levels 3.4 and 3.5 may be very different than the difference between grade levels 8.5 and 8.6 or even 3.5 and 3.6.
- They cannot be added and subtracted as raw scores, as standard scores can.
- They cannot be compared with the student's current grade placement.

This last point is very important. For example, if Richard's current grade placement is 6.3 (sixth grade, third month) and his WRAT reading grade is 5.1 (fifth grade, first month), we might say that he is one year and two months behind. This is an incorrect use of scores. If Richard's intelligence quotient is 110, his expected WRAT reading score is 7.1. This is the score to compare with 5.1. Better yet is a comparison of standard scores 110 and 94, the standard score that corresponds to the 5.1 grade equivalent.

The implications of Brown *et al.* and Brill's statements are very clear. Never report only grade scores when standard scores and percentiles are available; preferably, report the standard scores and percentiles and omit the grade scores. If a test yields only grade scores, don't use it; if you must, report the results only through discussion without scores.

Evaluating Progress

Evaluating pupil progress is an essential part of every program for students with academic difficulties. Accountability demands that educators evaluate programs in terms of pupil progress, but measuring an individual student's growth is often not a simple process. The selection of tests that will not only provide valuable diagnostic information but also prove to be effective measures of pupil progress takes forethought and planning. The following factors may serve as general guidelines.

- Selecting tests that have equivalent alternate forms for retesting purposes may not be critical in determining student progress. Research studies regarding a "practice effect" on achievement tests are inconclusive. Curr and Gorlay (1960, pp. 155–167) reported a high practice effect in ninth-grade students tested in the mechanics of reading and reading comprehension at one-, three-, and six-month intervals. In contrast, Karlin and Jolly (1965, pp. 187–191) tested fourth through eighth graders in September and May in reading. Whether the same test was readministered or an alternate form was used, they found no differences between the results. These results give mixed information about the practice effect in normal students. Even less is known about the practice effect in students with learning disabilities. However, because the concept of practice effect is based on the assumption that the student will remember the first test's content, it is likely that students with learning disabilities will be less affected by the practice effect than normal students will be.

- Selecting an individual test, such as the Wide Range Achievement Test, or a coordinated series of tests, such as the Gates-MacGinitie Silent Reading Tests, that covers a wide age range allows for a measure of progress from year to year on the same instrument.

- Selecting tests with an appropriate level of difficulty for students is necessary in determining student progress. A test that is too hard or too easy gives little information on growth. (This particularly difficult issue for students with reading problems is discussed in the following section.)

- Issues of validity are important in measuring pupil progress. The test must reflect the curriculum content. As the example of the Maple School District (p. 6) demonstrates, tests that do not measure the skills being taught show little pupil progress and require much explanation. Another example deals with oral reading tests. Tests of oral reading usually include a high percentage of sight words. If the student has been taught all year in a systematic phonics program, the retest score may not reflect his or her progress because exposure to sight words has been minimal. In this case, a measure of phonic skills that reflects the curriculum should be included in the retesting procedures. Testing oral reading with a timed test when speed of reading has not been emphasized by the classroom teacher is another example of an impractical way to measure student progress.

For severely impaired students with learning disabilities, even the format of the test items should be familiar. Shifting from math computation in the vertical format

$$\begin{array}{r} 2 \\ +6 \\ \hline \end{array}$$

to the horizontal format (2 + 6 = ____) may be enough to confuse the student so that the test score does not reflect progress in math computation.

- Reliability is a critical factor in selecting measures of pupil progress. In addition to the factors within the student and the test that affect reliability (discussed on p. 7), the teacher needs to be aware of several other reliability factors that affect measurement of progress. Difference scores are frequently used to document pupil progress; that is, a student is given a test in September and the same test (or its equivalent form) in May. The lower score (hopefully September's) is subtracted from the higher score, and the resulting difference score is used as an indication of growth or lack of progress. But several precautions are needed for this procedure. First, grade scores and percentile scores are not based on an equal-interval scale and should not be used for calculating differences. Raw scores or standard scores should be used. Second, difference scores are the most unreliable of test scores, because they combine the measurement errors of both test scores. Small gains or losses in achievement may not be reliable or statistically significant. Finally, difference scores that do reach statistical significance may not make any practical difference in instructional level and should not be overplayed.

- Tests with many subtests are particularly difficult to interpret in terms of student progress. Changes in the total test score often are used to document progress. However, total test scores are usually obtained by summing several subtest scores. Such a procedure often obscures progress in certain skills and lack of progress in others.

- Measuring progress in specific skill areas, such as auditory memory or math computation, often needs to be done at two intervals: immediately following the unit of instruction and a few months later. Immediate scores are often very high, whereas the later scores are lower but reflect the critical skills of retention and generalization.

The problems of evaluating pupil progress by test results are many, and clearly the reevaluation process should include less formal but in many ways more important data from the teacher. Anecdotal records and observational data on social-emotional skills, work habits, and attention are often the primary indicators of progress. Many curriculum materials now provide records of continuous progress in specific skills. These ongoing records of progress are the most important tools in future program planning. They provide measures of such behaviors as rate of learning and retention rate—critical factors that are not assessed in standardized, norm-referenced tests.

Standardized tests are also weak in another important area. Although they may be valid and reliable measurements of specific academic skills, they do not assess the degree to which those skills have been generalized to other curriculum areas and new learning situations. A good example is the student who makes a three-year gain on a test of listening comprehension but still cannot follow the flow of conversation in a classroom. Systematic observation of the student learning new materials and in larger instructional groups is an important part of the reevaluation process.

Who should do the pre- and posttesting on students in special programs? In some school districts the teacher does the testing; the rationale is that the teacher who does the testing gets information about the student's performance firsthand rather than through a diagnostician's translation. Having the teacher retest for progress gives the student the advantage of being tested by the most familiar person—presumably a less anxiety-producing situation. However, it is more desirable for someone other than the teacher, such as an administrator or diagnostician, to do the post-testing, for a number of reasons. First, the teacher has a great deal of personal need for the student to do well; the skill of the teacher is validated by the success of the students. In this situation, it is very difficult to be objective; in very subtle and unknowing ways the teacher may give the student more cues or more time. Second, having the teacher do the testing may in fact prove to be more stressful for a student. The student and the teacher often have a very close relationship, and the student may not want to disappoint the teacher. Although having a relative stranger do the testing may initially be stressful for the student, usually the neutral relationship results in less anxiety.

There are other advantages to having someone other than the teacher do the testing. A diagnostician, in the process of testing the whole class, gains an overall view of the group that may lead to suggestions for new groupings, materials, or instructional techniques. Because testing is time-consuming, this procedure allows the teacher to continue teaching—the teacher's most important responsibility.

Testing the Student with Reading Problems
Particular problems arise in evaluating the progress of students with significant reading problems. Standardized reading tests are designed to assess "normal" readers; students with identified reading problems are usually excluded from the norming sample. It is questionable practice to apply the norms of the "normal" population to students with reading problems, but we have no choice: One purpose of reading testing is to compare the poor reader with other students. It is that comparison that determines the degree of reading retardation.

One question that always arises is what level of test should be given to the student with reading problems—the level that is appropriate for the student's age and grade or the level that fits the student's reading functioning? Do you give Susan, a sixth grader reading at the third-grade level, a sixth-grade test that you know she cannot read? Or a third-grade test that will only tell you how she compares with third graders? This question only occurs on such tests as the Wide Range Achievement Test, the Gates-MacGinitie Silent Reading Tests, and the Slingerland Screening Tests for Identifying Children with Specific Language Disability, which specify different forms for different grade levels. Many reading tests use the same form for all age levels, and through a basal and ceiling procedure, ask the student to read only passages appropriate for his or her skill level.

When it is necessary to select a test level for a below-grade-level reader, the educational question being asked again determines which level to use. Here are three examples of when the below-grade-level reader should be given the test for his or her age and grade level:

1. If a standardized achievement test is being used to measure the progress of all the students in a special program, retarded readers must be given the test level for their age and grade, no matter how difficult it is for them. Otherwise, their scores cannot be included with the group.

2. Sometimes it is necessary to demonstrate that a student cannot do the academic work required in a regular classroom. In such cases, giving the student a test appropriate for that grade level clearly demonstrates skill deficiencies and makes the student eligible for special assistance.

3. Important clinical information is often acquired by giving a student a test that is too difficult. In the individual setting, the examiner can observe the student's reactions to stress. Does the student stop working or begin to guess wildly? How much encouragement does the student need to continue working? Such information is helpful to the diagnostician in program planning.

When a student is given a test that is obviously too difficult, other testing should be done both to provide a success experience for the student and to provide valid testing information. If the student achieves a score below the norms on the test for his or her grade level, then a lower-level test that the student can do well should be administered. Readministration of both levels of the test is necessary for the progress report. For diagnostic purposes, you may choose to use several other tests to assess specific skills taught during the year, and these will form additional measures of progress.

As discussed earlier, the usual procedure for measuring pupil progress is through difference scores (posttest minus pretest score). Given the unreliability of difference scores, what is the best way to measure growth? Bliesmer (1962, pp. 344–350) compared three methods of evaluating progress in retarded readers:

1. Determining gains by the usual pretest-and-posttest difference method
2. Comparing yearly gains in the remedial program with average yearly gains before entering the remedial program
3. Comparing the reading achievement–reading potential gaps at the beginning and end of a remedial program

Bliesmer found that the third method did not demonstrate significant improvement, probably because as reading achievement improved, reading potential as measured by listening comprehension also improved. The first method did demonstrate gains, but the students with reading disabilities gained at the same rate as normal readers. When the second method was used and difference scores were compared to an average of difference scores in previous years, the growth of the students in the special program was more dramatic. This concept of determining the achievement rate of a student before the remedial program begins and comparing it to the rate of progress in the program holds the most promise for effectively reporting pupil progress.

Another problem inherent in assessing progress in disabled readers is the "regression toward the mean" phenomenon. There is a high probability that the students with the lowest scores on a pretest will score nearer the mean on subsequent retests (Farr 1969, p. 145). Students are frequently selected for remedial programs because they are significantly below average in reading. Consequently, when retested, their scores have a tendency to move closer to the mean, thus inflating the amount of progress they appear to have made. This issue is clouded by the fact that the lowest-functioning students often make strong initial gains in a structured remedial program; it becomes difficult to sort out what is "true" gain and what can be attributed to the statistical regression phenomenon.

Measuring long-term gains in a remedial program is also a difficult task. Remedial programs often create a Hawthorne effect; that is, the individualized work, small class size, highly structured program, concerned teacher, students' reduced fear of failure, and other characteristics of the program result in improved performance within the program, which unfortunately has little carry-over into other settings and few long-term gains. Some school districts have now introduced "watch and consult" programs in which students who leave the remedial program to return to regular classes are carefully monitored to ensure continued success.

Given the difficulties of measuring reading progress by administering standardized tests to students with reading disabilities, teachers must develop continuous monitoring systems and charts that graph students' work on a daily basis. These are more reliable measures of growth.

Measuring Reading Comprehension
For many students with reading disabilities at the upper-elementary and secondary school levels, the reading problem is not decoding, or word reading, but reading comprehension. Tests available in the area of reading comprehension, oral or silent, yield grade-level or percentile scores but offer little diagnostic information about the types of reading comprehension problems that the student demonstrates. Many skills make up reading comprehension—decoding, knowing word meanings, understanding content, organizing, recognizing tone and mood, inferring meaning, and many others. A task analysis of the reading comprehension process and developmental studies of the progression of skills involved is needed. From these data, criterion-referenced tests can be designed. Meanwhile, diagnosticians need to remember that many factors of the test affect reading comprehension scores:

- Level of material read (too easy or too difficult)
- Type of questions asked (specific facts or inferential questions)
- Type of response required (written, oral, multiple-choice, or essay)
- Length of time between reading and responding (immediate or delayed recall)
- Speed factor (timed or untimed)
- Instructions to the student

No global score can accurately reflect a student's reading comprehension. The conditions of the test must be considered.

Teachers who are designing individual programs to remediate reading comprehension should also consider the following factors in the student that may cause poor reading comprehension:

- *Poor decoding skills*. The most usual explanation for poor comprehension is that the student is reading material too difficult for his or her decoding skills.
- *Deficits in underlying language skills*. Weaknesses in vocabulary and sentence comprehension, due to inadequate language comprehension, is a frequent cause of low reading comprehension.
- *Experiential deficits*. Students may not have the experience to understand the concepts being presented in the reading material.
- *Memory deficits*. Diagnosticians and teachers too often attempt to teach comprehension skills to students who already comprehend but who cannot recall the material.
- *Deficits in expressive skills*. Reading comprehension is often assessed by asking the student to express understanding of a passage verbally or in writing. The problem

may not be in the comprehension but in the expressive part of this process.

• *Specific comprehension deficits*. Many students need to be taught such specific skills as finding the main idea, recognizing mood and tone, and so forth.

When planning individualized reading programs, the teacher must study the diagnostic test information and the student's classroom performance to determine which of the above factors are contributing to the student's reading comprehension difficulties. The remediation program should be very different for the student who has significant language disabilities and for the student who needs to be taught specific comprehension skills.

In addition, predicting students' silent reading skills from their oral reading performance is risky. The average reader usually has better comprehension in silent reading, but the student with learning disabilities frequently reads aloud with greater accuracy and comprehension. Oral reading increases this student's attention, and hearing himself or herself read often improves comprehension. Measures of both kinds of reading should be included in a full diagnostic evaluation.

Determining Instructional Level
Deciding at what level to begin instruction is not always clear from test scores. Careful attention to each child's test protocols yields more useful information, and having the student read aloud in a series of graded instructional materials is perhaps the most useful process.

In 1946, Betts (pp. 445–454) divided reading levels into four categories depending on the student's accuracy rate. These categories are still our best guide for determining instructional level.

1. *Basal or independent level*. Student reads with 99 percent accuracy and 90 percent comprehension. Oral reading is fluent and well phrased. The student is free from tension and free to think about the content, because he or she is totally in control of the vocabulary, the sentence construction, and the content.

2. *Probable instructional level*. Student reads with 95 percent accuracy and 75 percent comprehension. He or she can use word analysis skills and makes good progress with teacher guidance.

3. *Frustration level*. Student reads with less than 90 percent accuracy and less than 50 percent comprehension. He or she becomes easily bogged down, tense, distractable, and sometimes resistive.

4. *Probable capacity*. Student comprehends material read aloud with 75 percent accuracy and can discuss it with good vocabulary.

It is questionable whether listening comprehension is a valid measure of reading capacity. However, Betts's other three categories are very relevant for planning classroom instruction. Many, many students are being instructed in materials at their frustration level; that is, they are misreading more than 1 word in every 10. Halting and struggling over almost every word, they become very tense. This is not instruction; it is frustration.

Students with good phonics instruction will often read with approximately the same accuracy rate in materials at a wide range of grade levels. In such cases, instructional level should be the highest level at which the student has 75 percent comprehension. Students with reading disabilities of the dyslexic type often make errors on little words (*the, he, they, from*). Their accuracy rate may also be the same across several grade levels, and they should be instructed at the highest level of good (75 percent) comprehension.

The Diagnostic Report
For many diagnosticians, the written report is the most difficult part of the educational assessment process. Describing a student's behavior during testing and analyzing the student's performance on several tests is a very difficult task. The written diagnostic report ranges in length from a 12-page dissertation about the student's performance (which few people take the time or make the effort to read) to a 1-page listing of test scores. Between these extremes is a thoughtfully prepared 3- or 4-page report that helps the teacher, parent, or doctor understand more fully the student's classroom performance.

The following general outline has been useful in preparing a written report.

1. Identifying data
2. Reason for referral
3. Behavioral observations during testing
4. Tests administered
5. Test results
6. Analysis of test results
7. Summary
8. Recommendations

Appendix C contains two examples of completed diagnostic reports using a similar format.

Identifying Data
The identifying data include such information as the student's name, birthdate, chronological age, grade, school, examiner's name, and date of testing.

Reason for Referral
This should be a brief statement of the present problem. It is helpful to know who referred the student, what behaviors were of concern, and the purpose of the testing.

Behavior during Testing
A most important section of the report is the description of the student's behavior during testing. Statements about the

student's cooperation, attention, persistence, anxiety level, and response to the testing are important in assessing the validity of the tests. Although the comments are subjective, based on the examiner's observation of the student, they do describe the student in the individual testing situation. The student may behave very differently from in the classroom—more attentive and cooperative or less so, more nervous and hyperactive or less so. The student's behavior may account for differences in performance and may provide clinical information critical to the assessment process.

Tests Administered
These tests are often listed separately or combined with test results. Whenever possible, a brief description of the test itself should be included for readers who are unfamiliar with the test format. Some diagnosticians prefer to describe the tests on a separate page attached to the test report.

Test Results
All test scores are listed for each test or subtest administered.

Analysis of Test Results
The essence of the test report is in the analysis of the test results. The examiner discusses the student's performance on each test, summarizes the student's strengths and weaknesses in skills, and analyzes the various learning processes assessed. Examples are given to illustrate the kinds of errors the student made. The examiner describes in detail the specific tasks the student has not mastered and summarizes the error pattern.

Summary Statement
The summary reviews the essential information about the student, reason for referral, behavior, and test performance.

Recommendations
These typically include a placement recommendation as well as teaching suggestions. In a well-written report, the recommendations flow logically from the description of the behavior and the performance. The suggestions for teaching are based on task analysis and error analysis. They should incorporate analyses of the student's interests and strengths. They lead the teacher directly into curriculum planning. This section may also specify a date for reevaluation.

The written report described in this section is similar in format to those prepared by many psychologists and educational diagnosticians. In recent years, shorter standardized forms have been devised that allow test results to be written in quickly with little or no narrative concerning the student's behavior or performance. But description of 16 separate tests with no analysis of their interrelationships is of little value. Such report forms, although expedient, often lead to stereotyped recommendations that do not follow logically from the student's behavior. The purpose of the written report is to communicate information about a student's performance that will enable teachers to plan and implement an appropriate instructional program and to communicate information to parents about their child's performance. As such, it is a critical document, deserving of time and effort in preparation.

Communicating Test Results to Parents
In addition to providing information to the student's classroom teacher, the assessment process should help parents understand their child. Conveying the results of the diagnostic assessment to parents is usually the responsibility of the special education administrator, teacher, or psychologist. Conducting a parent conference that conveys clear and helpful information to parents is a very important skill.

Parents want and have the right to know whatever you know about their child's abilities and disabilities. They have the right to know your concerns and to express theirs. They need to have all of the information necessary to participate knowledgeably in any decisions being made about their child's placement and program. This means that professionals involved in the assessment process have the responsibility to convey clear and accurate information. This does not mean giving the parents a list of numerical scores that have little meaning for them. Nor does it mean describing in detail a child's problems in terms like "perceptual disturbance" or "auditory closure." Nor does it mean talking with parents in such generalities ("Yes, Tom is a little behind in math") that they leave the office uncertain of the results of the assessment. The balance between being too technical and too general is very difficult, but essential, to achieve.

Some parents ask for specific numbers and terms. What is their child's IQ? What grade level is he or she reading at? Is the child dyslexic? Brain-damaged? Others ask few questions. But beneath the specific questions and the unasked questions, parents of all levels of sophistication are basically asking, "Is something the matter with my child? What is it? Is the child going to be all right? What is the school going to do? How can we help?"

The following guidelines can be used in preparing for a parent conference:

• Think about the most important information you want to share with the parents about their child. Be sure that the information is presented clearly and does not get lost in a morass of numbers and descriptions of behavior.

• Be certain you know what your recommendations will be. If the assessments have been done by a team, come to an agreement about recommendations before the parent conference. Parents want to hear the professional recommendations—not four conflicting views.

- Have all the information ready for the parent conference. Come prepared to answer such questions as Who is the teacher of the special class? When can we observe? Do you know a good math tutor? How do we go about getting some counseling?

In a recent study titled "What Parents of the Learning Disabled Really Want from Professionals," Dembinski and Mauser (1977, p. 53) found that parents wanted professionals (teachers, psychologists, and physicians) to use terminology they could understand. They overwhelmingly disapproved of professional jargon. But the use of educational and psychological jargon is such a part of the professional role that teachers and psychologists must make a conscious effort not to overwhelm the parents with "jargonese." The following techniques have proven helpful:

- Review with the parents the reasons for referral and the school's concerns about the child. If the parents initiated the assessment, ask them to restate their concerns. Review the assessment process. Name the professionals who worked with the child and explain what they did. Be certain the parents know the names and understand the roles of all the people involved in the assessment process.

- Show the parents a few of the actual test items to demonstrate the task the student was asked to perform and the performance. Be certain to include examples of both the student's strengths and deficits. Rockowitz and Davidson (1979, p. 6) found it was better to present information about the child's strengths early in the conference. Too often, parents cannot hear the good news after a discussion of problems.

- Illustrate with examples how the student's skill deficiencies may be noted in the classroom, at home, and with friends.

- Encourage parent questions and comments by your manner. Try to draw both parents into the discussion. Be certain to schedule enough time for questions and discussion.

- Don't avoid using terms such as *mental retardation, learning disability, dyslexia,* or *aphasia* if your evaluation clearly supports the diagnosis. Rockowitz and Davidson (1979, p. 6) echo the finding of several researchers that parents need a name for their child's problem.

- Give parents a written report. With some parents it is better to discuss the report point by point; with others it is better to just talk about the assessment results and have them read the report later. Explain clearly in the body of the report or on an attached sheet the meaning of terms such as *grade score, standard score, stanine,* and *percentile.*

- Before concluding, ask the parents to restate what they have learned from the conference. This gives the professional a chance to clarify any misconceptions.

- End the conference with a clear plan of what will happen next and whose responsibility it is to carry out each part of the process. Be aware of parents' feelings, and don't press them to make decisions until they have had a chance to think it over and talk to others.

THE TEST REVIEWS

The remaining chapters of this book present critical reviews of some of the most commonly used instruments in educational diagnosis. Each test is introduced with a data sheet that presents the essential data about the test. The purpose of the test, the major areas tested, and the age or grade range of the test are stated.

The data sheet also indicates whether the student's performance is timed, the amount of testing time required, and the amount of scoring/interpretation time necessary. If available, information on the norming sample is given. The data sheet also indicates whether a test has alternate forms for test-retest purposes.

Following the data sheet, the format of the test is described, and a critical review of the test's strengths and limiting factors is presented. Guidelines are given for the use of each test to minimize abuses and misuses of the test and to provide information for the diagnostician regarding administration and interpretation. But *75 Tests* is not intended to teach the reader how to administer any test. Even a person who is experienced in diagnostic testing needs to study the examiner's manuals and practice administering the test before using it with a student referred for testing.

Testing is one part of the educational assessment process—an important part but not the only part. The educational diagnostician must work with parents, teachers, and others who know the student to gather information that will answer important educational questions accurately. This, after all, is the goal of educational assessment—a field of challenges and responsibilities.

PART I
Skill Area Tests

Most tests used in special education assess one or more specific skill areas. The tests reviewed in Part I are grouped into five chapters according to the type of skills they assess. These chapters are: Academic Tests, Perception and Memory Tests, Speech and Language Tests, Bilingual (Spanish-English) Language Tests, and Gross Motor Tests. While it is difficult to categorize tests that cover a wide range of skills, two major considerations determined the placement of such tests in Part I: (1) when a test is commonly used to evaluate a particular skill or learning process, and/or (2) when the majority of a test's subtests relate to a particular skill or learning process.

The assessment of skills in basic academic areas is one of the primary purposes of educational testing. Chapter One contains 21 representative tests that assess student functioning in the basic academic skill areas. General achievement tests, as well as specific tests of reading, spelling and written language, and mathematics are included.

Ten tests of perception and memory are reviewed in Chapter Two. These tests are commonly used in conjunction with tests that assess basic academic skills. "Comprehensive tests," that is, tests that assess more than one of the primary modalities used in the learning process—auditory, visual, and kinesthetic or motor—are included as well as tests that principally assess either auditory perception and memory or visual and visual-motor perception and memory.

The 16 speech and language tests reviewed in Chapter Three include both tests that measure articulation or speech production and tests that measure receptive and expressive language skills. All of the tests in this chapter are designed for use with preschool children as well as those in the elementary grades. In addition to these language assessment tools, Chapter Four includes information on eight bilingual tests for Spanish-speaking children.

Chapter Five contains two test batteries whose primary contribution is the assessment of motor skills. Because developmental delays in physical coordination may be associated with learning disorders, these tests yield information valuable in the planning of many students' educational programs.

CHAPTER ONE: ACADEMIC TESTS   17
Achievement Tests   18
Reading Tests   33
Spelling and Written Language Tests   62
Mathematics Tests   80

CHAPTER TWO: PERCEPTION AND MEMORY TESTS   91
Comprehensive Tests   92
Auditory Tests   109
Visual and Visual-Motor Tests   117

CHAPTER THREE: SPEECH AND LANGUAGE TESTS   139

CHAPTER FOUR: BILINGUAL (SPANISH-ENGLISH) LANGUAGE TESTS   195

CHAPTER FIVE: GROSS MOTOR TESTS   219

Chapter One

Academic Tests

The assessment of skills in basic academic areas is one of the primary purposes of educational testing. This chapter contains 21 representative tests that assess student functioning in the basic academic skills of reading, writing, spelling, and mathematics.

The first section reviews four multiple-subject tests of academic achievement. The Wide Range Achievement Test is probably the best-known and most widely used individual achievement test. It assesses a student's skills in reading, spelling, and mathematics. The Peabody Individual Achievement Test includes those three areas as well as reading comprehension and general information. The Basic Achievement Skills Individual Screener, a newcomer to the field, assesses reading comprehension, math computation, math word problems, spelling, and written language. It is a standardized instrument that is also criterion-referenced. The Brigance Diagnostic Inventories are comprehensive, criterion-referenced instruments.

The second section of the chapter contains nine tests specific to the field of reading. Two very similar and well-known standardized tests of oral reading, the Gray Oral Reading Tests and the Gilmore Oral Reading Test, are reviewed. Next are five more-extensive batteries of reading skills: the Spache Diagnostic Reading Scales, the Durrell Analysis of Reading Difficulty, the Gates-McKillop-Horowitz Reading Diagnostic Tests, the McCarthy Individualized Diagnostic Reading Inventory, and the Woodcock Reading Mastery Tests. The section concludes with two tests of silent reading, the well-known Gates-MacGinitie Silent Reading Tests and the newer Test of Reading Comprehension. For a complete overview of the reading tests, see Appendix D.

In the spelling and written language section of this chapter, there are six tests. The Larsen-Hammill Test of Written Spelling is a norm-referenced spelling instrument. The Diagnostic Achievement Test in Spelling, the Diagnostic Analysis of Reading Errors, and the Diagnostic Spelling Potential Test assess spelling errors with an eye to remediation. Two tests of written language, the Myklebust Picture Story Language Test and the Test of Written Language, conclude this section.

As mathematics is included in the three multiple-subject tests, only two individual diagnostic tests for mathematics are reviewed in this chapter. The KeyMath Diagnostic Arithmetic Test assesses a wide range of math concepts and computation skills. The Enright™ Diagnostic Inventory of Basic Arithmetic Skills is a very new test which looks very promising in the assessment of computation. The Kraner Preschool Math Inventory and the Brigance Diagnostic Inventory of Early Development, which both include counting and other beginning math skills, are reviewed in Part II: Preschool and Kindergarten Tests.

Some tests are difficult to categorize. The Slingerland Screening Tests for Identifying Children with Specific Language Disability and the Malcomesius Specific Language Disability Test are clearly tools for assessing academic skills. They include sections related to writing, spelling, and phonics. However, the primary contribution of these tests to educational assessment is in the area of perception and memory, so they are reviewed in Chapter Two.

Achievement Tests

Wide Range Achievement Test 19
Peabody Individual Achievement Test 22
Basic Achievement Skills Individual Screener 26
Brigance Diagnostic Inventories 29

Wide Range Achievement Test (WRAT)

J. F. Jastak, S. R. Jastak, and S. W. Bijou
Jastak Associates, Inc., 1937; revised 1965; Manual revised 1976; renorming 1978
1526 Gilpin Ave., Wilmington, DE 19806

Purpose	To assess skills in reading (word recognition), written spelling, and arithmetic computation
Major Areas Tested	Reading, spelling, and arithmetic
Age or Grade Range	5 years–adult
Usually Given By	Classroom teacher Special education teacher Psychologist
Type of Test	Standardized Individual Group (some subtests) Norm-referenced
Scores Obtained	Grade level Standard Percentile Stanine
Student Performance Timed?	Yes (some subtests)
Testing Time	20–30 minutes
Scoring/Interpretation Time	15 minutes
Normed On	A large sample of children and adults from all socioeconomic groups and all ranges of intellectual ability in seven states
Alternate Forms Available?	No

FORMAT

The materials for administering the Wide Range Achievement Test (WRAT) include the manual of instructions and individual student record forms.

The test is divided into two levels. Level I is for students between the ages of 5 years, 0 months and 11 years, 11 months. Level II is for students 12 years of age and older. The same manual and student record forms are used with both levels of the test.

Each level of the WRAT contains three subtests:

1. *Reading*. Recognizing and naming letters and pronouncing single words; no measure of context reading or comprehension
2. *Spelling*. Copying marks (X, ⊓, ⊏), writing the name, and writing single words from dictation
3. *Arithmetic*. Counting dots, reading numerals, solving oral problems, and performing basic written computation skills; no measure of mathematical concepts

The three subtests can be given independently. When all three are given, no particular order is required. The WRAT usually is given individually, but group procedures for the Spelling and Arithmetic subtests are described in the manual.

In Level I, each of the subtests begins with some preacademic tasks. In the Reading section, the prereading skills assessed include naming letters in the student's name, matching 10 letters by form, and naming 13 letters of the alphabet. The prespelling test consists of copying 18 geometric marks and writing names. The prearithmetic test includes counting 15 dots, reading 5 digits, showing 3 and 5 fingers, identifying which number is more, and doing 3 oral addition and subtraction problems. Students between the ages of 5 and 7 years are routinely given the pretests. Older students are given the pretests only when they cannot achieve a basal level on the Reading, Spelling, or Arithmetic subtests. Level II students who cannot achieve a basal level are also given the pretests.

The items in each subtest are arranged in order of difficulty. The student continues working until a ceiling level is reached in Reading (12 consecutive errors) and Spelling (10 consecutive errors) or until the time limit expires in Arithmetic (10 minutes).

Raw scores are converted to grade scores immediately, using the norm tables printed on the student record forms. Standard scores and percentiles are available in the manual.

STRENGTHS OF THE WRAT

- The WRAT is undoubtedly the best known and most widely used quick measure of individual achievement in basic academic skills. Students of all ages and skill levels can be tested to get an estimate of academic performance that can serve as a first step in diagnostic evaluation.

Although equivalent forms of the WRAT are not available, the wide age range covered by the test makes it a valuable tool for assessing the progress of an individual student over several years. The WRAT is inexpensive in terms of materials and time. It is relatively quick to administer and score.

- Grade scores, standard scores, and percentiles are provided and should be reported. The use of these three types of scores makes interpretation of the student's performance clear to parents and teachers.
- Extensive research has been done on the WRAT, and reliability and validity data are presented in the manual.
- The manual also presents excellent discussions of such topics as the diagnostic evaluation, reading disability, speed reading, remedial techniques, and reading readiness, which are interesting to the teacher and helpful in test interpretation and program planning.
- Large-print editions of both levels of the WRAT are available for testing visually handicapped students.

LIMITING FACTORS OF THE WRAT

In *Uses and Misuses of the WRAT,* a technical report published by Jastak Associates, Inc., the limitations of the WRAT are described very well. The report is issued by the publisher to avoid misuse of the instrument. All examiners should read this report.

- Because the WRAT is so easy to give and to score, it is frequently overused and misused. It must be viewed as an initial estimate of a student's basic academic skills and not as a complete diagnostic instrument. Too often students are admitted to or excluded from special programs on the basis of their WRAT scores alone. An investigation of the content of each of the WRAT subtests indicates that such a use of the test is not warranted.

The Reading subtest assesses word recognition only. The student simply reads aloud a list of single words. There is no measure of sentence reading, paragraph reading, or comprehension. Because the student can obtain 25 points for the prereading items, a reading grade score of 1.4 is obtained by reading three preprimer words. Consequently, overestimations of students' reading levels are quite common on the WRAT, especially at the primary level.

Similarly, in Spelling a student may obtain a grade score of 1.3 by copying 18 marks and writing 2 letters in his or her name correctly. The relationship between design copying and written spelling is not well documented and raises questions about the validity of including 18 points from such a task on a measure of spelling.

The Arithmetic subtest raises many content questions. Because it is a straight computation test, student performance depends on the curriculum that has been taught. Students who have not been taught skills in fractions cannot obtain a fourth-grade score. Students instructed totally in the "new math" may get unrealistically low scores. Also, there is only one example of many types of problems. For example, on Level I

$$\begin{array}{r}\$62.04\\-5.30\\\hline\end{array}$$

is the only example of subtraction with regrouping; it clearly requires understanding of zeros and money as well. In addition, the 10-minute time limit on the arithmetic test affects the scores of older students, who may work slowly. If possible, they should be given an opportunity to complete as many problems as they can; then two scores should be reported, one within the 10-minute limit and one after the time limit was extended.

• A major limiting factor in the 1965 edition of the WRAT was the poor organization of its manual. Administration procedures were confusing, and examiner errors in administration and scoring were frequent. However, the most recent revision of the WRAT manual is well organized. Nevertheless, examiners who are new to the test are still cautioned to study the manual carefully and to practice giving the test several times before administering it to a student with academic difficulties.

• Although it is quick to administer and an easy source of grade scores, the WRAT is a limited diagnostic tool. Time should be taken to analyze a student's error pattern. Table 3 shows how an analysis of common WRAT spelling errors can be used to define a remedial program.

NOTE

A new edition of the WRAT will be available in the fall of 1983. Changes include:

• Minor changes in test items
• New grade-level norms, standard scores, and percentiles based on a national stratified sampling of 6,000 children and adults
• Separate test forms for levels I and II, allowing more space for presentation of the items

Table 3. Analysis of Spelling Errors

Word	Spelling	Error Type	Teaching Strategy
cat	ɔat	Letter reversal (kinesthetic)	Dictation, visual-motor training
boy	doy	b/d confusion (visual-kinesthetic)	Visual discrimination, visual-motor training
will	well	Vowel discrimination (auditory)	Auditory discrimination, word patterns (*ill*)
make	mack	Vowel error and visual recall	Silent-*e* rule, dictation
say	sae	Poor visual recall	Word patterns (*ay*), word tracing
grown explain	grone explane	Poor visual recall	Word tracing
enter advice	inter edvice	Vowel discrimination (auditory)	Auditory discrimination, dictation
surprise	suprise	Incorrect pronunciation (auditory)	Auditory-kinesthetic feedback, visual cuing, color coding
cut cook	kut kook	Poor visual recall	Word tracing
light dress watch	lite dres woch	Poor visual recall	Word tracing, color coding

Peabody Individual Achievement Test (PIAT)

Lloyd M. Dunn and Frederick C. Markwardt, Jr.
American Guidance Service, Inc., 1970
Publishers' Bldg., Circle Pines, MN 55014

Purpose	To provide a wide-range screening measure of reading, spelling, mathematics, and general achievement
Major Areas Tested	Mathematics, reading, spelling, and general achievement
Age or Grade Range	Grades K–12
Usually Given By	Classroom teacher Paraprofessional Special education teacher Any trained person Psychologist
Type of Test	Standardized Individual Norm-referenced
Scores Obtained	Age level Grade level Standard Percentile
Student Performance Timed?	No
Testing Time	30–40 minutes
Scoring/Interpretation Time	20 minutes
Normed On	Public school children from 27 urban, suburban, and rural communities across the United States; sample balanced for sex, race, and parents' occupations
Alternate Forms Available?	No

Achievement Tests

FORMAT

The Peabody Individual Achievement Test (PIAT) materials consist of individual record booklets, the examiner's manual, and two easel kits that contain the test items, practice items, and instructions for administration. A training tape that provides a guide for acceptable pronunciation of reading and spelling words is also available.

The two easel kits are arranged as follows:

Volume I
    Subtest 1: Mathematics
    Subtest 2: Reading Recognition
Volume II
    Subtest 3: Reading Comprehension
    Subtest 4: Spelling
    Subtest 5: General Information

The PIAT was standardized on all five subtests given in the above order. However, it is possible to give selected subtests rather than the complete test. The PIAT combines short-answer and multiple-choice questions. No writing is required. Suggested starting points are given for each subtest, and the basal level is five consecutive correct responses. Testing continues until the student makes five errors in seven consecutive responses. With this procedure, students are tested only on items within their range of ability. The five subtests are:

1. *Mathematics*. This subtest contains 84 multiple-choice items, ranging from such kindergarten-level tasks as matching numbers to high school concepts in algebra and geometry. The questions are read to the student, who selects the answer from four visually-presented choices (see Figures 1 and 2). All computation must be done mentally.

2. *Reading Recognition*. This subtest contains 84 items, including 18 readiness tasks such as letter matching and letter naming. The remaining 66 items are single words that the student reads aloud (see Figure 3). The words were selected from basic reading series using both the "look-say" and phonic approaches.

3. *Reading Comprehension*. This subtest contains 66 multiple-choice items. On each one, the student is presented with a page that contains one sentence to be read silently; the second page has four pictures, and the student selects the picture that best illustrates the meaning of the sentence just read (see Figure 4).

4. *Spelling*. This subtest contains 84 multiple-choice items. The first 14 are readiness tasks, such as finding the "different" symbol in a group of four and letter recognition. The remaining 70 items require the student to select the correct spelling of a word pronounced by the examiner from four choices, as shown in Figures 5 and 6. No written spelling is required.

5. *General Information*. This subtest contains 84 questions that are read to the student and answered orally. The content includes science, social studies, fine arts, and sports. Examples of the test items might include the following:

How are birds and fish different?

Which boy has the least money?

David has three dimes and two pennies.	John has six nickles and one dime.
Jim has three quarters.	Bill has twenty cents.

Figure 1. PIAT Mathematics

Which set of lines are *not* parallel?

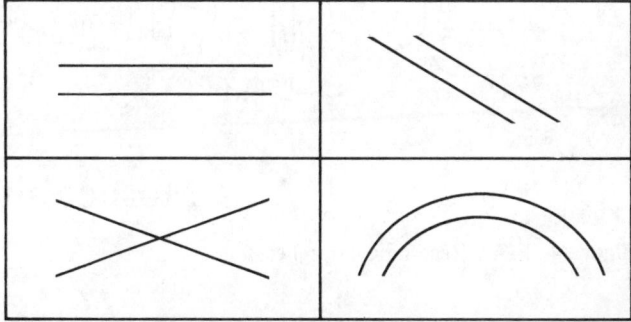

Figure 2. PIAT Mathematics

come	down	yellow	fast
huge	warm	century	artist
impede	caution	survey	knead

Figure 3. PIAT Reading Recognition

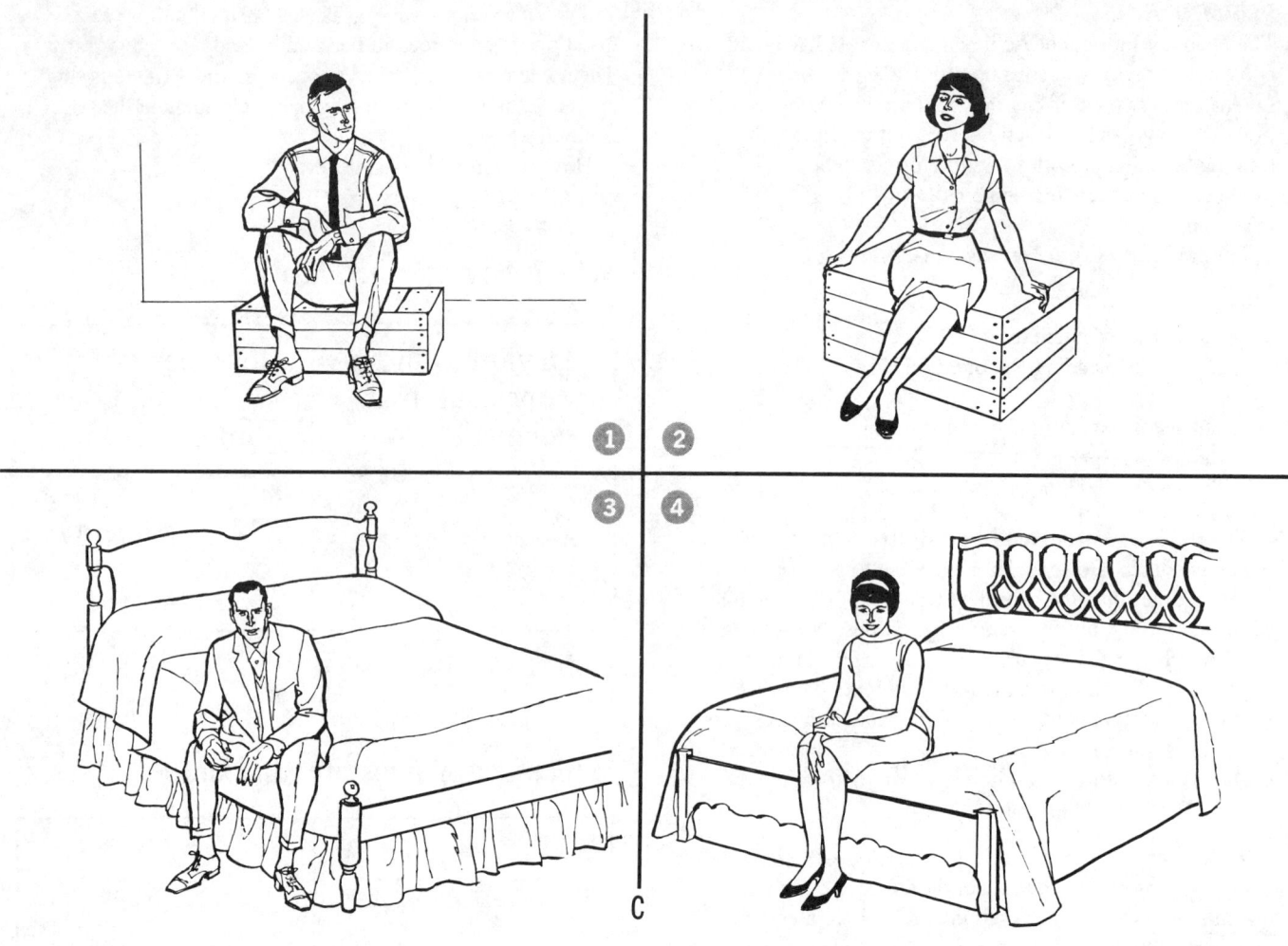

Mother sits on the bed.

Figure 4. PIAT Reading Comprehension

What do you call a large group of people who play musical instruments together?

By what process do the people select their government officials?

What is a common belief of the Catholic and Protestant religions as contrasted with Judaism?

Grade level, age level, percentile, and standard scores are obtained for each of the five subtests as well as for the total test. Using these derived scores, together with chronological and mental ages, a variety of types of profiles can be plotted to represent graphically a student's achievement in the five subtest areas.

Alternate forms for test-retest purposes are not available, but the wide age range of the PIAT makes it a usable test for documenting progress over time.

lok	loc
looke	look

Figure 5. PIAT Spelling

excillent	excellent
excelant	excellant

Figure 6. PIAT Spelling

STRENGTHS OF THE PIAT

- The PIAT provides a quick rough estimate of achievement levels. The multiple-choice format allows the test taker to move quickly, and the variety of items holds students' interest. The items appeal to a wide age range, which makes the PIAT very useful for underachieving secondary students.

- The subtests of the PIAT, used in conjunction with other diagnostic tests, can provide useful information. The Mathematics subtest includes items that assess a student's problem-solving skills more effectively than a straight computation test would. The picture format of the Reading Comprehension subtest is a unique way to measure the important skill of sentence comprehension. For students who have not previously had an intelligence test, the General Information subtest can provide a quick estimate of overall functioning.

- Perhaps most useful is a comparison of a student's Spelling score on the PIAT (which requires only recognition of the correct spelling) with written spelling performance on a test such as the Wide Range Achievement Test (p. 19) or the Larsen-Hammill Test of Written Spelling (p. 63). For example, suppose two sixth-grade students obtained the grade scores shown here:

	WRAT Spelling	PIAT Spelling
Student A	4.3	5.8
Student B	4.5	4.7

Both students are performing significantly below grade level on written spelling. Student A, however, has the ability to recognize correct spelling, as her PIAT score indicates, thus demonstrating some visual memory skills. The remedial program for Student A would attempt to capitalize on that visual memory, and the expectations for performance in such skills as proofreading and dictionary work would be higher than they would be for Student B.

LIMITING FACTORS OF THE PIAT

- The PIAT was not intended to be a comprehensive diagnostic instrument in any of the subtest areas. For students with academic problems, it should serve only as a guide for further in-depth testing.

- When interpreting a student's performance on the PIAT, it is necessary to keep in mind the exact task presented on each subtest. The broad general subtest names (Mathematics, Reading Recognition, Reading Comprehension, Spelling, and General Information) do not describe the tasks. For example, the examiner must be careful not to make general statements about a student's spelling based on the PIAT alone, because the task of recognizing correct spelling is quite different from written spelling (the more usual classroom task). Such a statement as "Student C is two years below grade level in math" may be very inaccurate if based on the PIAT alone; the student's computation skills may be excellent.

- The multiple-choice format used on the Mathematics, Reading Comprehension, and Spelling subtests is appropriate for a screening tool but may yield very inaccurate results for individual students. For example, the impulsive student often selects an answer without thinking, whereas the student with sophisticated test-taking skills may puzzle out an answer by the process of elimination without really knowing the information.

- As with any test made up of subtests, there is a tendency to focus attention on a comparison of subtest scores; that is, to discuss Student A's performance in spelling compared to her performance in math. The PIAT manual discusses the problems in this type of analysis and presents guidelines for interpreting differences between raw scores on subtests. The examiner should study these guidelines carefully to avoid overinterpretation of subtest differences.

- The arrangement of subtest materials in the easel kit is confusing; the examiner needs to practice locating materials quickly before administering the test. There is little room for writing comments in the individual record book.

- PIAT reliability varies with the subtest and the age of the students. In general, the Reading Recognition and Total Test scores are most reliable, and the Spelling and Reading Comprehension subtest scores are least reliable. The reliability of performance of kindergarten students is low, suggesting that the PIAT is not a good test for students at the preacademic level.

- Studies on the validity of the PIAT are notably lacking, again suggesting that the best use of the PIAT is as a quick screening device.

Basic Achievement Skills Individual Screener (BASIS)

The Psychological Corporation, 1982 (standardization form); 1983
7500 Old Oak Blvd., Middleburg Heights, OH 44130

Purpose	To provide both norm-referenced and criterion-referenced information in basic academic skills
Major Areas Tested	Mathematics, reading, spelling, and writing
Age or Grade Range	Grades 1–12
Usually Given By	Psychologist Educational diagnostician Counselor Administrator Special education teacher Any trained person
Type of Test	Individual Criterion-referenced Norm-referenced Standardized
Scores Obtained	Grade level Percentile Age level Stanine
Student Performance Timed?	Yes (Writing subtest)
Testing Time	1 hour
Scoring/Interpretation Time	15–30 minutes
Normed On	National demographically controlled standardization in process
Alternate Forms Available?	No

Achievement Tests

FORMAT

The Basic Achievement Skills Individual Screener (BASIS) is an individual test of reading, math, spelling, and writing achievement. It covers grades 1 through 12 and provides both norm-referenced and criterion-referenced information.

The materials consist of the manual, containing directions for administration and scoring, as well as technical information; the BASIS content booklet, including the reading passages and readiness activities; and BASIS record forms. The student writes directly on these consumable forms for the Mathematics, Spelling, and Writing subtests. The forms also include a summary of the student's performance in both norm-referenced and criterion-referenced scores.

Four subject areas are assessed by the BASIS:

1. *Mathematics*. This subtest includes five items at the readiness level; addition, subtraction, multiplication, and division of whole numbers, fractions, and decimals; and word problems using basic computation skills.

2. *Reading*. This subtest includes a few items at the readiness and beginning reading levels (letter naming, word matching, word reading, and sentence reading). It primarily assesses reading comprehension through a cloze procedure. The student reads orally a passage with two or more words missing and fills in an appropriate word.

3. *Spelling*. In this subtest, the student writes single words dictated by the examiner.

4. *Writing*. This subtest consists of a 10-minute writing sample on a standardized topic ("Your Favorite Place"). The examiner reads the sample for an overall or holistic impression of its content, organization, vocabulary, sentence structure, and mechanics. The impression is then matched against an average sample for the student's grade, and the student's sample is rated average, above average, or below average as compared to the sample.

A student may be given all four subtest areas or single areas selected by the examiner. When the complete test is given, the Mathematics subtest is given first.

The grade-referenced cluster is the basic unit of administration of the BASIS. The content of each subtest area is divided into eight clusters of items, a cluster for each grade level, 1 through 8. All of the items in each cluster for each subject area must be administered at one time. If the student passes the criterion or minimum number of items for each cluster, he or she moves on to the next level. If the student does not pass the criterion, the examiner drops two grade-level clusters to obtain a basal. The basal/ceiling process, then, is done through levels rather than through single items. The basal is the lowest level at which the student passes criterion; the ceiling is the lowest level at which the student does not pass the criterion.

A grade-referenced cluster in Mathematics consists of six computation items and two word problems (see Figure 7).

7

(a) $\begin{array}{r} 4283 \\ \times\ 315 \\ \hline \end{array}$

(b) $\dfrac{2}{3} = \dfrac{6}{\Box}$

(c) $67\overline{)7303}$

(d) $\begin{array}{r} 7.03 \\ \times\ 4.6 \\ \hline \end{array}$

(e) $5.94 + 3.4 =$

(f) $.14\overline{)7.42}$

DICTATED:

(g) In the gym, we set up 10 rows of chairs with 12 chairs in each row. 125 more people can sit on the bleachers. How many people can sit in the gym in all?

DICTATED:

(h) Jan has $3\frac{4}{5}$ yards of canvas cloth. She needs $1\frac{2}{5}$ yards to make a floor for her tent. How many extra yards of cloth will Jan have?

Figure 7. BASIS Mathematics Cluster

Criterion is usually five out of eight correct. A grade-referenced cluster in Reading is one paragraph with six omitted words; criterion is usually four out of six. The Spelling grade-referenced cluster is six dictated words with the usual criterion being four correct.

Following the test completion, raw score points for items correct, plus those below the basal level, are totaled in each subject area and converted to a variety of scores, grade equivalents, stanines, and percentile ranks based on grade and age. In addition, a grade-referenced placement is determined. The grade-referenced placement score describes the student's instructional level in each subject area. In Reading, it represents the last level at which a student reached criterion, a level of 50–67 percent accuracy on the cloze procedure. In Mathematics and Spelling, it represents the first level at which the student did not achieve criterion, a level of about 60–70 percent accuracy. In addition to these norm-referenced and criterion-referenced scores, other diagnostic information is elicited by error analysis of math, reading, and spelling performance.

STRENGTHS OF THE BASIS

- The BASIS is obviously designed to provide the quick screening information usually obtained through the Wide Range Achievement Test (p. 19). Many of the limitations of the Wide Range Achievement Test have been eliminated by including reading comprehension, word problems, and written language. The advantages of a single instrument measuring the four basic skills quickly and over a wide age range have been maintained. The BASIS shows good promise as an initial screening tool.
- The combining of norm-referenced scores with criterion-referenced information is a unique feature of the BASIS. It should allow for more meaningful interpretation of student performance.
- The testing materials, forms, and manual are clear and well designed.

LIMITING FACTORS OF THE BASIS

The BASIS was available only in its experimental form for standardization purposes at the time of writing this review. Information on standardization procedures and norms tables had not been completed; thus, it was not possible to administer the test to children and score the results. The instrument's reliability and validity have not yet been documented.

Achievement Tests

Brigance Diagnostic Inventories (Brigance Inventories)
Albert H. Brigance
Curriculum Associates, Inc., 1981
5 Esquire Rd., North Billerica, MA 01862

Purpose	To assess preacademic, academic, and vocational skills and to provide a systematic performance record to help teachers define instructional objectives and plan individualized educational programs
Major Areas Tested	Reading, writing, spelling, mathematics, language, and motor skills
Age or Grade Range	Preschool–grade 12
Usually Given By	Classroom teacher Administrator Special education teacher Paraprofessional Psychologist Teaching aide
Type of Test	Informal Individual (some group subtests) Criterion-referenced
Scores Obtained	Grade level (some subtests) Age level (some subtests)
Student Performance Timed?	No
Testing Time	15–90 minutes (depending on purpose of testing)
Scoring/Interpretation Time	15–30 minutes
Normed On	Not normed, but field-tested in 30 states and 2 provinces of Canada
Alternate Forms Available?	No, except for some subtests in the Diagnostic Comprehensive Inventory of Basic Skills

FORMAT

There are four Brigance Diagnostic Inventories (Brigance Inventories) designed to assess basic competencies at different grade levels. Together, the four instruments evaluate more than 500 skill sequences from preschool through grade 12. The skills assessed in each are outlined in Table 4. The materials for each Brigance Inventory consist of an examiner's notebook and individual record books. The notebook is designed to lie flat on the table between the examiner and the student. It includes directions for administering each subtest, test items, scoring criteria, and instructional objectives in behavioral terms. A sample page from the examiner's notebook is shown in Figure 8, and the corresponding test items are shown in Figure 9. When the assessment is oral, the student works directly from the student page; when a test requires writing or when group testing is done, the student page is reproduced in multiple copies.

The individual student record books provide a means of recording ongoing progress. The student's responses are recorded by the examiner in the record book in a different color each time the test is administered. A grade-level profile is charted after each administration to provide a graphic summary of student achievement. Observation of student behavior can also be noted.

The Brigance Inventories are informal. Administration directions are given, but the examiner is encouraged to adjust the procedures to meet the needs of the student. The only question being asked in each subtest is: "Has the student mastered this skill, or is more instruction needed?" Developmental ages or grade-level scores are provided for a few key subtests in each inventory, but, basically, the tests are not norm-referenced. Their purpose is to assess basic skills, define instructional objectives, assist teachers in program planning, and provide a continuous measure of progress.

INITIAL CLUSTERS VISUALLY

SKILL: Can articulate correct sound when cluster is presented visually.

DIRECTIONS: Point to the first letters (sh).

Say: Look at these letters. Tell me the sound they have when they are together at the beginning of a word.

If the student does not understand, explain the first blend.

Say: These letters have the sound of sh as in shock or shape.

See NOTE #2 and the next page for alternate method of administration.

NOTES:

1. You may wish to check the student's understanding of the voiced and unvoiced "th."

   Say: Can you tell me the other sound "th" makes?, after the student has given one sound.

2. An alternate method of assessing this skill is to present the initial clusters in combination with a vowel. The results of the alternate method may have more validity if the student has been taught by a method which always presents the clusters in combination with a vowel such as Duggins or *Words in Color*. See next page for alternate administration.

DISCONTINUE: After three consecutive errors.

TIME: 10 seconds per response.

ACCURACY: Give credit for each correct response.

OBJECTIVE: When presented with a list of 33 blends and digraphs (clusters) listed in an order commonly taught, the student will indicate the sound_____(quantity) of the consonants have or make in the initial position.

–56–

Initial Clusters Visually C-10

Figure 8. Brigance Inventories Examiner's Page for Initial Clusters Visually

Achievement Tests

STRENGTHS OF THE BRIGANCE INVENTORIES
- Each inventory is a comprehensive battery of assessments, including many skills for a wide age range of students. By careful selection of subtests appropriate for each student's age and skill level and for the purpose of the testing, assessment can be completed quickly.
- The Brigance Inventories are intended to lead directly to instructional objectives and program planning; if used correctly, they do.
- The inventories can be administered by teaching aides or paraprofessionals under supervision.
- The inventories provide a well-organized recordkeeping system.
- The inventories include some unique subtests. Skills such as alphabetizing, dictionary and reference book use, interpretation of graphs and maps, and knowledge of geometry are not assessed in other instruments.
- The Spanish Edition is very helpful in assessing the instructional needs of Spanish-speaking students.

LIMITING FACTORS OF THE BRIGANCE INVENTORIES
- Although the Brigance Inventories claim to be a measure of progress, informal tests should not be used as the only measure of progress. Reliability is difficult to establish, since the tests are not administered in a standardized manner. The grade-level scores should *not* be used as a measure of progress.
- The informal format somewhat encourages teachers or teaching aides to administer the Brigance Inventories without preparation. This often results in too lengthy, inappropriate, or haphazard assessment. Careful selection of tests, preparation of materials, and study of data-recording procedures is essential if the instruments are to be valuable.

sh →	wh	th (v)	th (u)	st
sw	gr	sp	fl	gl
sl	pl	cl	bl	tr
cr	sc	dr	ch	fr
pr	br	sm	sk	wr
qu	spr	thr	scr	shr
str	spl	squ		

Figure 9. Brigance Inventories Initial Clusters Visually

Table 4. Scope of the Brigance Inventories

Inventory	Grade Range	Skills Assessed	Comments
Diagnostic Inventory of Early Development (Yellow Notebook)	Preschool–2	Preambulatory motor Gross and fine motor Self-help Prespeech Speech and language General knowledge Readiness Reading Writing Math	

Diagnostic Inventory of Basic Skills (Blue Notebook)	K–6	Readiness
		Reading
		   Word recognition
		   Fluency
		   Analysis
		Vocabulary
		Handwriting
		Grammar
		Spelling
		Math
		   Computation
		   Measurement
		   Geometry
			Comprises the original Brigance Inventory with 141 subtests covering a variety of academic tasks in key subject areas. A small pamphlet lists which subtests are appropriate to administer for a particular grade.

Diagnostic Inventory of Essential Skills (Red Notebook)	4–12	Reading
		   Word recognition
		   Oral reading
		   Comprehension
		   Analysis
		   Reference
		Writing
		Spelling
		Math
		   Computation
		   Fractions
		   Decimals
		   Percents
		   Measurement
			Designed for use with secondary students in special-education programs. Measures minimal competencies in academic and vocational skills. Provides grade-placement scores in word recognition, oral reading, comprehension, sentence writing, spelling, and math. Includes rating scales for health practices and attitudes, self-concept, attitude, personality, responsibility, job interview skills, auto safety, and speaking and listening skills. A guide lists tests appropriate for each grade level.

Diagnostic Comprehensive Inventory of Basic Skills (Green Notebook)	K–9	All skills in Diagnostic Inventory of Basic Skills Speech Listening Percents Metrics Reading comprehension	Designed for use in elementary and middle schools. Expands Diagnostic Inventory of Basic Skills to grade 9. Adds new subtests, particularly in the areas of speech, listening, and reading comprehension. More than half of the skills can be assessed in groups. A guide lists tests appropriate for each grade level. Has two forms for many subtests to provide for pre- and posttesting. The Assessment of Basic Skills Spanish Edition contains 112 subtests from this inventory translated into Spanish.

Reading Tests

Gray Oral Reading Tests 34
Gilmore Oral Reading Test 36
Spache Diagnostic Reading Scales 39
Durrell Analysis of Reading Difficulty 42
Gates-McKillop-Horowitz Reading Diagnostic Tests 46
McCarthy Individualized Diagnostic Reading Inventory 49
Woodcock Reading Mastery Tests 53
Gates-MacGinitie Silent Reading Tests 56
Test of Reading Comprehension 59

Gray Oral Reading Tests (Gray Oral)

William S. Gray
Pro-Ed, 1967
5341 Industrial Oaks Blvd., Austin, TX 78735

Purpose	To measure growth in oral reading and to aid in the diagnosis of oral reading problems
Major Areas Tested	Oral reading
Age or Grade Range	Grades 1–college
Usually Given By	Special education teacher Psychologist Diagnostician trained in reading disorders
Type of Test	Standardized Individual Norm-referenced
Scores Obtained	Grade level
Student Performance Timed?	Yes
Testing Time	15–20 minutes
Scoring/Interpretation Time	15 minutes
Normed On	Public school children in two districts in Florida and in several schools in metropolitan and suburban Chicago, Illinois
Alternate Forms Available?	Yes

FORMAT

The Gray Oral Reading Tests (Gray Oral) consist of four equivalent forms—A, B, C, and D. The materials include a spiral-bound set of reading passages for each form, the corresponding examiner's record booklets, and an examiner's manual. A stopwatch is also needed for administration.

The first passage of each form is introduced by a picture that provides the setting for the paragraph. Each of the 12 passages that follow is self-contained, so that the test may be started with any paragraph. The student reads aloud while the examiner marks errors in the examiner's record booklet and notes observations of the student's reading style and behavior on a checklist. Each passage is timed, and each is followed by four comprehension questions that are read to the student and answered orally. The passages within a form increase in difficulty in several ways: higher-level vocabulary, longer words, longer and more complex sentences, and higher-level concepts. The 13 paragraphs cover the range from preprimer to adult reading; 8 of the 13 paragraphs contain material at the elementary school level.

The student begins the test by reading a passage two years below grade level. If necessary, the examiner proceeds with easier paragraphs until the student reads one passage without error. Then the student progresses through more difficult paragraphs until seven or more errors are made on two successive paragraphs. The average student reads five or six paragraphs: two relatively easy, one or two at the achievement level, and two that are more difficult.

The Gray Oral tests are scored by combining the number of errors made in each paragraph with the time needed to read that paragraph. The resultant passage scores are then totaled to yield a test score that is converted into a grade equivalent. (The comprehension questions do not contribute to the grade-equivalent score.) Separate norms are provided for boys and girls.

STRENGTHS OF THE GRAY ORAL

- The Gray Oral is one of several good oral reading tests that all follow the same general format. With its wide age range and four equivalent forms, it is designed for measuring progress. (However, only grade scores are provided, and they should not be used for measuring progress.) The unique feature of the Gray Oral is that speed of reading is an integral part of the grade score. In other oral reading tests, timing is optional, but in the Gray Oral, rate of reading is considered of equal importance to number of errors. Particularly with older students, combined assessment of accuracy and speed yields a grade-equivalent score that is more predictive of classroom performance.

- In addition to the scores, the Gray Oral tests yield a variety of diagnostic information. Oral reading errors are recorded and grouped into eight categories. Errors include gross or partial mispronunciations, omissions, additions, substitutions, repetitions, changes in word order, and requests for examiner assistance. Analysis of these types of errors, together with observations of reading style noted on the checklist (lack of expression, loss of place, and so on), enables the examiner to plan an individualized reading program. In addition, the four comprehension questions that accompany each passage require only comprehension of literal meaning and immediate recall of facts, but they give some estimate of oral reading comprehension.

- The examiner's manual is clear and well organized. It presents many good suggestions for interpreting students' oral reading performance.

LIMITING FACTORS OF THE GRAY ORAL

- For students with reading disabilities, the timing aspect of the Gray Oral causes increased pressure. Because these are the students for whom the most accurate diagnostic data is needed, another test may need to be used with students whose performance is significantly affected by the stopwatch.

- It is questionable whether speed of reading is an important criterion for beginning readers. The beginning reader who reads slowly and cautiously but without errors is penalized by the Gray Oral scoring system. And for students with reading difficulties related to impulsiveness, reading speed may not be a desirable characteristic.

- While emphasizing reading speed, Gray has eliminated comprehension as a factor in determining grade scores. The test would be strengthened by the addition of other types of comprehension questions and of norms or guidelines for interpreting student performance in this area.

- The norms on the Gray Oral are described as "tentative" in the examiner's manual. Only about 40 students were tested at each grade level (20 boys and 20 girls). No efforts were made to obtain a balanced sample on such variables as race, IQ level, or socioeconomic class. All students with physical or emotional problems, with speech defects, or who had repeated or skipped a grade were eliminated from the sample. As a result, caution should be taken before applying the norms to groups of varying abilities and ethnic backgrounds. Local norms should be developed. Of particular interest are the different norms provided by the Gray Oral for boys and girls. Other achievement tests in reading have not found that sex difference requires different norms.

- Validity and reliability studies are notably lacking. The tests base their claim to validity on careful test construction, but research studies are needed.

NOTE

The rights to the Gray Oral have recently been purchased by Pro-Ed, and the test is undergoing revision and restandardization.

Gilmore Oral Reading Test

John V. Gilmore and Eunice C. Gilmore
Harcourt Brace Jovanovich, Inc., 1968
The Psychological Corporation
7500 Old Oak Blvd., Middleburg Heights, OH 44130

Purpose	To assess oral reading accuracy and comprehension skills
Major Areas Tested	Oral reading
Age or Grade Range	Grades 1–8
Usually Given By	Classroom teacher Special education teacher
Type of Test	Standardized Individual Norm-referenced
Scores Obtained	Grade level Percentile Stanine Rating scale
Student Performance Timed?	Optional
Testing Time	15–25 minutes
Scoring/Interpretation Time	15 minutes
Normed On	Over 4,000 students from a wide range of socioeconomic levels in six school districts throughout the United States
Alternate Forms Available?	Yes

FORMAT

The materials for the Gilmore Oral Reading Test consist of a manual of directions, the booklet from which the student reads paragraphs, and the individual record blanks for recording the student's reading errors and answers to comprehension questions.

Two equivalent forms are available—Forms C and D (A and B are out of print). Each form consists of 10 paragraphs carefully constructed from graded vocabulary in basal readers. The paragraphs are graduated in length and difficulty from the primer through the eighth-grade level. The 10 paragraphs form a continuous story that is introduced with an illustration. Forms C and D are both printed in the same booklet, but separate record blanks are provided for each.

The examiner introduces the test through the illustration and selects a paragraph about two years below the student's expected reading level. The student reads the paragraph aloud, and the examiner times the reading with a stopwatch and marks any errors. The examiner reads the five comprehension questions following each paragraph, and the student answers orally. The testing stops when the student makes 10 or more accuracy errors in one paragraph.

Separate grade-equivalent, percentile, and stanine scores are obtained for accuracy, comprehension, and rate of reading. Performance ratings are also provided. Table 5 is an example of what a sixth grader's scores might look like.

Table 5. A Sixth Grader's Scores on the Gilmore Oral Reading Test

Score	Accuracy	Comprehension	Rate
Stanine	3	8	
Percentile band	11–22	89–95	
Grade equivalent	4.2	5.3	
Performance rating	Below average	Above average	Fast

STRENGTHS OF THE GILMORE ORAL READING TEST

• This is one of several good standardized oral reading tests. It provides a means of assessing a student's oral reading accuracy, comprehension, and rate. A system for analyzing the student's oral reading errors is built into the test format. Table 6 summarizes the types of errors that are possible.

• Careful analysis of the error pattern of an individual student can lead directly to planning a corrective program. For example, a student who waits for prompting from the examiner needs to be taught how to use word analysis skills and needs to be encouraged to sound out new words; the student who makes frequent "substitutions" may need to learn to monitor oral reading with comprehension clues.

• The wide grade range of the Gilmore Oral Reading Test, together with its equivalent Forms C and D, make it a good instrument for measuring pupil progress through test-retest procedures. An added advantage of the test is that the timing is optional and separate from the scoring for accuracy and comprehension. The examiner may decide whether using the stopwatch will cause anxiety in a student that would significantly affect performance. Eliminating the timing simplifies test administration and does not affect the accuracy and comprehension scores.

LIMITING FACTORS OF THE GILMORE ORAL READING TEST

Users of this test should be aware of several factors that significantly affect interpretation of test results.

• The accuracy score is the only reliable and valid score on the test. The system for obtaining a comprehension score often results in a spuriously high score. This is because of a procedure that gives "bonus" points for paragraphs above the ceiling level. The authors make the assumption that, if a student could read the next paragraph after reaching the ceiling (that is, after making 10 errors), he or she would be able to answer almost the same number of questions as on the ceiling paragraph. The result of this assumption is the scoring system shown in Table 7.

Students frequently receive comprehension scores high above their accuracy scores, not because they answered the questions correctly, but simply because of the bonus system. Also, because the comprehension questions on the Gilmore Oral Reading Test require only recall of specific facts from the paragraph and no interpretation or abstract reasoning, comprehension scores rarely reflect the student's functioning level in classroom materials. It is safe to say that, if the student's comprehension score is higher than the accuracy score, it means little in terms of actual skills. However, if the student's comprehension score is lower than the accuracy score, beware! Given the types of questions and the bonus scoring system, a low comprehension score may reflect serious comprehension or memory problems that require further assessment.

• The vocabulary of the test is drawn from basal readers, which usually have a sight-word emphasis. Particularly at the lower levels, students who are being instructed in a phonic or linguistic approach are often unable to demonstrate their reading gains. For example, a student may have made great progress during the year in learning letter names, sounds, and phonically regular three- and four-letter words. These gains will not be seen on pre- and posttesting, because linguistically regular words are not featured. Parents

Table 6. Error Types on the Gilmore Oral Reading Test

Error Type	Definition	Example
Substitution	Real word is replaced by another	*Step* for *stop*; *father* for *farther*
Mispronunciation	Word produced is not a real word	*Frist* for *first*; *at'end* for *attend*
Lack of response	Student does not attempt word within five seconds	
Disregard of punctuation	Student does not pause for periods or commas	
Insertion	An extra word or words are added	*the* The boy and girl came home.
Hesitation	Student pauses at least two seconds before attempting word	
Repetition	A word, phrase, or sentence is repeated	
Omission	One or more words are omitted	This is the best place to (have a) picnic.

and teachers need to understand that the Gilmore Oral Reading Test will not reflect growth until the child also masters a basic sight-word vocabulary.

• The content of the upper-grade paragraphs of this test deals with the vocational aspirations of male and female students. Professionals today may find the orientation offensive (Dick prepares to be a doctor or scientist, but Mary considers secretarial work or nursing).

Table 7. Scoring System for the Comprehension Section of the Gilmore Oral Reading Test

Paragraph Number	Comprehension (number correct)	
1	5	
2	5	Credited
3	4	
4 Basal	3	
5	4	
6	3	Actually read
7 Ceiling	4	
8	3	
9	2	"Bonus points"
10	1	

Spache Diagnostic Reading Scales (DRS)

George D. Spache
CTB/McGraw-Hill Division, 1963; revised editions 1972, 1981
Del Monte Research Park, Monterey, CA 93940

Purpose	To evaluate oral and silent reading abilities and auditory comprehension
Major Areas Tested	Oral and silent reading and listening comprehension
Age or Grade Range	Grades 1–7
Usually Given By	Special education teacher Diagnostician trained in reading assessment
Type of Test	Standardized Individual Criterion-referenced (supplementary phonics tests)
Scores Obtained	Grade level
Student Performance Timed?	Optional
Testing Time	30–45 minutes
Scoring/Interpretation Time	15 minutes
Normed On	3,081 rural and urban students in southern and eastern United States originally; 534 students in grades 1–8 in 1981
Alternate Forms Available?	Yes

FORMAT

The Spache Diagnostic Reading Scales (DRS) materials consist of an examiner's manual, an individual expandable record book for use by the examiner, and a reusable spiral-bound book for use by the students.

An examiner's cassette provides a model for administration of the DRS, and a technical manual provides more extensive statistical data.

The battery includes 3 graded word recognition lists, 2 reading selections at each of 11 levels (ranging from grades 1.6 to 7.5 in difficulty), and 12 supplementary word analysis and phonics tests:

Initial Consonants
Final Consonants
Consonant Digraphs
Consonant Blends
Initial Consonant Substitution
Auditory Recognition of Initial Consonant Sounds
Auditory Discrimination
Short and Long Vowel Sounds
Vowels with *r*
Vowel Diphthongs and Digraphs
Common Syllables
Blending

1. *Word Recognition Lists*. These graded word lists yield a tentative level of performance and are used to determine the level of the initial passage the student should be able to read orally in the next part of the test.

2. *Oral Reading*. The student reads each paragraph aloud and answers orally questions asked by the examiner. Most of the seven or eight questions for each paragraph require factual recall, but a few interpretive questions are included. Oral reading errors, including reversals, omissions, substitutions, mispronunciations, repetitions, and hesitations, are recorded by the examiner. Oral Reading stops when the student makes more accuracy errors than the maximum allowed for the paragraph or does not answer the minimum number of comprehension questions required.

3. *Silent Reading*. The student reads silently the paragraph just higher in difficulty than the last one read orally. Comprehension is assessed again by oral answers to questions asked by the examiner. Silent Reading stops when the student does not answer the minimum number of questions required on a given paragraph.

4. *Auditory Comprehension*. The examiner reads to the student the paragraph just higher than the last one read silently. Comprehension is assessed in the same manner.

5. *Supplementary Phonics Tests*. Any or all of the phonics tests (see the list above) may be administered to the student to obtain a detailed analysis of the student's word attack skills and phonics knowledge. The phonics tests are essentially criterion-referenced rather than norm-referenced.

Two forms of the reading passages (R and S) are provided for test-retest purposes.

The scores obtained on the DRS are Instructional Level (Oral Reading), Independent Level (Silent Reading), and Potential Level (Auditory Comprehension).

Instructional Level is defined as "the level at which the student reads orally and comprehends as well as 68 percent of the standardization population at that level." The author feels that this level is likely to be found acceptable by the average classroom teacher for group reading practice.

Independent Level is the highest level the student can read silently with no less than 60 percent comprehension. It represents the upper limit for materials the student is expected to read independently.

Potential Level is the highest level to which the student can listen with at least 60 percent comprehension. It represents the level to which a student's reading level can theoretically be raised as a result of an appropriate remedial program.

STRENGTHS OF THE DRS

- The DRS assesses word recognition and oral and silent reading in one battery. It is fairly easy to administer and takes relatively little time. Scores are not useful but provide good information about a student's reading skills. For example, an analysis of specific errors gives clues to how the student attempts to read. Error analysis is crucial for determining the instructional needs of a student. To facilitate analysis of types of errors, the student record book contains a Work Analysis Checklist and a Checklist of Reading Difficulties.

- The Supplementary Phonics Tests are helpful in revealing the nature of word analysis skills. They include tasks involving initial and final consonants, blends, vowels, and word endings. These criterion-referenced tests can identify specific skills that need to be mastered.

- In addition to the standard test procedures, the manual contains useful suggestions for further informal analysis of reading difficulties. For example, the examiner may wish to present to the student words in isolation that were misread in context. Then the examiner can compare a student's success with words in context to success with them in isolation.

- Students failing in reading often feel threatened by a reading test. In the DRS, the passages that the student reads are not marked by grade level, an important and sensitive consideration.

- The author is sensitive to the problems of assessing oral reading in students with nonstandard English. The manual contains an excellent section on typical pronunciations of certain words by students who speak Black dialect or are of Hispanic background. The pronunciation tendencies of Puerto Rican immigrants are carefully outlined, and an outline of procedures for testing any student with a dialect is included.

- The author's knowledge of reading is shared with the examiner through the excellent manual, which should be read by every examiner.

LIMITING FACTORS OF THE DRS
- The DRS must be administered by a person with considerable clinical experience in reading diagnosis because analysis of reading performance is often a subjective evaluation. Accurate recording of oral reading errors depends heavily on the judgment of the examiner.
- The terms *Instructional*, *Independent* and *Potential Reading Levels* have been used consistently with informal reading inventories. They have certain meanings within that context. In the DRS, the terms have a different meaning. Examiners need to be aware of these differences as they interpret scores to teachers who are more familiar with the informal reading inventories.
- The comprehension questions at all levels are short-answer questions, the majority of which are straight recall of facts. For the student with a short-term memory problem, the comprehension score can be quite misleading. An alternative way of assessing comprehension that does not depend so heavily on immediate memory would add to the test's usefulness.

Adding other fundamental types of comprehension questions would be helpful at the upper grade levels. For example, the test does not cover such skills as the ability to grasp the main idea, the ability to weave together the ideas in a selection, or the ability to draw inferences from a short passage.

The short-answer comprehension questions pose some real concerns. Questions designed on the yes-or-no model are handicapped by a 50 percent probability of getting any question correct simply by guessing. This kind of question is all too prevalent at the upper-grade levels. For example, seventh-grade-level questions include "Can we skim all kinds of reading?" and "Is marble always white?"

Answers to many other questions seem quite obvious, so that any student with sufficient experience and knowledge can derive the correct answer regardless of how well he or she read the passage. Typical questions are "What color was his wagon?" (second grade); "How do birds help us?" (fifth grade); "What kind of flowers do poppies have?" (fifth grade). The superficial understanding required by such comprehension questions is a serious drawback.

- The measurement of reading rate as fast, average, or slow similarly presents special concern. A student may have many reading rates, depending on such factors as the difficulty of the material, the content of the passage, and the purpose for which it is being read. In view of these factors, the silent reading rate on the DRS does not appear to be too meaningful.
- The examiner should keep in mind that performance on the Supplementary Phonics Tests can be directly related to the type of reading instruction a student receives. For instance, a student in a phonics-oriented program may perform much better on these tests than a student who is being taught by sight-word methods. As the manual states, the phonics tests do not possess any degree of reliability to justify grade norms.

Durrell Analysis of Reading Difficulty
(Durrell Analysis)

Donald D. Durrell and Jane H. Catterson
Harcourt Brace Jovanovich, Inc., 1937; revised 1955, 1980
The Psychological Corporation
7500 Old Oak Blvd., Middleburg Heights, OH 44130

Purpose	To assess strengths and weaknesses in various reading skills and subskills
Major Areas Tested	Oral and silent reading, listening comprehension, word analysis skills, spelling, and handwriting
Age or Grade Range	Grades 1–6
Usually Given By	Special education teacher
Type of Test	Standardized Individual Norm-referenced
Scores Obtained	Grade level
Student Performance Timed?	Yes (some subtests)
Testing Time	30–90 minutes (depending on number of subtests given)
Scoring/Interpretation Time	15–30 minutes
Normed On	200 students at each grade level, 1–6, from five states representing each region of the U.S.; included only children in the average range of the Metropolitan Achievement Test; consideration given to language backgrounds, socioeconomic status, ethnicity, and curriculum
Alternate Forms Available?	No

Reading Tests

FORMAT

The materials for the Durrell Analysis of Reading Difficulty (Durrell Analysis) consist of the examiner's manual of directions, individual record booklets for recording each student's responses, a tachistoscope with word lists to accompany specific subtests, and a book containing the paragraphs for the Oral Reading, Silent Reading, and Listening Comprehension subtests. The manual includes directions for administering and scoring tests and for interpreting test results, and brief information on test construction and standardization.

The Durrell Analysis contains 19 subtests designed to assess a student's performance on various types of reading tasks. The subtests are described in Table 8. The examiner selects only those subtests appropriate for each student's reading level.

Following the administration of each subtest, the examiner scores the test and calculates the grade-level score

Table 8. Durrell Analysis Subtests

Subtest	Reading Grade Level	Task	Timed?	Normed?	Additional Information Gained?
Oral Reading	1–6	Reading aloud a series of paragraphs graded for difficulty; answering comprehension questions	Yes	Yes	Error patterns in oral reading
Silent Reading	1–6	Reading silently a series of graded paragraphs; aided and unaided recall	Yes	Yes	Eye movements per line, imagery, sequential recall
Listening Comprehension	1–6	Listening to graded paragraphs; answering comprehension questions	No	No	Comparison to silent reading
Word Recognition	1–6	Reading word lists of graded difficulty, presented by tachistoscope; time for analysis given on words not recognized	Yes	Yes	Comparison of sight-word vocabulary and word analysis skills
Listening Vocabulary	1–6	Listening to a series of words and indicating the category to which they belong by pointing to a picture (Child hears the words *glow* and *elated* and points to a picture of the sun and a smiling face, respectively.)	No	Yes	Comparison of reading vocabulary and listening vocabulary
Sounds in Isolation	1–6	Giving sounds of letters, digraphs, blends, phonograms, prefixes, suffixes	No	Yes	
Spelling Test	2–6	Writing dictated spelling words correctly from a graded list	No	Yes	Comparison of phonic and sight spelling
Phonic Spelling	4–6	Writing dictated words exactly as they sound	No	Yes	Patterns of spelling errors
Visual Memory of Words (Primary)	3 and below	Recalling words presented visually and locating them in a list of similar words	Yes	Yes	

Table 8.—*Continued*

Subtest	Reading Grade Level	Task	Timed?	Normed?	Additional Information Gained?
Visual Memory of Words (Intermediate)	3–6	Recalling words presented visually and writing them	Yes	Yes	
Identifying Sounds in Words	3 and below	Listening to a word pronounced by the examiner and finding one that begins with the same sound from three printed choices	No	Yes	Ability to perceive beginning blends and ending sounds
Prereading Phonics Abilities Inventories					
Syntax Matching	Nonreaders–1	Recognizing that a sentence is composed of single words (Child looks at the phrase *come here*. Examiner says, "Come here," and asks, "Which word is *here*?")	No	Yes	
Identifying Letter Names in Spoken Words	Nonreaders–1	Listening to a word and giving the initial letter by name	No	Yes	
Identifying Phonemes (Letter Sounds) in Spoken Words	Nonreaders–1	Listening to a word and giving the initial sound	No	Yes	
Naming Lowercase Letters	Nonreaders–1	Naming lowercase letters in printed words	No	Yes	
Writing Letters from Dictation	Nonreaders–1	Writing letters from dictation with picture cues provided ("Write a *t* in the box next to the picture of a tree.")	No	Yes	
Writing from Copy	Nonreaders–1	Copying four words (given only to children who are unable to write from dictation)	No	No	
Naming Uppercase Letters	Nonreaders–1	Naming uppercase letters in isolation	No	No	
Identifying Letters Named	Nonreaders–1	Pointing to letters, either lowercase or uppercase, named by the examiner (given to children who are unable to name letters)	No	No	

according to procedures in the manual. The results of the major subtests are plotted by grade-level scores on the profile chart on the front of the individual record booklet. The profile provides a graphic representation of the student's strengths and weaknesses in reading. A checklist of instructional needs is also included in the individual record booklets, as are specific checklists of difficulties on individual subtests. These checklists, together with the profile chart, form the basis for an individualized remedial program.

STRENGTHS OF THE DURRELL ANALYSIS

• The Durrell Analysis was developed to help reading teachers understand the reading process and plan individual reading programs. To reach this goal, a wide variety of subtests are included. When used wisely, they yield a wealth of information about a student. The Durrell Analysis is one of the few tests that allow assessment of oral and silent reading, listening comprehension, word analysis skills, and spelling all in the same battery. The variety of subtests allows for testing of nonreaders as well as readers with high intermediate-grade skills.

• While maintaining the same general format, the revised Durrell Analysis includes several important changes in the third edition. The content of the reading and listening paragraphs has been updated for sex and ethnic balance. New normative data using a wider geographic sample is included. New measures of listening vocabulary allow direct comparison between reading and listening skills. New measures have been added to the prereading skills section.

• The manual is well organized and clearly written, and the checklists for recording reading difficulties are helpful in bridging the gap between test scores and daily performance.

• The Durrell Analysis includes several unique subtests. Listening Vocabulary provides a measure of a student's understanding of single spoken words by assessing the student's ability to place them in categories. Phonic Spelling is a good measure of auditory analysis for intermediate students. Syntax Matching is a creative measure of the basic concept that sentences are made up of single separate words.

LIMITING FACTORS OF THE DURRELL ANALYSIS

• Although the third edition of the Durrell Analysis has been renormed, only grade scores are provided. No standard scores are included, and the grade scores themselves are of little value. On the Oral Reading and Silent Reading subtests, the grade scores are based on speed and vague scoring of comprehension questions. For example, the manual states, "Generally speaking, the scoring of the comprehension questions should be generous. . . . If the child . . . answered that the little brown dog played with 'three or four other dogs,' one might assume that knowing that there was more than one other dog was worth half-credit.'' (The story says ''two dogs.'') Such vague scoring criteria invalidate the use of the grade scores, which were questionable to begin with. While some studies of reliability and validity are reported in the manual, the Durrell Analysis is best thought of as an informal inventory of reading skills.

• In considering the Durrell Analysis as an informal inventory, it is important to note which reading skills are poorly assessed or omitted. First, reading comprehension on both the Oral Reading and Silent Reading subtests is limited to recall of specific facts. No interpretation or generalization is required. Second, tachistoscopic presentation, such as that used on the Word Recognition subtest, is often confusing for poor readers and gives inaccurate information regarding their word recognition skills. Word lists or flashcard procedures are often more accurate. Third, no subtests assessing discrimination or recognition of vowel sounds (long or short) are included. Fourth, no pure auditory tests of discrimination or blending are included.

• The authors of the Durrell Analysis discuss the comparison of the student's raw score on Listening Vocabulary and Word Recognition. While the equivalency of lists of words is well done, the tasks are too dissimilar to compare. Word Recognition is decoding only, while Listening Vocabulary requires both comprehension of the single words and categorization skills.

Gates-McKillop-Horowitz Reading Diagnostic Tests (Gates-McKillop-Horowitz)

Arthur Gates, Anne McKillop, and Elizabeth Horowitz
Teachers College Press, second edition 1981
Teachers College, Columbia University, 1234 Amsterdam Ave., New York, NY 10027

Purpose	To assess strengths and weaknesses in reading and related areas
Major Areas Tested	Oral reading, word analysis, and related skills
Age or Grade Range	Grades 1–6
Usually Given By	Classroom teacher Special education teacher Diagnostician trained in reading disorders
Type of Test	Standardized Individual
Scores Obtained	Grade level Age level (some subtests) Rating scale
Student Performance Timed?	No
Testing Time	40–60 minutes (depending on number of subtests given)
Scoring/Interpretation Time	15 minutes
Normed On	600 children in grades 1–6 from public and private schools, urban and rural areas, and minority groups (Black and Spanish)
Alternate Forms Available?	No

FORMAT

The Gates-McKillop-Horowitz Reading Diagnostic Tests (Gates-McKillop-Horowitz) are a revised edition of the 1962 Gates-McKillop Tests. They are a battery of subtests designed to measure the subskills of reading. They are designed to be used with individual students in elementary school and include tasks from the readiness level through such advanced skills as syllabication. Subtests are selected based on the student's reading level and particular reading difficulties. No specific order of administration is required.

The materials consist of a reusable booklet that contains the materials to be read by the student; a booklet in which the student and the examiner record responses; and a manual that includes the rationale for the tests, directions for administering and scoring, grade-level scores, and interpretive ratings.

The 15 subtests included in the Gates-McKillop-Horowitz are shown in Table 9. As the table shows, the tests yield two types of scores. Grade scores that may be converted into a rating of high, medium, low, or very low are given for the four general ability tests that assess oral reading, word recognition, and spelling. These grade scores allow comparison of each student with others at the same grade level. On the diagnostic tests of specific skills, such as recognition of vowel sounds, the student's raw score or number correct is compared with the norming sample and is rated average, above average, or below average.

STRENGTHS OF THE GATES-McKILLOP-HOROWITZ

- The most obvious advantage of the Gates-McKillop-Horowitz battery is that many critical skills are included. Through thoughtful selection of subtests, the skilled examiner can develop a testing battery appropriate for a beginning reader or a struggling intermediate student. Careful selection of subtests allows every student some successful reading experiences during testing, while the examiner obtains maximum diagnostic information. The variety in the format and the informal tone of the procedures hold the interest of most students.

- Comparison of students' performances on various subtest pairs also yields invaluable diagnostic information. A few examples:

1. Words: Flash Presentation and Words: Untimed allow the examiner to compare sight-word vocabulary and word analysis skills on words of equivalent difficulty.

2. Auditory Blending and Recognizing and Blending Common Word Parts offer an auditory-visual comparison, blending with auditory stimuli only, and blending skills with printed words.

This type of diagnostic information can be obtained when the Gates-McKillop-Horowitz is used by a skilled examiner. Other features, such as the checklist of difficulties for the Oral Reading subtest and the discussion of interpretation of test results in the manual, are excellent.

LIMITING FACTORS OF THE GATES-McKILLOP-HOROWITZ

- The test was normed on 600 children. Only limited information regarding the composition of the norming sample is given, and no studies of reliability or validity are reported. The lack of these critical pieces of information strongly suggests that the Gates-McKillop-Horowitz should be used as an informal battery to obtain information about a student's skills in a variety of reading tasks. The information is excellent, but the grade scores are of little value.

- The Oral Reading passages are stilted in style and content. No measure of comprehension is included. The examiner should substitute another oral reading test (Gilmore Oral Reading Test, Gray Oral Reading Tests, Spache Diagnostic Reading Scales) or devise comprehension questions for the Gates-McKillop-Horowitz in order to get some measure of oral reading comprehension.

- The first edition of these tests included three subtests that were of great diagnostic value: Recognizing the Visual Form of Sounds in Nonsense Words, in Initial Letters, and in Final Letters. The new edition has added nothing in technical soundness and is less valuable as an informal diagnostic instrument.

Table 9. Gates–McKillop-Horowitz Subtests

Subtest	Task	Grade Score Obtained?
Oral Reading	Student reads orally seven paragraphs ranging in difficulty from grades 1 to 6. Errors recorded by the examiner and classified by type. No comprehension questions included.	Yes
Reading Sentences	Student reads four sentences with phonetically regular words.	No
Words: Flash Presentation	Tachistoscope presents a graded list of words at half-second intervals. Tests sight recognition of single words.	Yes
Words: Untimed	Presentation of same word list as above, but student is given opportunity to use word analysis skills.	Yes
Knowledge of Word Parts: Word Attack		
Syllabication	Student is asked to read a list of nonsense words (*rivlov*, *kangadee*). The skill being measured is syllable blending.	No
Recognizing and Blending Common Word Parts	Student reads a list of nonsense words made up of common word parts (*stade*, *shemp*, *whast*). If student is unable to read the whole word, the examiner may show how to break it into an initial blend and a common ending and then blend it back together (*wh-ast—whast*).	No
Reading Words	Student reads 15 one-syllable nonsense words.	No
Letter Sounds	Student is shown printed letter and is asked to give its sound.	No
Naming Capital Letters	Student is shown printed uppercase letter and is asked to name it.	No
Naming Lowercase Letters	Student is shown printed lowercase letter and is asked to name it.	No
Recognizing the Visual Form (Word Equivalents) of Sounds		
Vowels	Student is shown five vowels and is asked to indicate which one is in a nonsense word pronounced by examiner (*vum*, *keb*, *hote*, *sate*).	No
Auditory Tests		
Auditory Blending	Student listens to word pronounced by examiner, with parts separated by quarter-second intervals; student pronounces whole word (*d-ar-k—dark*).	No
Auditory Discrimination	Examiner pronounces pairs of words, and student identifies them as same or different (*dim—din*, *weather—wetter*).	No
Written Expression		
Spelling	Words from Words: Flash Presentation and Words: Untimed are presented to the student for oral spelling.	Yes
Informal Writing	Student is encouraged to write an original paragraph on a topic of his or her choice.	No

McCarthy Individualized Diagnostic Reading Inventory (IDRI)

William G. McCarthy
Educators Publishing Service, Inc., 1971; revised 1976
75 Moulton St., Cambridge, MA 02188

Purpose	To assess developmental skills necessary for effective reading
Major Areas Tested	Reading fluency, comprehension, thinking skills, phonics, word recognition, and study skills
Age or Grade Range	Grades 1–9
Usually Given By	Classroom teacher Reading specialist
Type of Test	Individual Informal Criterion-referenced
Scores Obtained	Independent reading level Instructional reading level Frustration reading level Reading expectancy
Student Performance Timed?	No
Testing Time	35–90 minutes
Scoring/Interpretation Time	30–40 minutes
Normed On	Not normed
Alternate Forms Available?	No

FORMAT

The McCarthy Individualized Diagnostic Reading Inventory (IDRI) is an informal reading inventory that provides a comprehensive measure of reading skills for students in grades 1 through 9. The materials consist of:

- An information booklet explaining the rationale behind the inventory and procedures for its use
- A student booklet containing word lists, reading selections, and skills subtests
- A teacher administration booklet, which is a plastic, reusable booklet for recording student responses
- An individual record form for recording test results, background information, and instructional plans
- A classroom chart that organizes instruction for individual students or small groups

The IDRI assesses a wide variety of reading skills. Table 10 describes the inventory organization.

Table 10. IDRI Organization

Part One: Placement for Instruction in Reading, Fluency, Comprehension, and Thinking Skills

Controlled Vocabulary Word Lists
Graded Oral Reading Paragraphs
   Fluency
   Comprehension
Thinking Skills

Part Two: Phonics, Word Recognition, and Study Skills

Phonics
   Letter Names
   Initial, Final Consonants
   Short, Long Vowels
   Digraphs, Diphthongs, Blends
   Prefixes, Suffixes
   Reversals
Contractions, Compound Words, Syllables
Vocabulary Development
   Antonyms, Synonyms, Homonyms
   Context Level
Essential Sight-Word Vocabulary
Study Skills
   Alphabetizing
   Index, Encyclopedia

Part Three: The Pupil and the Pupil's Environment

Reading Interests
School Information
Reading Expectancy Score
Physical and Psychosocial Factors

Part Four: Let's Get Started

Instructional Planning

In Part One, word recognition is quickly assessed through the Controlled Vocabulary Word Lists. The student's score determines at which level to begin the graded paragraphs. By having the student read higher- or lower-level paragraphs, independent, instructional, and frustration levels are determined using the chart in Figure 10. Systematic scoring procedures are printed immediately following each paragraph.

A unique feature of the IDRI is the set of eight comprehensive questions for each paragraph. Each question assesses a different type of reading comprehension, as shown below.

Recall	1. Sequence: *Did mother call before or after dinner?* 2. Exact Detail: *Name the four major blood types.*
Interpretive	3. Cause-Effect: *Why does a dog learn to shake hands?* 4. Main Idea: *Make up a title for this story.*
Creative-Critical	5. Author's Intent: *What is something you thought about as you read the story?* 6. Logic: *What is something you read in the story? Does it seem sensible to you? Why?* 7. Mood: *How does the story end? Which word represents your feeling at the end? Why?* 8. Language: *Find the sentence that begins, "Suddenly she. . . ." Do you ever use the word* loomed? *How could you say the sentence in a different way?*

A wide variety of phonics skills, vocabulary, and study skills are assessed in Part Two. The examiner selects those subtests that are appropriate for each student. Ninety percent accuracy on subskills is considered mastery level. Following testing in Part Two, the teacher completes Part Three, regarding the student's interests and other factors related to the student's reading performance. The reading expectancy score is derived from an equation using mental and chronological ages and the number of years in school. Data from the reading tests is recorded on the individual record form and the instructional plan is completed in Part Four.

STRENGTHS OF THE IDRI

- The IDRI is a comprehensive inventory with many excellent features. In particular, the test provides more than the usual number of comprehension questions. By assessing the same types of comprehension questions (sequence,

detail, author's intent, etc.) in each paragraph, a pattern of specific comprehension strengths and weaknesses often emerges.
- Having the student read the paragraph silently prior to reading aloud is a customary classroom procedure incorporated into administration of this test.
- The scoring procedures that appear immediately below each paragraph facilitate the recording of data.
- The concept of instructional, independent, and frustration reading levels is the basis of this test and offers a classroom teacher a different type of information than standard scores and percentiles. Pairing the IDRI with a norm-referenced silent reading test provides a comprehensive picture of a student's reading skills.

\multicolumn{6}{c	}{READING PROFICIENCY LEVELS}
Level	Purpose	Miscues	Approximate Accuracy	Comprehension Questions	Observations
Independent or Library	For library reading, recreational reading, homework, free study	2% About 2 words miscued out of 100 running words	98%	7 or 8 correct out of 8, or about 90% right	There is high pupil interest. Pupil has no difficulty in reading and uses good phrasing. Fluent reading with speed, ease, and expression is achieved.
Instructional	For classroom learning under teacher direction	3% to 6% About 6 words miscued out of 100 running words	94%	5 or 6 correct out of 8, or about 70% right	Material is challenging but not too difficult. Good phrasing in a conversational tone is achieved. There is no vocalizing in silent reading. Selection is enjoyed.
Frustration	Notifies us that the reading is too difficult for this pupil	7% or more More than 7 words miscued out of 100 running words	Below 93%	Fewer than 5 correct out of 8, or less than 70% right	Lowest level of readability at which a pupil is able to understand. There is nervous word-by-word reading, with frequent miscues such as repetitions, insertions, omissions, substitutions, and fingerpointing. Pupil fails to pay attention. Material is too difficult to provide a basis for developing good reading habits.
Capacity or listening	The highest level a pupil is able to understand when read to	Not tested	Not tested	About 6 out of 8 correct or about 75% right	The pupil can answer questions in language similar to the selection. He can supply additional information from background experience.

Figure 10. IDRI Reading Proficiency Levels

LIMITING FACTORS OF THE IDRI

• The test materials are confusing. Administration procedures are in both the information booklet and the teacher administration booklet. Data is recorded first in the teacher administration booklet and then on the individual record form. The reusable booklet is more confusing than helpful.

• The author's intent to assess thinking skills is applauded, but the four questions selected do not seem to add information about the student's thinking process. The questions to assess creative-critical thinking skills are poorly stated (*What is something you thought about as you read the story? What is something you read in the story? Does it seem sensible?*) and many students don't understand them. The questions evoke personal answers; however, answers that come from personal experience cannot be scored as correct. Scoring criteria are vague. Since this is an informal test, the examiner should modify these questions to make them more meaningful.

• The paragraphs for oral reading vary in organization. Some are well organized with a topic sentence, elaboration, and conclusion, but others seem to begin in the middle of a story and do not come to a conclusion. Students have much more difficulty with the less-structured paragraphs, which may affect their reading level scores.

• The reading expectancy score should be omitted or used with great caution since it focuses upon grade scores.

Woodcock Reading Mastery Tests (Woodcock)

Richard W. Woodcock
American Guidance Service, Inc., 1973
Publishers' Bldg., Circle Pines, MN 55014

Purpose	To measure a wide range of reading skills and to provide new types of scores to allow more useful interpretations of a student's reading ability
Major Areas Tested	Reading
Age or Grade Range	Grades K–12
Usually Given By	Classroom teacher Special education teacher Psychologist Paraprofessional
Type of Test	Standardized Individual Criterion-referenced Norm-referenced
Scores Obtained	Grade level Achievement index Percentile Reading range Relative mastery
Student Performance Timed?	No
Testing Time	30–45 minutes
Scoring/Interpretation Time	20–30 minutes
Normed On	5,000 students from various racial and socioeconomic groups and geographical regions
Alternate Forms Available?	Yes

FORMAT

The Woodcock Reading Mastery Tests (Woodcock) are a battery of five individually administered reading subtests for use with students from kindergarten through twelfth grade. The materials include a test manual, an easel kit for presenting the test materials, and the response forms. On the examiner's side of the easel kit, the test items are presented with directions for administration. Simultaneously, the student sees the test items on the other side of the easel kit. The items require verbal responses. Multiple-choice and yes-or-no items are not included.

The five subtests are:

1. *Letter Identification.* The 45 items of this subtest assess the student's ability to name letters of the alphabet. A variety of common letter forms in uppercase and lowercase, manuscript and cursive, are presented.

2. *Word Identification.* The student reads aloud 150 words ranging in difficulty from preprimer to twelfth-grade level (for example, *the, go, and; facetious, beatitude, picayune*).

3. *Word Attack.* The 50 items included here assess the student's ability to pronounce nonsense words (like *dee, lat, idpan, depnonlel*) using phonic and structural-analysis skills.

4. *Word Comprehension.* The subtest contains 70 items that test knowledge of word meaning using an analogy format. The student reads three words silently and then tells the examiner a word to complete the analogy (for example, *bird-fly, fish-_____*).

5. *Passage Comprehension.* This subtest includes 85 items selected to assess reading comprehension using a cloze format. The student reads the one- or two-sentence passage and fills in the blank with an appropriate word. For example:

"Be sure to read all the signs. We don't want to _____ lost," said Mother.

Whizz! The ball slammed into the hornet's nest. Debby could _____ the wild angry buzzing.

The Woodcock is constructed so that students are tested only on those items within their operating range. The operating range is assumed to extend from a basal level marked by five consecutive correct responses to a ceiling level of five consecutive incorrect responses. On two subtests, Letter Identification and Word Attack, all students begin at the first item. For the other three subtests, a starting-point table based on estimated reading grade level is provided.

Forms A and B are equivalent and may be used for test-retest purposes. The manual suggests that both forms be given to the same student to obtain a more reliable score.

The Woodcock tests were designed as both criterion-referenced and norm-referenced tests. The tests yield a variety of scores, including relative mastery scores, grade-level scores, a reading range, an achievement index, and percentile ranks. The concept underlying the Woodcock's construction is the mastery score. Based on the equal-interval mastery scale, it allows the examiner to predict a student's performance on grade-level tasks. It makes possible such statements as "John can be expected to perform with 50 percent accuracy on word recognition tests performed with 90 percent accuracy by average students at his grade level." These relative mastery scores are then translated into percentile ranks, which are readily understandable by teachers and parents.

The Woodcock provides a mastery profile, on which the student's performance on each subtest is graphically displayed. An instructional range for each subtest is plotted. Figure 11 is an example of the interpretation page, completed for a seventh-grade boy.

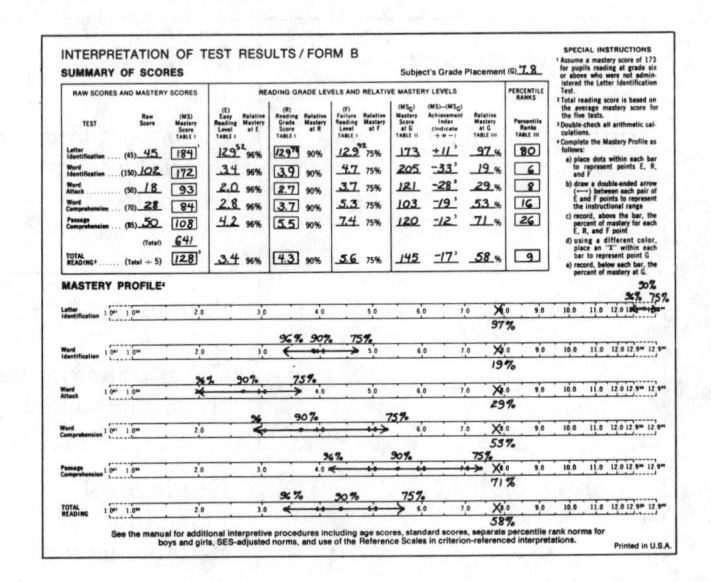

Figure 11. Woodcock Test Manual, Page 37

Modified norms are available for students performing above grade level 12.9 and below 1.0. Adjusted norms are also available for populations with differing socioeconomic status. Separate percentile ranks for boys and girls, means for converting mastery scores into age-equivalent scores, and procedures for converting percentile ranks into standard scores and stanines are available in the manual.

STRENGTHS OF THE WOODCOCK

• The Woodcock is a valuable addition to the field of individual oral reading tests. The five subtests present a variety of reading tasks over a wide age range. The easel kit format is easy to use and generally less formidable to the student. The suggested starting points, basal and

ceiling procedures, and variety of tasks allow the examiner to move quickly and to hold the interest of the student.
- Test instructions are clear, and the test manual is unusually complete and well organized.
- Several of the subtests of the Woodcock are unique in the tasks they present. Letter Identification provides a measure of form constancy, or the recognition of many types of print, which may provide some interesting information on beginning readers. The Word Comprehension subtest assesses verbal analogy skills in reading and gives the teacher an understanding of the language functioning of the student. The cloze procedure used on Passage Comprehension is a well-established technique for assessing comprehension of reading in the content areas, but before the Woodcock, it was available only on informal tests.
- The most important contribution of the Woodcock is its concept of relative mastery. Teachers have long recognized that different types of reading skills develop at different rates. Letter identification is acquired fairly rapidly, but passage comprehension begins later and develops gradually over several years. Teachers also know that, within a given grade level, the students have a wide range of reading skills; this wide range of skills is normal. Other tests that provide only grade-level scores may make a student's performance look very low or very high when actually it falls within the normal range for students of that grade level. Woodcock's concept of relative mastery provides a more realistic statement of what we can expect of a student in reading tasks.
- The concept of instructional range is a helpful one as well. Students do not perform on every word recognition task at a specific grade level, such as 3.2. They have a range of word recognition skills and on a given task may be somewhat higher or lower. By looking at the student's instructional range on the five subtests and seeing whether the actual grade placement falls within that instructional range, the examiner can make decisions about whether the student's reading program can be provided in the regular classroom.
- Extensive reliability data are included for each subtest and for the test as a whole. Split-half reliability and alternate form reliability, as well as standard error of measurement, are all provided. Several validity studies are also reported in the manual. For a relatively new test, the Woodcock has good reliability and validity data.

LIMITING FACTORS OF THE WOODCOCK
- The test construction and the concepts underlying the Woodcock are unfamiliar to most diagnosticians and teachers. Examiners need to administer the test to several students at various grade levels and to study the manual very carefully before they can feel confident about their interpretation of test scores.

- Because of the unique format of such subtests as Word Comprehension and Passage Comprehension, examiners must be cautious in generalizing scores on these subtests to all reading comprehension tasks. A student may have difficulty with the process of verbal analogies or the cloze procedure and not necessarily have difficulty with other kinds of reading comprehension. Supplementing the Woodcock with another reading comprehension test, such as the Gates-MacGinitie Silent Reading Tests (p. 56) is advisable for students with low scores.
- The Word Comprehension and Passage Comprehension tasks are unusual in format and often difficult initially for students to understand. It is usually necessary to go back several items below the recommended starting point before a basal level is achieved. Because of the uniqueness of the tasks, students tend to read aloud, although the directions are to read silently. Although oral reading gives a great deal of diagnostic information about the student's performance, the student should be encouraged to read silently, because that is how the norms were obtained.
- The order of items in the Word Comprehension and Passage Comprehension subtests is questionable, because it seems difficult to obtain basal and ceiling levels.

Gates-MacGinitie Silent Reading Tests
(Gates-MacGinitie Tests)

Arthur Gates and Walter MacGinitie
Teachers College Press, first edition 1965
Teachers College, Columbia University, 1234 Amsterdam Ave., New York, NY 10027
The Riverside Publishing Co., second edition 1978
1919 S. Highland Ave., Lombard, IL 60148

Purpose	To measure silent reading skills
Major Areas Tested	Silent reading vocabulary and comprehension
Age or Grade Range	Grades 1–12
Usually Given By	Classroom teacher Special education teacher
Type of Test	Standardized Group Norm-referenced
Scores Obtained	Grade level Standard Percentile
Student Performance Timed?	Yes
Testing Time	50–60 minutes
Scoring/Interpretation Time	15 minutes
Normed On	40,000 students of various educational and socioeconomic levels in 38 communities, varying in size and geographic location, throughout the United States
Alternate Forms Available?	Yes

FORMAT

The first edition of the Gates-MacGinitie Silent Reading Tests (Gates-MacGinitie Tests) is a series of multiple-choice, pencil-and-paper tests designed for group administration. Eight levels of tests are available, each with two or three forms for test-retest purposes. The available tests are:

1. *Readiness Skills*. Eight subtests for the end of kindergarten and beginning of grade 1.
2. *Primary A*. Vocabulary and Comprehension subtests for grade 1, Forms 1 and 2.
3. *Primary B*. Vocabulary and Comprehension subtests for grade 2, Forms 1 and 2.
4. *Primary C*. Vocabulary and Comprehension subtests for grade 3, Forms 1 and 2.
5. *Primary CS*. Speed and Accuracy subtests for grades 2 and 3, Forms 1, 2, and 3.
6. *Survey D*. Speed, Vocabulary, and Comprehension subtests for grades 4 through 6, Forms 1, 2, and 3 (Forms 1M, 2M, and 3M for machine scoring).
7. *Survey E*. Speed, Vocabulary, and Comprehension subtests for grades 7 through 9, Forms 1, 2, and 3 (Forms 1M, 2M, and 3M for machine scoring).
8. *Survey F*. Speed, Vocabulary, and Comprehension subtests for grades 10 through 12, Forms 1 and 2 (Forms 1M and 2M for machine scoring).

The test materials consist of a teacher's manual for each level of the test, separate test booklets for the students for each grade level and form, and three technical manuals: one for Readiness Skills, one for Primary A through Survey E, and one for Survey F. The teacher's manuals describe the tests and give directions for administration and scoring. Tables of standard scores, grade-level scores, and percentile scores are also in the teacher's manuals. More technical information about the construction and standardization of the tests, as well as interpretation, is available in the technical manuals.

Because of their different purpose and content, the Readiness Skills subtests are not reviewed here. The other levels of the Gates-MacGinitie Tests measure three basic silent reading skills: vocabulary, comprehension, and rate of reading. The Vocabulary subtests assess a student's ability to recognize and comprehend single words in isolation. At the primary levels, the student selects a word to match a picture (see Figure 12). In the Survey tests, the student selects one of five words that has the same meaning as the key word (see Figure 13). The Comprehension subtests assess the student's ability to read and understand complete sentences and short paragraphs (see Figures 14, 15, and 16). The Speed and Accuracy subtests are considered supplementary tests and should be given when more information on a student's rate of reading is desired. The students read short paragraphs of uniform difficulty, so that speed of reading is the primary factor being measured. Time limits are imposed on the Vocabulary and Comprehension subtests for ease in group administration, but the limits are very liberal and present no serious constraints for most students.

Figure 12. Gates-MacGinitie Vocabulary, Primary A, Form 1

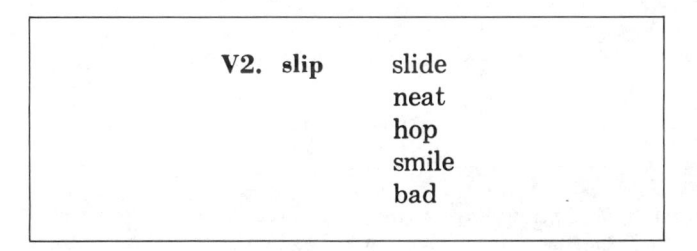

Figure 13. Gates-MacGinitie Vocabulary, Survey D, Form 1

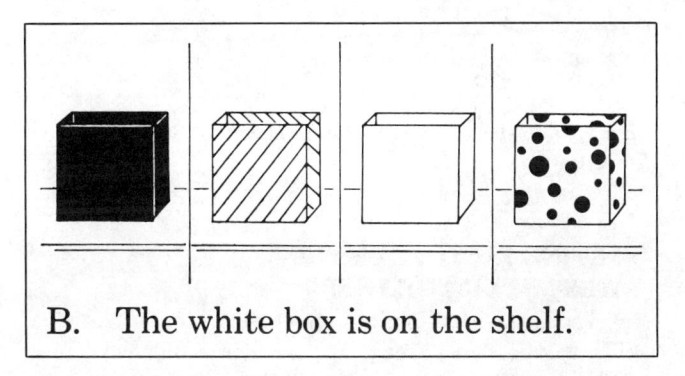

Figure 14. Gates-MacGinitie Comprehension, Primary A, Form 1

STRENGTHS OF THE GATES-MACGINITIE TESTS

• The Gates-MacGinitie Tests are well known and well normed. Because they are group tests, they are very appropriate for screening purposes, to determine which students are in need of more diagnostic testing.

• Their wide age range and alternate forms make the Gates-MacGinitie Tests excellent for test-retest procedures, to determine the progress an individual student has made in a remedial reading program. Many school districts use them routinely, fall and spring, to evaluate pupil progress in special and regular education programs. Each subtest is scored independently, so a student may be given one or all of the three test parts.

• The teachers' manuals and technical supplements are well prepared and easy to use.

Last year, for his seventh birthday, Eddie had a party at home. On his birthday this year, Eddie's father is taking him and his friend Bill to the circus.

A. Who will go with Eddie and his father?

his mother   Bill   Sally   an uncle

B. Eddie is going to the circus on

Friday   his vacation   his birthday   Hallowe'en

Figure 15. Gates-MacGinitie Comprehension, Primary C, Form 1

We have a playroom in our ___C1___. It is down in the basement, so we need to turn on an electric ___C2___ even on sunny days.

C1. stove	house	bed	car	lake
C2. storm	friend	ladder	room	light

Figure 16. Gates-MacGinitie Comprehension, Survey D, Form 1

LIMITING FACTORS OF THE GATES-MacGINITIE TESTS

• The Gates-MacGinitie Tests measure silent reading skills, a critical area of reading competence. In any silent reading test, analysis of errors is difficult. For example, in the Vocabulary subtest, the item shown in Figure 13 offers *slide, neat, hop, smile,* and *bad* as possible synonyms for *slip*. If the student marks *hop* as the word closest in meaning to *slip*, the examiner does not know which of the following occurred: (1) the student could not read the word *slip*; (2) the student could not read the word *slide*; (3) the student did not know the meaning of the word *slip*; or (4) the student did not know the meaning of the word *slide*. Because analysis of errors on group silent reading tests is difficult, low-scoring students should be administered individual tests such as the Spache Diagnostic Reading Scales (p. 39) or the Gates-McKillop-Horowitz Reading Diagnostic Tests (p. 46) to determine more specifically the nature of their reading difficulties.

• The Comprehension sections of the Gates-MacGinitie Tests have two other important weaknesses. First, they rely on a student's vocabulary and general knowledge of facts not present in the paragraph itself. Second, they measure a very low level of comprehension. They do not assess the reader's ability to interrelate information and draw conclusions. Particularly in older students, the comprehension skills that are not measured may be crucial for classroom success.

• It is also important to remember that students being instructed in a specific phonic or linguistic reading program may not show significant gains on the Gates-MacGinitie Tests until they have mastered a basic sight-word vocabulary. Teachers of primary students need to be aware of this aspect of standardized testing and to develop supplementary informal tests on which their students can demonstrate their progress.

CHANGES IN THE SECOND EDITION

• Speed and accuracy tests are not included.

• Two tests levels are available for first grade.

• Norms are provided for students above and below test level; that is, norms for first and third graders taking the second-grade test.

• Careful attention has been given to content. Minority-, culturally, and sex-biased items have been avoided.

• A Decoding Skills Analysis form has been included to improve the diagnostic use of the test.

Test of Reading Comprehension (TORC)

Virginia L. Brown, Donald D. Hammill, and J. Lee Wiederholt
Pro-Ed, 1978
5341 Industrial Oaks Blvd., Austin, TX 78735

Purpose	To provide a normed measure of silent reading comprehension independent of specific curriculum
Major Areas Tested	Reading comprehension
Age or Grade Range	6½–14½ years
Usually Given By	Classroom teacher Special education teacher
Type of Test	Standardized Individual Group Norm-referenced
Scores Obtained	Scaled (each subtest) Standard (total test)
Student Performance Timed?	No
Testing Time	½–2 hours
Scoring/Interpretation Time	30–60 minutes
Normed On	2,707 students in 10 states balanced for sex, age, and city and rural populations
Alternate Forms Available?	No

FORMAT

The Test of Reading Comprehension (TORC) is an instrument for measuring silent reading comprehension in students from grades 1 through 8. The test may be individually or group administered. The materials consist of an examiner's manual, student booklets, answer sheets, individual student profile sheets, and separate response forms for the Reading the Directions of Schoolwork subtest.

Three subtests form the General Reading Comprehension Core:

1. *General Vocabulary* (25 items). The student reads three stimulus words that are related in some way (*teeth, nose, arm*) and selects two words from a group of four (*hair, air, legs, too*) that are related to the stimulus words. Both answers must be correct.

2. *Syntactic Similarities* (20 items). The student reads five sentences and selects the two that are most nearly alike in meaning. For example:

> *It was her wagon.*
> *It was not her wagon.*
> *It was his wagon.*
> *The wagon was not hers.*
> *It was not his wagon.*

Both responses (in this example, the second and fourth sentences) must be correct.

3. *Paragraph Reading* (6 paragraphs). The student reads a paragraph and five questions. A multiple-choice format is used for all five questions, which requires selecting the "best" title, recalling story details, drawing an inference, and drawing a negative inference (for example: *Which sentence could* not *go in the story?*).

Diagnostic Supplements, five additional subtests, are used to gain a more comprehensive evaluation of strengths and weaknesses in a student's reading comprehension:

4. *Mathematics Vocabulary* (25 items). The student reads three stimulus items (*more than, longer, bigger*) and selects two words from a group of four (*blue, larger, food, greater*) that are related to the stimulus words. Both answers must be correct.

5. *Social Studies Vocabulary* (25 items). The student reads three stimulus items (*Florida, Georgia, Mississippi*) and selects two words from a group of four (*Louisiana, Alabama, Massachusetts, California*) that are related to the stimulus words. Both answers must be correct.

6. *Science Vocabulary* (25 items). The student reads three stimulus items (*corpuscles, plasma, serum*) and selects two words from a group of four (*lungs, red, types, intestine*) that are related to the stimulus words. Both answers must be correct.

7. *Reading the Directions of Schoolwork* (25 items). The student reads a common teaching instruction and carries it out. This subtest is designed to be used with younger or remedial readers (below fourth-grade level).

8. *Sentence Sequencing* (10 items). Each item includes five randomly ordered sentences that, when ordered properly, will create a meaningful paragraph. The student orders the sentences. Scoring is based on relational order rather than specific sequence.

This subtest may be used to substitute for one of the three core subtests when one is believed to be clinically invalid. It may also be used to supply additional information about a student's reading comprehension. It is always recommended for students older than 14½ years.

On all subtests, the student begins with item 1 and proceeds until a ceiling is reached. Ceiling criteria are clear in the examiner's manual. For each subtest, a raw score (number correct) is computed and converted into a scaled score using tables based on age. Scaled scores have a mean of 10 and a standard deviation of 3. The three core tests are combined into a reading comprehension quotient (RCQ) with a mean of 100 and a standard deviation of 15, allowing easy comparison of a student's TORC scores with other measures of intellectual and language functioning.

STRENGTHS OF THE TORC

- The TORC is subtitled *A Method for Assessing the Understanding of Written Language*. It is based upon the latest research on reading comprehension and psycholinguistics. Subtests are designed to assess the reader's ability to "construct meaning" from the printed word. Examiners are urged to read the manual carefully to understand the rationale for the test and avoid misinterpretation.

- Several of the subtests are unique in content and format and offer new understandings of the reading comprehension process.

- The examiner's manual is clear and complete. Directions for administration and scoring are easy to follow. The addition of Sentence Sequencing as an alternative subtest to one of the three core tests is a helpful feature.

- Administrative options, such as answer sheets or booklets, one sitting or several, are included, making administration easier.

- Attention has been paid to reliability, validity, and construction of norms, all of which are clearly reported in the manual.

- No grade-equivalent scores are provided. Since the statistical problems of grade scores are overwhelming, it is to the authors' credit that they do not provide them.

LIMITING FACTORS OF THE TORC

- No description of the standardization population regarding race, linguistic background, or degree of reading facility is included. The authors urge the development of local norms; unless that is done, scores of learning-disabled students or students from minorities should be interpreted cautiously.

• Several of the TORC subtests measure abilities rarely taught in classrooms. In particular, Syntactic Similarities measures the ability to recognize that two sentences mean the same thing, a very unfamiliar task. Many students need more teaching of this type of task than that provided in two examples. Because of this, scores on the subtest and, therefore, the RCQ, are suspect.

• The content area vocabulary tests are recommended to be used for students in the intermediate and upper grades to screen their readiness for reading in content areas. The vocabulary is so specific to topics previously taught, it has little value as either a screening test or a measure of progress.

• The theoretical constructs underlying the TORC are new and complex. Interpretation of scores is difficult. The TORC is best used in conjunction with other measures of reading skills.

Spelling and Written Language Tests

Larsen-Hammill Test of Written Spelling 63
Diagnostic Achievement Test in Spelling 66
Diagnostic Analysis of Reading Errors 69
Diagnostic Spelling Potential Test 71
Myklebust Picture Story Language Test 73
Test of Written Language 77

Larsen-Hammill Test of Written Spelling (TWS)

Stephen Larsen and Donald Hammill
Pro-Ed, 1976
5341 Industrial Oaks Blvd., Austin, TX 78735

Purpose	To provide an adequately standardized, reliable, and valid measure of written spelling
Major Areas Tested	Written spelling
Age or Grade Range	5–15 years
Usually Given By	Classroom teacher Special education teacher
Type of Test	Standardized Individual Group Norm-referenced
Scores Obtained	Age level Grade level Spelling quotient
Student Performance Timed?	No
Testing Time	15–20 minutes
Scoring/Interpretation Time	10 minutes
Normed On	A random sample of 4,544 children in 22 states
Alternate Forms Available?	No

FORMAT

The Larsen-Hammill Test of Written Spelling (TWS) materials consists of a teacher's manual and a set of individual forms on which the students write the dictated words. The student forms are not necessary; ordinary notebook paper may be used.

The TWS includes two subtests or lists of spelling words. The first list includes 35 Predictable Words—words that follow basic spelling rules; the second list contains 25 Unpredictable Words—words that essentially have to be memorized. For example:

Predictable Words	Unpredictable Words
dog	*music*
trip	*sure*
spend	*fountain*
hardly	*awful*
tardy	*collar*
district	*campaign*

The examiner pronounces each word, uses it in a sentence, and pronounces it again. The student writes each word.

The same word lists are used with students at all grade levels. All students begin with the first word, and the testing is discontinued when the student misspells five consecutive words on each of the two word lists.

In addition to raw scores, the TWS yields three scores on each subtest. The spelling age score allows a comparison with other students of the same age; the grade-equivalent score allows a comparison with other students of the same grade. The spelling quotient is calculated by the following formula:

$$\text{Spelling quotient (SQ)} = \frac{\text{Spelling age (SA)} \times 100}{\text{Chronological age (CA)}}$$

STRENGTHS OF THE TWS

- The TWS is a well-constructed, well-normed test. Good reliability and validity studies are reported. Information on item validity and percentage of difficulty for each of the 60 spelling words is presented.
- Dividing the words into two types allows the classroom teacher to plan an appropriate individualized spelling program. For example, two beginning fourth-grade students might receive the scores shown in Table 11. As the table shows, Student A has significantly more difficulty with unpredictable words than with predictable words and needs a spelling program that focuses on techniques for memorizing sight words. Student B is having difficulty with rule-based words as well and needs a systematic approach to this type of spelling.
- The teacher's manual contains clearly written instructions for administration and scoring and a description of the theoretical basis for the test. Reliability and validity data and some guidelines for interpretation are also included.
- The first 10 or 12 words on the Predictable Word list are generally familiar to all students past the first grade and allow even the very weak speller to experience success.

LIMITING FACTORS OF THE TWS

- The first few words on the Unpredictable Word list are much more difficult than those on the Predictable Word list, not only because they are not rule-based, but also because they are less familiar. For example:

Predictable Words	Unpredictable Words
up	*myself*
that	*people*
it	*knew*
bed	*uncle*
dog	*music*

If the authors wished to provide a comparison of the student's skills on predictable versus unpredictable words,

Table 11. Two Fourth Graders' Scores on the TWS

	Predictable Words	Unpredictable Words	Total Test
Student A			
Age score	10.1	8.7	9.4
Grade score	4.6	3.3	3.9
Spelling quotient	98.0	83.0	91.0
Student B			
Age score	8.11	8.1	8.8
Grade score	3.3	2.7	3.2
Spelling quotient	87.0	79.0	84.0

they should have selected words of equal familiarity.
- The Unpredictable Word list is too difficult for first-, second-, and third-grade students. Because the unique feature of this test is a comparison of the student's skills with both types of words, the test is most effectively used with fourth-grade or older students.
- The spelling quotient score has little meaning. The spelling age and grade-equivalent scores allow a comparison between each student and others of the same age and grade. Deriving a spelling quotient (similar to an intelligence quotient) adds little information.

Diagnostic Achievement Test in Spelling (DATS)

William Wittenberg
Barnell Loft, Ltd., 1980
958 Church St., Baldwin, NY, 11510

Purpose	To measure spelling ability and to diagnose specific spelling deficiencies
Major Areas Tested	Written spelling
Age or Grade Range	Grades 2–8
Usually Given By	Classroom teacher Remedial specialist Paraprofessional
Type of Test	Group Standardized Criterion-referenced
Scores Obtained	Grade level
Student Performance Timed?	No
Testing Time	20–25 minutes
Scoring/Interpretation Time	10–15 minutes
Normed On	14,400 students; information on sample not available
Alternate Forms Available?	Yes

Spelling and Written Language Tests

FORMAT

A Diagnostic Achievement Test in Spelling (DATS) is part of the Diagnostic and Prescriptive Spelling Program, a remedial program for students with spelling levels between grades 2 and 8. The DATS is designed to measure a student's spelling ability and diagnose specific spelling deficiencies. The test materials consist of an administration and scoring manual, spirit masters for answer sheets, and individualized evaluation forms that profile a student's skills and deficiencies in spelling. Four 100-word lists of equal difficulty are included in the manual, one form for assessment and the other three for measuring achievement. The words are grouped according to spelling principles, short vowels, silent *e*, vowel digraphs, and others.

Raw scores of number correct are converted into grade-level scores through a table in the manual. The number of correctly spelled words for each spelling principle is plotted on the individualized evaluation form (see Figure 17). The resulting profile allows the teacher to place each student in the appropriate workbook in the prescriptive program and depicts which skills need reinforcement or instruction.

STRENGTHS OF THE DATS

- The DATS is a carefully constructed diagnostic spelling test which leads directly to instruction.
- The test has inexpensive materials and efficient group administration procedures.
- Remedial materials are available from the publisher.

INDIVIDUALIZED EVALUATION FORM
Barnell Loft Diagnostic Spelling Test

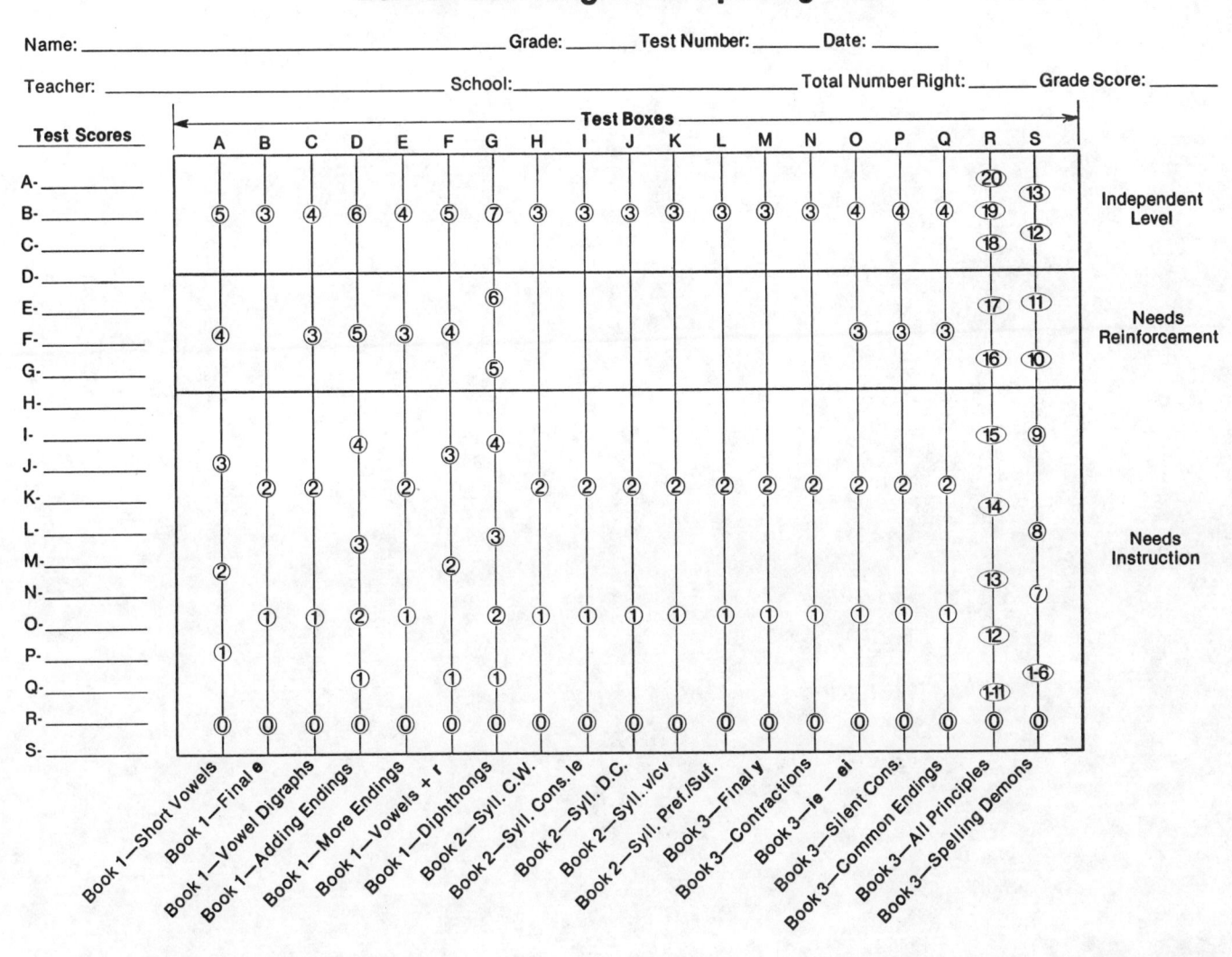

Figure 17. DATS Individualized Evaluation Form

LIMITING FACTORS OF THE DATS

- No standardization information is available in the manual. The information available in the author's report is too meager to determine the composition of the standardization sample. Therefore, the grade level scores have little meaning.
- The lack of standard scores is a serious limitation. Although four forms are available to measure progress, only grade-level scores are available. Users should not use pre- and postgrade-level scores as a measure of progress. (See p. 8.)

Diagnostic Analysis of Reading Errors (DARE)

Jacquelyn Gillespie and Jacqueline Shohet
Jastak Associates, Inc., 1979
1526 Gilpin Ave., Wilmington, DE 19806

Purpose	To identify adults and adolescents with language-related learning disabilities through group testing and to provide individual diagnostic information about the nature of the disability
Major Areas Tested	Auditory-visual integration affecting reading and spelling
Age or Grade Range	Grade 6–junior college
Usually Given By	Classroom teacher Special education teacher Psychologist Any trained person
Type of Test	Standardized Norm-referenced Individual Criterion-referenced Group
Scores Obtained	Grade level Standard Percentile Mastery level
Student Performance Timed?	No
Testing Time	20–30 minutes
Scoring/Interpretation Time	15 minutes
Normed On	Approximately 1,500 junior and senior high students from suburban southern California public schools
Alternate Forms Available?	No

FORMAT

The Diagnostic Analysis of Reading Errors (DARE) is a 46-item, multiple-choice spelling test. The word list used is the Wide Range Achievement Test (p. 19) Spelling, Level II. Test materials for the DARE include an examiner's manual, individual student response forms for either hand or machine scoring, individual profile forms, and a scoring template.

The test is administered by the examiner reading the word list while the students select the correct spelling of each word from four alternatives. The alternative spellings have been selected to provide diagnostic information about a student's difficulties with sound substitutions, omissions, and reversals.

The DARE may be given either individually or in groups; a taped presentation is also available for reading lab situations. Each student completes the entire test.

Using the scoring template, four scores are calculated for each student. The C score is the total number of *correct responses*. The S score indicates the number of errors due to *sound substitutions*. The O score reflects *omissions* of letters or syllables, and the R score indicates the number of *reversals*. Table 12 illustrates how sample items are scored on the DARE.

Table 12. Example of DARE Scoring

Item	Score
• gorl	S
• gril	R
• girl	C
• gill	O

Standard scores and percentiles for the C score, or total correct score, are provided for age and grade level, male and female. Standard scores are based on a mean of 100 and a standard deviation of 15 to facilitate comparison with the Wide Range Achievement Test (p. 19), the Wechsler Intelligence Scale for Children—Revised (p. 265), and the Wechsler Adult Intelligence Scale (p. 275). A table of error expectancies provides the number of errors of each type (S, R, O) for each C score. For example, a typical error pattern for a student with 27 correct responses would be 7 sound substitutions, 7 omissions, and 5 reversals. Error patterns that vary from the expected by more than two are considered indicators of strengths and weaknesses in auditory-visual transcoding. A high number of sound errors might reflect auditory discrimination problems or unfamiliarity with English sounds. Omissions are indicative of confusion in sound-symbol association, and reversals are a demonstration of difficulty in sound sequencing. An individual profile is completed demonstrating the relationship between the number of errors of each type and the total correct.

STRENGTHS OF THE DARE

- Few diagnostic tests are designed particularly for the junior high school through junior college population.
- The DARE manual is clearly written and contains valuable information regarding the theoretical background of the test, test construction, standardization, reliability and validity, as well as remedial principles and case studies.
- The DARE is designed as a group test and provides an efficient way to obtain individual diagnostic information. This diagnostic information is enhanced by using the Wide Range Achievement Test (WRAT) Spelling word list. A comparison of a student's written spelling proficiency and word reading facility on the WRAT with the student's ability to recognize correct spelling is often very interesting and has remedial implications. For example, students who perform significantly better in spelling on the WRAT than on the DARE may be students who need kinesthetic input and would do well with multisensory teaching techniques.

LIMITING FACTORS OF THE DARE

- The DARE is based on the concept of modality patterns related to learning disabilities. This concept has questionable validity (see p. 4 of the Introduction to this book).
- Throughout the manual, the authors describe the purpose of the DARE as "identifying" adolescents with learning disabilities. Although they mention comparing the DARE with other tests, they imply that diagnosis can be made on the basis of the DARE alone—obviously a faulty implication.
- The standardization population for the DARE is very narrow, including, primarily, regular high school students from suburban Los Angeles. Small numbers of Hispanic students are included, as well as one group of Continuation High School students. Since the DARE is intended to be useful for non-English-speaking or limited-English-speaking students and for remedial students, the norms need to be expanded.
- The manual does not clearly state the number of students at each age and grade level in the norming population. Since the authors report some unusual findings in terms of scores (no differences among grades 7 to 10, sex differences at all age levels), expansion of norms to confirm these findings is critical.
- The absence of basal/ceiling procedures is understandable in a group test. However, for students with very low spelling ability, the second half of the test can be very frustrating.

Diagnostic Spelling Potential Test (DSPT)

John Arena
Academic Therapy Publications, 1982
20 Commercial Blvd., Novato, CA 94947

Purpose	To assess written spelling level and "spelling potential" skills
Major Areas Tested	Spelling
Age or Grade Range	7 years–adult
Usually Given By	Special education teacher Psychologist Remedial specialist
Type of Test	Individual Group Standardized Norm-referenced
Scores Obtained	Grade level Standard Percentile
Student Performance Timed?	No
Testing Time	25–40 minutes
Scoring/Interpretation Time	15–20 minutes
Normed On	967 students in grades 1–12 in the San Francisco Bay Area
Alternate Forms Available?	Yes

FORMAT

The Diagnostic Spelling Potential Test (DSPT) is a comprehensive spelling test covering a wide age range. The materials are an examiner's manual and record forms for two alternate forms, A and B. The DSPT is composed of four subtests, each with 90 items:

1. *Spelling*. A dictated written spelling list.
2. *Word Recognition*. A decoding test that yields two scores: a sight recognition score and a phonic recognition score.
3. *Visual Recognition*. Recognition of the correctly spelled word in four choices without an auditory stimulus.
4. *Auditory-Visual Recognition*. The same as Visual Recognition but with an auditory stimulus.

Through a basal and ceiling process, students are tested only on items within a critical range.

The DSPT is based on the concept of "spelling potential." This term refers to skills that will enable the student to learn new words efficiently. The author suggests that the Spelling subtest be given and scored. If the student's spelling is below expectation, then the remaining subtests should be given so that specific strengths and weaknesses can be detected.

Five raw scores are obtained (two from the Word Recognition subtest) and converted into standard scores, percentile ranks, and grade ratings using tables in the manual. Standard scores have a mean of 100 and a standard deviation of 15 for easy comparison with other tests. All of the scores are transferred to the face sheet of the record form, giving a visual profile of the student's performance.

Next, a spelling error analysis is done. The student's errors on the Spelling subtest are classified into two types: Category 1, phonetically correct misspellings (*wellcum* for *welcome*), and Category 2, nonphonetic omissions, additions, and substitutions (*bog* for *dog*). Based on the assumption that students with phonetically correct misspellings have greater spelling potential, students with more than 50 percent of their errors in Category 1 are rated high potential while students with less than 50 percent of their errors in Category 1 are rated low potential.

Through an analysis of the student's spelling level, types of errors, and performance on the other three subtests, a remedial program can be defined. For example:

John's written spelling was below average but his errors fell into Category 1, indicating a high spelling potential. Remediation that focuses on visual perception and memory will enhance his basically strong phonics skills.

Carol's score on Visual Recognition was quite low, but when the auditory stimulus was introduced, she performed much better. This would indicate that a multisensory approach that utilizes verbalization skills should be used initially until Carol's visual recall and visualization skills improve.

STRENGTHS OF THE DSPT

• Throughout the manual, the author's knowledge of, and sensitivity to, students with spelling problems is apparent. Flexibility in basal and ceiling procedures, markers for younger children, the use of phrases instead of sentences for the dictation, and the recording procedures are all designed to help the student feel at ease.

• The basic assumption of the DSPT, that phonetic misspellings are better than nonphonetic misspellings, seems sound. Some research (Compton, Bisagno, and Tretten 1979) on written language skills in learning-disabled students suggests that the only variable that clearly separated learning-disabled and non-learning-disabled students was phonetic versus nonphonetic misspellings.

• Careful attention to the item selection for each subtest is apparent. The word lists allow for a good sampling of student spelling at all grade levels.

• The DSPT is clearly designed to lead to remediation. Forty pages in the manual are devoted to remedial activities and materials related to subtest performance.

LIMITING FACTORS OF THE DSPT

• The DSPT was standardized by equating each subtest with the Spelling subtest of the Wide Range Achievement Test (WRAT), 1978 norming. While this procedure is statistically sound, whatever problems are inherent in the WRAT standardization (p. 19) then become part of the DSPT.

• The long length of the DSPT is a factor. In group testing, students with poor spelling may experience great frustration.

• The DSPT is similar to the Diagnostic Analysis of Reading Errors (p. 69) in that it is based on the premise that modality assessment should form the basis for remedial programs. This assumption is highly questionable. (See p. 4.)

Myklebust Picture Story Language Test (PSLT)

Helmer R. Myklebust
Grune & Stratton, Inc., 1965
111 Fifth Ave., New York, NY 10003

Purpose	To assess various written language skills
Major Areas Tested	Written language
Age or Grade Range	7–17 years
Usually Given By	Special education teacher Speech/language clinician
Type of Test	Standardized Individual Group Norm-referenced
Scores Obtained	Age level Percentile Stanine
Student Performance Timed?	No
Testing Time	20–30 minutes
Scoring/Interpretation Time	20–30 minutes
Normed On	Metropolitan, rural, and suburban school populations in one midwestern state
Alternate Forms Available?	No

FORMAT

The Myklebust Picture Story Language Test (PSLT) is a test of written language most often administered individually, but it can be given to groups ranging in size from 8 to 10 students. More than 10 students may be tested simultaneously if additional test pictures are available. The test picture is a black-and-white photograph, 10½ by 13½ inches, that shows a young boy playing with dollhouse figures (see photo).

Other materials needed to administer the PSLT include the test manual and the printed record forms used for scoring. The manual is a clothbound book *(Development and Disorders of Written Language, Volume One)* containing administration and scoring procedures, as well as chapters discussing the author's ideas about the development of written language skills.

The examiner must supply the type of writing paper and pencils that the students are familiar with. Standard-sized writing paper is suggested, because it affords the same potential story length for all students.

Administration of the PSLT requires simple oral directions. The examiner holds up the picture so that all can see and says, "Look at this picture carefully." The examiner waits 20 seconds and says, "You are to write a story about it. You may look at it as much and as often as you care to. Be sure to write the best story you can. Begin writing whenever you are ready."

The picture is then placed in a central position, where it can be viewed by all students. It is permissible for a student to pick up the picture for close inspection. It should be replaced in a central position after the student finishes examining it.

Questions are answered neutrally. For example, a student might ask, "Should I write about how the boy is dressed?" A typical reply would be, "If you want to. Write the story the way you think is best." The examiner may encourage

PSLT Stimulus Picture

students to write something if they are having difficulty thinking of a story but must refrain from offering any suggestions that might influence the content of the story.

The PSLT is not timed; the students continue to write until they have completed their story. Alternate, equivalent forms for test-retest purposes are not available.

STRENGTHS OF THE PSLT

• Tests measuring written expression are virtually nonexistent. The PSLT then, being the first of its kind, is a landmark test.

• The PSLT is easy to administer and requires no special training. The wide age range makes it a particularly good instrument for measuring the progress of a student's writing skills in relation to age. Separate norms are provided for boys and girls, reflecting sex differences in the development of written language at different age levels. Provision has been made for converting the raw scores into age and percentile equivalents and stanine ranks.

• Three attributes of language usage are evaluated by the PSLT. Scores are provided for the following scales: *Productivity* measures the length of the expression and includes counts of total words, total sentences, and words per sentence; *Syntax* measures the correctness of what is expressed and includes accuracy of word usage, of word endings, and of punctuation (errors of additions, omissions, substitutions, and word order are counted); *Abstract-Concrete* measures the meaning of the ideas being expressed on a continuum ranging from concrete to abstract. Norms for each of these measures were established developmentally for both boys and girls.

• The three aspects of language that are measured are useful because they make it possible to obtain a profile of a student's strengths and weaknesses in written language. For example, one student may write a story deficient in syntax but highly imaginative and abstract. Another student may write a syntactically correct story that is limited in ideation, tending toward the concrete. In planning a writing program, the teacher would study the student's performance on each of the three scales.

• Another diagnostic use of the PSLT is to compare the student's facility with the spoken and the written word. Initially the test may be administered by having the student tell a story about the picture. The next day the student is asked to write a story. Although the PSLT has not been standardized for spoken language, the findings from an oral test may be significant for remediation.

• The manual includes scored stories (illustrating normal and handicapped children), which are particularly helpful for the examiner who is learning how to score and interpret the PSLT. It will often be necessary to refer to these sample stories for comparison.

• The PSLT answered a critical need for a test of written language. In addition, volume 2 of *Development and Disorders of Written Language: Studies of Normal and Exceptional Children* (Myklebust 1973) includes further analyses of the PSLT results for normal students and comparative findings for exceptional students—learning disabled, mentally retarded, socially and/or emotionally disturbed, speech handicapped, and reading disabled.

LIMITING FACTORS OF THE PSLT

• The norming procedures described in the test manual are inadequate. The sample came from only one midwestern state, and as yet there is no information available on geographic differences in written language development.

The author claims that a wide range of socioeconomic levels and cultural backgrounds were included in the standardization sample. However, data regarding the racial breakdown or number of minority students included in the study are lacking. Caution should be the rule when using the PSLT norms with students from different cultural backgrounds.

• Another consideration concerning standardization is that only odd ages from 7 to 17 were sampled. The author interpolates scores for ages not tested. This is a questionable practice, especially because the standard deviations for the sampled ages are quite large.

• The author makes the statement that the PSLT appears to be a valid test but offers no evidence to support this assumption. No attempt was made to evaluate the face validity of the test. How motivating, for example, is the test picture in comparison with other pictures that might have been used?

• The author states that the test-retest reliability coefficients were statistically significant but does not report the data. The coefficients for the syntax scale seem to indicate that there is not sufficient interscorer reliability, especially with untrained examiners. This should be noted in the information on test administration.

• Scoring the PSLT is a time-consuming, tedious job that requires a highly skilled clinician. Training in the use of the syntax scale is essential for its correct use. Scoring is also not entirely objective. Judgment of the level of abstraction of the stories in relation to criteria given in the manual is very subjective. Even after carefully studying each criterion and the illustrative examples, it is still difficult in many cases to determine the appropriate level.

• Principles for scoring the syntax scale pose some concern. The scale was designed to measure accuracy of usage only. Thus the student who writes productively or who attempts to use more complex sentence constructions has a higher probability of making more errors and receiving a lower syntax score than the student who writes simply (subject-verb sentences), using a limited range of punctuation marks. Consider the samples below, both written by 8-year-old boys.

Story A: *This is a picture of a boy playing with dollhouse people. He is having fun.*

Story B: *A young boy Jimmy is playing with some dolls his brother in law gave him. He said, "I like my new toys." After an hour or so he went to lunch and said to his brother, what a fun day this is.*

Story A contains no errors of syntax and would receive a high score. Story B has several scorable errors (comma, hyphen, and quotation mark omissions) and would receive a lower syntax score. This seems misleading. The second student tried to use a variety of punctuation marks, mastery of which he has not yet achieved. Hence the scoring procedures actually penalize, unfairly, the student who attempts to write complex structures requiring a wider range of punctuation marks. Perhaps criterion-referenced evaluation, designed to discriminate between mastery and nonmastery of specific objectives, would be more meaningful than the traditional norm-referenced evaluation in the assessment of written language skills.

Test of Written Language (TOWL)

Donald D. Hammill and Stephen C. Larsen
Pro-Ed, 1978; 1983
5341 Industrial Oaks Blvd., Austin, TX 78735

Purpose	To identify students with written language disabilities, to identify strengths and weaknesses in writing, and to document progress in writing
Major Areas Tested	Written language
Age or Grade Range	Grades 2–12
Usually Given By	Classroom teacher Special education teacher Educational diagnostician Psychologist
Type of Test	Individual Group Standardized Norm-referenced
Scores Obtained	Percentile Standard
Student Performance Timed?	No
Testing Time	40–60 minutes
Scoring/Interpretation Time	15–20 minutes
Normed On	3,418 students balanced for sex, place of residence, and grade level in 14 states
Alternate Forms Available?	No

FORMAT

The Test of Written Language (TOWL) is one of the few standardized assessments of students' written language skills. The materials consist of a manual containing administration and scoring directions, as well as theoretical and statistical background, individual student answer booklets, and a summary and profile sheet for recording each student's scores.

On the student answer form is printed a three-part picture depicting life on another planet, shown in Figure 18. In scene one, the environment of the planet is deteriorating; scene two shows the movement by spaceships to a new planet; in scene three, humans and space creatures join together in a cooperative life. Using this stimulus, the student is asked to write a story using all three pictures. This sample of spontaneous writing and other measures compose the six subtests of the TOWL:

1. *Vocabulary*. Students receive one point for every correctly spelled word that contains seven or more letters.

2. *Thematic Maturity*. Students receive one point for each of 20 criteria included in their stories. Among the criteria are writing in paragraphs, giving personal names to the characters, having a definite ending, and expressing a philosophical or moral theme.

3. *Handwriting*. If the student wrote in cursive, the handwriting is matched against five samples in the manual demonstrating degrees of legibility. A score of 0 to 10 is obtained. Students who wrote in manuscript do not receive a handwriting score.

4. *Spelling*. The student is given a separate 25-word spelling test. The test is a shortened form of the Larsen-Hammill Test of Written Spelling (p. 63) using words from both the Predictable Words list and the Unpredictable Words list. One point is given for each word spelled correctly.

5. *Word Usage*. The student is given 25 sentences with missing words to complete. The word usage test assesses the student's knowledge of correct grammar (regular and irregular plurals, past tenses, comparatives, and pronouns). (For example: *He built the house all by* _____ . *One sheep is in the barn; two other* _____ *are in the field*.)

6. *Style*. The student rewrites 25 sentences with correct punctuation and capitalization. (For example: *she is mrs smith*.) The sentence must be totally correct to receive one point.

Raw scores for each section are converted into percentiles and standard scores. The standard scores for the six subtests are totaled and transformed into a total test score, the written language quotient (WLQ). The WLQ has a mean of 100 and a standard deviation of 15. If a student did not obtain a score on a specific section (such as handwriting), a score for that section is prorated by averaging the student's other standard scores.

No grade scores are provided in the 1983 edition, in line with the author's position that grade scores are too often misinterpreted and are less statistically reliable than standard scores.

STRENGTHS OF THE TOWL

• The need for a standardized test to measure written language is apparent to every diagnostician in the field. The other highly used instrument, the Myklebust Picture Story Language Test, has serious drawbacks (see p. 73). The use of the standardized picture stimulus to gather a spontaneous

Figure 18. TOWL Stimulus Picture

writing sample together with standardized measures of spelling, grammar, and mechanics is a creative approach to this difficult assessment problem.

- The TOWL picture is interesting to students of all ages and generally produces a good writing sample.

- The TOWL is technically sound in terms of standardization and reliability. This is impressive in such a nebulous area as written expression.

- The group format allows for efficient testing of a whole class, followed by individual analysis of strengths and weaknesses.

- Administration and scoring procedures for the TOWL are very clear. The addition of sample stories for scoring practice is a helpful feature.

- The TOWL manual is clear and well written. The section on informal assessment of written language is very helpful to the teacher.

LIMITING FACTORS OF THE TOWL

- While the TOWL picture produces a reasonably good spontaneous writing sample, the assessments of that sample seem contrived and of little value in evaluating a student's program needs. For example, while rating vocabulary on the length of the words used may be theoretically sound, it is not as meaningful as a system that indicates the types of words (parts of speech, common or unusual words) a student is currently using and not using.

- Also, the Thematic Maturity criteria seem very arbitrary. A student who writes dialogue or a story personalizing the characters in the picture will receive a very high score that may have little to say about the writer's overall thematic maturity.

- There are many standardized spelling tests. Therefore, it is disappointing that the authors did not assess the student's spelling *in the context of the story*. Difficulties with standardizing that procedure are obvious, but an attempt would be applauded. A way of assessing Word Usage and Style in the context of the story also would have made the TOWL a much more valuable assessment tool.

- Even though the TOWL reports many validity studies comparing the TOWL with the Myklebust Picture Story Language Test (p. 73), the Test of Reading Comprehension (p. 59), the Test of Adolescent Language (p. 191), and the Test of Language Development (p. 187), impressions of clinicians are that the validity is questionable. For students in suburban communities, the subtest scores and WLQ seem to overestimate a student's abilities. Many students reported by their teachers to be doing very poorly in written language in school obtain average or higher scores on the TOWL. Such results may be due to the inherent problems of assessing such a global skill as written language with one writing sample, or they may be due to the limitations in the subtests described above. In either case, examiners should be extremely cautious about reporting individual students' scores without information about their writing skills in other situations.

- Although the TOWL was designed to measure progress in a writing program, the lack of an alternate picture or other subtests makes it inappropriate to use as a pre- and posttest. A student could make great gains in written language that would not be reflected in retesting on the TOWL.

Mathematics Tests

KeyMath Diagnostic Arithmetic Test 81
Enright™ Diagnostic Inventory of Basic Arithmetic Skills 86

KeyMath Diagnostic Arithmetic Test (KeyMath)
Austin J. Connolly, William Nachtman, and E. Milo Pritchett
American Guidance Service, Inc., 1971; 1976
Publishers' Bldg., Circle Pines, MN 55014

Purpose	To assess mathematics skills
Major Areas Tested	Mathematics
Age or Grade Range	Preschool–grade 6
Usually Given By	Classroom teacher Special education teacher Psychologist Paraprofessional
Type of Test	Standardized Individual Criterion-referenced
Scores Obtained	Grade level Percentile
Student Performance Timed?	No
Testing Time	30–45 minutes
Scoring/Interpretation Time	10–15 minutes
Normed On	Children from urban, suburban, and rural areas of the West, Midwest, and East with wide range of racial representation, based on the 1970 census
Alternate Forms Available?	No

FORMAT

The KeyMath Diagnostic Arithmetic Test (KeyMath) materials include a test manual, an easel kit, and individual diagnostic record forms on which the examiner records the students' responses. Stimulus materials and directions for administering each item are sequentially displayed to the examiner in the easel kit. Most subtests require verbal responses to open-ended questions that are presented orally in conjunction with colorful pictorial materials. The easel kit is durable and has a convenient flip-page arrangement for presentation.

The KeyMath is an individually administered test consisting of 14 untimed subtests grouped into three major areas: Content, Operations, and Applications. Following is a description of the three areas, along with a listing of their respective subtests.

The subtests in the Content area investigate basic mathematics concepts and knowledge essential to an understanding and practical application of the number system. The subtests are:

A. Numeration
B. Fractions
C. Geometry and Symbols

The subtests in Operations include the basic computational processes. Some problems are of a pencil-and-paper variety. These problems are presented on the back of the diagnostic record form. Other subtests in Operations evaluate the ability to perform more than one computational process. The subtests in the Operations are:

D. Addition
E. Subtraction
F. Multiplication
G. Division
H. Mental Computation
I. Numerical Reasoning.

The subtests in Applications focus on the functional use of mathematics. The content is designed to evaluate school arithmetic skills necessary and relevant in daily life. The subtests are:

J. Word Problems
K. Missing Elements
L. Money
M. Measurement (assesses standard weights and measures of the United States; a recently developed Metric Supplement is now available)
N. Time

For all of the subtests on the KeyMath, students complete only those items appropriate to their range of ability. This range extends from a basal level established by three consecutive correct responses to a ceiling level marked by three consecutive errors. Alternate, equivalent forms of the KeyMath are not available for test-retest purposes.

STRENGTHS OF THE KEYMATH

- The KeyMath has many excellent features. It is a criterion-referenced instrument based on the developmental sequence of skill acquisition and logical thinking. Extensive clinical training and experience in test administration are not required for the KeyMath, making it a helpful screening and diagnostic tool.

- Responses are easily recorded during administration on the record form (see Figure 19). A general pattern is identified according to student performance in the three major areas—Content, Operations, and Applications. The record form also graphically profiles a student's strengths and weaknesses in the 14 subtest areas. In addition, the examiner is provided with a comprehensive evaluation of the student's performance on individual items. A description of each item, stated as a behavioral objective, can be found in the appendix of the manual. For example, the objective for the Measurement subtest (item 8) reads: "Given the concept of a dozen, [the student] indicates the number of its elements." The objective for item 15 of the same subtest reads: "Given a common object, [the student] estimates its weight." Thus the teacher can quickly determine whether the student has or has not mastered a certain objective. This knowledge helps the teacher establish with certainty where instruction in the different areas should begin.

- Another level of information provided by the KeyMath is a grade-equivalent score, ranging from preschool to grade 6, based on total test performance. Separate grade scores for each of the 14 subtests are not provided. Scoring the test is simple and objective, taking approximately 10 minutes.

- The KeyMath is a highly motivating test for students because of the broad range and diversity of item content and the colorful and stimulating materials. The pictures that it uses are very much in the realm of experience of today's students (for example, illustrations of Raisin Bran cereal and Campbell's soup). Contemporary pictures contribute greatly to student interest in the test.

- Because of its diagnostic structure and almost total lack of reading and writing requirements, the test is particularly useful for students with a wide range of intellectual abilities and those who are learning disabled.

- In addition to measuring the usual math skills, the KeyMath also includes some unique subtests, one of which is Missing Elements. The word problems in this subtest are novel in that some missing information impedes their solution. For example: "Susan is 4 feet tall. She is how much taller than her brother?" The student must specify the missing information, which emphasizes the application of logical thinking and directly taps the student's ability to analyze and understand the structure of a verbal problem.

This is a skill generally not included in other math tests.
- In terms of standardization, the KeyMath sample contained a wide range of geographic and racial types. The sample was weighted on the demographic variables of race and community size to conform to the proportions obtained in the 1970 U.S. census.
- Reliability coefficients for total test performance are consistently high across grade levels. Moderate subtest reliabilities are reported in the manual. The manual also lists the standard errors of measurement for the total test and for each of its subtests, as well as for each grade level. These indices provide the range within which the student's performance may be expected to vary.
- Curriculum materials of two types are available to supplement remedial programs based on KeyMath results. Early Steps is a program appropriate for kindergarten through grade 1, and KeyMath Activity Pacs are available in each area measured by the test. Activity Pacs are intended for children in kindergarten through grade 6.

LIMITING FACTORS OF THE KEYMATH
- Although the primary value of the KeyMath is its use as a criterion-referenced instrument, grade norms for the total score are provided. However, the grade scores tend to be inflated and often do not correspond accurately to the student's day-to-day classwork in mathematics. Tables of normal curve equivalents and percentile ranks by grade are available in a separate manual from the publisher.
- There is a tendency to report grade-level scores on KeyMath subtests by using the graph at the bottom of the record form. This should not be done; the grade score norms were obtained by using total test scores only.
- A further caution concerns the use of KeyMath grade scores alone to determine a student's eligibility for special instruction in mathematics (as is the case in some school systems). As with any test, scores alone are of little value. The degree of subtest variability as seen on the diagnostic profile is a very important factor, because it demonstrates the variability in a student's math skills. Some students have superior abilities in math concepts and specific disabilities in computation, whereas for others the reverse is true.
- The norms for the KeyMath extend to the 8.8 grade level. But the number of students in the standardization sample at the junior high level is insufficient to warrant the test's use with regular seventh- and eighth-grade students. As stated in the manual, the test is intended for use from preschool through grade 6. Inclusion of test items appropriate for older students and extension of the standardization sample to include upper grade levels would greatly increase the test's usefulness.
- The KeyMath provides basal and ceiling levels, which are convenient testing features that allow the examiner to administer less than the entire test. Some subtests, however, have fewer numbers of items than others, so that significant gaps occur at different points on the grade-level continuum for those particular subtests. For example, in the Fractions subtest, item 2 has a relative grade-level difficulty of 1.3. Item 3 corresponds to a relative grade-level difficulty of 3.6, a jump of over two years from the previous item. If the ceiling level procedure of three consecutive errors is followed, a kindergarten student might have to be administered item 3 (which is beyond his or her ability range) to reach the described ceiling. More items are needed in some subtests to cover the grade-level gaps so that the examiner does not have to administer superfluous items that are too difficult.

84　　　　　　　　　　　　　　　　　　　　　　　　　　　　　　　　Part I　Skill Area: Academic Tests

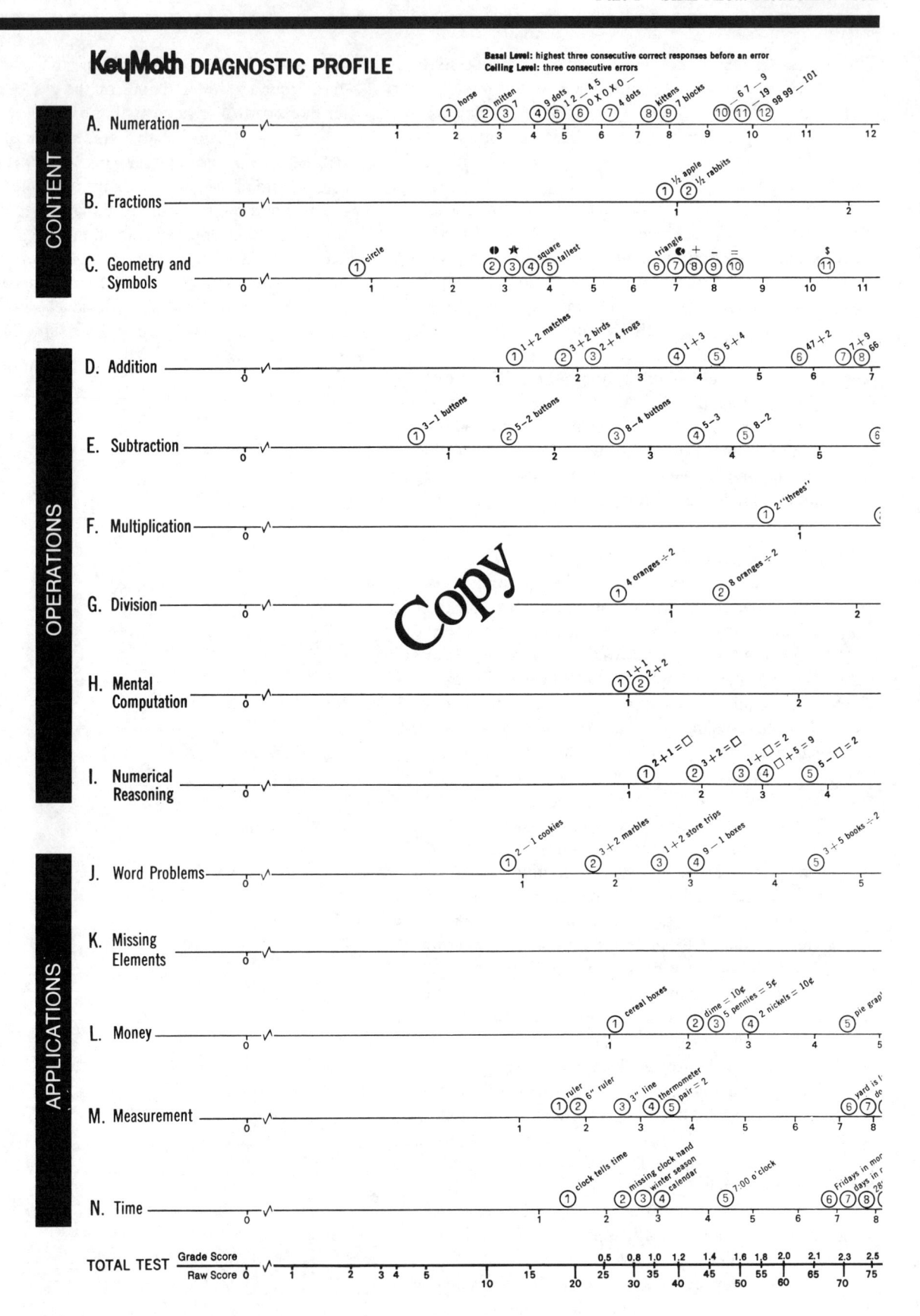

Figure 19. KeyMath Diagnostic Profile

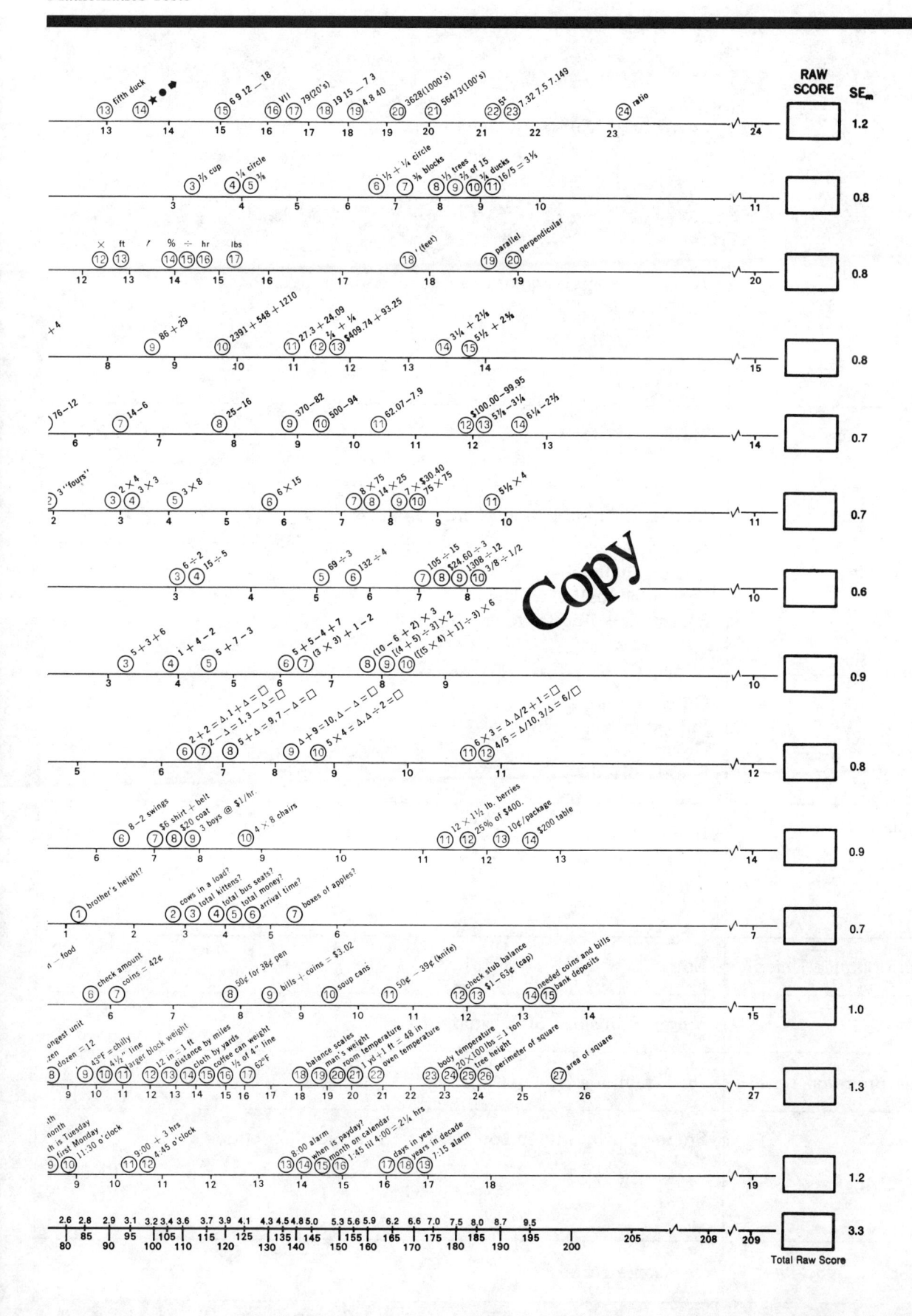

Mathematics Tests

Enright™ Diagnostic Inventory of Basic Arithmetic Skills (Enright™)

Brian E. Enright
Curriculum Associates, Inc., 1983
5 Esquire Rd., North Billerica, MA 01862

Purpose	To assess knowledge of basic facts and computation skills in mathematics
Major Areas Tested	Math computation
Age or Grade Range	Grades 1–6 (and remedial classes in secondary school)
Usually Given By	Classroom teacher Special education teacher Educational diagnostician
Type of Test	Criterion-referenced Individual Group Standardized
Scores Obtained	None
Student Performance Timed?	No
Testing Time	Varies with skills of the student
Scoring/Interpretation Time	15–30 minutes
Normed On	Students primarily in Louisiana and in five other states
Alternate Forms Available?	Yes (some parts)

Mathematics Tests

FORMAT

The Enright™ Diagnostic Inventory of Basic Arithmetic Skills (Enright™) is a comprehensive instrument for assessing a student's math computation skills. The materials consist of an examiner's notebook and individual arithmetic record books. The loose-leaf examiner's notebook is designed to lie flat on the table between the examiner and the student for individual testing. The Skill Test pages can be duplicated for use with a group.

The Enright™ provides three levels of information:

1. The grade level at which basic math computation skills are commonly taught
2. Assessments of 144 basic computational skills
3. An analysis of error patterns

Each of the basic skills assessed has been referenced to five basal mathematics series selected for their nationwide use. Through tables in the examiner's notebook, it is possible to determine the grade level at which a particular skill, such as adding two-digit numbers and regrouping ones, is typically taught. This information is useful in determining sequential curriculum.

The 144 basic computational skills are assessed in a very systematic manner. First, the student is administered the Wide Range Placement Test. This 26-problem screening test establishes a starting point for assessing a student's competency in addition, subtraction, multiplication, and division of whole numbers, fractions, and decimals. For students whose area of difficulty is known, this step may be omitted.

Once it is determined which operations the student needs help with, the Skill Placement Test for that operation is given. Figure 20 is the Skill Placement Test for addition of whole numbers. The purpose of this test is to determine the student's competency within the sequence of skills required in adding whole numbers. One problem for each critical step in the sequence is provided. The examiner's page corresponding to this Skill Test, Figure 21, provides the grade level at which the skills are usually taught, a description of each type of problem, and an instructional objective for the skill sequence.

The student's first error on the Skill Placement Test determines what Skill Test is then given. For example, if a student's first error is adding and regrouping two three-digit numbers from left to right (see item 12 in Figure 20), the student is given the Skill Test (A-12) for that step in the

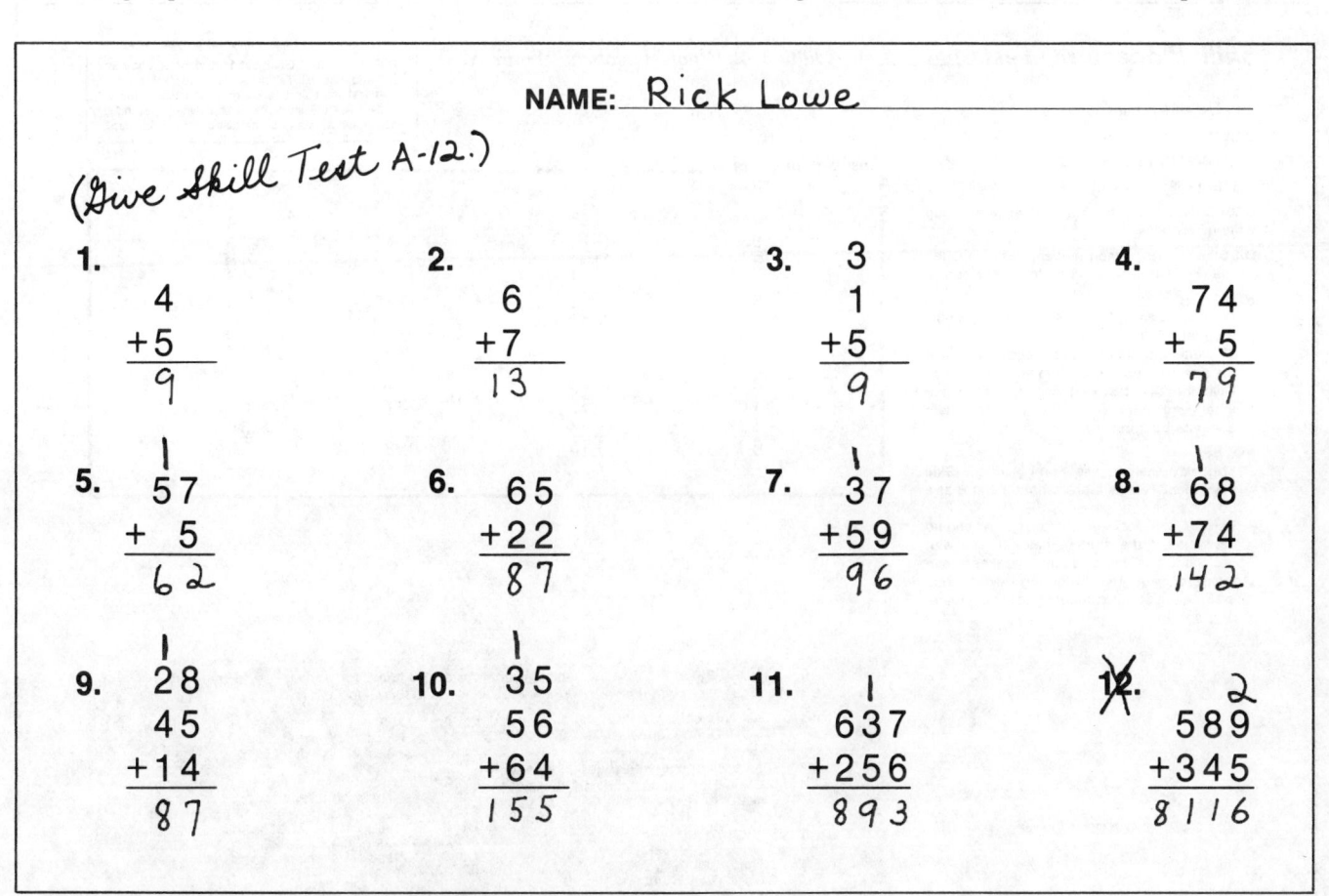

NAME: Rick Lowe

(Give Skill Test A-12.)

1. 4
   +5

    9

2. 6
   +7

   13

3. 3
    1
   +5

    9

4. 74
   + 5

   79

5. ⁱ57
   + 5

   62

6. 65
   +22

   87

7. ⁱ37
   +59

   96

8. ⁱ68
   +74

   142

9. ⁱ28
    45
   +14

   87

10. ⁱ35
    56
   +64

   155

11. ⁱ
    637
   +256

    893

12. ²
    589
   +345

   8116

Figure 20. Enright™ Skill Placement Test, Addition of Whole Numbers

88   Part I   Skill Area: Academic Tests

operation, shown in Figure 22. Figure 23 is the examiner's page for this particular Skill Test.

This part of the process is a unique feature of the Enright.™ The student computes five problems. On the examiner's page, each test item is printed with the correct response. The most common incorrect responses are also provided. By matching the student's response with one of the incorrect responses, the examiner can determine which type of error a student has made. The Enright™ identifies 198 distinct error types. These have been grouped into seven error clusters, shown in Table 13. The error pattern information clarifies for teachers the approach a student is taking to arrive at an answer. This information leads directly to an individualized remedial program. Students with errors in the same error clusters may be grouped for instruction. Following remediation, the second five items on the Skill Test are administered as a posttest. A criterion of 80 percent accuracy is recommended. When all of the skills in an operation that the student had made errors on have been retaught, the alternate form of the Skill Placement Test may be given as a posttest.

A Basic Fact Test is provided for addition, subtraction, multiplication, and division. Two forms are available for each operation. Each form consists of 50 basic facts. One form of the Basic Fact Test is usually given after the Skill Placement Test. Students who do not know the basic facts may still understand the computational process and should be allowed to use manipulatives or facts tables for the Skill Placement Test. Calculators are not permitted because they give a complete answer and do not allow error analysis. The alternate form of the Basic Facts Test may be used as a posttest.

The student's performance is recorded in the arithmetic record book. The booklet has 13 sections to correspond with the 13 operations assessed in the Enright™. The record tracks a student's progress in the acquisition of computation skills by dates and also provides information about error types. A color-coding system allows one record book for each student to be used throughout the elementary grades. A class record sheet and individual progress record forms that may be used for discussions with parents are also available.

Skill Placement Test — A. Addition of Whole Numbers   Form A

SKILL: Adds whole numbers.
GRADE LEVELS TAUGHT: 1.0 to 3.0
ARITHMETIC RECORD BOOK: Page 2
MATERIALS: Copy of S-8 and a pencil.
ASSESSMENT METHODS: Individual or group written response.
DISCONTINUE: When student has completed as many of the test items as he or she can.
NEXT:
1. Give **Basic Facts Test: Addition**, pages 38–39. (See **NOTE** 2.)
2. The letter and number above each test item in the **Answers** represent the matching skill test. Give the skill test that corresponds to the letter and number of the first test item computed incorrectly.

NOTES:
1. You may wish to use Form A of the **Skill Placement Test** as a pretest and Form B as a post test.
2. Before skill testing, the examiner should determine if the student has difficulty with basic addition facts. Such a weakness can interfere with the gathering of accurate information about student ability to compute.

DIRECTIONS: Give each student a copy of S-8 and a pencil. Tell the students to start with the first test item and to compute the test items *in order*. Tell the students to stop when they have computed as many of the test items as they can.

Answers for Form A

A-1 $^{1.0}$ 4 +5 / 9
A-2 $^{1.6}$ 6 +7 / 13
A-3 $^{1.6}$ 1 6 +1 / 8
A-4 $^{1.6}$ 74 + 5 / 79
A-5 $^{2.3}$ 57 + 5 / 62
A-6 $^{2.2}$ 65 +22 / 87
A-7 $^{2.3}$ 37 +59 / 96
A-8 $^{2.9}$ 68 +74 / 142
A-9 $^{3.0}$ 28 45 +14 / 87
A-10 $^{3.0}$ 35 56 +64 / 155
A-11 $^{2.7}$ 637 +256 / 893
A-12 $^{2.9}$ 589 +345 / 934

OBJECTIVE: By _____ (date), when given twelve test items for adding whole numbers, _____ (student's name) will compute with 100% accuracy: (list as appropriate)

- A-1 Two Numbers with Sum Less Than 10
- A-2 Two 1-Digit Numbers with Sum Greater Than 10
- A-3 Three Numbers with Sum Less Than 10
- A-4 2-Digit Number to a 1-Digit Number, with No Regrouping
- A-5 2-Digit Number to a 1-Digit Number, Regrouping Ones
- A-6 Two 2-Digit Numbers, with No Regrouping
- A-7 Two 2-Digit Numbers, Regrouping Ones
- A-8 Two 2-Digit Numbers, Regrouping Ones and Tens
- A-9 Three 2-Digit Numbers, Regrouping Ones
- A-10 Three 2-Digit Numbers, Regrouping Ones and Tens
- A-11 Two 3-Digit Numbers, Regrouping Ones
- A-12 Two 3-Digit Numbers, Regrouping Ones and Tens

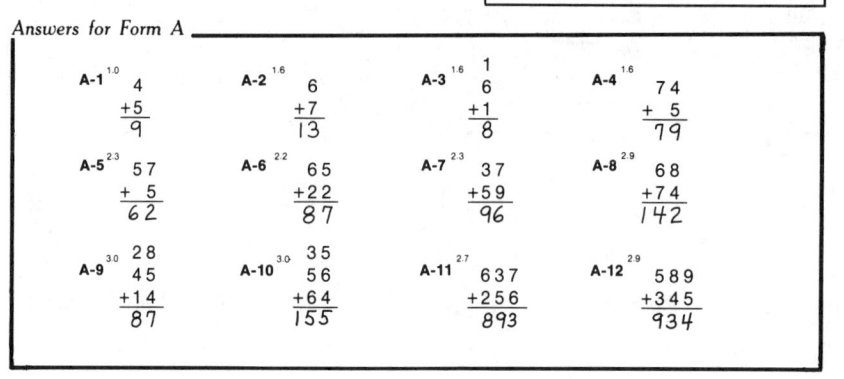

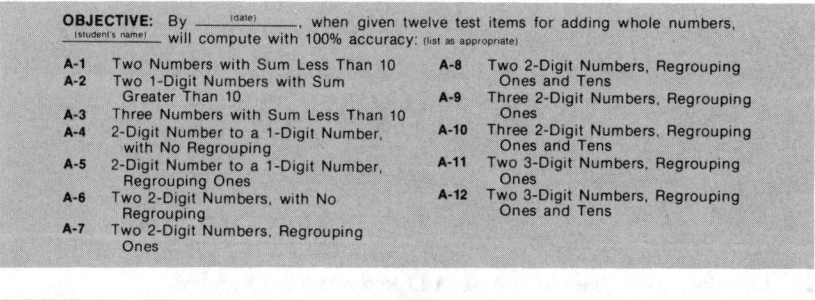

Figure 21. Enright™ Examiner's Page for Addition of Whole Numbers

Mathematics Tests

Table 13. Enright™ Error Clusters

Error Cluster	Definition	Example
Regrouping	Little understanding of place value	68 +74 ――― 1312
Process Substitution	Process changed in mid problem	$\overset{2}{\cancel{3}}\overset{1}{2}7$ −164 ――― 363
Omission	Step in process or part of answer left out	51 6)346 30 ―― 6 6 ―― 0
Directional	Steps performed in wrong direction or order	$\overset{3}{6}8$ +74 ――― 115
Placement	Correct computation, but numbers written in wrong place	6 +7 ―― 31
Attention to Sign	Wrong operation performed	4 +5 ―― 20
Guessing	Lack of basic understanding; random answers	3 1 +5 ―― 315

STRENGTHS OF THE ENRIGHT™

• This very new instrument promises to be very useful for diagnosticians and classroom teachers. There are few good math tests, and the Enright™ provides not only a sequential assessment of computational skills but also an analysis of errors, which leads directly to objectives and curriculum planning.

• Although the test is designed for elementary grade students, it obviously can be used effectively with students with poor computation skills in junior or senior high school.

• The record book for tracking progress of an individual student over the years is very helpful.

• Although the initial cost of the Enright™ is high, by duplicating student pages and designing an alternate record-keeping system, the materials can be used to assess large numbers of students over several years.

LIMITING FACTORS OF THE ENRIGHT™

• Although the Enright™ can be used with first and second graders, it is of limited value until the process of regrouping in addition and subtraction has been introduced.

• The grade-level information provided on each Skill Test should be used only to identify the grade level at which the skill is commonly taught. It is not appropriate to attach grade-level scores to a student's performance.

• The Enright™ is a test of computation skills only. Math concepts and applications are not assessed. A complete math curriculum would need to include many other skill areas.

(Directional 105.) NAME: Rick Lowe

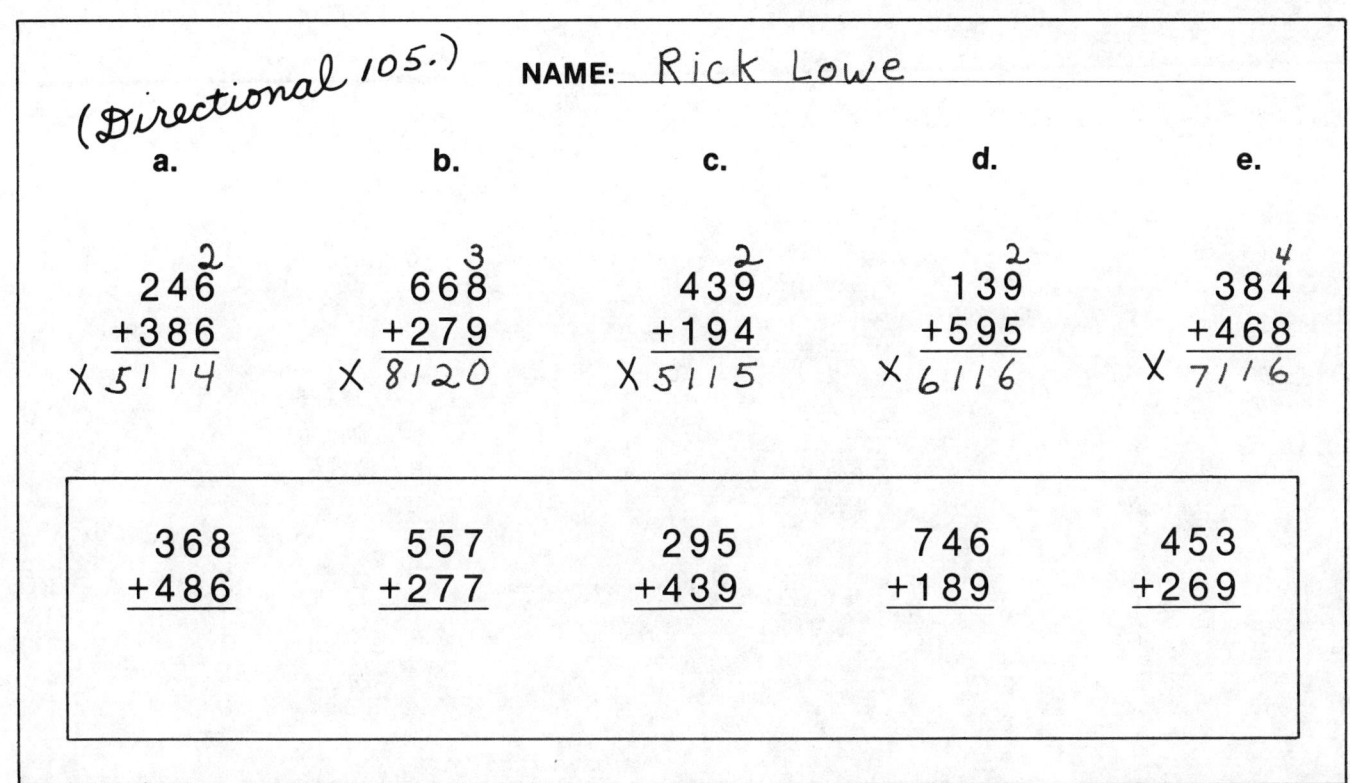

a.	b.	c.	d.	e.
$24\overset{2}{6}$ +386 ―――― X 5114	$66\overset{3}{8}$ +279 ―――― X 8120	$43\overset{2}{9}$ +194 ―――― X 5115	$13\overset{2}{9}$ +595 ―――― X 6116	$38\overset{4}{4}$ +468 ―――― X 7116

368	557	295	746	453
+486	+277	+439	+189	+269

Figure 22. Enright™ Skill Test A-12

ADDITION: TWO 3-DIGIT NUMBERS, REGROUPING ONES AND TENS

SKILL: Add two 3-digit numbers, regrouping ones and tens.

GRADE LEVEL TAUGHT: 2.9

STUDENT RECORD BOOK: Page 2

ASSESSMENT METHODS: Individual or group written response.

ACCURACY: At least 4/5 (80%) on the test items. When the review items are used for post testing, 4/5 (80%) is also required.

NOTES:
1. **Uses Fingers** Check to see if student adds by using his or her fingers.
2. **Addition Facts** Refer to page 2 of the *Student Record Book* if the student's error does not fit an error pattern. These kinds of random errors indicate a need for basic fact instruction and practice.

REVIEW ITEMS:

a. 368	b. 557	c. 295
+486	+277	+439
854	**834**	**734**

d. 746	e. 453
+189	+269
935	**722**

(A-12)
OBJECTIVE: By ____(date)____, when given five test items for adding two 3-digit numbers, regrouping ones and tens, ___(student's name)___ will compute the numbers with at least 4/5 (80%) accuracy.

	a.	b.	c.	d.	e.
	246	668	439	139	384
	+386	+279	+194	+595	+468
	632	**947**	**633**	**734**	**852**
	51212	81317	51213	61214	71412
	522	837	523	624	742
	722	1037	723	824	942
	5114	8120	5115	6116	7116

ERROR ANALYSIS

Regrouping 1: Writes entire sum of each column without regrouping.*

```
  6 8
+ 7 4
13 12
```

Regrouping 4: Writes ones in ones place, but does not regroup tens.

```
  ①
  5 7
+   5
  5 2
```

Regrouping 5: Regroups tens from ones column into hundreds column.†

```
  1
  6 3 7
+ 2 5 6
  9 8 3
```

Directional 105: Adds left to right, writes tens, regroups ones, and writes sum of ones column.

```
A  3  B
  6|8
+ 7|4
  1|1 5
```

* If the student is adding from left to right, he or she will have the same answer shown here. Check to see if the student is adding from left to right instead of from right to left.

† These answers show that the student correctly regroups tens from tens column into hundreds column.

Figure 23. Enright™ Examiner's Page for Skill Test A-12

Chapter Two

Perception and Memory Tests

Despite controversy over their concurrent and predictive validity, tests of perception and memory are routinely used in assessing students' academic skills. Although their relationship to academic skills may require further definition, perception and memory are clearly processes required for learning. As mentioned in the Introduction, if these process tests are used in conjunction with tests that assess basic academic skills, they can provide information that is useful in planning a student's instructional program.

This chapter begins with reviews of three comprehensive tests. The Detroit Tests of Learning Aptitude is an extensive battery of subtests containing measures of language, verbal comprehension and reasoning, fine motor coordination, spatial perception, and number skills. It has been placed in this chapter because several of its subtests assess visual and auditory perception and memory. A unique series of tests, the Slingerland Screening Tests for Identifying Children with Specific Language Disability, measures visual and auditory perception and memory, as well as kinesthetic memory skills. The Malcomesius Specific Language Disability Test, for students in grades 6 through 8, has the same format and content as the Slingerland Tests.

Following these comprehensive tests, three tests of auditory perception are reviewed. The Wepman Auditory Discrimination Test was one of the first diagnostic tests of auditory skills, whereas the Goldman-Fristoe-Woodcock Test of Auditory Discrimination is a more recent addition to the field. The Lindamood Auditory Conceptualization Test expands the range of auditory processes assessed to include not only discrimination, but sequencing and syllable analysis as well.

The last section of this chapter includes four tests in the area of visual perception. The first two tests—the Marianne Frostig Developmental Test of Visual Perception, a forerunner in the field of perceptual assessment, and the Motor-Free Visual Perception Test—assess a wide range of visual perception processes. In contrast, the Bender Visual Motor Gestalt Test and the Beery-Buktenica Developmental Test of Visual-Motor Integration focus on the assessment of eye-hand coordination through design-copying tasks.

In addition to these 10 tests, other tests containing subtests that assess perception and memory are reviewed in the remaining chapters. These tests are found in Chapter Five: Gross Motor Tests, Part II: Preschool and Kindergarten Tests, and Part III: General Intelligence Tests and Developmental Scales. Readers who are specifically interested in this area are referred to these sections.

Comprehensive Tests

Detroit Tests of Learning Aptitude 93
**Slingerland Screening Tests for Identifying Children
   with Specific Language Disability** 102
Malcomesius Specific Language Disability Test 106

Detroit Tests of Learning Aptitude (Detroit)

Harry J. Baker and Bernice Leland
Pro-Ed, 1935; Handbook revised 1967
5341 Industrial Oaks Blvd., Austin, TX 78735

Purpose	To assess a wide range of intellectual functioning, including reasoning and comprehension, practical judgment, verbal ability, time and space relationships, number ability, auditory and visual attention, and motor ability
Major Areas Tested	General intelligence functions
Age or Grade Range	3–19 years
Usually Given By	Special education teacher Psychologist Speech/language clinician
Type of Test	Standardized Individual
Scores Obtained	Mental age IQ
Student Performance Timed?	Yes (some subtests)
Testing Time	60–75 minutes (9–13 subtests)
Scoring/Interpretation Time	20–30 minutes
Normed On	600 public school children in Detroit, Michigan
Alternate Forms Available?	No

FORMAT

Test materials for the Detroit Tests of Learning Aptitude (Detroit) include the examiner's handbook, the student's record booklet, and a reusable spiral-bound book containing pictorial material.

The Detroit contains 19 tests measuring various aspects of intellectual functioning. No student is given all 19; only those tests that tap the particular range of abilities and that focus on the skills of particular interest should be given. The authors recommend that from 9 to 13 tests be administered individually and that they include one or more for each of the specific faculties (see Figure 24). A general idea of the nature of each test is given in Table 14. Detailed directions for scoring each test are given in the examiner's handbook. The raw score for each test is converted to a mental-age score. To obtain a total test score, the mental-age scores from all the tests are put in rank order to find the midpoint. This midpoint is the median mental-age score. The individual test results are also plotted on a profile to give a graphic representation of the student's strengths and weaknesses.

STRENGTHS OF THE DETROIT

- The Detroit provides a broad sampling of a student's mental processes and specific intellectual, perceptual, and cognitive functions.

- The provision for separate mental-age scores for each test increases the flexibility of the scale, because it allows for specific analysis of a student's strengths and weaknesses. An individual profile may be obtained, outlining a student's abilities and disabilities in a way that teachers and parents can readily understand. For example: "Sally is good at dealing with language and auditory tasks, as reflected by her strong performance on tests 2, 4, and 6, but she has difficulty when she must process, interpret, and remember information presented visually, as seen by her poor performance on tests 9 and 16."

- The profile of abilities and disabilities is much more useful diagnostically than the overall median mental age, and accordingly, less emphasis should be placed on the tests as an entity. Instead, the astute clinician will analyze performances on the various tests that together use many different combinations of modalities in order to determine which combinations facilitate or hinder the learning process. For example, when assessing auditory memory, the examiner might compare performance on Oral Directions (test 18) with performances on Auditory Attention Span for Unrelated Words (test 6) and Auditory Attention Span for Related Syllables (test 13). Questions might include, Is memory better when a motor response is required and input is visual as well as auditory (test 18)? Or is it better when response is oral and no visual material is viewed (tests 6 and 13)? What strategies does the student employ to aid recall? Verbal rehearsal? Shutting eyes to block out distracting

THE TESTS AND SPECIFIC MENTAL FACULTIES

Test	Reasoning and Comprehension	Practical Judgment	Verbal Ability	Time and Space Relationships	Number Ability	Auditory Attentive Ability	Visual Attentive Ability	Motor Ability
1. Pictorial Absurdities	X						X	
2. Verbal Absurdities	X		X					
3. Pictorial Opposites							X	
4. Verbal Opposites			X					
5. Motor Speed and Precision		X						X
6. Auditory Attention Span for Unrelated Words						X		
7. Oral Commissions		X				X	X	X
8. Social Adjustment A	X							
9. Visual Attention Span for Objects							X	
10. Orientation	X	X		X				
11. Free Association			X					
12. Memory for Designs				X			X	X
13. Auditory Attention Span for Related Syllables						X		
14. Number Ability					X			
15. Social Adjustment B	X							
16. Visual Attention Span for Letters							X	
17. Disarranged Pictures	X			X			X	
18. Oral Directions		X				X	X	X
19. Likenesses and Differences				X				

Figure 24. Detroit Tests

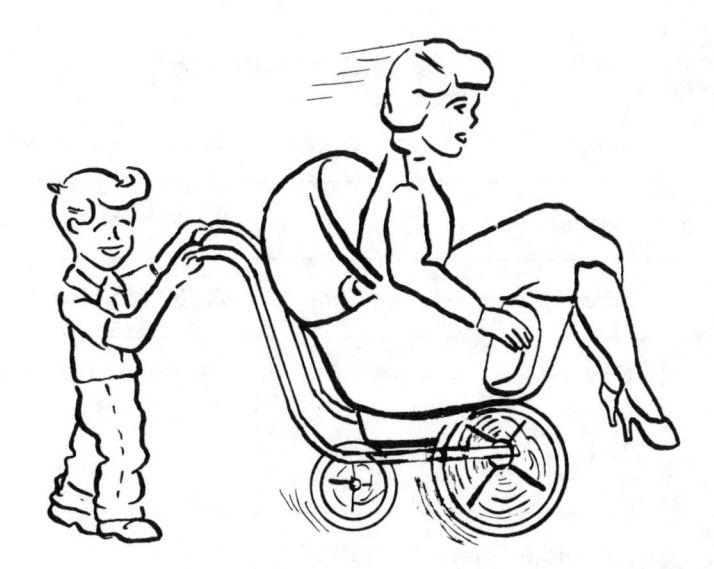

Figure 25. Detroit Pictorial Absurdities, Test 1

Comprehensive Tests

Table 14. Detroit Subtests

Subtest	Age Range	Presentation	Response	Task Description	Timed?
1. Pictorial Absurdities	3.0–10.0	Visual	Oral	Student must detect absurdities in pictures (see Figure 25 on p. 94)	No
2. Verbal Absurdities	5.3–16.6	Oral	Oral	Student must listen to statement and identify the illogical or erroneous cause-effect relationship (*I knew my father had walked all the way from Europe because his shoes were covered with mud.*)	No
3. Pictorial Opposites	3.0–9.3	Visual	Pointing	Student must examine sample picture and select from two choices the picture that shows the opposite relationship (see Figure 26 on p. 96)	No
4. Verbal Opposites	5.3–19.0	Oral	Oral	Student must name antonyms for sample words that gradually increase in difficulty (*deep-shallow*)	No
5. Motor Speed and Precision	4.6–18.6	Visual	Visual-motor	Student must make Xs in circles gradually decreasing in size (see Figure 27 on p. 97)	Yes
6. Auditory Attention Span for Unrelated Words	3.0–19.0	Oral	Oral	Student must remember and repeat series of unrelated words that increase in number from two to eight per span, after the examiner says them (*man-horse-song*)	No
7. Oral Commissions	3.0–8.3	Oral	Performance of task	Student must perform series of commissions, the units increasing in number from one to four (*Show me the window.*)	No
8. Social Adjustment A	3.6–13.6	Oral	Oral	Student must answer questions reflecting an ability to make judgments about social situations (*What is the thing to do if you break a school window?*)	No
9. Visual Attention Span for Objects	3.0–18.9	Visual	Oral	After viewing cards briefly, student must remember and recall sets of pictures on cards, the pictures increasing in number from two to eight per card (see Figure 28 on p. 98)	Yes
10. Orientation	3.0–13.6	Oral	Oral or performance of task	Student must answer questions and perform tasks reflecting temporal-sequential and spatial concepts (*What year is it now? Put your left foot behind you.*)	No
11. Free Association	5.3–19.0	Oral	Oral	Student must show verbal fluency by saying as many words as possible in a specified time period (*book, paper, pencil*)	Yes
12. Memory for Designs	3.0–15.9	Visual	Visual-motor	Student must either copy geometric forms from a model or reproduce them from memory after viewing them for a few seconds (see Figure 29 on p. 99)	Yes

Table 14. —*Continued*

Subtest	Age Range	Presentation	Response	Task Description	Timed?
13. Auditory Attention Span for Related Syllables	3.0–19.0	Oral	Oral	Student must repeat sentences of increasing length and complexity, after the examiner says them (*We will go for a walk.*)	No
14. Number Ability	3.0–11.0	Oral	Visual-motor or oral	Student must answer questions reflecting knowledge of arithmetic (*Count by 5s.*)	No
15. Social Adjustment B	3.0–17.9	Oral	Oral	Student must answer questions about civic affairs and common objects (*What is a jail?*)	No
16. Visual Attention Span for Letters	5.9–15.9	Visual	Oral	After viewing cards briefly, student must remember and recall sets of letters on cards, the letters increasing in number from two to seven (see Figure 30 on p. 100)	Yes
17. Disarranged Pictures	5.6–17.6	Visual	Visual-motor	Student must mentally rearrange pictures that are broken into sections and mark the correct answer in the test booklet (see Figure 31 on p. 100)	Yes
18. Oral Directions	6.3–19.0	Oral and visual	Visual-motor	Student must remember sets of oral directions, the units increasing in number from 2 to 5, and then carry out the directions by marking in the test booklet (see Figure 32 on p. 101)	Yes
19. Likenesses and Differences	6.9–19.0	Oral	Oral	Student must express similarities and differences between pairs of terms that gradually become more abstract (*sofa-bed, effort-achievement*)	No

Figure 26. Detroit Pictorial Opposites, Test 3

Comprehensive Tests 97

5. Motor Speed and Precision
(See pages 29-32 of Handbook)

Score ....

☐ Right or ☐ Left

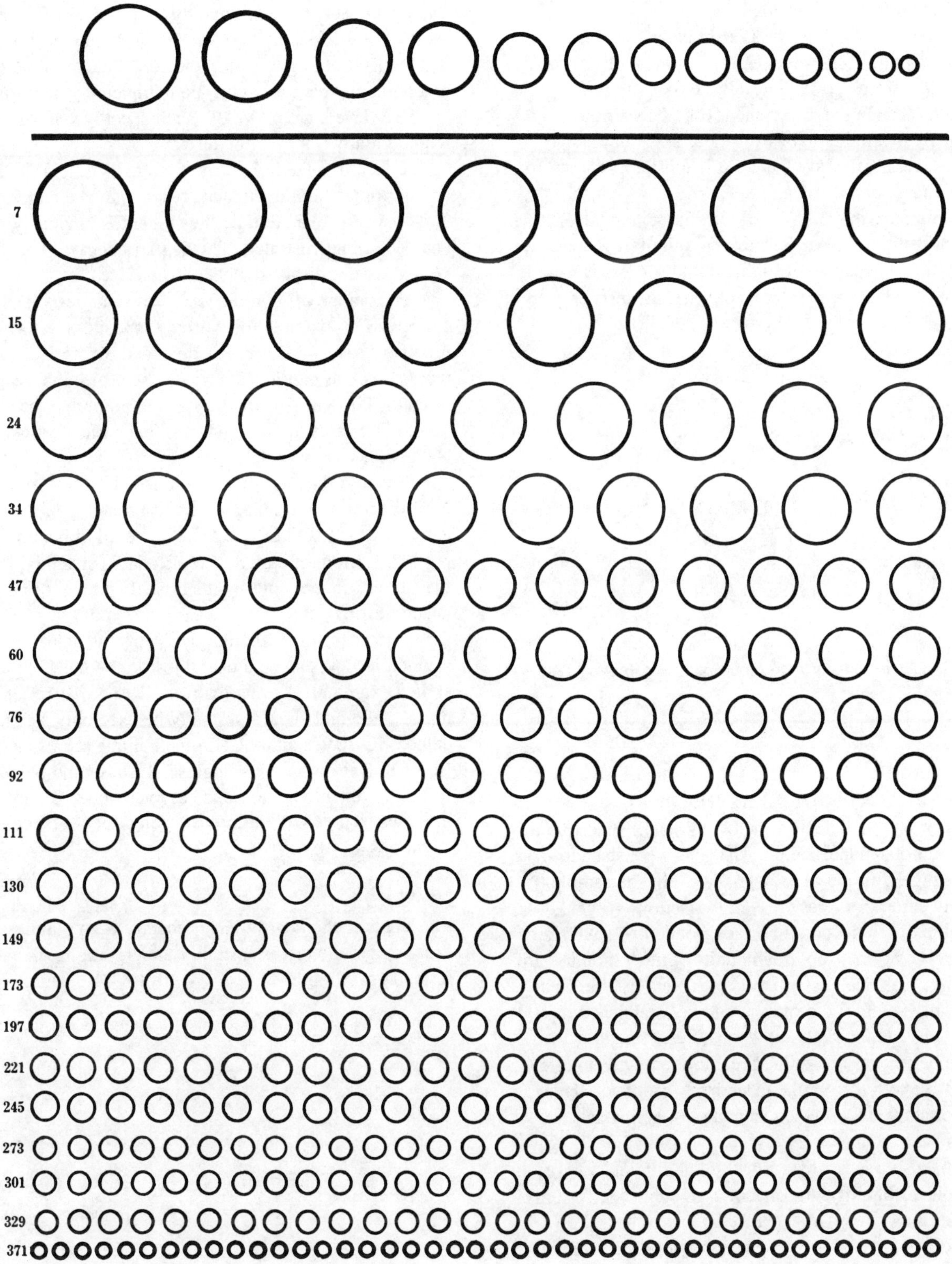

Figure 27. Detroit Motor Speed and Precision, Test 5

visual stimuli? Grouping the information by intonation or stress? In this example, the examiner will gain some information about whether auditory or visual approaches will enhance or inhibit learning.

- Another advantage of the Detroit is the wide age range it covers—from 3 to 19 years. Although many tests reach their ceiling before age 19, most of the memory and language tests span the upper age levels. Few instruments are currently available that assess these skills in older students. Overall, however, the test is most appropriate for the elementary school student.

- In summary, the Detroit is a flexible scale with easily added or substituted tests. The tests require few materials, tasks begin at an easy level so that initial success is usually guaranteed, and examiners generally find the tests easy to administer.

Figure 28. Detroit Visual Attention Span for Objects, Test 9

LIMITING FACTORS OF THE DETROIT

- A very serious defect of the Detroit is the inadequate and haphazard standardization. The tests were standardized on 50 average children at each grade level. The sample apparently came from only one city—Detroit. A breakdown of the sample's socioeconomic background and sex is not reported. The norms, reported in units of three months, are misleading, inasmuch as only 50 cases were used in each *year* group. Preferably, scores should be established in less-frequent age intervals, with means and standard deviations given, to make interpretation more meaningful. It is impossible to tell from the examiner's handbook the exact number of students on which any one test item was standardized.

There is also a lack of statistical reliability and validity in the Detroit. Reliability information was published for only one test of the battery. In general, the test authors draw many conclusions about its soundness but fail to provide supporting data. In particular, the concept of "specific mental faculties" is not backed by any evidence.

- Some of the administration procedures for the tests are ambiguous and need to be made more explicit. For example, on Likenesses and Differences (test 19), the handbook states that testing should "continue through three or four zero scores in succession." On Verbal Opposites (test 4), the handbook states that testing for older students should "begin at a point at which all items are completed successfully." No basal levels are provided; such specific starting points would greatly improve the tests.

The lack of a ceiling on some memory tests is still another procedural drawback. A test must be administered in its entirety, even though the student is obviously failing and becoming frustrated. This is particularly difficult for the young or very disabled student to endure.

- Poor range of item difficulty on some tests is also a concern. For example, on Verbal Opposites (test 4), the relatively easy word *begin* is preceded by more difficult words, such as *public* and *cruel*. Therefore, the assignment of credit for items below the starting point may be misleading; it cannot be assumed that earlier items have been successively easier.

- Because the Detroit was published in 1935 and has never been revised, many of the test materials are very dated. Questions like "What is the board of health?" are not in the realm of experience of today's students. Pictures that show potatoes sold by the bushel and a quill pen are anachronisms.

- In conclusion, although the Detroit is poorly standardized, it can be a useful test in the hands of a highly skilled examiner. Age scores from the normative tables may not be valid and should probably be used only as a ranking device. IQ scores and median mental-age scores calculated from the Detroit are meaningless. Tests should be examined for their content and not taken at face value. Comparison of these test scores with other test scores should be done with caution.

NOTE
The rights to the Detroit have recently been purchased by Pro-Ed, and the test is currently undergoing revision and restandardization.

Comprehensive Tests

12. Memory for Designs

(See pages 58-68 of Handbook)
GROUP A

Score A..............
B..............
C..............

Total ....

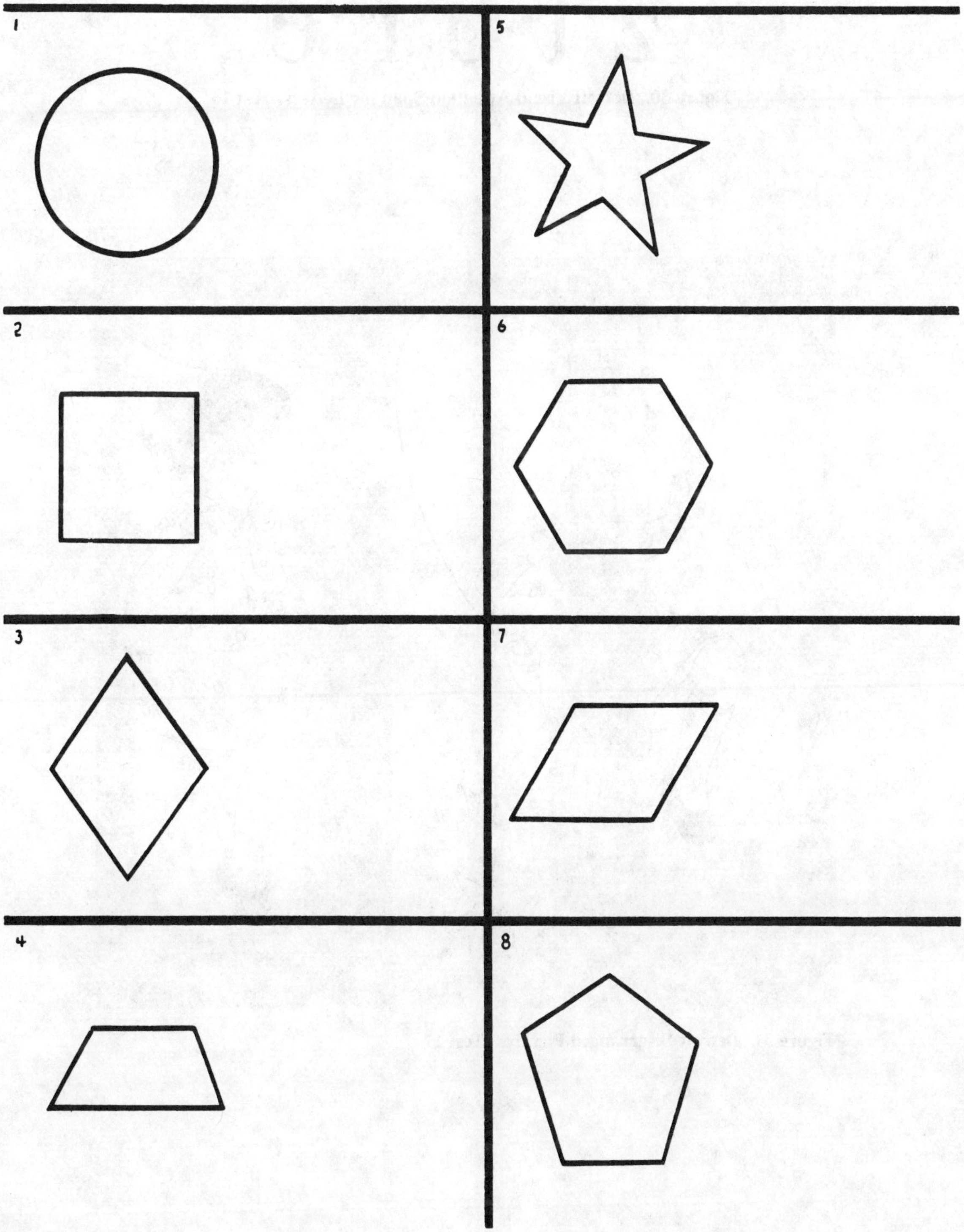

Figure 29. Detroit Memory for Designs, Test 12

z t b r c

Figure 30. Detroit Visual Attention Span for Letters, Test 16

Figure 31. Detroit Disarranged Pictures, Test 17

Comprehensive Tests

18. Oral Directions
(See pages 87-91 of Handbook)

Score..........................

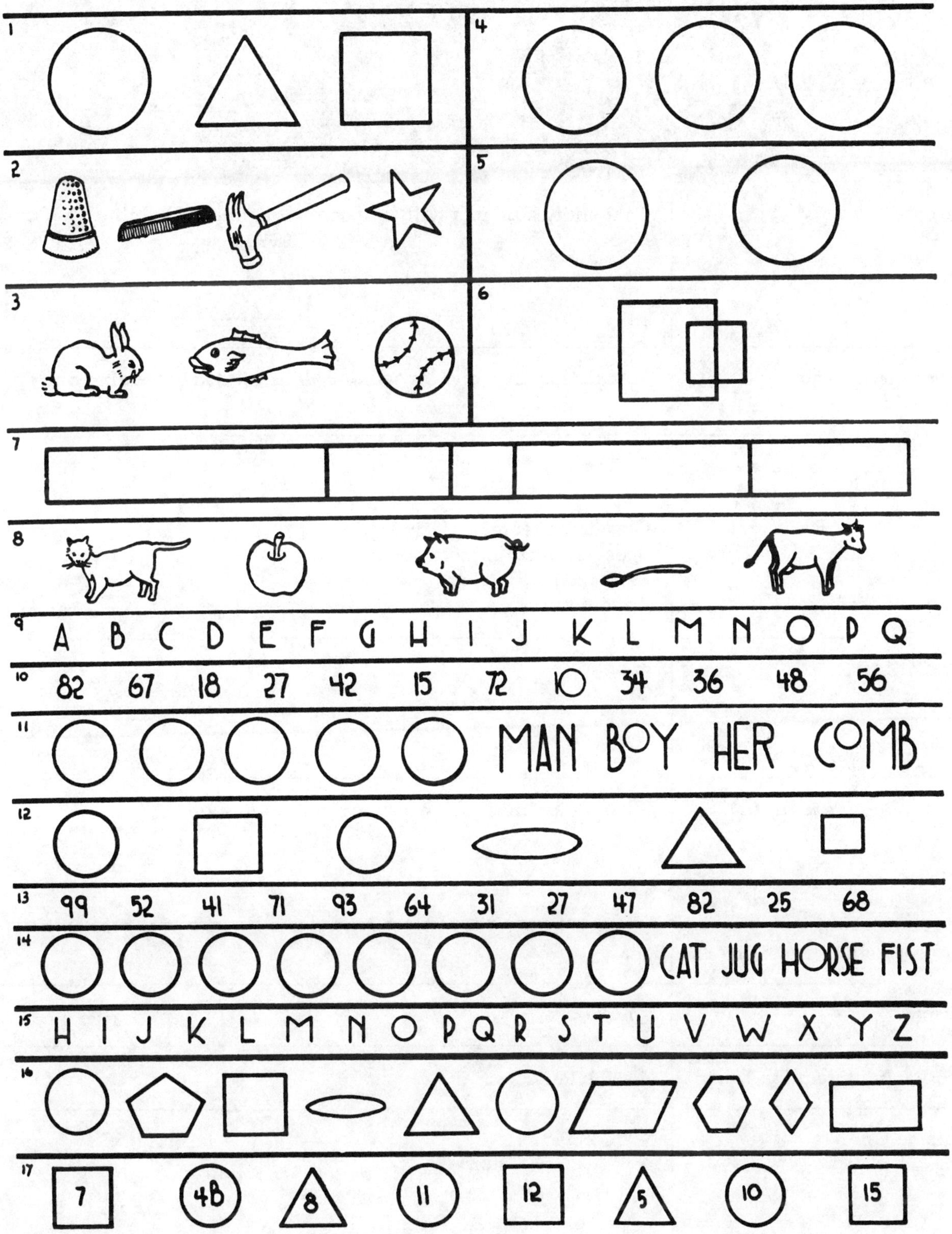

Figure 32. Detroit Oral Directions, Test 18

Slingerland Screening Tests for Identifying Children with Specific Language Disability
(Slingerland Tests)

Beth Slingerland
Educators Publishing Service, Inc., Forms A, B, C, 1962; revised 1970; Form D, 1974
75 Moulton St., Cambridge, MA 02188

Purpose	To identify students with a specific language disability
Major Areas Tested	Visual, auditory, and kinesthetic skills related to reading and spelling
Age or Grade Range	6–12 years
Usually Given By	Classroom teacher Special education teacher Psychologist Administrator
Type of Test	Informal Group
Scores Obtained	None (guidelines for evaluating test performance)
Student Performance Timed?	Yes
Testing Time	1–1½ hours
Scoring/Interpretation Time	30–40 minutes
Normed On	Not normed
Alternate Forms Available?	No

FORMAT

The Slingerland Screening Tests for Identifying Children with Specific Language Disability (Slingerland Tests) are a series of pencil-and-paper tests published in five forms for various grade levels.

Form	Grade Level
Pre-Reading	End of kindergarten to beginning of first grade
A	End of first grade to beginning of second grade
B	End of second grade to beginning of third grade
C	End of third grade to beginning of fourth grade
D	Fifth and sixth grades

The materials for each form include the students' booklets, in which they write their answers, and a set of cards and charts for the examiner. Although the Slingerland Tests are not normed and therefore provide no age- or grade-level scores, standardized administration procedures are described in the examiner's manuals. One manual is provided for the Pre-Reading Test; a second includes the instructions for Forms A, B, and C; and a third is available for Form D. Directions for scoring and guidelines for evaluating test performance are also included in the manuals.

The Slingerland Tests (and the teaching method) are based on Orton-Gillingham techniques for teaching reading and spelling through a multisensory approach. The linkages among auditory, visual, and kinesthetic modalities are the essence of the model. The tests are designed to assess these linkages.

Forms A, B, C, and D of the Slingerland Tests include the same eight group subtests. Form D includes an additional group subtest. Forms A, B, C, and D also include a series of auditory subtests to be given individually at the conclusion of the group subtests. The eight basic subtests and the individual auditory tests are described in Table 15. Although the number and difficulty of the items within each subtest vary, the skill being measured remains the same. This format allows assessment of student progress on the same series of tasks in grades 1 through 6.

Because of their different format, the Slingerland Pre-Reading Screening Procedures are reviewed separately in Part II (see p. 257).

STRENGTHS OF THE SLINGERLAND TESTS

- Beth Slingerland, the author of the tests, is an experienced teacher of students with specific language disability. She developed the tests for use in public schools, and they reflect her knowledge of teaching. The subtests measure skills that are directly related to classroom performance.

- Students with specific language disability have deficits in auditory, visual, and kinesthetic skills and the integration of these three systems, or modalities. Through careful analysis of a student's errors on the Slingerland Tests, a teacher can determine which modalities are the weakest and plan a remedial program accordingly. In contrast to the Illinois Test of Psycholinguistic Abilities (p. 141), the Slingerland subtests measure the modalities with regular academic tasks, which makes them much more usable for the classroom teacher.

- The Slingerland Tests were designed as screening instruments. They can be administered by classroom teachers to total classroom groups. They are an economical way to identify students with difficulties in visual, auditory, or kinesthetic skills. Although no norms are available, there is increasing research data to support the tests' validity as useful predictive instruments.

- As in all test batteries, some subtests are better than others. The three subtests measuring visual processing are particularly useful in determining the level of a visual perception problem. For example, the following performance on these three tests is very typical of students who have difficulty reading:

Visual Perception Memory (test 3): 80 percent correct
Visual Discrimination (test 4): 100 percent correct
Visual Kinesthetic Memory (test 5): 50 percent correct

These scores are interpreted to mean that, as the visual process becomes more complex, and when memory and a written response are required, the student's performance is poorer. In contrast is this typical performance of another student with reading difficulty:

Visual Perception Memory (test 3): 50 percent correct
Visual Discrimination (test 4): 70 percent correct
Visual Kinesthetic Memory (test 5): 95 percent correct

In this case, the kinesthetic (written) response seems to increase the efficiency of the visual processes.

LIMITING FACTORS OF THE SLINGERLAND TESTS

- At the present time, the Slingerland Tests must be viewed as informal tests. Although very specific directions for administration are given and complex scoring procedures are presented, no norms are provided. Thus, judgments about an individual student's performance are very subjective, depending on the sophistication of the examiner. The author stresses the need to develop local norms, which is probably true but not very realistic. Reliability and validity data are limited to unpublished manuscripts that have little value for the classroom teacher or school psychologist.

Table 15. Slingerland Subtests

Subtest	Description	Modality	Relationship to Classroom Skills
1. Far-Point Copying	Student copies paragraph from a chart on the wall	Visual, kinesthetic	Assesses visual-motor skills related to handwriting
2. Near-Point Copying	Student copies single words printed at top of page on lines at bottom	Visual, kinesthetic	Assesses visual-motor skills related to handwriting
3. Visual Perception Memory	Student is shown a word card for 10 seconds and then asked to find the word in a group of four visually similar words (*mnoey, mouey, woney, money*)	Visual	Assesses visual memory skills related to reading and spelling
4. Visual Discrimination	Student is asked to match words containing many easily confused letters (*lady, daly, laby, baby, lady*)	Visual	Assesses basic visual discrimination without memory component or written response
5. Visual Kinesthetic Memory	Student is shown word or design card for 10 seconds and then asked to write or draw the word or design	Visual, kinesthetic	Assesses the combination of visual memory and written response, which is necessary for written spelling
6. Auditory Kinesthetic Memory	Examiner dictates sequences of letters, numbers, and words, and then the student writes what the examiner dictated	Auditory, visual, kinesthetic	Combines auditory perception and memory with written response, skills necessary for dictation lessons
7. Initial and Final Sounds (Level D includes vowel sounds)	Examiner pronounces a word, and the student writes the initial or final sound (*shimmer—sh; clasp—p*)	Auditory, visual, kinesthetic	Assesses auditory discrimination and sequencing related to basic phonics with a written response
8. Auditory-Visual Integration	Examiner pronounces a word, and the student selects it from a group of four visually similar words (*baddy, babby, dabby, daddy*)	Auditory, visual	Assesses visual discrimination related to word recognition
9. Following Directions (Form D only)	Examiner gives a series of directions requiring a written response (*Write the alphabet. Do not use capital letters. Put a comma after each letter.*)	Auditory, kinesthetic	Assesses auditory memory and attention with a written response
Individual Auditory Tests (Forms A, B, C, and D)			
Echolalia	Examiner pronounces a word or phrase and the student repeats it four or five times aloud (*animal-animal-animal-animal*)	Auditory, kinesthetic	Assesses auditory-kinesthetic confusion related to pronunciation
Word Finding	Examiner reads a sentence with a missing word, and the student fills in the missing word (*A long yellow fruit is called a _____ .*)	Auditory	Assesses comprehension and the ability to produce a specific word on demand; word-finding problems often identify children with specific language disability
Story Telling	Examiner reads a story aloud, and the student retells it	Auditory	Assesses auditory memory and verbal expression of content material

- One advantage of the Slingerland Tests is the fact that they use skills related to classroom tasks. But precisely because they measure classroom tasks, the tests are long and difficult for many students to take. Several subtests require extensive writing, and many students become discouraged. Because the items were selected to produce the visual and auditory sequencing and discrimination errors characteristic of students with specific language disability, many students become frustrated and require a great deal of emotional support to complete the test.
- There seems to be no rationale for the number or order of items within a subtest. There is no systematic increase in the difficulty of items, other than increasing vocabulary difficulty from Form A through Form D.
- Administration procedures are complex and difficult: scoring procedures are long and also difficult, especially in view of the fact that the tests are not normed. The tests require considerable study before they can be used successfully.
- The terminology of the Slingerland Tests is very confusing. The term *specific language disability* requires explanation because it is often confused with oral language problems of other types. The titles of the subtests have no meaning to teachers or parents who have not seen the subtest items. School districts that choose to use this test need to devise a system of scoring, reporting scores, and describing results that is easily understood.
- Of great concern is the fact that the Slingerland Tests are frequently used as the only instrument to diagnose a student as having specific language disability. Such a practice is highly questionable for any single test and particularly for a nonstandardized, nonnormed instrument.

Malcomesius Specific Language Disability Test (Malcomesius Test)

Neva Malcomesius
Educators Publishing Service, Inc., 1967
75 Moulton St., Cambridge, MA 02188

Purpose	To identify students with a specific language disability
Major Areas Tested	Auditory, visual, and kinesthetic skills related to reading, writing, and spelling
Age or Grade Range	Grades 6–8
Usually Given By	Classroom teacher Special education teacher
Type of Test	Informal Group
Scores Obtained	None (guidelines for evaluating test performance)
Student Performance Timed?	Yes
Testing Time	1½ hours
Scoring/Interpretation Time	20–30 minutes
Normed On	Not normed
Alternate Forms Available?	No

FORMAT

The materials for the Malcomesius Specific Language Disability Test (Malcomesius Test) consist of a teacher's manual, test booklets for the students, and a set of cards and charts used in administering the test.

Because the Malcomesius Test was designed as an upward extension of the Slingerland Tests (junior high school level), the 10 subtests are almost identical to those in the Slingerland Tests, Forms A to D. The tests are also designed for group administration. Table 16 compares the Malcomesius subtests to those of the Slingerland. (Refer also to Table 15, page 104.) It is interesting that, in the Spelling—Auditory to Motor subtest (subtest 10), the focus is on sound-symbol association rather than correct spelling. Thus the following words would all be considered correct: *dubious-doobious; exceed-excead*.

The Malcomesius Test does not include any of the individual auditory tests that are found in the lower levels of the Slingerland Tests.

STRENGTHS OF THE MALCOMESIUS TEST

- As in the Slingerland Tests, the Malcomesius Test battery includes a series of school-related tests to aid the classroom teacher in identifying students with specific language disability. There are few tests designed for adolescents, and the Malcomesius Test provides a means of assessing the auditory, visual, and kinesthetic skills of this age group on tasks related to classroom performance.

LIMITING FACTORS OF THE MALCOMESIUS TEST

- The Malcomesius Test is subject to the same limiting factors as the Slingerland Tests, the most serious of which is the lack of norms. No reliability or validity studies are reported. In addition, the author seems to assume that the only difference between beginning readers and more mature readers is the length of the words they can process and the speed with which they can process them. This is shown by the fact that the items for sixth, seventh, and eighth graders are all the same; only time limits differentiate them. It may well be that an entirely different set of tasks should be used to identify these older disabled readers, rather than those used with the elementary students assessed by the Slingerland Tests.

- Subtests 9 and 10 are particularly poorly labeled. Subtest 9 is much more a measure of written language skills

Table 16. Comparison of the Malcomesius and Slingerland Subtests

Malcomesius Subtest	Description	Corresponding Slingerland Subtest
1. Paragraph Copying	Requires copying paragraphs from a wall chart	1
2. Near-Point Copying	Requires copying a list of words	2
3. Visual Discrimination	Requires matching visually similar words (*innuendo, inunendo, innuendo, inuennbo, innuenbo*)	4
4. Visual Perception and Recall	Requires identifying correct words and number sequences presented visually (*barbraian, barbarian, bardarian, darbraian*)	3
5. Visual Kinesthetic Recall	Requires writing phrases after a visual presentation (*Keep quite quiet.*)	5
6. Auditory Discrimination	Requires discrimination of words that sound very much alike (*trick, trek*)	None
7. Auditory Kinesthetic Memory	Requires writing phrases from dictation (*parents of the girl*)	6
8. Auditory-Visual Integration	Requires listening to a word or sequence of numbers and selecting it from four similar choices presented visually (*9,586; 6,589; 9,856; 9,589*)	8
9. Comprehension	Requires listening to a paragraph and writing it	None
10. Spelling—Auditory to Motor	Requires writing a list of 20 dictated words with focus on sound-symbol association, *not* correct spelling (*dubious-doobious, exceed-excead*)	None

and sequential memory than it is of comprehension, and subtest 10 cannot be called spelling when the scoring directions specifically say, "Do not count spelling."

• The teacher's manual includes a page of "General Directions for Evaluating the Tests." This page contains a number of statements about specific language disability that are presented as fact when they really represent the author's opinion. The person using the Malcomesius Test needs to be alert to these statements and to avoid conclusions about a student's learning disability based on performance on this test alone.

Auditory Tests

Wepman Auditory Discrimination Test 110
Goldman-Fristoe-Woodcock Test of Auditory Discrimination 112
Lindamood Auditory Conceptualization Test 114

Wepman Auditory Discrimination Test

Joseph M. Wepman
Language Research Associates, 1958; revised 1978
950 E. 59th St., Chicago, IL 60621

Purpose	To evaluate the student's ability to recognize fine differences that exist between phonemes in English speech
Major Areas Tested	Auditory discrimination
Age or Grade Range	5–8 years
Usually Given By	Special education teacher Speech/language clinician
Type of Test	Standardized Individual
Scores Obtained	Rating scale
Student Performance Timed?	No
Testing Time	10–15 minutes
Scoring/Interpretation Time	5–10 minutes
Normed On	Children from urban and nonurban communities
Alternate Forms Available?	Yes

FORMAT

The materials for the Wepman Auditory Discrimination Test include a brief manual and forms for recording individual responses. The manual contains some information on test development, directions for administration, and guidance in the interpretation of test results.

The test consists of 40 pairs of monosyllabic meaningful words. The words were selected from the *Lorge-Thorndike Teacher's Word Book of 30,000 Words* (1944). Of the 40 word pairs, 30 differ by only one sound: *muss-mush*. The 10 word pairs that do not differ are included as false choices and aid in the judgment of test validity.

The words in each pair are of equal length. Comparisons are made between 13 initial consonants, 13 final consonants, and 4 medial vowels. Consonants chosen for contrast are within the same phonetic category—for example, the stops /p/, /t/, and /k/. Vowel comparisons are based on such criteria as (1) the part of the tongue that is raised, (2) the height of the tongue, and (3) the position of the lips.

The word pairs are read by the examiner. The student indicates whether the words pronounced were the same or different. No pictures are used, and the examiner pronounces the words with lips covered. Thus, visual skills are not involved. A rating scale is used to interpret a student's performance. The scale provides descriptions of ability ranging from "very good development" to "below the level of the threshold of adequacy" for the ages 5 to 8 years.

STRENGTHS OF THE WEPMAN AUDITORY DISCRIMINATION TEST

- This test is a brief, inexpensive, and relatively simple tool for assessing auditory discrimination ability. The test is carefully constructed. Word length and complexity of test items are controlled.
- Test-retest reliability is high. The existence of equivalent forms provides the examiner with a good reevaluation procedure.

LIMITING FACTORS OF THE WEPMAN AUDITORY DISCRIMINATION TEST

- Some young handicapped children may have difficulty understanding the concept of *same/different*. A low score may represent difficulty in grasping that concept or in sustaining attention for the task, rather than auditory discrimination difficulty. This problem was found in clinical practice and was verified by Blank (1968) in her research.
- This test provides a measure of auditory discrimination of isolated word pairs. Additional testing or observation is necessary to assess discrimination skills of other types and in other situations, such as conversational speech and discrimination of sound against a background of noise.
- Although many phonemic contrasts are presented, others are missing. For instance, the sounds /ng/, /l/, /r/, /j/, and /ch/ are not included in the discrimination tasks. In addition, the contrast of voiced/voiceless consonants (for example, *bad-bat*) is not included. Also, only a limited number of vowel discriminations are assessed.
- Some of the contrasts presented in the test are not commonly made in nonstandard English—for example, ĕ/ĭ and v/*th*(voiced). Consequently, a low score by a student speaking nonstandard English may not indicate an auditory discrimination problem. Interpretation of the performance of this group of students, as well as students from bilingual backgrounds, should be made with caution, because no information on the norming population is available.

NOTES

In addition to the Wepman Auditory Discrimination Test, Joseph Wepman and his associates have since published two additional tests of auditory processing. The Auditory Memory Span Test (Wepman and Morency 1973*a*) requires the student to repeat a series of unrelated words pronounced by the examiner. Series of two, three, four, five, and six words are presented, three trials on each. The series does not have to be recalled in sequence. The student's raw score consists of the number of words recalled; performance is interpreted through the use of the rating scale, as on the Auditory Discrimination Test.

The Auditory Sequential Memory Span Test (Wepman and Morency 1973*b*) requires the student to repeat a series of digits pronounced by the examiner. The number of digits in each series increases from two to eight, and the series must be repeated in sequence. Two trials are given for each series length. Here, again, raw scores are interpreted through the use of the rating scale.

The three tests—Auditory Discrimination, Auditory Memory Span, and Auditory Sequential Memory Span—can be used together as a quick screening of auditory processes to identify students who need further assessment of their auditory skills.

Goldman-Fristoe-Woodcock Test of Auditory Discrimination (GFW)

R. Goldman, M. Fristoe, and R. Woodcock
American Guidance Service, Inc., 1970
Publishers' Bldg., Circle Pines, MN 55014

Purpose	To identify individuals who have difficulty discriminating speech sounds and to provide a measure of discrimination under ideal listening conditions and in the presence of controlled background noise
Major Areas Tested	Speech-sound discrimination
Age or Grade Range	4–70 years and over
Usually Given By	Reading specialist Psychologist Speech/language clinician Educational diagnostician Audiologist
Type of Test	Standardized Individual Norm-referenced
Scores Obtained	Standard Percentile
Student Performance Timed?	No
Testing Time	20–30 minutes
Scoring/Interpretation Time	10–15 minutes
Normed On	745 subjects from an eastern, a midwestern, and a southern state
Alternate Forms Available?	No

FORMAT

Materials for the Goldman-Fristoe-Woodcock Test of Auditory Discrimination (GFW) consist of a manual, response forms, a spiral-bound book of pictures, a prerecorded test tape, and a set of 61 large training plates. The manual contains information on test development, directions for administering and scoring the test, and technical data on validity and reliability. Appendixes include suggestions for teaching the vocabulary, a description of the distinctive-feature classification used in constructing the GFW, and the norms.

The response form provides a place to record performance on the three parts of the test: the training procedure and two subtests, one with and one without background noise. An error-analysis matrix on the response form aids in the analysis of errors according to distinctive features.

The test contains a set of 61 large test plates, and the test book contains 16 training plates. There are four black-and-white line drawings on each page. The book can be set up as an easel during administration. Instructions and directions for the subtests are contained on the prerecorded tape. The training procedure, which ensures familiarity with the vocabulary, is administered orally by the examiner. Large training plates are available for training students with inadequately developed vocabulary. Each plate is a simple enlarged picture from the test.

On each of the test's training plates, four monosyllabic words having little phonemic similarity (for example, *lake, nail, pear,* and *tea*) are pictured. On the test plates, either all initial or all final consonants differ (for example, *night, bite, write,* and *light*; or *core, coal, comb,* and *cone*). Sounds for contrast were selected on the basis of the distinctive-feature analysis of consonants. The stimulus word differs from the foils by only one or two features, including voicing, nasality, and manner of production (such as plosive). These are summarized in the manual. The voiced and voiceless /th/ contrast and vowel discrimination are not included.

Background noise on the noise subtest consists of typical cafeteria sounds. Three training stimuli are presented, with the noise intensity gradually increased to the point where it remains throughout the administration of that subtest.

A pointing response is used. The student points to the picture denoting the stimulus word on the tape. Headphones are suggested for student and examiner; normative data was obtained using headphones. Standard scores and percentiles are provided for each subtest for 32 age groups, from 3 years to over 70.

STRENGTHS OF THE GFW

- The authors have attempted to limit the variables involved in assessing auditory discrimination skills. As much time as needed may be allotted to training the vocabulary. Brief directions and the use of a pointing response simplify the task. Control of the examiner's voice is accomplished by the use of a prerecorded taped presentation.
- The GFW is applicable to a wide age range and is useful in a variety of settings (clinical, educational, and industrial). It is easy to administer. The manual provides clear instructions for administering the test and information that is helpful in understanding the results. In addition to the normative data on the standard population, selected data on clinical populations is also given. Data is available on limited numbers of hard-of-hearing, culturally disadvantaged, retarded, and learning-disabled children, and on children with speech and language problems.
- Test construction is well thought out. Most of the vocabulary that is used is familiar to young children. Words are all monosyllabic, and only one label is applied to each picture. The application of distinctive-feature theory is well described in the manual.
- Extensive information on reliability and validity has been compiled and is discussed in the manual.

LIMITING FACTORS OF THE GFW

- To keep pace with the taped presentation, the examiner must be familiar with the material. For some students, the pace of presentation may be too rapid. The examiner may momentarily stop the tape, but the stimulus should not be repeated.
- Some of the vocabulary included on the test requires flexible thinking. For instance, *Jack* is pictured as a jack-in-the-box and *we* as two friends. Younger children and those with significant conceptual delays may be slow to grasp such concepts, in spite of the training procedure.
- Although error analysis by distinctive features is included on the response form, it lacks satisfactory reliability and should be used only for clinical exploration and research.

NOTES

For a more in-depth look at auditory processing following the GFW, the same authors have prepared the GFW Auditory Skills Battery. The battery includes five independent tests measuring the areas of auditory attention, auditory discrimination, auditory memory, and sound-symbol associations. The tests are normed on individuals from 3 to 80 years old and are especially helpful for some clinic populations.

Lindamood Auditory Conceptualization Test (LAC)

Charles Lindamood and Patricia Lindamood
Teaching Resources Corporation, 1971
50 Pond Park Rd., Hingham, MA 02043

Purpose	To measure auditory discrimination and the ability to identify the number and order of sounds in a sequence
Major Areas Tested	Auditory perception
Age or Grade Range	Preschool–adult
Usually Given By	Special education teacher Speech/language clinician Remedial reading teacher Paraprofessional
Type of Test	Standardized Individual
Scores Obtained	Grade level
Student Performance Timed?	No
Testing Time	10–15 minutes
Scoring/Interpretation Time	10–15 minutes
Normed On	660 students in grades K-12 from a range of socioeconomic and ethnic backgrounds in a California school district
Alternate Forms Available?	Yes

FORMAT

The materials for administering the Lindamood Auditory Conceptualization Test (LAC) include a manual, individual record sheets, and a set of 18 half-inch colored cubes (three each of red, yellow, blue, green, white, and black). The manual contains directions for administration and scoring, information on test construction, and suggestions for interpreting results. A record is provided for the examiner to use as a guide for the pronunciation of individual sounds and syllable patterns.

The LAC Test consists of four parts:

1. *The Precheck*. This part contains five items designed to determine whether the student can demonstrate knowledge of the following concepts: same/different, numbers to 4, left-to-right order, and first/last.

2. *Category I, Part A*. The student must identify the number of isolated sounds heard from a list of 10 items, and decide whether they are the same or different.

3. *Category I, Part B*. The student is given six items and asked to identify not only the number of isolated sounds heard and their sameness or difference, but also their order.

4. *Category II*. From a list of 12 items, the student must determine the number of sounds in a syllable and changes in the sound pattern when sounds are added, omitted, substituted, shifted, or repeated.

The Precheck is given to determine that the student understands the basic concepts necessary to obtain a valid test score. If knowledge of the Precheck concepts is not demonstrated, the test is discontinued. Categories I and II are each preceded by demonstration procedures.

In the LAC, the student manipulates colored blocks to indicate understanding of sound patterns. Each block represents a sound. There is no constant relationship between a specific color and a specific sound, so the student may select any colors. Different sounds within a pattern are represented by different colors. Table 17 illustrates the test format.

As the examiner pronounces each sound pattern, the student may use visual cues (the examiner's lip movements) to aid discrimination; the examiner notes this diagnostic information. Patterns may not be repeated unless an environmental noise interferes with the student's hearing. Testing is discontinued after five consecutive errors in Category I. In Category II, the student is given an opportunity to do another similar pattern after an error. Testing is discontinued after five errors in Category II.

Points are given for each correct block pattern, and on that basis a raw score is obtained. The raw score is converted to a weighted score (one point for each correct response in Category I, Part A; three in Category I, Part B; and six in Category II). A single weighted score is obtained for the total test; no subtest scores are provided. The examiner then compares the weighted score with a table that provides recommended minimum scores for each grade level. These minimum scores should be considered predictive of success in reading or spelling at or above that grade level.

Two equivalent forms, A and B, are available for reevaluation purposes.

STRENGTHS OF THE LAC

- The LAC provides a means of evaluating auditory perception skills related to reading and spelling without using written symbols. The student need not have knowledge of sound-symbol associations to demonstrate auditory perception skills. This makes the LAC a valuable tool for assessing auditory perception in beginning or remedial readers.
- Many tests are available for assessing auditory

Table 17. LAC Test Format

Category	Examiner Pronounces	Student's Block Pattern
Category I, Part A	Three same sounds (/b/, /b/, /b/)	Three same colors
	Two different sounds (/t/, /m/)	Two different colors
Category I, Part B	Two same sounds followed by one different sound (/s/, /s/, /p/)	Two same colors followed by one different color
Category II	Two different sounds in a syllable (/al/)	Two different colors
	New sound added at beginning of a syllable (/pal/)	New color added at beginning
	Change in last sound of a syllable (/pab/)	Change in last color

discrimination of whole words (including the Wepman Auditory Discrimination Test, p. 110, and the Goldman-Fristoe-Woodcock Test of Auditory Discrimination, p. 112). Other tests assess sound blending or auditory synthesis (see the Illinois Test of Psycholinguistic Abilities, p. 141). The LAC, however, assesses analysis of the number and order of sounds as well as discrimination. These skills are crucial in reading and spelling.

- The Precheck section of the LAC is excellent. It allows the examiner to assess quickly the student's knowledge of the basic concepts necessary to take the test. Once it is determined that the student understands these basic concepts, errors on the test can more accurately be related to skill deficiencies in auditory perception.
- The manual provides an excellent discussion of the relationship among auditory perception, reading, and spelling. Teachers and clinicians will find the discussion of follow-up remediation techniques helpful, as well as the authors' interpretation of test performance.
- The LAC can be used with a wide age range of students. The alternate test forms make it a usable tool for evaluating progress in a remediation program.
- The norming sample, although small, was reportedly carefully selected to include various socioeconomic groups and ethnic backgrounds. Reliability and validity studies are reported in the manual.

LIMITING FACTORS OF THE LAC

- The LAC is not an easy test to administer, and extensive practice is recommended before using it with students suspected of auditory disorders. Although the administration manual is clearly written, the process of using colored blocks to illustrate sound patterns is a difficult one. Category II, in particular, requires extensive verbal explanation, and many students become confused if the examiner is not quite skilled in test administration. The order of items in Category II is particularly difficult to administer.
- Students with intellectual deficits or delays in concept development have difficulty learning the relationship between the colors and the sounds. They may continue to believe that there is a direct relationship between color and sound, such as red always equals /p/. This confusion is seen in such statements as "There aren't enough colors." Such students may actually be able to spell the syllables in Category II (illustrating good auditory analysis) without being able to do the block patterns.
- The LAC authors have chosen to allow students to use visual cues (lip movements) to aid their auditory discrimination. It is true that visual cues are usually available in natural conversations. However, it is important for the examiner to note carefully whether or not the student uses visual cues. If the student does not, teaching him or her to do so is a good first step in remediation. If they are used extensively, it is important for the teacher to realize that, in activities where the student does not have direct contact with the speaker, auditory perception may be quite poor.
- The score obtained on the LAC is difficult to interpret. For example, suppose a third-grade student obtains a total test score of 60. According to the minimum scores table in the manual, a score of 60 is the minimum score predicting high probability of successful reading and spelling performance in high-first-grade material. Does this mean that the third-grade student's auditory perception skills are at a first-grade level? Or that the student should be instructed in first-grade material? The interpretation becomes even more confusing with an older student. A score of 93 is the minimal score for predicting reading and spelling success for the second half of fourth and fifth grades, but 94 is the minimum recommended score for sixth through twelfth grades. The lack of clarity in test score interpretation suggests that the LAC is better used as an informal test—a task-analysis approach to auditory perception, rather than a standardized test yielding grade-level scores.
- Throughout the manual, reading and spelling are treated as identical tasks requiring the same auditory perception skills. Validity studies should be done to separate these two processes. Although the authors feel that the reading method the student has been taught does not affect performance on the LAC, this seems questionable. Students with phonics training have clearly had more practice with auditory analysis than sight-word readers.

Visual and Visual-Motor Tests

Marianne Frostig Developmental Test of Visual Perception 118
Motor-Free Visual Perception Test 125
The Bender Visual Motor Gestalt Test 130
Beery-Buktenica Developmental Test of Visual-Motor Integration 134

Marianne Frostig Developmental Test of Visual Perception (DTVP)

Marianne Frostig, in collaboration with Welty Lefever and John R. B. Whittlessey
Consulting Psychologists Press, Inc., 1961; Manual revised 1966
577 College Ave., Palo Alto, CA 94306

Purpose	To measure certain visual perceptual abilities and to detect difficulties in visual perception at an early age
Major Areas Tested	Visual perception
Age or Grade Range	3–8 years
Usually Given By	Special education teacher Occupational therapist Psychologist
Type of Test	Standardized Individual Group
Scores Obtained	Age level Scaled Perceptual quotient (PQ)
Student Performance Timed?	No
Testing Time	30–45 minutes (individual administration); 40–60 minutes (group administration)
Scoring/Interpretation Time	10–15 minutes
Normed On	2,116 white, middle-class students from southern California
Alternate Forms Available?	No

Visual and Visual-Motor Tests

FORMAT

The Marianne Frostig Developmental Test of Visual Perception (DTVP) is a paper-and-pencil test. The test materials consist of an examiner's manual and monograph, expendable test booklets for the students, demonstration cards, and plastic scoring keys. The examiner must also supply four colored pencils or crayons (red, blue, green, and brown) and a pencil without an eraser for each student. For group administration, access to a blackboard is necessary, for demonstration purposes.

During the testing session, the student completes tasks arranged in order of increasing difficulty in five areas of visual perception. The subtests and selected items from each are described below.

1. *Eye-Motor Coordination* (16 items). The student must draw continuous straight, curved, or angled lines between increasingly narrow boundaries or draw straight lines to a target (see Figure 33).

2. *Figure-Ground* (8 items). The student must distinguish between intersecting shapes and find embedded figures (see Figure 34). The student must outline the hidden geometric forms with a colored pencil or crayon.

3. *Constancy of Shape* (17 items). The student must

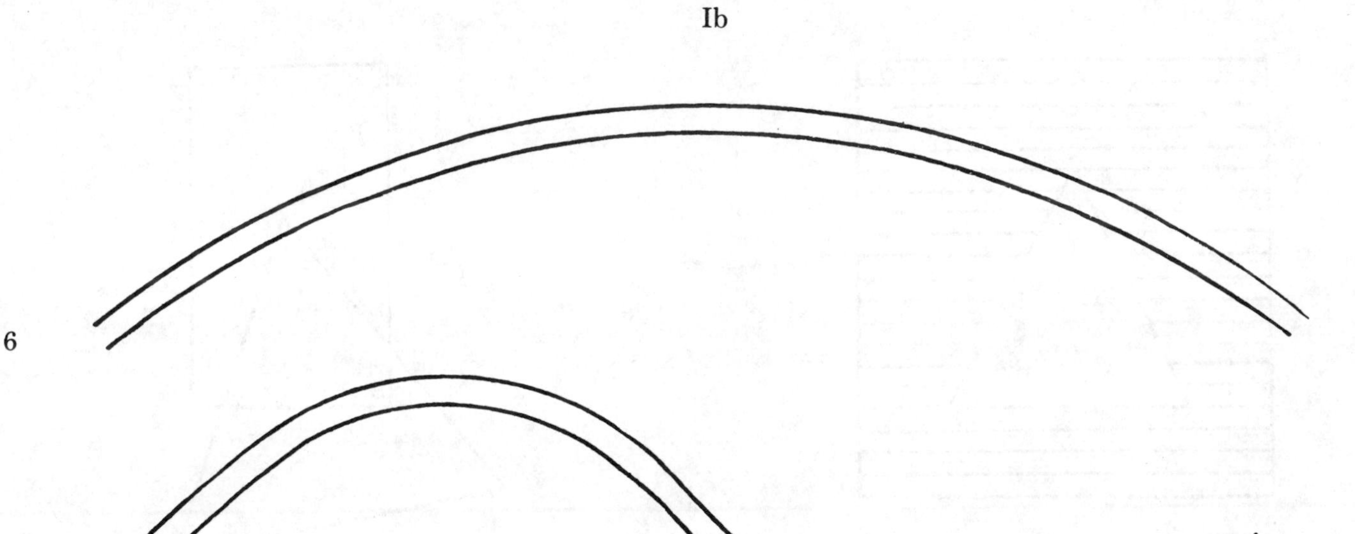

Figure 33. DTVP Eye-Motor Coordination

discriminate common geometric shapes (circles and squares), presented in different sizes, shadings, textures, and positions, from other similar shapes (see Figure 35). The student must outline the recognized figures with a colored pencil or crayon.

4. *Position in Space* (8 items). The student must distinguish between figures in an identical position and those in a reversed or rotated position (see Figure 36), marking the different figure.

5. *Spatial Relations* (8 items). The student must copy simple forms and patterns by joining dots (see Figure 37).

The DTVP may be administered individually or in groups. The optimum number of students in a group depends on the age of the students. For example, a group of 8 to 10 is appropriate for kindergarten students, whereas 10 to 20 second graders may be tested simultaneously. Large groups require paraprofessionals who can circulate among the students to help monitor the test.

Instructions for the test are verbal, but there is an adaptation of the manual for hard-of-hearing, deaf, and non-English-speaking students. Additional examples and gestures are used.

IIa

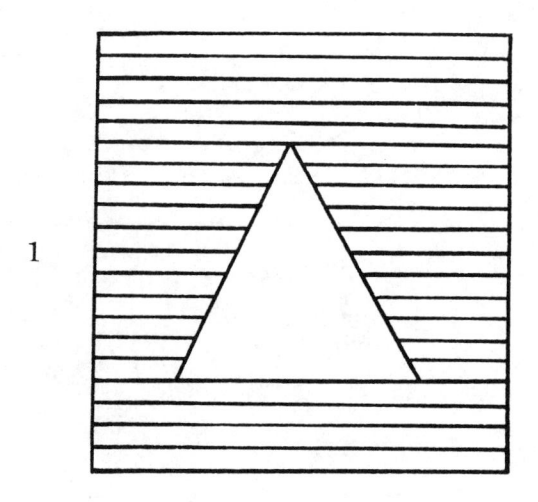

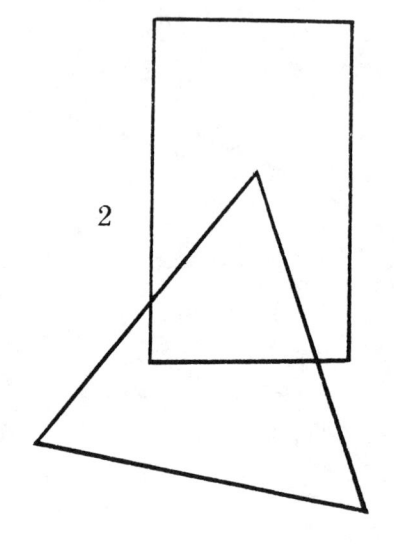

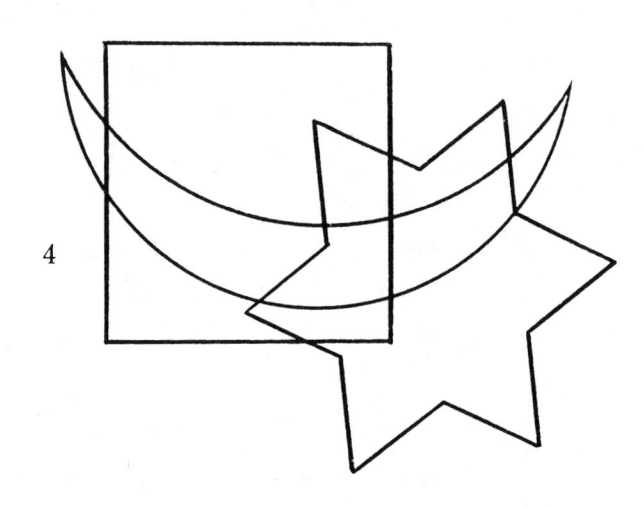

Figure 34. DTVP Figure Ground

Visual and Visual-Motor Tests

Although the items are presented in one test booklet, parts of the test are omitted for nursery school and kindergarten students. The student may not erase, make corrections, or turn the test booklet. The test is not timed. Alternate, equivalent forms of the DTVP are not available.

Raw scores on each subtest are converted to age scores and scaled scores. The scaled scores on the five subtests are added to obtain a total test score; when divided by a student's age, the total score yields a perceptual quotient. Subtest scaled scores range from 0 to 20, with 10 as average and 8 or below indicating need for remediation. A perceptual quotient of 90 is suggested as the cutoff for children entering first grade; lower scores indicate the need for perceptual training.

STRENGTHS OF THE DTVP

- The DTVP is a well-known test, a forerunner in the field. It evaluates both visual perception and eye-hand coordination in young students. No expensive equipment is required. In addition to individual testing, the DTVP is useful as a screening instrument with groups of students. The test can also be used by the experienced clinician to

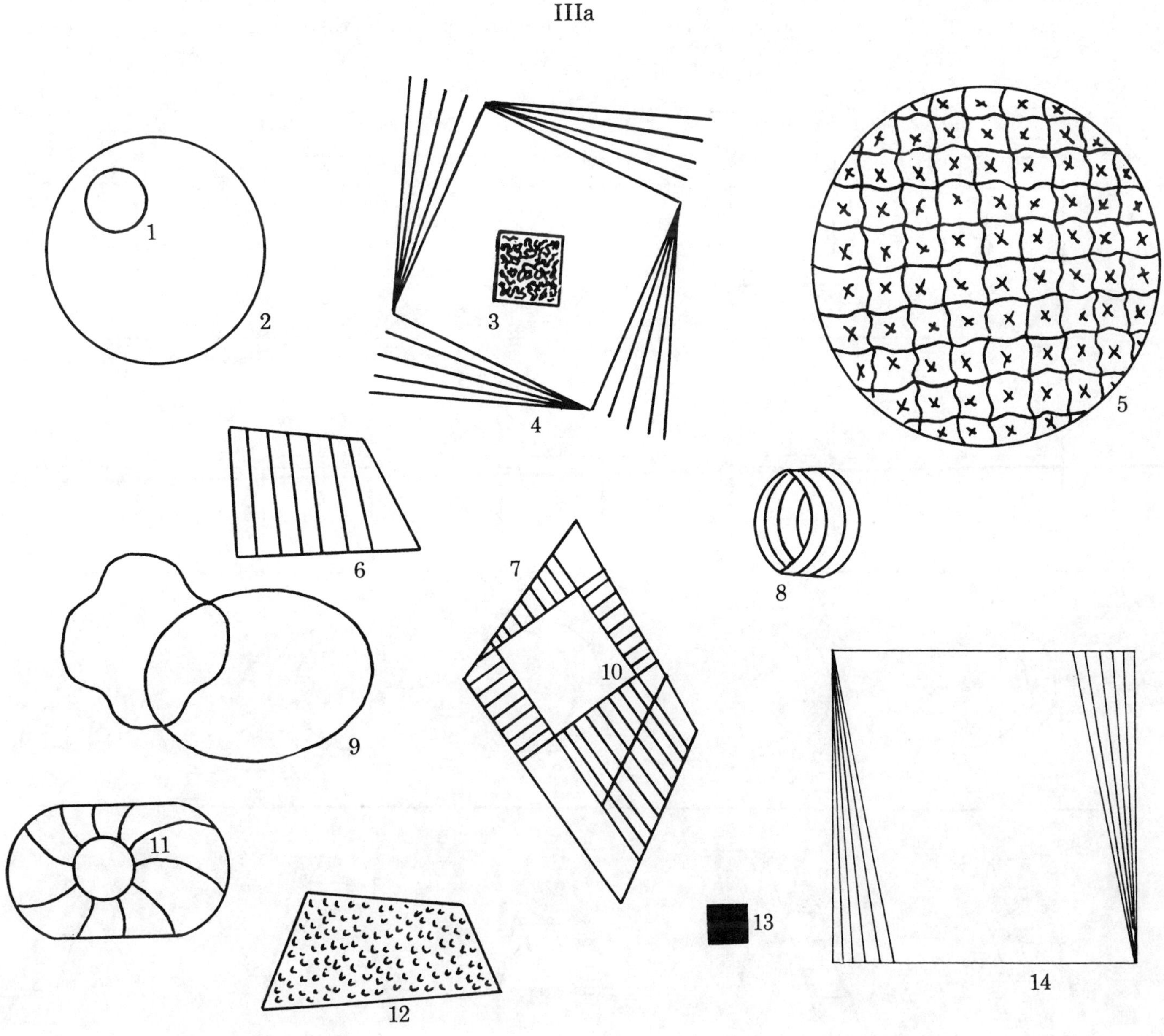

Figure 35. DTVP Constancy of Shape

gain diagnostic information on older students who have learning problems.

- The particular tasks on the DTVP are simple in design and arranged in order of increasing difficulty. The subtests can generally be performed quickly. For the most part, the directions for administering the test are clear. Examiner demonstration of each subtest, either on the blackboard or with demonstration materials, is especially helpful for the young student.
- The instructions for scoring the DTVP are fairly explicit. Examples are given that illustrate criteria for scoring each item. Scoring stencils provided for some items further increase objectivity. Time required for scoring is relatively short—approximately 10 minutes.
- The test-retest reliability coefficient for the whole DTVP is adequate. In studies of predictive validity, the test scores have been found to discriminate poor readers from good readers at the first-grade level with modest correlations.
- A particular advantage of the test is the accompanying training program for remediation of perceptual difficulties. This program is directly related to a student's performance on the DTVP and includes motor and worksheet activities for each subtest. For example, if a student scores low on the Position in Space subtest, he or she is provided with activities to improve that skill (training in body image, body schema, and body concept). Thus the DTVP and the corresponding training materials are of value to experienced teachers; when used wisely, they provide good supplementary curricular activities.

Figure 36. DTVP Position in Space

Visual and Visual-Motor Tests

LIMITING FACTORS OF THE DTVP

- The DTVP purports to measure five distinct aspects of visual perception. Frostig's correlation studies indicate independence of the subtests. However, contradictory evidence has been found in several other investigations. Such studies show that the DTVP subtests do not measure five different and relatively independent visual perceptual abilities. More research seems warranted to evaluate with certainty the independence of the subtests. The degree to which the subtests measure one or more general visual perceptual factors also needs to be established (Hammill and Wiederholt 1972).

- The process of transforming raw scores to scaled scores is very confusing. For example, in students over 8 years of age, someone who receives a perfect score on a subtest receives a scaled score of only 10, whereas younger students can make errors and get a higher score. Salvia and Ysseldyke (1978, p. 311) state, "The transformed scores for the DTVP are not only confusing; they are questionably derived and therefore absolutely must not be used in making diagnostic decisions."

- The test items on the DTVP consist only of geometric forms and shapes; no letters or numbers are used. Although students may be able to distinguish a particular form from

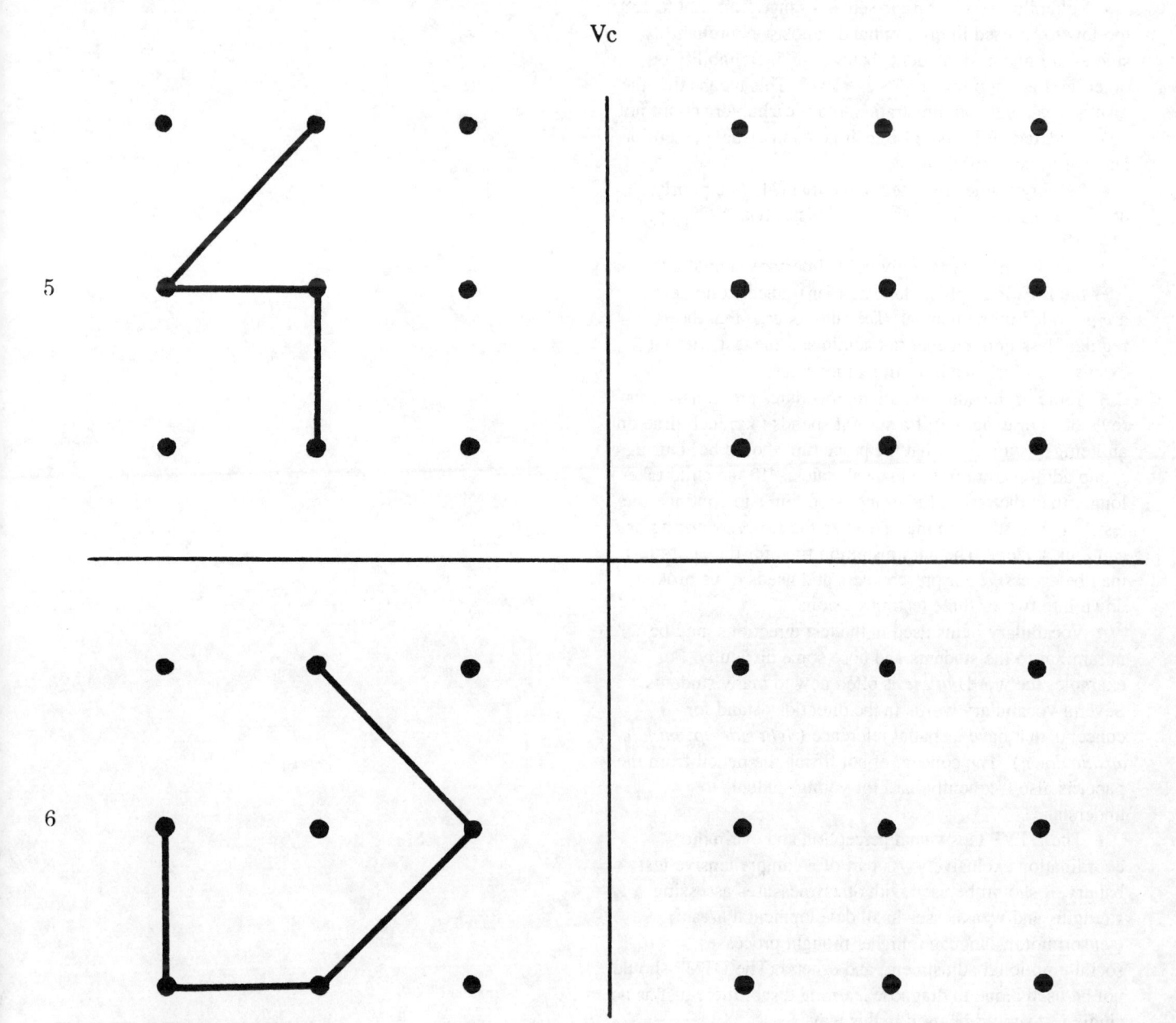

Figure 37. DTVP Spatial Relations

other figures presented in an identical, rotated, or reversed position, they still may not be able to differentiate letters having the same form but different positions (for example, *b* and *d*). The examiner should not conclude that a student's good performance on the DTVP automatically rules out difficulties in perceiving the symbols for language.

- Another difficulty with the DTVP is that visual perceptual skills are not measured apart from motor skills. The added motor component (tracing with a pencil), especially on the Figure-Ground subtest, contaminates the purity of the visual perceptual process. Visual perceptual abilities and motor skills should be measured as separate entities as well as integrative functions.

- Reliability results on the subtests range from .29 to .68, too low to be used in differential diagnosis. No reliability studies are given for students below age 5. Reliability on other tests is often low at this age level. This means that the results of a single administration to a preschooler should not be considered definitive of impairments in visual perception and eye-motor coordination.

- Validity studies reported in the manual were poorly designed and controlled (Salvia and Ysseldyke 1978, pp. 314–316).

- As with most tests, only trained persons should administer the DTVP. Explicit standards for trained examiners are provided in the manual. The authors urge that the regular classroom teacher not administer the test without extensive experience in testing procedures.

- Some of the administration procedures are in need of revision. For example, if a student spends too much time on an item, it is unclear what the procedure should be. During group administration, the manual states, "If one child takes longer than the rest of the group, stop him and continue the test." This instruction may penalize the slower-working or cautious student. The administration time for the entire test may be excessive for preschoolers and needs to be broken down into two or three testing sessions.

- Vocabulary items used in the test directions may be unfamiliar to the students and pose some difficulty. For example, the word *outline* is often new to many students. Several vocabulary words in the directions stand for concepts that have a spatial reference (*right side up, middle, upside down*). The concept of not lifting the pencil from the paper is also frequently hard for young students to understand.

- The DTVP taps visual perception and eye-motor coordination exclusively. As part of a comprehensive test battery, it should be used with other measures assessing strengths and weaknesses in all developmental areas (sensorimotor, language, higher thought processes, social-emotional adjustment, and others). The DTVP should not be used alone to diagnose learning disabilities, just as no single test should be used in this way.

Motor-Free Visual Perception Test (MVPT)
Ronald P. Colarusso and Donald D. Hammill
Academic Therapy Publications, 1972
20 Commercial Blvd., Novato, CA 94947

Purpose	To measure overall visual perceptual processing ability
Major Areas Tested	Visual perception
Age or Grade Range	4–9 years
Usually Given By	Classroom teacher Special education teacher Occupational therapist
Type of Test	Standardized Individual
Scores Obtained	Age level Perceptual quotient (PQ)
Student Performance Timed?	No
Testing Time	10–15 minutes
Scoring/Interpretation Time	15–20 minutes
Normed On	881 urban, suburban, and rural children from all races and economic levels in 22 states
Alternate Forms Available?	No

FORMAT

The materials required for administering the Motor-Free Visual Perception Test (MVPT) are the test manual, the book of test plates, and an individual scoring sheet. The test consists of 36 items arranged into five sections, each section with its own demonstration item and instructions.

Section 1. From an array of four drawings, the student selects a drawing of a geometric form that matches a stimulus drawing. The first three items in this section require matching by spatial orientation; the remaining five items require recognizing the correct form in a rival background, as shown in Figure 38.

Section 2. The student selects the geometric form that is the same shape as the model but is rotated, darker, or a different size. On some items in this section, the correct figure must also be distinguished from a rival background, as shown in Figure 39.

Section 3. The student is first shown a stimulus drawing and then is asked to choose it from memory from an array of four similar drawings (see Figure 40).

Section 4. The student selects, from an array of incomplete drawings, the drawing that would, if completed, match the model (see Figure 41).

Section 5. The student selects from four drawings the one that is different. The difference involves a change in spatial orientation of the drawing or a part of the drawing (see Figure 42).

The examiner tallies the number of correct responses in all five sections to determine the raw score. This score can then be converted to an age equivalent, a perceptual quotient, and with some computation, a standard score. Each of these scores represents the student's performance on the total test; separate scores are not given for each section.

STRENGTHS OF THE MVPT

- The motor-free aspect of this test makes it a useful diagnostic tool, because it helps to detect which component of visual-motor integration activities may be causing an individual student's difficulty. When used as part of a test battery that includes tests of visual-motor integration and various aspects of coordination, it can make an important contribution to delineating the specific problem area and setting up an appropriate intervention program.

- The MVPT is easy to administer, and although it must be given individually, it is not excessively time consuming. The scoring procedure is simple and objective. Admin-

Figure 38. MVPT, Section 1, Item 6

Visual and Visual-Motor Tests

istering the test requires no disposable materials, except for the one-page scoring sheet, making it a relatively inexpensive test to give.

- The method of reporting scores is quite useful; the availability of age scores, perceptual quotients, and standard scores makes it easy to compare a student's performance on this test to performance on other tests. In addition, the availability of scores in several forms serves as a system of checks and balances against the pitfalls of the individual scoring systems.

- The authors' use of the standard error of measurement in reporting age-equivalent scores is useful because it requires the examiner to view the student's score as a range within which the "true" score is likely to fall. The examiner is also cautioned to take into account the standard error of measurement when interpreting perceptual quotients, although this is not "built into" the reporting of these scores (unlike the age-equivalent scores).

- The test directions are, for the most part, clear and simple. However, language-impaired students sometimes have difficulty understanding what is expected on the visual closure items, and the standard procedure outlined in the manual does not permit much additional explanation.

- The MVPT's reliability is acceptable for students aged 5 years to 8 years, 11 months but is borderline for 4-year-olds. Construct validity is acceptable for students aged 5 years to 7 years, 11 months.

LIMITING FACTORS OF THE MVPT

- The authors caution that guessing, random answering, and perseveration are factors that must be considered in interpreting scores on this and most other tests. A raw score of less than 10 indicates less than chance performance and cannot be interpreted with confidence.

- No information is given about the selection of the normative sample nor about the proportions of subgroups included in the sample.

- The sample populations for students aged 4 years through 4 years, 11 months and for students aged 8 years, 6 months through 8 years, 11 months were too small to allow confident test interpretation for students in these age groups.

- The high success rate on each item for 7-year-olds makes the MVPT nondiscriminatory at the upper age limits.

- The content validity of the test is open to question. The authors state that the test assesses five areas of visual perception: spatial relationships, visual discrimination, figure-ground perception, visual closure, and visual mem-

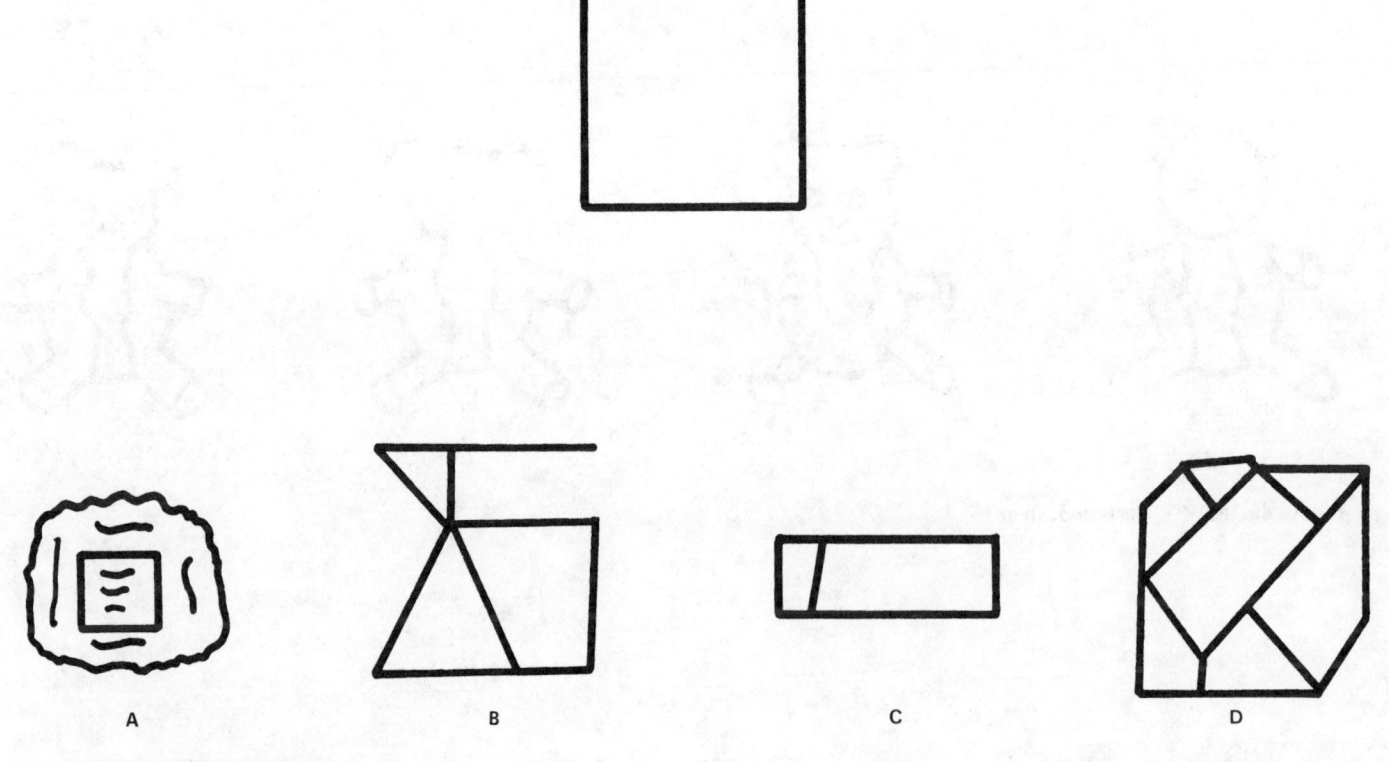

Figure 39. MVPT, Section 2, Item 12

ory. For each of the five types, other researchers are cited who have measured similar aspects of visual perception. However, the authors do not establish adequately that these five areas are mutually exclusive nor that they represent all aspects of visual perception.

• Some of the definitions of perceptual categories are vague and confusing. This is complicated by the division of the test into five unlabeled sections that do not seem to correspond in all cases with the perceptual categories the authors have defined. Section 1, for example, includes five figure-ground items, as well as three items that the authors would, it seems, include in their definition of spatial relations.

• The number of items in each perceptual category ranges from 5 to 11. Because the test provides only a total score, the larger percentage of items on visual closure, for example, means that a student with this difficulty may achieve an unrealistically low score.

• No information is provided about the test's construct validity for 4-year-olds and 8-year-olds.

• In studying the MVPT's criterion-related validity, the authors did not correlate MVPT scores exclusively with other motor-free tests, thus introducing too many variables for accurate interpretation. This problem was further complicated by using a homogeneous sample for the intertest correlations.

Figure 40. MVPT, Section 3, Item 15

Visual and Visual-Motor Tests 129

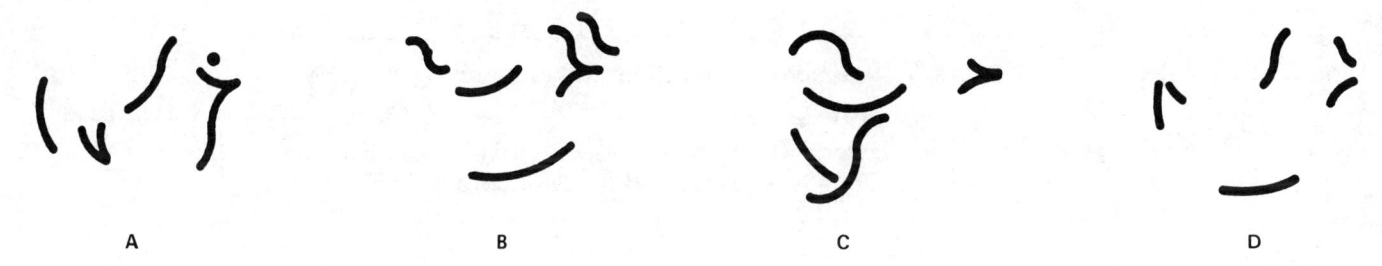

Figure 41. MVPT, Section 4, Item 29

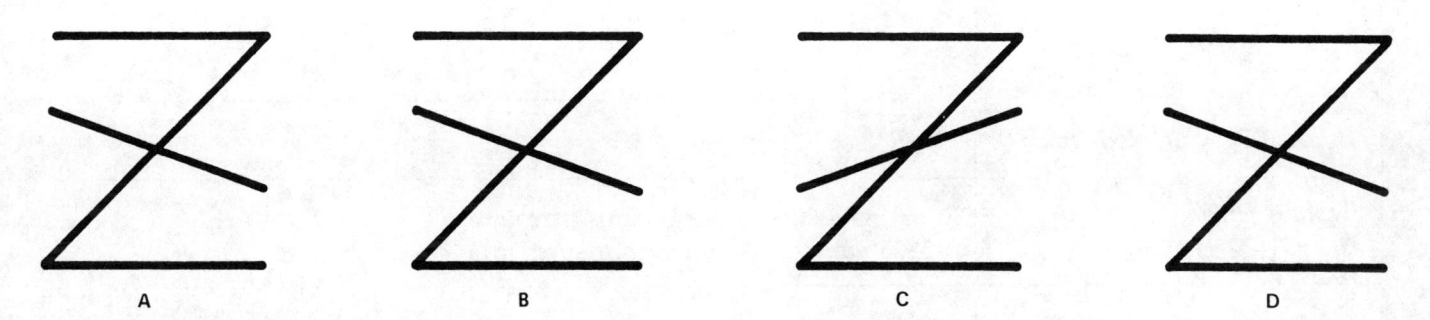

Figure 42. MVPT, Section 5, Item 34

The Bender Visual Motor Gestalt Test (Bender)

Lauretta Bender
The American Orthopsychiatric Association, Inc., 1946; Koppitz Developmental Scoring System, 1963, revised 1975; Pascal and Suttell Scoring System, 1951
1775 Broadway, New York, NY 10019

Purpose	To assess level of maturity in visual-motor perception and to detect emotional disturbances
Major Areas Tested	Visual-motor integration and emotional adjustment
Age or Grade Range	5–11 years (Koppitz Developmental Scoring System) 15–50 years (Pascal and Suttell Scoring System)
Usually Given By	Psychologist
Type of Test	Standardized Individual Group
Scores Obtained	Age level Percentile
Student Performance Timed?	No
Testing Time	10 minutes (individual administration) 15–25 minutes (group administration)
Scoring/Interpretation Time	10–20 minutes
Normed On	1,100 students from the Midwest and East, including public school children in rural, small town, suburban, and urban areas; 1974 sample included Blacks, Orientals, Mexican-Americans, and Puerto Ricans (norms refer to Koppitz standardization)
Alternate Forms Available?	No

FORMAT

The Bender Visual Motor Gestalt Test (Bender) is a series of nine abstract designs to be copied in pencil by the student (see Figure 43). The figures illustrate certain principles of Gestalt psychology. The designs, printed on four-inch by six-inch cards, are presented one at a time. The student copies each design, with the sample before him or her. When the student finishes drawing a figure, the card is removed, and the next card is placed at the top of the paper. A modification of the test requires the student to recall the designs from memory after initial performance.

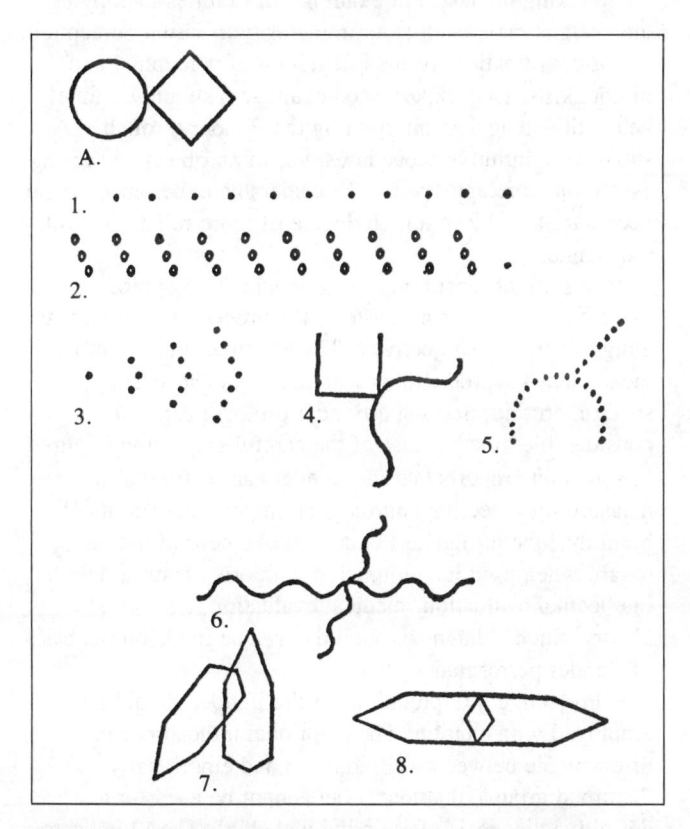

Figure 43. Bender, Plate I

The Bender is usually administered individually but can be given to a group of students. As a group test, different techniques have been devised for administration: projecting the designs onto a screen or wall, using enlarged stimulus cards, using individual decks of cards for each student, or using special copying booklets.

The standard individual administration of the Bender permits the student to erase and rework the reproductions. More than one sheet of paper may be used, and although there is no time limit on this test, data presented by Koppitz (1963) shows the average time required to complete the test along with the critical time limits. Timing the test, then, can be useful. Manipulation of the stimulus cards is allowed, but they must be replaced in the original position before the student begins copying. If the student rotates the paper while copying a design, it should be returned to its original position before the next figure is presented.

There is no basal or ceiling level on the Bender. The student copies all nine designs, which are presented in a specified order. Alternate, equivalent forms for test-retest purposes are not available.

The original Bender did not include any formal scoring system. However, as the test became more popular in clinics and schools, several scoring systems were developed. One of the most frequently used was devised by Elizabeth Koppitz, a clinical psychologist who used the test extensively with children with learning and emotional disorders. Koppitz's book, *The Bender-Gestalt Test for Young Children* (1963), describes a scoring system, age norms for children between the ages of 5 and 11 years, and reliability and validity data. Volume 2 of the same book (Koppitz 1975) presents a revised scoring system, a norming population expanded to include minority groups, and a compilation of the research available on the test. These two books are essential for scoring and interpreting test performance.

In the Koppitz scoring system (described in detail in her books), errors are counted for distorting the shape of the design, perseverating, falsely integrating two forms, and rotating forms. The student's total error score is converted to a developmental-age score. Volume 2 provides tables for converting the total number of errors to both age-equivalent and percentile scores. Examples of error types are found in Figure 44. Koppitz reports that these types of errors are most indicative of minimal brain dysfunction.

STRENGTHS OF THE BENDER

- The Bender is a quick, reliable, easy-to-administer test that is generally nonthreatening and appealing to students. It is popular with psychologists and a widely used clinical instrument. The test is inexpensive and requires few materials.

- The Bender provides developmental data about a student's maturity in visual-motor integration. Of equal value is the important clinical information that can be obtained by observing a student's behavior while taking the test. For example, the experienced examiner notes such behaviors as excessive erasing and reworking of the designs, rotation of the drawing paper, time needed to complete the test, the spatial organization of the designs on the paper, and the student's attitude during testing. Two students may achieve the same score on the Bender, even producing similar-looking finished protocols, but the clinical observations of the two students may be very different. The behaviors observed during testing provide valuable diagnostic insight.

- Research has also supported the use of the Bender to detect emotional problems. Koppitz (1975) has developed two new emotional indicators (Box around Design and Spontaneous Elaboration, or Addition to Design) to add to her previous list of 10 (Confused Order, Wavy Line, Dashes Substituted for Circles, Increasing Size, Large Size, Small Size, Fine Line, Careless Overwork or Heavily Reinforced Lines, Second Attempt, and Expansion). She reports that the presence of three or more emotional indicators on a student's final product suggests the need for further psychological evaluation.

- The group adaptation of the Bender is particularly economical in terms of time. Combined with other brief tests, it is moderately effective as a screening instrument, to identify high-risk students in need of further evaluation. Used in a pretest-posttest manner, the Bender can also be used as a means of evaluating the effectiveness of perceptual-motor training programs.

- The development of various scoring systems to meaningfully quantify a student's performance on the Bender has increased the test's utility. In addition to the Koppitz system for children, the Pascal and Suttel Scoring System has proven useful for adult protocols.

LIMITING FACTORS OF THE BENDER

- The Bender can be interpreted both intuitively and objectively. In either case, the examiner must be highly trained and experienced to effectively analyze the test protocols and to observe and evaluate the student's behavior while taking the test. For example, difficulties in copying the designs may result from immaturity in visual perception, motor coordination, or the integration of perceptual and motor skills. Less experienced examiners should definitely be cautioned against interpreting the Bender through subjective, intuitive procedures; use of an objective scoring system is more appropriate. Considerable experience is also necessary to achieve a high degree of score reliability with the Bender.

- In spite of recent improvements in the Koppitz Developmental Scoring System, the procedures still contain a high degree of subjectivity. The examiner must compare the student's reproductions with the model according to specific criteria. Scoring a Bender protocol can take considerable time because of the careful inspection required.

- Koppitz reports that the Bender can be used as a measure for detecting neurological impairment (minimal brain dysfunction). The Bender may be helpful in this regard when used in conjunction with other tests and with intellectual evaluation, medical evaluation, and social history. Such a diagnosis should *never* be made on the basis of Bender performance alone.

- Projective interpretations of the Bender should be employed with caution. The emotional indicators can discriminate between well-adjusted and emotionally disturbed groups of students but cannot be used for a definitive diagnosis of an individual child. The 12 indicators can differentiate neurotic, psychotic, and brain-damaged students only when accompanied by other tests and background data.

- The Bender is limited by age because of its developmental ceiling. The test distinguishes between students with outstanding or average visual-motor perception and those with immature perception only for students between the ages of 5 and 8. Most normal 10-year-old students can copy the Bender designs without any difficulty. Scores are meaningful for older students only if their perceptual-motor development is below the 9-year-old level.

- As a group test, the Bender has certain drawbacks. The examiner cannot observe and supervise each student individually; therefore some of the clinical value of the test

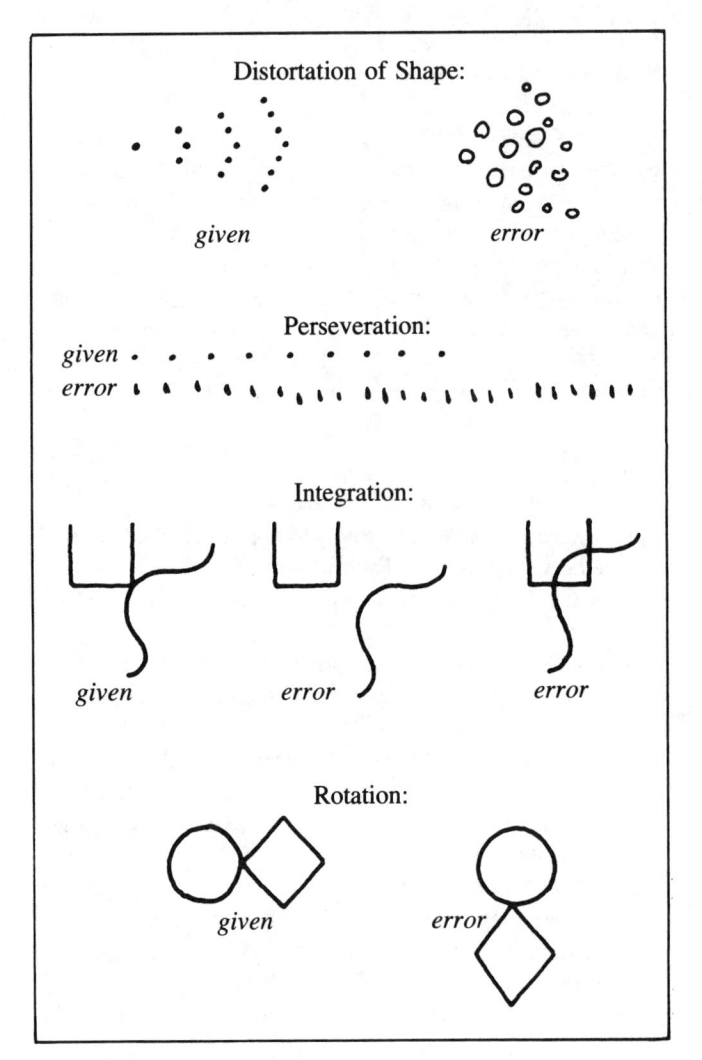

Figure 44. Bender Error Types

is lost through group administration. For very immature and hyperactive students who cannot work independently, individual administration is more appropriate.

- A last consideration is the use of the Bender in research studies. The reported findings on using the test as a means of predicting academic achievement have often been contradictory. Further investigation might clarify these discrepant findings. More research is also needed to determine what the recall method of the Bender measures and what diagnostic implications this procedural variation holds. Another area that needs to be more fully explored and substantiated concerns the recent finding that the rate of development in visual-motor perceptual skills differs among students of various ethnic groups.
- Given the conflicting results of research using the Bender, it is best to think of this test as a measure of visual-motor integration through design copying, rather than as a test of intelligence, emotional disturbance, or minimal brain damage.

Beery-Buktenica Developmental Test of Visual-Motor Integration (VMI)

Keith E. Beery and Norman Buktenica
Follett Publishing Company, 1967; renorming 1982
1010 W. Washington Blvd., Chicago, IL 60607

Purpose	To assess visual-perception and fine-motor coordination
Major Areas Tested	Visual-motor integration
Age or Grade Range	2–15 years
Usually Given By	Classroom teacher Special education teacher Occupational therapist Psychologist
Type of Test	Standardized Individual Group
Scores Obtained	Age level Percentile Standard
Student Performance Timed?	No
Testing Time	10–15 minutes
Scoring/Interpretation Time	10 minutes
Normed On	3,090 students between the ages of 2 years, 9 months and 19 years, 8 months, balanced for ethnicity, income level, place of residence, and sex
Alternate Forms Available?	No

Visual and Visual-Motor Tests   135

FORMAT
The materials for the Beery-Buktenica Developmental Test of Visual-Motor Integration (VMI) consist of the manual and individual test booklets. The VMI is a pencil-and-paper test. It may be presented to groups of students but is more often used individually. The test booklet presents 24 geometric forms for the student to copy. The forms are printed in heavy black outlines and arranged three to a page, with a space below each one for the student to copy the form. The format is clear and uncluttered, and the forms are arranged from the simplest to the most complex (see Figures 45, 46, and 47). The student copies the forms and may not erase or rotate the book. The test is not timed, and the student continues working until three consecutive errors are made. Although the same booklet is used for students of a wide age range, the student only copies forms within his or her ability. The raw score consists of the total number of forms copied correctly before reaching the ceiling; this score is converted to an age score, standard score, and percentile using the tables in the manual.

The VMI is published in two forms. The Long Form contains all 24 geometric forms and covers the age range of 2 to 15 years. The Short Form is somewhat less expensive, contains only the first 15 geometric forms, and is recommended for students between 2 and 8 years of age. Alternate, equivalent forms for test-retest purposes are not available.

STRENGTHS OF THE VMI
- The VMI is a well-constructed test. The 24 geometric forms were chosen over letter forms because they were equally familiar to children of varying backgrounds. The forms are developmentally sequenced, with careful thought to increasing task complexity. The wide age range makes the VMI a good instrument for screening purposes as well as measurement of student progress. Renorming eliminated the separate age norms for boys and girls. The addition of new norms, standard scores, and percentiles has greatly increased the value of the test.

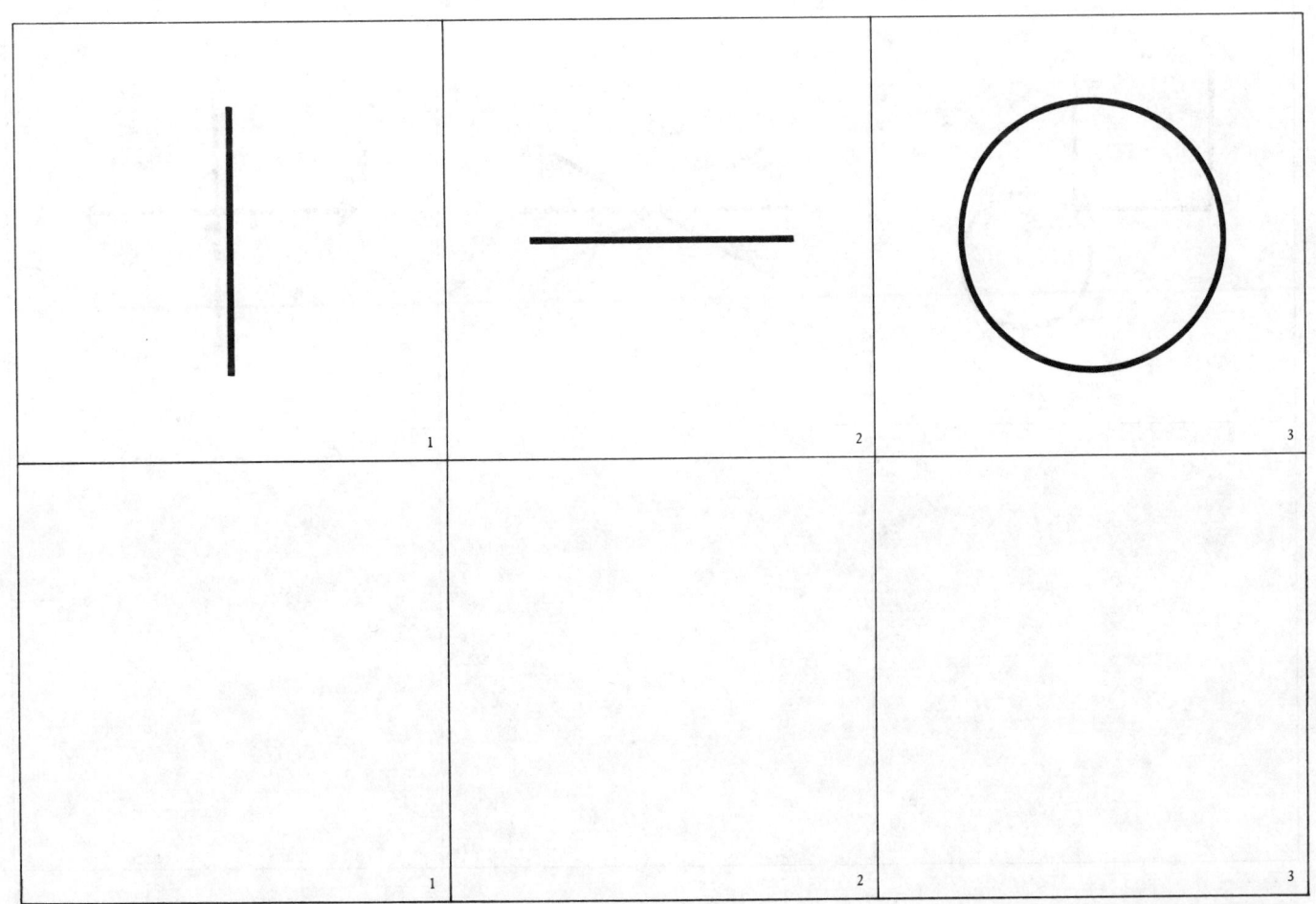

DEVELOPMENTAL TEST OF VISUAL-MOTOR INTEGRATION
Copyright © 1967 by Keith E. Beery and Norman A. Buktenica

Figure 45. VMI, Items 1, 2, 3

- The VMI is an enjoyable test for most students. The directions are clear and easy to understand. The beginning forms allow even young or seriously impaired students to experience success, whereas the more complex forms present a challenge for the adolescent student.

- The VMI has clear directions for administration and is a good instrument for the classroom teacher to use with small groups of students. The provision of age norms for each item provides the teacher with a basis for understanding which types of geometric forms can be expected to be mastered next. That is, if a student can complete the right oblique line (/) and the left oblique line (\ ) successfully, we can expect that next the student will probably learn to reproduce the oblique cross (×).

- The VMI manual is particularly helpful in describing the process of visual-motor integration and outlining a sequence of visual-motor training activities.

LIMITING FACTORS OF THE VMI

- The VMI measures visual-motor integration. As in all tests of this type, it is often difficult to determine whether the student's difficulty lies only in the visual perception process, only in the motor response, or in both. Low scores on the VMI suggest that further testing or diagnostic teaching procedures be used to separate the two processes. One clue is often the student's frustration level on the test. If the student becomes very frustrated when he or she recognizes that the reproduction does not match the stimulus form, the student is probably perceiving it correctly but having difficulty with the motor response. Another student may not see that the reproduction and the stimuli are different, indicating that visual perception may also be impaired.

- Although the VMI has age norms for students up to 15 years old, it seems most useful with preschool and

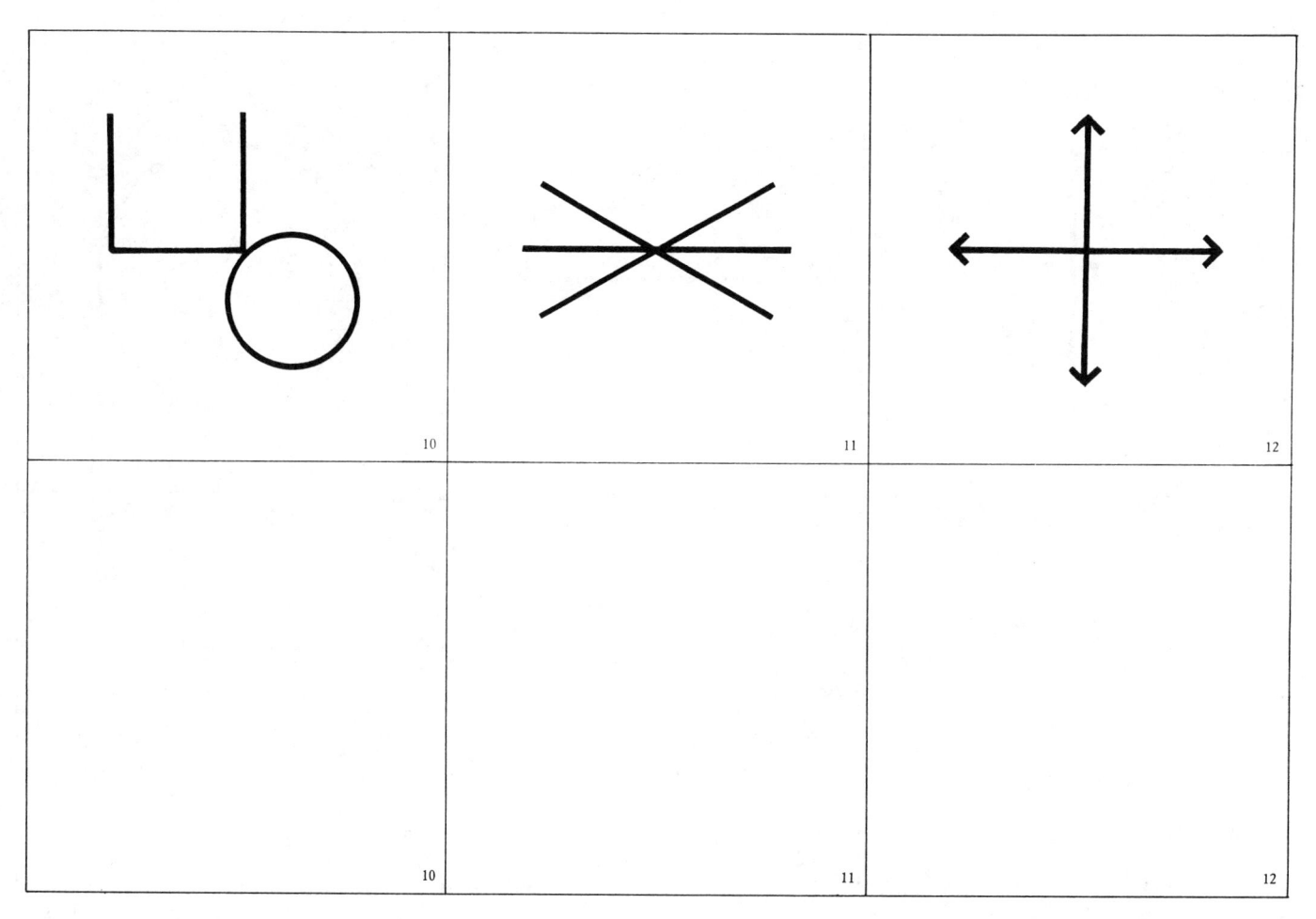

DEVELOPMENTAL TEST OF VISUAL-MOTOR INTEGRATION
Copyright © 1967 by Keith E. Beery and Norman A. Buktenica

Figure 46. VMI, Items 10, 11, 12

Visual and Visual-Motor Tests

primary-age students. It can be used as either an individual or group test with one set of age norms. If used as a group test, monitors should be provided to keep students from rotating the book or skipping forms.

- The scoring procedures for the VMI are somewhat inconsistent. On some items, great precision is required, and the examiner must use a protractor to score the item; on others, scoring is very subjective. It is important that the examiner emphasize to students that they do their best. Some students view the test as "so easy" that they work carelessly and then are penalized by the precise scoring system. In some places in the scoring system, the student who gets one more form correct gets a significantly higher age score.
- The size and composition of the standardization sample indicates that the norms are most adequate for the 5- to 13-year-old age range.
- The VMI does not measure spatial organizational skills. Each form is copied in the space provided. A student may have much more difficulty on a test like the Bender Visual Motor Gestalt Test, where nine forms are copied on a blank piece of paper. A very low score on the VMI often reflects an impulsive, careless approach to the test, and this must be sorted out from true deficits in visual-motor integration.

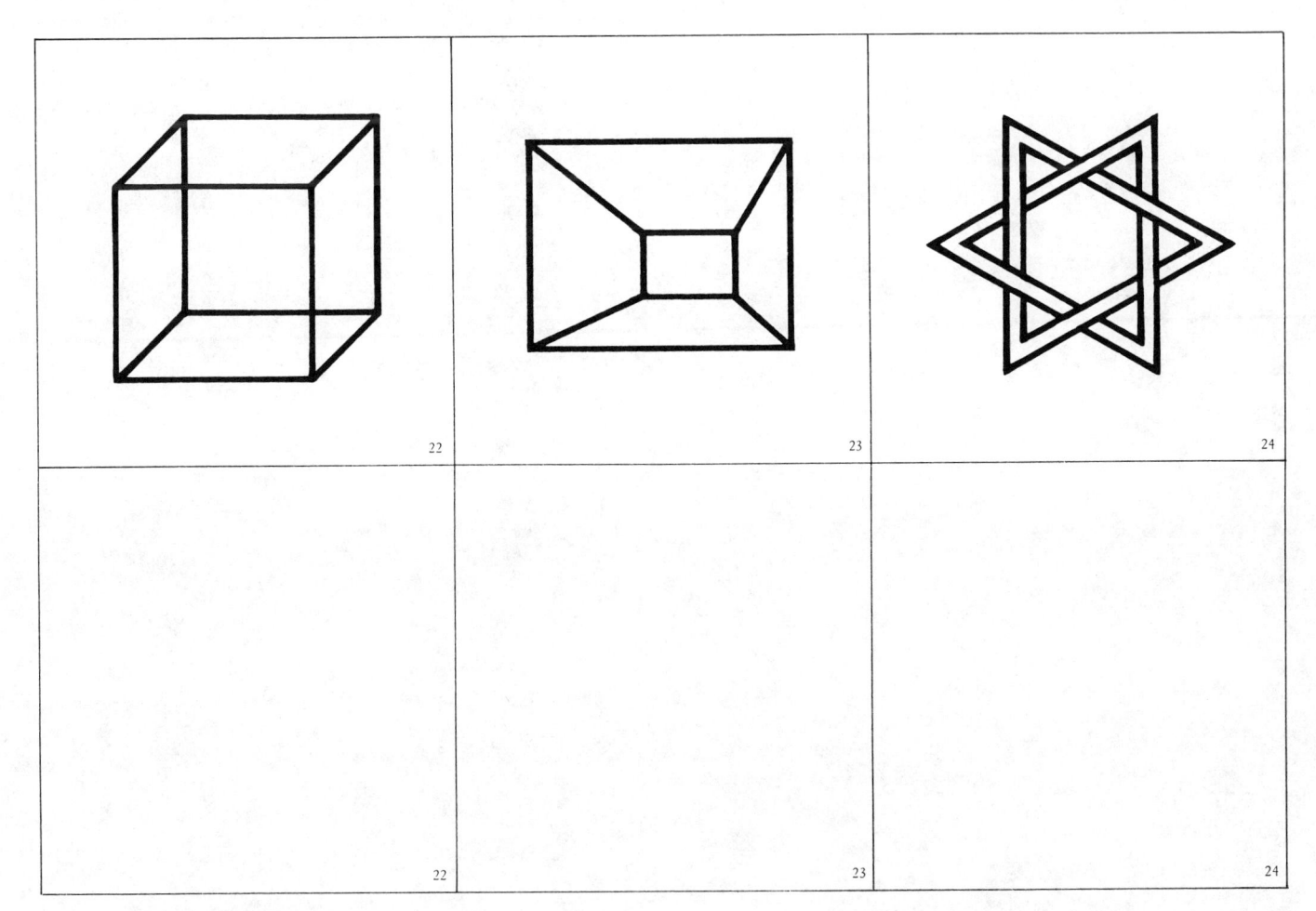

DEVELOPMENTAL TEST OF VISUAL-MOTOR INTEGRATION
Copyright © 1967 by Keith E. Beery and Norman A. Buktenica

Figure 47. VMI, Items 22, 23, 24

Chapter Three

Speech and Language Tests

The primary, first-learned language system is oral. Long before children come to school, they develop skills of listening and speaking that enable them to communicate with others. The secondary language system, written language, is learned in school. Difficulties in the acquisition of reading and writing often have their basis in the student's oral language skills. This chapter deals with the assessment of oral language—its reception and expression. The 16 tests reviewed here are usually given by speech and language therapists or clinicians.

A complete speech and language evaluation includes assessment in the five major components of language:

1. *Phonology*. This is the sound system that constitutes spoken language. Phonemes such as /k/ and /f/ have no meaning in isolation, but their combination in specific sequences creates words.

2. *Morphology*. Morphemes are the smallest meaningful units of language. They are usually words like *picnic*, *work*, or *slow*, but they may also be grammatical markers signifying specific concepts, such as plurality (picnic*s*), tense (work*ed*), or shifts from adjective to adverb (slow*ly*).

3. *Syntax*. This is the grammatical aspect of spoken language, the system for ordering words into meaningful sequences. Grammatical structure plays an important role in the comprehension and production of spoken language.

4. *Semantics*. This includes the meaning of words, sentences, and paragraphs. Vocabulary is a basic part of semantics.

5. *Pragmatics*. This includes the rules governing the use of language in context. Such features as conversational turn-taking and topic maintenance affect the ability to communicate effectively.

A speech and language clinician assesses both the receptive and expressive processes of each of these five components. For example, in the area of syntax:
- *Receptive*. Can the student comprehend past tense?
- *Expressive*. Can the student express ideas in past tense?

In the area of semantics:
- *Receptive*. What is the level of the student's listening vocabulary?
- *Expressive*. What is the level of the student's spoken vocabulary?

The tests reviewed in this chapter include measures of receptive and expressive language. This section includes 16 language tests, beginning with a comprehensive measure, the Illinois Test of Psycholinguistic Abilities (ITPA). The ITPA contains a variety of subtests that assess perception, memory, and language skills in both reception and expression. Some critics feel that it probably should not be called a language test; however, it does measure aspects of phonology, morphology, syntax, and semantics and is routinely given by speech and language clinicians. Therefore, it is reviewed in this chapter.

Following the ITPA is a newer comprehensive test battery, the Clinical Evaluation of Language Functions (CELF). The CELF assesses a variety of language-processing and language-production skills in school-age children.

Following these batteries are five measures of receptive language. The Peabody Picture Vocabulary Test—Revised assesses single-word receptive vocabulary; the Assessment of Children's Language Comprehension and the Test for Auditory Comprehension of Language include not only reception of single words but also phrases, sentences, and grammatical markers. The Boehm Test of Basic Concepts assesses knowledge of familiar concepts. The Token Test for Children assesses understanding of commands of gradually increasing complexity.

Two tests, the Northwestern Syntax Screening Test and the Sequenced Inventory of Communication Development, include measures of both receptive and expressive skills. The latter is a developmental test containing both verbal and nonverbal communication tasks.

The section continues with two measures of assessing spontaneous speech, Developmental Sentence Scoring (DSS) and the Environmental Language Inventory (ELI), which are not tests but rather methods for gathering and assessing language samples. The DSS evaluates sentence structure while the ELI assesses early semantic-grammatical rules in two- to four-word utterances.

The Multilevel Informal Language Inventory is a new diagnostic tool that combines elements of language sampling and formal assessment of grammar, syntax, and semantics. The Expressive One-Word Picture Vocabulary Test assesses only single-word expressive vocabulary. The Word Test, a new test, evaluates the semantic aspects of expressive language.

While the above tests are usually used by language pathologists to assess children with language deficits, two new tests specialize in the language problems of students with learning disabilities. The Test of Language Development and the Test of Adolescent Language assess not only oral language but also reading comprehension and written language.

Many of the tests in this chapter were designed to be used with preschool children, attesting to the importance of the speech and language area in the assessment of very young children. The tests reviewed in Part II: Preschool and Kindergarten Tests all include significant language components. Those who are interested in the language assessment of young children are referred to that material.

Many of the tests reviewed in this chapter lack validity for students from bilingual backgrounds. Those who are interested in the assessment of Spanish-speaking children are referred to the bilingual (Spanish-English) language tests in Chapter Four.

Due to space limitations, this chapter does not include any measures of articulation. Three major tests of articulation are outlined in Appendix E.

Illinois Test of Psycholinguistic Abilities   141
Clinical Evaluation of Language Functions   148
Peabody Picture Vocabulary Test—Revised   155
Assessment of Children's Language
  Comprehension   157
Test for Auditory Comprehension of Language   159
Boehm Test of Basic Concepts   162
Token Test for Children   165

Northwestern Syntax Screening Test   167
Sequenced Inventory of Communication
  Development   169
Developmental Sentence Scoring   172
Environmental Language Inventory   176
Multilevel Informal Language Inventory   180
Expressive One-Word Picture Vocabulary Test   182
The Word Test   184
Test of Language Development   187
Test of Adolescent Language   191

Illinois Test of Psycholinguistic Abilities (ITPA)
S. A. Kirk, J. J. McCarthy, and W. D. Kirk
University of Illinois Press, 1961; revised 1968
Urbana, IL 61801

Purpose	To assess how a child communicates with and receives communication from the environment and to provide a framework for planning remediation and developing instructional programs
Major Areas Tested	Visual-motor and auditory-vocal skills
Age or Grade Range	2–10 years
Usually Given By	Psychologist Speech/language clinician
Type of Test	Standardized Individual
Scores Obtained	Age level Scaled
Student Performance Timed?	Yes (some subtests)
Testing Time	1½ hours
Scoring/Interpretation Time	30–40 minutes
Normed On	962 average children from medium-sized towns and cities in the Midwest; 4 percent Black students
Alternate Forms Available?	No

FORMAT

The Illinois Test of Psycholinguistic Abilities (ITPA) materials consist of a manual, two books of test pictures, objects for description, visual-closure picture strips, and individual student record forms, all packaged in a carrying case.

The ITPA is based on Osgood's model of communication (Osgood 1957), which postulates three dimensions to cognitive abilities: *channels* (auditory, visual, vocal, motor), *processes* (reception, association, expression), and *levels* (automatic, representational). The subtests of the ITPA represent these dimensions. There are ten basic subtests and two other supplementary tests. The summary sheet (see Figure 48) shows how the ITPA is organized.

The two levels postulated by Osgood are the representational and the automatic. At the *representational level* (or meaningful level), the processes of *reception, association,* and *expression* are assessed in the two major channels, auditory and visual. Functioning at the *automatic level* is assessed in the two major channels in terms of closure and sequential memory skills. The two supplementary tests provide additional information about automatic functioning in the auditory channel. The supplementary scores are not included when deriving the total or mean scores for the test.

Precise directions for administrating and scoring each subtest are contained in the manual. Raw scores are converted to age scores and scaled scores and recorded on the summary sheet. Scaled scores are plotted on the profile sheet to provide a graphic representation of a student's performance (see Figure 49).

An individual's test performance may be viewed in several ways. The total of the raw scores from the ten basic

Summary Sheet

| SUBTEST | REPRESENTATIONAL LEVEL ||||||| AUTOMATIC LEVEL |||||||
| | AUDITORY-VOCAL ||| VISUAL-MOTOR ||| AUDITORY-VOCAL ||| VISUAL-MOTOR |||
	Raw Score	Age Score	Scaled Score	Raw Score	Age Score	Scaled Score	Raw Score	Age Score	Scaled Score	Raw Score	Age Score	Scaled Score
AUDITORY RECEPTION												
VISUAL RECEPTION												
VISUAL MEMORY												
AUDITORY ASSOCIATION												
AUDITORY MEMORY												
VISUAL ASSOCIATION												
VISUAL CLOSURE												
VERBAL EXPRESSION												
GRAMMATIC CLOSURE												
MANUAL EXPRESSION												
(Supplementary tests) AUDITORY CLOSURE SOUND BLENDING												

SUMMARY SCORES: Sum of Raw Scores | Composite PLA | Sum of SS | Mean SS | Median SS

Figure 48. ITPA Summary Sheet

Speech and Language Tests

subtests is converted into a "psycholinguistic age," which provides an overall index of the student's level of psycholinguistic development. The raw scores are also translated individually into scaled scores. The mean scaled score for the normative population is 36, with a standard deviation of plus or minus 6. The student's own mean is derived by averaging the scaled scores of the ten basic subtests. Discrepancies of plus or minus 10 from the student's own mean or the median scaled score are considered substantial. Using the student's mean or median scaled score as a reference point assists the examiner in viewing strengths and weaknesses.

In addition, patterns of performance may be found by analyzing the results further. Several ways of doing this are described by Kirk and Kirk in *Psycholinguistic Learning Disabilities* (1971). For example:

1. *Comparison of levels of organization.* The representational-level score is obtained by averaging age scores and scaled scores of tests at the representational level. The automatic-level score is obtained by averaging age scores and scaled scores of tests at the automatic level.

2. *Comparison of channels.* The auditory-vocal score is obtained by averaging age scores and scaled scores from auditory and verbal subtests. The visual-motor score is obtained by averaging age scores and scaled scores from visual and motor subtests.

3. *Comparison of psycholinguistic processes.* Scores for reception, association, and expression are obtained by averaging scaled scores for each process.

Table 18 describes and comments on the individual subtests.

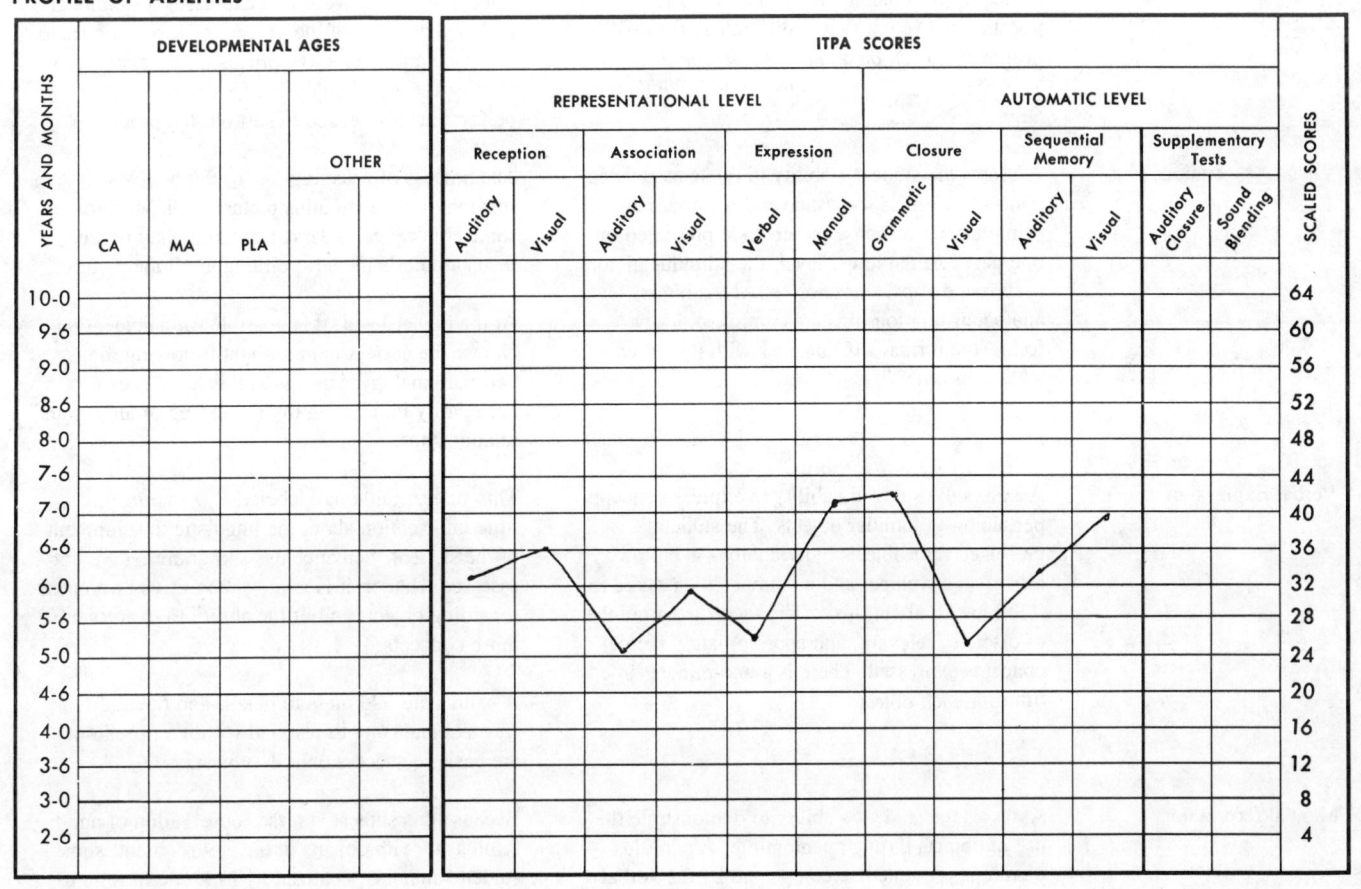

Figure 49. ITPA Profile Sheet

Table 18. ITPA Subtests

Subtest	Description	Comments
Auditory Reception	Assesses the student's ability to derive meaning from verbally presented material. Questions of controlled length and structure are presented by the examiner. Vocabulary increases in difficulty. A simple yes or no response is required of the student. (*Do dogs eat? Do cosmetics celebrate?*)	The examiner is cautioned not to influence the student's response by inflection or facial expression. The simple response that is required makes it possible to test nonverbal children. However, some students may be tempted to give minimal involvement to the task and thereby respond in random fashion.
Visual Reception	Assesses the student's ability to match concepts presented visually. After brief exposure to a single stimulus picture, the student selects the correct match from four choices on the following page. Objects and situations conceptually similar to the stimulus are to be chosen.	Mild and moderate visual handicaps do not appear to affect performance on this subtest. It appears to measure central rather than peripheral processes (Bateman 1963).
Auditory Association	Assesses the student's ability to complete verbal analogies presented by the examiner. The vocabulary becomes more difficult as the task progresses. (*I sit on a chair; I sleep on a _____. Years have seasons; dollars have _____.*)	The student needs to grasp the analogy and to select the correct word that expresses it. Although included as a test of the process of association, the receptive and expressive processes are also involved. Careful analysis of a student's performance is needed to sort out the processes.
Visual Association	Assesses the student's ability to relate associated concepts, such as sock/shoe and hammer/nail. Stimulus and response pictures are presented on one page. At the lower level, the stimulus picture is surrounded by four choices. At the higher level, analogous relationships are employed. They follow the format "If this goes with this, then what goes with this?"	The process of selecting one of the pictures surrounding the stimulus picture is difficult for some children to understand. Some may imitate the examiner's model, pointing to all the pictures. At the higher level, it is possible for a student to choose the correct item without following the two-part analogy. Success at this level does not necessarily indicate an understanding of analogous relationships.
Verbal Expression	Assesses the student's ability to express concepts pertaining to familiar objects. The student is presented four objects individually—a ball, a block, an envelope, and a button—then asked to "Tell me all about this." The score is the number of discrete, relevant, and approximately factual concepts expressed. There is a one-minute time limit for each object.	This subtest, although labeled *Expression*, gives little information about the linguistic development of the student. Sentence use and grammar are not assessed. Rather, it is a test of cognitive awareness regarding objects and of the ability to express those concepts. A calm state, alertness to detail, and the ability to free associate and to respond within a time limit are basic to success on this subtest.
Manual Expression	Assesses the student's ability to demonstrate the use of objects through pantomime. A stimulus picture is presented, accompanied by the verbal request to "Show me what you do with a _____." The student's movements are recorded on a checklist of behaviors. Objects pictured include a guitar and binoculars.	Because this subtest assesses observation of and familiarity with objects in the environment, some students may be penalized by lack of exposure to such items as guitars and binoculars. Students respond best to this task when relaxed and uninhibited.

Speech and Language Tests

Table 18.—*Continued*

Subtest	Description	Comments
Manual Expression—*continued*		A study by McCarthy, reported in Kirk and Kirk (1971), found Down's Syndrome children to be superior in this area to other retarded children, and in relation to their other abilities. Many children with severe verbal language deficits do well on this measure of gestural language.
Grammatic Closure	Assesses the student's ability to complete verbal statements presented by the examiner. Each item consists of a complete statement followed by one to be completed with the correct word or grammatical inflection. Pictures serve as stimuli. (*Here is a boy. Here are two _____. Each child has a ball. This is hers and this is _____.*)	The ITPA was standardized on a basically Caucasian population. Standard American dialect was predominant. Therefore, responses of students from other populations may be informative, but they should not be scored. Students with speech defects were found to be deficient on this subtest in studies done by Ferrier (1966) and Foster (1963). This subtest does not provide complete analysis of grammatical form. Language sampling should be employed for more complete information.
Visual Closure	Assesses the student's ability to recognize a pictured object (or objects) when partially obscured in a scene. The task requires visual closure and figure-ground discrimination. A pointing response is used. There is a 30-second time limit.	Scanning ability and a reasonable searching procedure assist the student on this task. Also, an ability to function under time pressure is involved, although not explicitly stated.
Auditory Memory	Assesses the student's short-term memory for digits presented at the rate of two per second. Two trials are allowed. The digit series increase in length from two to eight numbers.	This subtest assesses immediate recall of unstructured, nonsyntactic material. Performance may be unrelated to short-term memory for other material, such as sentences. Because it requires verbal output, it may also be unrelated to tests of short-term retention of directions that are acted out rather than spoken. Performance on this subtest requires attention, a calm state, and retention of sequential material.
Visual Memory	Assesses the student's ability to reproduce sequences of nonmeaningful figures from memory. A pictured sequence is shown for five seconds; then the student places corresponding tiles in the same order. Two trials are allowed. Sequences increase in length from two to eight designs and include such patterns as lines and triangles.	This subtest requires a minimum of accumulated knowledge. Performance may be influenced by the ability to focus attention, function within a time limit, and retain sequential patterns. Patience and tolerance for a frustrating task are an aid. Some students are assisted by their verbal description of the designs. This helps the examiner understand a student's strategy but diminishes the test's value as a discrete measure of visual memory. This subtest only assesses memory of nonmeaningful pictorial material.

Table 18. —Continued

Subtest	Description	Comments
Auditory Closure (Supplementary)	Assesses the student's ability to supply mentally, then verbally, the sounds omitted in word(s) presented by the examiner. A progression from easier to more difficult vocabulary is used. Stimuli include "airpla/" (*airplane*) and "auto/o/ile" (*automobile*).	The student needs adequate hearing, good vocabulary, and attentive behavior to accomplish this task.
Sound Blending (Supplementary)	Assesses the student's ability to blend sounds spoken by the examiner at half-second intervals into words. At the lower end of the test, pictures are employed. The test progresses through synthesis of words with no picture clue (*f-i-s-h*) to nonsense words (*t-e-k-o*).	The upper limit for this subtest is below that for the test as a whole, specifically 8 years, 7 months. Adequate hearing, auditory discrimination, and retention of sounds in sequence are required for adequate performance. Performance may also reflect training approaches. For instance, students in the primary grades who have been instructed in a phonic approach often do not reach a ceiling. A recording is provided to ensure correct presentation.

STRENGTHS OF THE ITPA

• The ITPA is widely used and highly respected. It has been carefully constructed, its organization derived from the Osgood and Sebeok (1965) model of communication. This model makes it possible to view an individual's strengths and weaknesses in terms of channels, levels of organization, and processes. The ITPA provides a basis for making observations about an individual's pattern of performance. Supplemented by other diagnostic measures, it assists in accurate diagnosis of learning and language problems.

• Directions for presenting and scoring the ITPA are well stated in the manual. The examiner will find the profile sheet useful in viewing an individual's strengths and weaknesses.

• The variety of tasks included in the test enables the examiner to alter task presentation to meet the needs of the student. Tasks requiring the greatest concentration can be presented when attention and interest are adequate. The visual tests provide a means for evaluating children with poor language skills and give them the opportunity to demonstrate normal functioning.

• The ITPA has been widely studied. Many publications are available to increase the examiner's understanding of the test. Courses are taught on its construction and administration, and a film is available to help prepare examiners.

LIMITING FACTORS OF THE ITPA

• The term *psycholinguistic abilities* used in the title of this test is misleading. The ITPA samples cognitive functioning in verbal and nonverbal areas through different processes, but it does not analyze a student's psycholinguistic abilities.

• The ITPA purports to measure "discrete" functions. However, it is difficult to define, and to develop, tests that measure "discrete" functions. Subtests that are designed to assess nonlanguage functioning, such as Visual Memory, may still involve the use of vocabulary. Some students use labeling to retain the visual patterns.

• The ITPA was standardized on a limited sample of the population, drawn from medium-sized towns and cities in the Midwest. Rural and metropolitan areas were not represented. Only 4 percent of the population was Black, and the number of Spanish-Americans is not even reported. Thus the usefulness of the ITPA for minority populations is extremely limited. The results must be interpreted with caution when used with minorities or students from lower socioeconomic classes. Reference to research on the use of the ITPA with these groups is included in Kirk and Kirk's book (1971).

• Caution is also advised in the interpretation of scores. Within the age range of 2 to 10 years, scores should be compared to the student's scaled score. To do this, all ten subtests must be given. Age scores should not be compared at these ages. Interpretation of scores is difficult at both the lower and upper ends of the age range. Many of the ITPA subtests do not provide a high enough ceiling. Above age 10, language-age scores, rather than scaled scores, should be used to describe performance.

- Accurate administration and meaningful interpretation of the ITPA require good preparation and experience. Its use by untrained and inexperienced people is fraught with danger, much as the use of IQ tests is. Its administration is also more time-consuming than the manual would suggest. Usually an hour and a half are required for its presentation, and another hour for scoring and interpretation.

- The ITPA does not, and should not, stand alone as a diagnostic tool. The examiner needs to know how to interpret the results and to supplement the testing to obtain needed information, whether academic, cognitive, or linguistic.

- Studies on the validity of the ITPA are limited. Factor-analytic studies of the ITPA have neither proven nor disproven the construct validity of the test, according to the authors (Kirk and Kirk 1978, p. 64). A study by Elkins (1972) analyzed construct validity and found that the process and channel dimensions were verified but that the representational and automatic levels were not clear. Evidence of predictive validity is not presented. Although Paraskevopoulos and Kirk (1969) state that scores deviating from the child's mean make it more likely that the child will have learning disabilities, no data is provided to support this conclusion.

- Reliability data is summarized by Salvia and Ysseldyke in their book on assessment (1978, p. 357). Internal consistency is generally high in the ITPA, but particular caution should be taken in interpreting the Visual Closure and Auditory Closure subtests. Test-retest reliability is significantly lower than internal-consistency reliability. Salvia and Ysseldyke (1978) provide a summary of the reliability data.

Clinical Evaluation of Language Functions (CELF)

Eleanor M. Semel-Mintz and Elisabeth H. Wiig
Charles E. Merrill Publishing Company, 1980
1300 Alum Creek Dr., Columbus, OH 43216

Purpose	To identify the nature and degree of language disabilities in school-age children
Major Areas Tested	Phonology, syntax, semantics, memory, word finding, and word retrieval
Age or Grade Range	Grades K–12
Usually Given By	Speech/language clinician Special education teacher Psychologist
Type of Test	Individual Standardized Norm-referenced
Scores Obtained	Age level Percentile
Student Performance Timed?	Yes (some subtests)
Testing Time	1¼ hours
Scoring/Interpretation Time	45–60 minutes
Normed On	1,378 students in grades K–12 across the United States who demonstrated normal development in all areas; minority-group children well represented
Alternate Forms Available?	No

FORMAT

The Clinical Evaluation of Language Functions (CELF) is a comprehensive diagnostic battery providing differentiated measures of selected language functions in the areas of phonology, syntax, semantics, memory, word finding, and word retrieval. Studies by Wiig and Semel-Mintz (1976 and 1980) and other researchers have indicated that a sizable portion of school-age children with learning disabilities (approximately 39–63 percent) also exhibit a language disorder that can hinder academic progress. Development of the CELF is an outgrowth of this research into the nature of learning and language disabilities in children and adolescents.

The CELF diagnostic battery is administered individually and consists of 3 timed subtests and 10 untimed subtests. The materials include an examiner's manual, a booklet of stimulus/score forms, two visual stimulus manuals, and an audiotape of test stimuli for training purposes. The test manual is clearly written and informative. It contains a description of the test design, standardization information, administration and scoring procedures, and guidelines for error analysis and extension testing for each subtest. A description of each subtest is given in Table 19.

The CELF stimulus score forms are well designed and easy to use. For each subtest, trial and stimulus items are listed, correct responses are indicated (by underlining or bold type), and space for recording responses is provided. The student's responses are credited two points if correct, one point if correct after a second reading of the stimulus, and zero points if incorrect or if the student does not respond. Many subtests contain error analysis grids that permit a detailed evaluation of error response patterns and calculation of error percentages in each item group. The front sheet of the protocol booklet, Figure 50, contains a summary profile grid for plotting raw scores in relation to expected criterion scores for kindergarten through grade 12. A computation grid for indicating whether individual raw scores are at or above criterion (+) or below criterion (−) is included, as well as space for recording the norm-referenced comparisons between language processing and language production subtest scores.

With the original printing of the CELF in 1980, only experimental grade-level criterion scores were available. These scores were based on the performance of a limited sample of students (159), a large percentage of whom were considered below average. A norming study with a larger sample of normal children was completed in the fall of 1981, and the pass/fail criteria were updated. In partial response to consistent feedback from CELF users that the original criteria had been set too low, the new grade-level scores are roughly equivalent to a twentieth percentile cutoff, as compared to one standard deviation on the first criteria. As a result of the 1981 norming, raw scores from the language-processing subtests (1, 2, 3, 4, 5, 6) and language-production subtests (8, 9, 10, 11) may be converted to language-age scores and percentiles at each grade level.

The authors state that failure on a single subtest may not be uncommon among normal children. As a general guideline, they suggest that failure on any three subtests may be indicative of a potential language disorder. Since results from the norming study indicated that language performance on the CELF did not change significantly after the age of 12 years, language-age scores should be used cautiously with children over 12 years old. The authors suggest using only percentile scores for this age group.

STRENGTHS OF THE CELF

- The CELF is a thorough, carefully constructed test battery that makes an important contribution to the area of oral language assessment. It contains a diversity of linguistic tasks, which enables the examiner to select subtests to meet the diagnostic needs of a particular student. Subtest presentation can be altered for the student with obvious oral communication handicaps so that language production tasks are interspersed with processing tasks.

- Many of the tasks contained in the CELF battery are unique. There are few diagnostic instruments appropriate for assessing the oral language abilities of older school-age children. The CELF tasks and test materials are usually appealing and interesting to this age group. The inclusion of word recall and retrieval tasks enhances its value for adolescents.

- The CELF diagnostic battery is considered to be an integral part of Wiig and Semel-Mintz's assessment process, which consists of Screening, Diagnosis, Extension Testing, Assessment for Intervention, and Assessment for Progress. Based on an error analysis of CELF responses, extension or additional testing can be completed. Wiig and Semel-Mintz's book, *Language Assessment and Intervention for the Learning Disabled* (1980), is a valuable resource for criterion-referenced assessment tasks and intervention strategies following the administration of the CELF.

- Studies indicate that significant positive correlations at the .05 and .01 levels exist among several CELF subtests, including those probing processing, recall, and formulation of sentence structure.

- Strong test-retest reliability is reported for the total CELF diagnosis battery (.96) as well as for individual subtests.

LIMITING FACTORS OF THE CELF

- The authors responded to criticism concerning the original grade-level criterion scores by completing a norming study in 1981. Although these scores are now adjusted upward slightly, they are still limited in usefulness. Criterion scores for some CELF tasks vary quite insignificantly across several grade levels. For example, subtest 4,

TABLE 1: Age-Expected Grade Level Criteria

Subtest	1	2	3	4	5	6	7	8 (120 Sec. Minus Time)	9	10	11
GRADE Total Possible	52	44	44	64	50	34	7	12	?	60	96
10-12	43	37	39	49	43	17		12	59 Sec.	33	42	41
9	43	36	38	48	42	15		12	52 Sec.	30	41	40
8	43	35	38	47	42	14		12	51 Sec.	28	40	39
7	42	35	37	47	42	14		10	50 Sec.	28	40	39
6	42	35	37	47	41	13		10	47 Sec.	27	39	37
5	41	33	36	45	39	12		10	36 Sec.	25	37	37
4	40	32	34	42	36	11	7	9	32 Sec.	23	33	35
3	38	28	33	38	33	9	7		21 Sec.	20	30	32
2	36	22	30	33	26	8	7		30 Corr*	17	23	25
1	27	12	28	25	15	6	5		28 Corr*	15	18	15
K	24	10	27	21	9	4	3		26 Corr*	11	14	12

*Accuracy within 120 seconds.

Clinical Evaluation of Language Functions
Diagnostic Battery
Eleanor Semel-Mintz
Elisabeth H. Wiig

Name _____ Birthdate _____ Grade _____ Sex _____
Date of Testing _____ School _____ Teacher _____
Other Relevant Background Information _____

Total Raw Score Computation Grid

SUBTEST RAW SCORES/TOTAL RAW SCORES

Criterion-Referenced Comparisons (See Table 1) — Above Criterion / Below Criterion

Norm-Referenced Comparisons — Language Age (See Table 2) — Percentile Rank (See Table 3)

1. Word & Sentence Structure _____ [+ / −]
2. Word Classes _____ [+ / −]
3. Linguistic Concepts _____ [+ / −]
4. Relationships & Ambiguities _____ [+ / −]
5. Oral Directions _____ [+ / −]
6. Spoken Paragraphs _____

Total Processing Raw Score _____

7. Word Series _____ (Do not include in totals) [+ / −]
8. Confrontation Naming
   120 secs. − _____ (card III time) = _____ [+ / −]
9. Word Associations—Series I + Series II _____ [+ / −]
10. Model Sentences _____ [+ / −]
11. Formulated Sentences _____

Total Production Raw Score _____

☐ = Number of Subtests Below Criterion.

Figure 50. CELF Summary of Scores

Table 19. CELF Subtests

Subtest	Description	Areas Measured	Timed?	Comments
1. Processing Word and Sentence Structure	Student points to a pictorial representation of the meaning of 26 stimulus sentences from four choices (*The boy is being followed by the dog.*).	Receptive morphology and syntax	No	Three foils associated with each sentence feature a minimal grammatical contrast that influences the meaning. Some stimulus sentences are designed to assess more than one grammatical feature, such as personal and demonstrative pronouns.
2. Processing Word Classes	Student identifies two words that are associatively related after three or four words are presented verbally (*tiger-lion-tree-baby*).	Verbal concept development	No	Deficits in the ability to classify and categorize verbal concepts and identify associatively related words may be related to problems in input organization, according to the authors. Difficulties in auditory memory can affect performance on this task. For further diagnostic information, the examiner can ask the student why a particular word pair was chosen.
3. Processing Linguistic Concepts	Student executes 22 oral directions requiring logical operations by pointing to a series of six colored lines (*Before you point to the blue line, point to a red line.*).	Understanding of linguistic concepts and logical operations, including coordination, conditionals, inclusion, exclusion, temporal, and instrumental	No	Among the critical linguistic concepts found to differentiate the language- and learning-disabled from academically achieving children were those reflecting inclusion-exclusion, temporal, and instrumental relationships.
4. Processing Relationships and Ambiguities	Student answers a series of 32 yes/no questions (*Judy was pulled by Sue. Was Sue pulled?*).	Processing and interpretation of logico-grammatical relationships and ambiguities, such as comparatives, temporal-sequential idioms, metaphors, and proverbs	No	This subtest is an adaptation and expansion of the Wiig-Semel Test of Logico-Grammatical Sentences, an experimental edition (Wiig and Semel 1974). The yes/no format can result in minimal involvement with the task and frequent guessing responses.
5. Processing Oral Directions	Student executes 25 oral commands ranging in length from 5 to 18 words by pointing to black or white circles, squares, and/or triangles in two or three different sizes (*Point to the smallest black square.*).	Serial and left-right orientation and auditory memory	No	Interaction among level of commands, orientation expressed, and length of modifier sequences featured can be evaluated by use of the error analysis grid. This task seems least affected by the student's cultural background.

Table 19.—*Continued*

Subtest	Description	Areas Measured	Timed?	Comments
6. Processing Spoken Paragraphs	Student recalls salient information presented in four oral paragraphs of increasing length and complexity by responding to verbal questions.	Receptive language recall and retrieval	No	Stimulus questions involve recall of specific facts and do not require the understanding and processing of oral paragraphs as a whole unit. The increase in length and complexity between the third and fourth paragraphs is enormous. Few children seem able to retain much information from this final narrative.
7. Producing Word Series	Student recites the days of the week or the months of the year. Responses are scored for accuracy and speed.	Accuracy, fluency, and speed in recall of automatic-sequential word series	Yes	The days of the week item is administered to grades K–4, and the months of the year item is administered to grades 4–12. Since the total subtest is not given to every student, the raw score is not included in calculation of language age or percentile scores. Analysis of error types (omissions, substitutions, repetitions, transpositions) provides useful diagnostic information.
8. Producing Names on Confrontation	Student names colors (Card I), geometric forms (Card II), and colored geometric forms (Card III). Only the responses for Card III are scored for accuracy and speed.	Word recall and retrieval	Yes	Analysis of the student's performance in the areas of response latencies, mislabelings, and omissions is useful in planning a remediation program for word retrieval.
9. Producing Word Associations	Student produces names of foods and animals in two 60-second periods. Performance is measured by the total number of different words produced in both categories.	Vocabulary and word recall and retrieval	Yes	Controlled association tasks have been observed to differentiate language- and learning-disabled students from academically achieving adolescents (Wiig and Semel 1975). Although the responses are scored with respect to *quantity* (number of words recalled), evaluation of *quality* (number of semantic subclasses represented and shifts between various subclasses) is also possible.
10. Producing Model Sentences	Student repeats 23 sentences, which may or may not be structurally and semantically acceptable and appropriate (*Were delivered the flowers by the messenger?*). Items are sequenced in approximate order of difficulty in regard to vocabulary, sentence length, and complexity.	Morphology, syntax, recall and retrieval of words, and sentence structure	No	The two sentence types are included to probe adherence to word meaning and predictability in immediate sentence recall. A study by Wiig and Semel (1975) suggested that recall of utterances violating syntactic-semantic rules differentiated language- and learning-disabled students from academically achieving adolescents.

Speech and Language Tests

Table 19.—*Continued*

Subtest	Description	Areas Measured	Timed?	Comments
11. Producing Formulated Sentences	Student verbally formulates a sentence using each one of 12 stimulus words. Sentences are scored for level of structural complexity.	Morphology and syntax	No	The scoring criteria in the manual is vague. The authors responded to examiners' comments about this by including additional guidelines and examples of creditable responses in an update mailed to all CELF purchasers in 1981.
12. Supplementary: Processing Speech Sounds	Student identifies whether words featured in a spoken word pair are the *same* (phonemically identical) or *not the same/different*. The test includes 60 minimally different and identical word pairs.	Auditory discrimination	No	This test format is commonly used in auditory discrimination testing. This test, however, contrasts a wider range of speech sounds (consonants, vowels, consonant blends, diphthongs) than the Wepman Auditory Discrimination Test (p. 110). The error analysis grid is useful in isolating the consonant or vowel phonemes or phoneme combinations confused by the student.
13. Supplementary: Producing Speech Sounds	Student names pictured objects and attributes. Picture naming is elicited in the context of orally read cloze paragraphs in which target words are omitted.	Articulation of consonants and consonant blends	No	This test format was selected to approximate conditions in spontaneous speech production. Target words were selected to elicit the phonemes most frequently misarticulated.

Processing Relationships and Ambiguities, has a range of only two points over six grade levels (grades 6 through 12). Standardized scores, such as means and standard deviations, for individual grade levels and subtests are sorely needed. Often time constraints prevent administration of the entire set of language-processing or language-production subtests necessary for obtaining age scores or percentiles with the current norming data.

• The CELF is a complex collection of subtests that requires a substantial time commitment on the part of the examiner, in both administration and interpretation of the battery. Fortunately, a videotape is available from the publisher for training in administration of the diagnostic battery. Clinicians may need to present portions of the CELF over several sessions with their students to complete the entire battery. In addition, completion of split-half reliability and related studies would be useful in determining whether the battery could be shortened without loss of important diagnostic information.

• Although the CELF is a comprehensive diagnostic tool, the authors suggest that a standardized measure of receptive vocabulary and analysis of a spontaneous speech sample be included as part of the testing process. Academic and intellectual testing may also be needed to complete an assessment of a school-age child.

• Even though the test manual does describe dialectal variations in morphology and syntax, the authors caution clinicians about interpreting the performance of culturally and ethnically different students. Consideration should be given to the development of a Spanish version of this battery in the future.

• Validity studies of the CELF are sparse and need to be expanded.

CELF ELEMENTARY AND ADVANCED LEVEL SCREENING TESTS

These two tests were developed by the authors of the CELF diagnostic battery, Elisabeth Wiig and Eleanor Semel-Mintz, to provide a measure for screening language-processing and language-production abilities of school-age children.

Each screening test contains separate language-processing and language-production sections that can be administered and scored in approximately 15 minutes. The Elementary

Level test covers kindergarten through grade 5 and consists of an adaptation of the "Simon Says" game and a set of expressive language tasks (phrase completions, repetition of sentences and polysyllabic words, serial recall, and word opposites). The Advanced Level, spanning grades 5 to 12, involves a series of oral directions using an array of playing cards and a higher-level version of language-production tasks.

The language-processing sections of both screening tests probe aspects of the following:

1. Accuracy in phoneme discrimination
2. Sentence formation rules
3. Interpretation of words and logical relationships among sentence components and linguistic concepts
4. Retention and recall of word and action sequences

Language-production items assess the following areas:

1. Agility and accuracy in phoneme production
2. Ability to recall, identify, and retrieve words and concepts
3. Accuracy in serial recall
4. Immediate recall of model sentences

Both screening tests were standardized in order to identify children who need an in-depth assessment of oral language. Percentile ranks by grade level are provided for the language-processing section, the language-production section, and the total test. The authors suggest that the CELF diagnostic battery be administered to students scoring below the fifteenth percentile on the total screening test or below the tenth percentile on either portion of the test. The same norming population was used to standardize the CELF screening tests and diagnostic battery.

Peabody Picture Vocabulary Test—Revised (PPVT-R)

Lloyd M. Dunn and Leota M. Dunn
American Guidance Service, Inc., 1959; revised 1965; 1981
Publishers' Bldg., Circle Pines, MN 55014

Purpose	To assess an individual's receptive (hearing) vocabulary for standard American English
Major Areas Tested	Receptive single-word vocabulary
Age or Grade Range	2½–40 years
Usually Given By	Special education teacher Psychologist Speech/language clinician
Type of Test	Standardized Individual
Scores Obtained	Age level Standard Percentile Stanine
Student Performance Timed?	No
Testing Time	10–20 minutes
Scoring/Interpretation Time	10–15 minutes
Normed On	Carefully selected nationwide sample of 5,028 persons, including 4,200 children, balanced for age, sex, geographic region, socioeconomic level, ethnicity, and community size
Alternate Forms Available?	Yes

FORMAT

The Peabody Picture Vocabulary Test—Revised (PPVT-R) consists of two equivalent forms, L and M. For each form there is an easel-book of line drawings printed four on a page and individual student record forms. There is one examiner's manual including administration and scoring procedures and norms tables covering both forms. A technical supplement provides more detailed information on test construction and standardization.

To administer the test, the examiner pronounces a word, and the student selects the corresponding picture ("Show me *meringue*."). No verbal response is needed because the student can simply point to the correct picture. The vocabulary words gradually increase in difficulty, from such items as *arrow, furry,* and *vase* to *ascending* and *trajectory*.

Although all the items are together in one picture book, the student is tested on only the vocabulary appropriate for his or her age and language development. There are no subtests. Equivalent forms L and M may be given in alternate sessions to increase the reliability of the score, or they may be used as pre- and posttests for evaluating a student's progress. The manual includes detailed directions for administering and scoring, as well as tables for converting raw scores to age equivalents, standard scores, percentiles, and stanines.

The primary changes in the PPVT-R over the 1965 edition include the following:

1. The test was standardized nationwide and the sample was balanced for age, sex, geographic region, socioeconomic level, ethnicity, and community size.

2. The terms "mental age" and "intelligence quotient" were changed to "age equivalent" and "standard score equivalent."

3. Two-thirds of the stimulus items were replaced with new items and 25 items were added to each form to increase the instrument's sensitivity and reliability.

4. The racial, ethnic, and sex balance in the line drawings was improved.

STRENGTHS OF THE PPVT-R

• The PPVT-R is well designed and well normed. The format of presenting a picture to elicit a pointing response makes it a nonthreatening test that even the young or seriously impaired student can take successfully. It is frequently used as the first in a battery of tests, because its easy format makes it a good warm-up for more difficult material. The wide age range covered by the PPVT-R and its alternate forms make it a good instrument for test-retest purposes; it can be administered every year to assess a student's progress in specific language therapy or in general language development. The PPVT-R is relatively quick to administer and interpret. Although it is usually used as a global measure of receptive vocabulary, analysis of a student's errors can reveal information about the specific nature of a vocabulary deficit. For example, student errors on such items as *filing, assaulting,* and *lecturing* would seem to indicate difficulty with verbs.

LIMITING FACTORS OF THE PPVT-R

• The PPVT-R is a test of single-word vocabulary only. The comprehension of spoken language in context is a different skill, and the examiner must not assume that a student's receptive language is adequate simply because he or she obtains a high PPVT-R score. Knowing the meaning of *group* when it is pronounced clearly and represented by a picture of five children is quite different from understanding the word when the teacher says, "First do the group of subtraction problems on page 10, and then do the group on page 14, starting with line 3." In addition, the PPVT-R assesses only receptive vocabulary. A high PPVT-R score may not predict high verbal performance in the classroom. Understanding a word and using it correctly in spoken language are two different skills.

• The PPVT-R does not assess all parts of speech. Only nouns, verbs, and adjectives are included. The understanding of prepositions, a critical skill, is not included.

• The standardization sample of the PPVT-R is greatly improved over the original sample and includes students of various ethnic backgrounds, races, and socioeconomic levels. However, it is still important to consider the effects of different cultural backgrounds on test performance. Students from different cultures or disadvantaged homes may not have had experience with the pictured items. In a student from a middle-class home and community, a low score may reflect a true deficit in ability to comprehend spoken language, but in a student from a culturally different or disadvantaged background, a low score may reflect lack of language stimulation or experience. The program for developing language skills in these two students would be quite different.

• As in all tests, the student's attention span is a big factor in performance. Low scores on the PPVT-R may be related to impulsive responses caused by an inability to scan four pictures. Or they may result from perseveration—continued pointing to the same position on the page. Such behavior is not unusual in low-functioning children with physical, emotional, or attention problems. A low PPVT-R score therefore may not reflect low vocabulary development but rather an inability to scan and select visual material.

• In the PPVT-R, hearing vocabulary is measured through picture stimuli. Clearly, two processes are involved in doing this: the understanding of the spoken word and the understanding of the line drawings. A low score may not necessarily reflect a problem in receptive vocabulary but possibly a problem in comprehending pictures. For example, a student may know the meaning of the word *exterior* but be unable to interpret which drawing is the *outside* of the house and which is the *inside*. Other measures of receptive vocabulary and picture comprehension are needed to confirm the results of the PPVT-R if a specific definition of the disability is needed.

Assessment of Children's Language Comprehension (ACLC)

R. Foster, J. Gidden, and J. Stark
Consulting Psychologists Press, Inc., 1973
577 College Ave., Palo Alto, CA 94306

Purpose	To define receptive language problems in young children using single-word vocabulary and phrases
Major Areas Tested	Receptive language
Age or Grade Range	3–7 years
Usually Given By	Speech/language clinician
Type of Test	Standardized Individual Group
Scores Obtained	Ratio Percentage
Student Performance Timed?	No
Testing Time	15–20 minutes
Scoring/Interpretation Time	5 minutes
Normed On	A small sample of normal nursery school and kindergarten children from diverse socioeconomic levels and ethnic groups in Florida and California
Alternate Forms Available?	No

FORMAT

The Assessment of Children's Language Comprehension (ACLC) materials consist of a spiral-bound book of silhouette and line drawings, a teacher's manual, and record sheets. The test has four sections. Part A assesses the student's comprehension of a core vocabulary of 50 single words (nouns, verbs, prepositions, and modifiers). The examiner pronounces the words one at a time, and the student responds by pointing to the correct drawing from a group of five. Testing is terminated if it becomes apparent that the student does not know the core vocabulary.

Parts B, C, and D each consist of 10 items using the core vocabulary in phrases of two, three, and four critical elements. For example: *horse standing, broken cup* (two critical elements); *chicken in the basket, happy lady sleeping* (three critical elements); *happy little girl jumping, cat standing under the bed* (four critical elements). The examiner pronounces the phrase, and the student points to the correct drawing. A record sheet for each student is used to note the error patterns.

A group form of the ACLC also exists, composed of 17 plates from the complete version. This is used as a screening test for groups. Each student receives a booklet and marks the appropriate pictures in response to the words and phrases given by the teacher.

STRENGTHS OF THE ACLC

- The ACLC is an inexpensive test and is easy to give and score. Very young and nonverbal children can be assessed with this measure, because it requires no verbal responses. The pictures are generally clear and unconfusing. Simple directions, easy responses, and a relatively fast pace hold the attention of most young children.

- The analysis of error patterns yields good information for planning therapy and for communicating information to parents. For instance, knowing that their young child cannot retain more than two critical elements (for example, *broken cup*) helps parents understand why the child cannot retain and comprehend longer utterances and directions. If analysis of error patterns indicates difficulty primarily in a certain area, such as verbs in isolation and in phrases, a remediation program is suggested. Such information is clearly observable on the well-organized score sheet.

- The manual presents an overview of language development and impairment as well as information on the design of the ACLC. Guidelines are given for language training based on expansion of critical elements.

- The new ACLC protocols contain a Spanish translation of stimulus items on the reverse side. Although normative data has not been developed for this translation, it is useful in the assessment of receptive language skills in bilingual or monolingual Spanish-speaking students.

LIMITING FACTORS OF THE ACLC

- Normative data are considered tentative and are based on an earlier form, but new and more complete norms are being collected. The numbers tested at certain age levels are very small: 16 children at 3 years to 3 years, 5 months. Data comparing performance on the group screening test with performance on the complete, individually administered scale are not yet available.

- Interpretation of the results is easiest for students with significant language problems. Only percentage scores are given; without the aid of standard deviations, it is difficult to interpret borderline performance accurately.

- Young children with visual scanning problems may have difficulty attending to all the pictures prior to selecting the appropriate one. They need to be taught how to look at all the pictures on a page before their responses can be considered valid.

Test for Auditory Comprehension of Language (TACL)

Elizabeth Carrow
Learning Concepts, Inc., 1973; revised 1977
2501 N. Lamar Blvd., Austin, TX 78705

Purpose	To measure auditory comprehension of vocabulary and structure (syntax and grammar) in English- and Spanish-speaking students
Major Areas Tested	Receptive language
Age or Grade Range	3–7 years
Usually Given By	Speech/language clinician
Type of Test	Standardized Individual Group (Screening Test)
Scores Obtained	Age level Percentile
Student Performance Timed?	No
Testing Time	20–30 minutes
Scoring/Interpretation Time	10–15 minutes
Normed On	200 middle-class Black, Caucasian, and Mexican-American children
Alternate Forms Available?	No

FORMAT

The materials for the Test for Auditory Comprehension of Language (TACL) consist of the test manual and response sheets. In the manual are directions for administration and interpretation, information on test development, and 101 plates of test pictures. The pictures, arranged three per page, are black-and-white line drawings (see Figures 51 and 52).

With Figure 51, the examiner says, "His puppy is black and white" or "El perrito de él es blanco y negro." With Figure 52, the examiner says, "Second" or "Segundo." The student responds by pointing to the picture representing the vocabulary or structure given. No oral response is required. Responses are recorded on a form that includes information on the ages at which 75 percent and 90 percent of the normative sample passed each item. An analysis section organizes recorded errors under the headings Vocabulary, Morphology, and Syntax. Raw scores for the total test are converted to age-equivalent scores and percentiles.

A screening version of the TACL is also available, with 25 items from the longer version. It can be given to small groups of students. The author recommends that a student who scores below the tenth percentile for his or her age on the screening test be given the full test.

STRENGTHS OF THE TACL

- The TACL is relatively easy to administer and score. Directions for presentation are clear. Tables for the interpretation of scores are well organized and easy to use.
- Diagnostic information provided on the response sheet can be useful in planning remediation. Specific areas of need, such as pronouns, may emerge in the analysis of performance. However, further assessment would be necessary to determine thoroughly the deficits in such an area, because only a few items are provided in each category.
- The TACL demonstrates high test-retest reliability, according to several studies reported in the manual, and is valuable in showing a developmental progression in the comprehension of language. Scores increase with both age and subsequent language development.
- Words used to test linguistic structures have first been tested in their basic form. For instance, *tall* is tested prior to *taller*. Thus, there is some control in assessing acquisition of morphological features.
- The nonverbal response mode makes the test useful with young or nonverbal students.

LIMITING FACTORS OF THE TACL

- The entire test must be presented in order to make use

Figure 51. TACL, Item 28

Speech and Language Tests

of the normative data, but its length—101 plates—makes it tedious for young and immature students. Even normally developing children of lower age levels may miss half the items presented. The amount of failure and the resulting confusion may make this an inefficient means of assessing the language comprehension of young children delayed in development.

- The pictured stimuli make the TACL a test of visual processing as well as language processing. The student's ability to concentrate on, scan, and interpret the pictures should be noted in addition to performance on the test.

- Although mean scores and standard deviations are provided for six-month age intervals, they are not very discriminating. For example, a raw score of 58 is within normal limits for both a child of 3 years and a child of 4 years, 5 months. A raw score of 80 is within normal limits for children from 4 years to 6 years, 5 months. This means that only students with serious language problems can be identified with the TACL. Although a screening test of 25 items is available, it is of questionable value when the complete test is so imprecise and nondiscriminating. The long version of the TACL would more appropriately be thought of as a screening test except for its lengthy administration time.

- In the analysis section of the response sheet, the assignment of certain structure errors to Morphology is not clear. For instance, errors in prepositions would seem to be listed more correctly under Vocabulary than under Morphology. And errors in answering questions beginning with *who, what,* and *when* reflect problems in the comprehension of syntactic transformations rather than in morphology.

- The Spanish version of the TACL is a translation of the English test. This is a questionable procedure for obtaining information about a student's auditory understanding of Spanish. Differences in Spanish grammar, structure, and regional vocabulary may result in errors that do not reflect comprehension level. In addition, no norms are available for the Spanish version, making it interesting but of little diagnostic value.

Figure 52. TACL, Item 63

Boehm Test of Basic Concepts (Boehm)

Ann E. Boehm
The Psychological Corporation, 1967; Form A, 1969; Form B, 1971
7500 Old Oak Blvd., Middleburg Heights, OH 44130

Purpose	To assess knowledge of concepts basic to early academic success and to identify students with low-level concept mastery
Major Areas Tested	Comprehension of space, quantity, and time concepts
Age or Grade Range	Grades K–2
Usually Given By	Classroom teacher Special education teacher Speech/language clinician
Type of Test	Standardized Individual Group (Screening Test)
Scores Obtained	Percentile
Student Performance Timed?	No
Testing Time	30–40 minutes
Scoring/Interpretation Time	10 minutes
Normed On	More than 12,000 urban children from grades K–2 throughout the United States
Alternate Forms Available?	Yes

Speech and Language Tests

FORMAT

The Boehm Test of Basic Concepts (Boehm) materials include the manual, test booklets, and class record forms. The manual provides directions for administering, scoring, and interpreting the test and gives some information on test development and standardization.

Alternate test Forms A and B are available; each comprises Booklets I and II, containing 25 items each. Concepts of space, quantity, and time are assessed in approximate order of difficulty. For example, the concept *next to* occurs near the beginning of the test, and *half* is the last concept in Booklet I.

The test may be given either individually or to a small group. The teacher reads the directions for each item from the manual. In the test booklets, the students mark the picture or aspect of the picture that correctly portrays the concept presented. For example, in using the item shown in Figure 53, the examiner would say, "Look at the toys. Mark the toy that is *next to* the truck. Mark the toy that is *next to* the truck."

The number of correct responses is tallied, and the total is converted to a percentile score related to age, grade placement, and socioeconomic class.

On the class record form, space is provided for recording the success or failure of 30 students on each item. Such information leads directly to group language lessons.

STRENGTHS OF THE BOEHM

- The Boehm is an inexpensive way to assess the understanding of space, quantity, and time concepts in young school-aged students. Most young children find it interesting. The illustrations are clear, and the format is well organized. A gross marking response is adequate. A pointing response may also be used if the student is unable to handle a pencil or crayon and if the test is being individually administered.

- The manual is also well organized, and it is informative, providing extensive information on test development, analysis of results, normative data, and remediation approaches. Performance information on students from different socioeconomic levels is included from kindergarten to grade 2. Also included is information on students' performance at the beginning and middle of the year. The manual lists concepts known by most students of the ages tested and therefore not included on the test. These concepts include *bottom*, *flat*, *straight*, and *fast/slow*, and they should be assessed informally in students who have great difficulty with the Boehm material.

- The mechanics of presentation and scoring are simple. Thoughtfully employed, the test results can be useful to teachers in identifying the needs of individual students and planning remediation.

- Directions for the Boehm have been translated into Spanish, suitable for both Puerto Rican and Chicano children. Spanish-speaking aides or teachers can administer the test using the same picture booklets.

LIMITING FACTORS OF THE BOEHM

- The concepts were initially chosen through a review of curriculum materials in reading, math, and science. But the criteria for selection, described in the manual, are subjective and not well defined. They include (1) concepts occurring frequently in curriculum materials, (2) concepts not usually defined in curriculum materials, and (3) concepts representing relatively abstract basic ideas. The meanings of *frequently* and *relatively abstract* are not clarified.

- It is claimed that the concepts in the Boehm are basic to academic success in the early years of school. However, no

Figure 53. Boehm Test, Form A, Item 4

documentation of this is given. Both a review of the literature and validity data are missing.

• The Boehm is described as useful for kindergarten through grade 2. However, analysis of typical performances indicates that the test may be too easy to be of value for first graders from middle and upper socioeconomic levels and for second graders from all socioeconomic levels. For instance, at the second-grade level, all but two items from Booklet I were passed by 90 percent of the students.

• Knowledge of a concept in one context does not insure familiarity with it in another context. For example, a child may be able to identify *nearest* and *farthest* with objects but not recognize the concepts in pictured form. Furthermore, the concept may be understood, but the specific label called for in the test may not be known. For example, a student may understand the concept *same,* but when the direction labels it as *alike,* the student may not be able to equate that label with the concept he or she understands.

• Although this is a test of concept understanding, it presumes a certain level of language comprehension. The directions include complex language, such as, "Look at the pictures of the house and the boy. Mark the house with the boy *inside* it." It is possible for a student to fail to understand these directions but demonstrate comprehension of the concept *inside* in another context. The test manual does caution about the interpretation of errors.

• Individual and group presentations are described in the manual. However, individual administration is recommended for children suspected of having difficulty in this area. Analysis of the student's performance during testing will enable the examiner to interpret performance more accurately.

Token Test for Children (Token Test)
Frank DiSimoni
Teaching Resources Corporation, 1978
50 Pond Park Rd., Hingham, MA 02043

Purpose	To provide a quick measure of receptive language
Major Areas Tested	Receptive language
Age or Grade Range	3–12½ years
Usually Given By	Speech/language clinician
Type of Test	Standardized Individual Norm-referenced
Scores Obtained	Age level Grade level Standard
Student Performance Timed?	No
Testing Time	15 minutes
Scoring/Interpretation Time	10–15 minutes
Normed On	1,304 students with no language problems, ranging from 3 to 12½ years of age, from eastern United States suburban communities where standard American English was spoken; sample balanced for sex and socioeconomic status
Alternate Forms Available?	No

FORMAT

The Token Test for Children (Token Test) is an adaptation of the original Token Test developed by DeRenzi and Vignolo (1962) to assess subtle receptive language deficits in aphasic adults. A few years later, Noll (1970) developed the test format described below, and in 1978, the present author provided the normative data.

The materials consist of 20 wooden or plastic tokens; a manual including background of the test, administration and scoring procedures, and norms for children; and individual test protocols for recording student's responses and results. The 20 tokens include two shapes (square and circle), two sizes (small and large), and five colors (red, blue, yellow, green, and white).

The administration of the Token Test is very easy. The tokens are placed in a prescribed arrangement in front of the student. First, the examiner determines that the student knows the meaning of the words *square, circle, large,* and *small* and can recognize the five colors by name. Testing is discontinued if this criterion is not met. Then the examiner proceeds with the test, giving the student a series of commands involving the tokens. The 61 commands are divided into five subtests, increasing in linguistic complexity. Examples of items are given below.

Item 8. *Touch the white circle.*
Item 18. *Touch the small blue circle.*
Item 28. *Touch the green circle and the blue square.*
Item 38. *Touch the large blue circle and the large green circle.*
Item 48. *Put the white circle in front of the blue square.*

On some subtests all 20 tokens are used, on others only the 10 large tokens are used. Every student begins with the first item. Unless several errors are made in the first subtest, the student completes the entire test. The subtests must be given in consecutive order, and the entire test must be given to obtain a score. All commands may be given only once, and the student's response is scored as correct or incorrect. Correct responses are totaled for each subtest and for the total test. These raw scores are converted into scaled scores for age and grade. The scaled scores have a mean of 500 and a standard deviation of 5, therefore "average" performance is between 495 and 505. A rating of "superior" performance is given to scores of 506 or higher, while scores of 494 or lower are called "inferior." Since the Token Test is considered a rapid screening device providing a gross measure of functional language, students obtaining a low score should not be labeled "inferior" but should be referred for further testing of vocabulary and syntax.

STRENGTHS OF THE TOKEN TEST

- The Token Test is a quick measure of basic receptive skills. The test is easy to administer and score, and the manipulation of the tokens is an interesting format for most students.
- The test is well constructed. The vocabulary is carefully controlled, as is the increasing linguistic complexity. Commands are short to reduce auditory memory to a minimal level.
- The original Token Test has been used extensively as a measure of receptive language functioning in populations of aphasic adults. The standardization for children has been carefully done, and the validity and reliability studies are clearly reported in the manual.
- In addition to the scaled scores, means and standard deviations for the norming population by age and grade level are included, which is useful in interpreting scores.
- Analysis of the subtest scores, which really represent levels of complexity, allow the examiner to determine the length of utterance and complexity at which language processing breaks down.

LIMITING FACTORS OF THE TOKEN TEST

- The Token Test has some limitations for preschool children. Three-year-olds and 5-year-olds are not well represented in the norming sample. Even more important, the length of the test—61 commands—requires the child to continue long past the level he or she is supposed to get correct. For example, a scaled score of 500 for a 3-year-old requires only 20 correct responses, yet the child must complete the 61 items. A ceiling procedure would be very helpful for the young child.
- The older, language-impaired student also may find the test quite difficult and may experience a sense of failure.
- The age scores are more appropriate for comparisons than the grade scores, for several reasons. First, language skills such as those tested by the Token Test are more meaningful when discussed in relation to age. Second, the age scores are broken into norms for each six-month period, while grade scores cover the entire school year.
- The term "subtest" is misleading. The subtests on the Token Test represent not different linguistic skills but rather levels of linguistic complexity. Therefore, the total test score is more meaningful.
- The use of a scaled score with a mean of 500 and standard deviation of 5 is unusual and requires explanation in test reports or in interpretation to parents or teachers.

Northwestern Syntax Screening Test (NSST)

Laura Lee
Northwestern University Press, 1969; revised 1971
1735 Benson Ave., Evanston, IL 60201

Purpose	To provide a quick estimate of a student's syntactic development and to identify those students requiring more thorough language evaluation
Major Areas Tested	Receptive and expressive language
Age or Grade Range	3–7 years
Usually Given By	Speech/language clinician
Type of Test	Standardized Individual
Scores Obtained	Age level Percentile
Student Performance Timed?	No
Testing Time	15–25 minutes
Scoring/Interpretation Time	15 minutes
Normed On	344 children from the middle and upper-middle classes in suburban Chicago, Illinois
Alternate Forms Available?	No

FORMAT

The materials for the Northwestern Syntax Screening Test (NSST) include a spiral-bound book of test pictures, an examiner's manual, and individual record forms. The test consists of 40 items—20 receptive and 20 expressive. In the receptive section, four black-and-white line drawings are displayed on each page, and in the expressive section, two drawings are displayed on each page. A demonstration item precedes each section. The norms and the instructions for presentation, interpretation, and scoring are all included in the manual. The individual record forms provide for scoring of individual responses.

Sentence pairs are arranged in the order in which the normative population accomplished the tasks. Consequently, identical structures are presented in a somewhat different sequence in the two sections. Among the structures assessed are prepositional phrases, negation, and subject-verb agreement. Vocabulary and structure are controlled; only the structure being assessed varies.

In administering the receptive portion, the examiner verbally presents the two statements or question forms given on the record form. These are given without the use of stress or intonation. Each statement or question is then regiven individually, and the student indicates the picture best described by it.

For the expressive section, the examiner verbally presents the key statements pertaining to the two pictures. The student is then asked to repeat the appropriate statement or question as the examiner points to each picture.

STRENGTHS OF THE NSST

- The NSST provides a quick and relatively easy means of screening the receptive and expressive language abilities of 3- to 8-year-old middle- and upper-middle-class white children.
- A study by Ratusnik and Koenigsknecht (1975) has demonstrated the value of the NSST for differentiating among normal language development, severely delayed expressive language, and retarded language development. Internal consistency of the NSST was demonstrated in their findings.
- A student's performance on the NSST often provides the examiner with hints as to what area needs further evaluation. For example, a student who fails to discriminate between *the shelf* and *himself* may need in-depth assessment of auditory discrimination skills.
- The NSST may be useful in evaluating a student's progress in therapy. Comparison with the student's own past performances may reveal progress in the comprehension and expression of specific structures.
- A short method for screening large numbers of children is described in the introduction to the NSST (revised 1971).

LIMITING FACTORS OF THE NSST

- The NSST was standardized on a limited socio-economic population (middle- and upper-middle classes) from a single geographical area. Applicability of the norms to other populations is questionable, and the author has expressed the need for those using the test to develop local norms.
- A narrow range of performance is noted at the 7- to 8-year-old age level, with only a four-point difference between those scoring at the tenth and the ninetieth percentiles. The author of the test states that these scores were included so that examiners would note the cutoff at age 8.
- The norms were derived from a limited sampling. At three of the five given age levels, fewer than 50 subjects were included.
- The NSST is designed as a screening instrument only. More thorough investigation of structures, pronouns, and prepositions is necessary before making definitive diagnostic statements or planning remediation.
- Only limited information regarding test development, reliability, and validity has been published.

Sequenced Inventory of Communication Development (SICD)

E. Prather Hedrick and A. Tobin
University of Washington Press, 1975
4045 Brooklyn N.E., Seattle, WA 98105

Purpose	To evaluate development of verbal and nonverbal communication in very young children and to estimate levels of receptive and expressive language functioning
Major Areas Tested	Receptive and expressive communication
Age or Grade Range	4 months–4 years
Usually Given By	Special education teacher Speech/language clinician
Type of Test	Standardized Individual Criterion-referenced
Scores Obtained	Age level
Student Performance Timed?	No
Testing Time	30–75 minutes
Scoring/Interpretation Time	30 minutes
Normed On	252 Caucasian children from the upper, middle, and lower socioeconomic levels in Seattle, Washington
Alternate Forms Available?	No

FORMAT

The materials for the Sequenced Inventory of Communication Development (SICD) consist of a kit of objects used in administering the test, an examiner's manual, and two test booklets (receptive and expressive scales) for each student. The manual includes information on test development, directions for administration and scoring, and tables to aid in test interpretation. The "receptive" and "expressive" test booklets each include a profile sheet for recording responses and for viewing patterns of success and failure systematically.

The SICD is based on a model of early communication patterns and the interaction of behaviors. Many of these behaviors are not linguistic in nature but represent ways that a young child relates to the environment. Some test items have been adapted from well-established sources, such as the Denver Developmental Screening Test (p. 233) and the Illinois Test of Psycholinguistic Abilities (p. 141).

Factors included on the receptive scale are awareness, discrimination, and understanding. Skills are documented by observation of motor responses to sound or speech clues and by parental reports of the child's responses to sounds and speech at home. Examples of the skills evaluated in each area follow. These tasks are passed by 75 percent of the children at the given age levels.

Awareness
Sound: Baby turns to sound of rattle and cellophane (8 months).
Speech: Baby looks up or smiles in response to "Hi there" (8 months).

Discrimination
Sound: Baby responds to environmental sounds at home, such as phone ringing (16 months).
Speech: Child discriminates between words such as *socks* and *box, tree* and *key,* and *bear* and *chair* by pointing to objects (24 to 28 months).

Understanding
Words plus situational cues: Child responds to command "Give it to me" (28 months).
Words: Child indicates correct blocks as examiner names colors (36 to 44 months).

Communicative behaviors analyzed on the expressive scale are imitation, initiation, and response. Parental report of behaviors is also included on this scale. Examples of the skills evaluated in each area follow.

Imitation
Motor: Child imitates examiner, placing blocks in box (16 months).
Vocal: Child imitates intonation patterns heard at home (20 months).
Verbal: Child imitates common words on request (28 months).

Initiation
Motor: Child uses gestures to elicit labeling response from parent (24 months).
Vocal: Child uses questioning inflection (16 months).

Verbal: Child asks "Why?" at home (40 months).

Response
Vocal: Child responds vocally to parents' verbalizing (4 months).
Verbal: Child names objects such as car, spoon, and shoe (36 months).

Verbal output and articulation may be analyzed as expressive behaviors, but they are not included in the scoring of the expressive scale. An articulation profile sheet is included with each expressive scale test booklet. The language sample is obtained following the methods outlined by Johnson, Darley, and Spriestersbach (1963). A mean length response and a structural complexity score can be derived. A description of the child's language structure may also be recorded on the record form by indicating the structures observed—for example, use of adverbs (36 months).

STRENGTHS OF THE SICD

- The SICD provides a means of assessing the language skills of very young children through parent report and observation. The inclusion of nonverbal tasks that are precursors to later language development is what makes this test valuable with the very young, as well as with very impaired children.

- Interexaminer and test-retest reliability are high. A high correlation between the receptive communication age and expressive communication age would be expected and is reported in the manual. The mean scores obtained by normal subjects closely resemble chronological age.

- The manual is very thorough. Specific directions for administering and scoring are presented, and several tables help in understanding test construction and student performance. Mean scores and standard deviations assist the examiner in interpreting performance accurately.

- By incorporating supplemental information from articulation testing, language sampling, and other assessment tools with the SICD, a total communication diagnosis can be established. If the child's errors are viewed in terms of consistency and with reference to developmental stages and overall level of functioning, goals for remediation can be selected.

- With experience, the examiner will find the test flexible to administer. Receptive and expressive tasks can be interspersed, depending on the child's interest. The use of objects, as well as pictures, to elicit language appeals to young children.

LIMITING FACTORS OF THE SICD

- Practice is required to become comfortable with test administration. Tasks vary, and the manipulation of the objects can be confusing for the examiner and distracting for the child.

- As the authors of the test point out, caution should be

used in interpreting the results. Results should be integrated with performance on other assessment tools to provide a thorough picture of an individual child's functioning. The authors stress that differences between the receptive communication age and expressive communication age of one age level (4 months) are not significant diagnostically.

- The SICD was normed on white children from the Northwest, and caution must be used when interpreting the results of other racial and geographical groups.

Developmental Sentence Scoring (DSS)

Laura Lee and R. A. Koenigsknecht
Northwestern University Press, 1974
1735 Benson Ave., Evanston, IL 60201

Purpose	To provide a systematic procedure for analyzing a student's grammatical structure and for estimating the extent to which the student has learned generalized grammatical rules enough to use them in conversation
Major Areas Tested	Grammatical structure of spoken language
Age or Grade Range	2–7 years
Usually Given By	Speech/language clinician
Type of Test	Individual
Scores Obtained	Percentile
Student Performance Timed?	No
Testing Time	30–60 minutes
Scoring/Interpretation Time	2 hours
Normed On	200 white monolingual children between ages 2 and 7 years, from middle-income homes where standard American English was spoken
Alternate Forms Available?	No

FORMAT

Developmental Sentence Scoring (DSS) involves obtaining a conversational language sample by using stimulus materials that the student is interested in, such as toys or pictures provided by the clinician. A corpus of 50 different, consecutive, intelligible, nonecholalic, complete (subject and verb) sentences is used for analysis. The authors state that this procedure, therefore, is appropriate only for students who use complete sentence structures at least 50 percent of the time. Fragmentary utterances are discarded from the sample. Detailed information about elicitation of the sample and the acceptability of various utterances in the language corpus is provided by the authors in the book containing the test (Lee and Koenigsknecht 1974).

The utterances are evaluated in terms of eight grammatical features that psycholinguistic research has found to be early components of language. Research has also provided information about their developmental progression. These features are based on transformational generative grammar (Chomsky 1957, 1965) and case grammar (Brown 1973; Fillmore 1968). The grammatical criteria includes the following:

1. Indefinite pronouns and/or noun modifiers
2. Personal pronouns
3. Main verbs
4. Secondary verbs
5. Negatives
6. Conjunctions
7. Interrogative reversals
8. *Wh-* question words

Each grammatical form present in a sample utterance is independently assigned a score from 1 to 8 points according to a weighted scoring system. The weighted scores indicate a developmental sequence of grammatical growth within each category. Furthermore, an additional sentence point may be added if the entire utterance is correct in all aspects—syntactically as well as semantically. This sentence point is designed, in part, to account for other grammatical features not individually scored, such as plurals, possessive markers, word order, and prepositions.

Comprehensive scoring guidelines are provided by the authors in both tabular and narrative form. Emerging structures may be indicated by inserting attempt marks (–) under the appropriate categories. A model chart format for listing and scoring the transcribed sentences appears in the authors' book (Lee and Koenigsknecht 1974), but practical tables must be made by the clinician. The DSS scoring procedure is illustrated in Table 20.

Scores for the 50-sentence utterance sample are totaled; then the mean score per sentence is computed. This is the Developmental Sentence Score (DSS), which is compared with the normative data available for the student's chronological age. Percentile values have been computed for the ninetieth, seventy-fifth, fiftieth, twenty-fifth, and tenth percentile ranks at six-month intervals for ages 2 to 7. An estimate of the student's expressive language level can be obtained by finding the age range where the DSS is approximately equivalent to the fiftieth-percentile score.

The authors suggest, in addition, that students scoring close to the tenth percentile for their age receive further speech and language evaluation and be considered potential candidates for therapy. When the DSS is used to measure progress, the authors state that students might be dismissed from therapy when their scores approximate the lower limits of the normal range for their age group. However, other important factors, such as conceptual development and auditory skills, must be taken into consideration.

STRENGTHS OF DSS

- DSS is an inexpensive language assessment procedure, with an authors' book that provides all the information necessary for administration and interpretation. Transcription forms are not provided, but they can easily be designed by the clinician.

- Because DSS is a detailed, painstaking procedure, a thorough reading of the author's book is necessary. Comprehensive information about various utterance types in the language corpus is included. Numerous examples illustrate the method of developmental scoring. The convenient chart provided by the authors usually contains enough specific scoring information to meet the requirements of typical language samples. Background psycholinguistic research and essential language-sampling techniques are also concisely presented.

- It is felt that 50 spontaneous and complete sentences is a reasonable number to use in assessing language-impaired children. There is no sufficient evidence that supports the collection of larger samples for analysis purposes. In fact, established criteria do not yet exist for determining adequate sample size for linguistic analysis.

- A significant amount of diagnostic information can be obtained by examining the scatter of scores on DSS charts, because consistent error categories and stereotyped structures are indicated in repetitive scoring patterns. The chart makes it especially easy to see what structures are missing and what forms the child is consistently substituting for others.

- Many psycholinguistic researchers and therapists of language-disordered students have espoused language-sampling measures such as DSS over traditional tests of morphological and syntactic competency. They feel that conversational speech places a "grammatical load" on the student because it requires the student to combine several transformations into single sentences. As a student gains linguistic competence with age, one can expect progressive

Table 20. DSS Scoring Procedure*

Sentence	Indefinite Pronoun/ Noun Modifier	Personal Pronoun	Primary Verb	Secondary Verb	Negative	Conjunction	Interrogative Reversal	Wh- Question Word	Sentence Point	Total
I want to eat.		1 I	1 want	2 to eat					1	5
What you doing?		1 you	– are (omitted)					2 what	0	3
The dog won't go in the house.			4 won't go		5 won't				1	10
She's trying to take it off.	1 it	2 she	1 is trying	5 to take					1	10
He drinked all the milk.	3 all	2 he	– drinked/ drank						0	5
Look at me!		1 me	1 look						1	3
He said, "Where's my house?"		2, 1 he, my	2, 1 said, is				1 where is my house?	2 where	1	10

*Numbers in columns indicate points assigned to each element.

growth in the grammatical load of his or her utterances. This increasing load results from mastery of new, higher-level morphological forms and syntactic structures, as well as growth in the number of forms and structures that the student can incorporate into a single utterance. DSS assesses the impact of both these developmental aspects. In addition, rule consistency and frequency of usage can also be assessed more accurately in conversational speech than under rigid testing conditions.

- The validity of a test of conversational language behavior is difficult to assess directly because adequate and appropriate external criteria are lacking. Therefore, determining the internal consistency of DSS and the consistency of repeated applications with different clinicians and different stimulus materials becomes more significant.

Validity of the DSS construct was established when the test was normed on 200 children from middle-income homes. Validity was indicated by the significant differences between age groups in the overall scoring procedure, as well as by all the component grammatical categories. Further validity was obtained through verification of the grammatical hierarchies in a reciprocal averaging procedure that resulted in a minor revision of the original weighted scoring system of DSS, presented in 1971.

High reliability coefficients obtained by DSS lend major support to the scoring procedure. The overall internal consistency was .71 (estimated by coefficient Alpha), and the reliability coefficient for the overall DSS was .73.

LIMITING FACTORS OF DSS

- DSS is a highly time-consuming procedure as compared with other conventional language-assessment techniques. Inherent in it are great opportunities for errors in transcribing and scoring the language samples. To minimize such errors, it is recommended that clinicians transcribe and score their own samples, using the authors' book to clarify the scoring procedure when necessary.

- Caution should be exercised in comparing a student's DSS with the percentile scores presented by the authors. The sample used to obtain normative data for each six-month age period was small (20 individuals). Furthermore, criteria used to determine the "normalcy" of these subjects' language appears to have been inadequate. The only objective, standardized measure of adequate language skill was a score within one standard deviation of the mean for age on the Peabody Picture Vocabulary Test—Revised (p. 155). Other criteria included normal developmental histories without reports of overt hearing problems, severe misarticulations, or discernible behavioral problems. More intensive evaluation of language skills with other standardized measures should have been undertaken.

- The usefulness of DSS is limited by the fact that the end product is a score rather than a descriptive, composite picture of the student's linguistic performance. Errors merely reduce a student's overall score without specifying the incorrect generalizations he or she may be using. A score may be spuriously high simply because the student uses many words.

- The authors have stated that an essential purpose of DSS is the planning of remediation goals. However, the absence of a descriptive summary sheet that examines performance on individual grammatical criteria tends to defeat this purpose. In addition to the lengthy assessment process, the clinician must also summarize the student's linguistic performance by reviewing individual sentence errors. Moreover, appropriate goals for language therapy cannot be developed solely from examination of DSS error patterns but require more detailed knowledge found through other language measures.

- The DSS procedure is appropriate only for students who can produce 50 complete sentences within a reasonable time. Clinicians should be aware that Lee and Koenigsknecht (1974) have developed an alternate method of language-sampling analysis for students exhibiting lower-level language development.

- The DSS was designed solely to assess the linguistic performance of students who have learned standard American English. Further research is needed to systematize analysis of other dialects of English as well as other languages. Allen Toronto (1972) has developed a scoring system similar to DSS for the Spanish language (see Screening Test of Spanish Grammar, p. 196). It is not a translation of DSS but a developmental scale of Spanish grammatical forms, and it can help clinicians differentiate between bilingual interference with language development and a disability in the student's native language.

- DSS uses a limited number of discrete grammatical criteria. Although there is little doubt that these are essential components of language development, such basic grammatical criteria as plurals, possessive markers, adverbs, and prepositions have been omitted.

- The authors claim that DSS is a useful tool for evaluating progress during therapy, but it should be limited to the assessment of longitudinal changes and not applied to short-term changes. Research has shown that a significant practice effect can be produced when the DSS is repeated over a short time (four applications over two weeks). Furthermore, when DSS is used as an objective measure of grammatical growth during an interim and posttherapy assessment procedure, it is essential that the same stimulus materials be used to minimize test variables as much as possible.

Environmental Language Inventory (ELI)

James D. MacDonald
Charles E. Merrill Publishing Company, 1974; revised 1978
1300 Alum Creek Dr., Columbus, OH 43216

Purpose	To provide a diagnostic strategy for the assessment and training of children with severe delays in expressive language
Major Areas Tested	Expressive language
Age or Grade Range	2 years–adult
Usually Given By	Speech/language clinician
Type of Test	Individual Criterion-referenced Informal
Scores Obtained	None
Student Performance Timed?	No
Testing Time	30 minutes
Scoring/Interpretation Time	30 minutes
Normed On	Various groups of normal, language-delayed, and retarded preschoolers, school-age children, and adults in Ohio
Alternate Forms Available?	No

FORMAT

The Environmental Language Inventory (ELI) is a semantic-based assessment and treatment model for generalized communication. It is a formal method of sampling optimal natural language by the use of parallel linguistic and contextual cues. The procedures sample three production modes—imitation, conversation, and free play—to provide information to help students generalize speech for spontaneous social use.

The ELI materials include:

- A book describing the rationale and development of the inventory; procedures for administration, recording responses, and scoring; extensive reliability and validity data; and the inventory's application to the clinical treatment of delayed language
- An administration and recording form for the conversation and imitation procedures
- A recording form for the free play procedure

An assortment of objects, such as small and large balls, toy cars, blocks, a bag, a baby doll bottle, a small book, and others, must be provided by the examiner.

The ELI consists of 24 stimulus sets, three of which assess each of eight semantic-grammatical rules. These rules describe the functional relations among words in emerging language based on their semantic roles, not just on grammatical categories. The semantic-grammatical rules include:

1. Agent + Action (*Block fall*)
2. Action + Object (*Throw ball*)
3. Agent + Object (*Car [on] head*)
4. Modifier + Head
   a. Possession (*My pants*)
   b. Recurrence (*Want more drink*)
   c. Attribution (*Big ball*)
5. Negation + Object (*No dog*)
6. Agent/Object + Location (*Ball in cup*)
7. Action + Location (*Push ball here*)
8. Introducer + Object (*Hi, doll*)

Each stimulus set contains one nonlinguistic cue and two linguistic cues. The nonlinguistic cue provides an environmental event illustrating the meaning expressed by each semantic-grammatical rule, while the linguistic cues elicit the rule in conversation and imitation. The imitation and sound conversational cues are used only when the target rule is not elicited by the first conversational cue. For example, assessment of the Action + Object rule involves the following procedure:

Nonlinguistic cue: Pretend to throw the ball to the child.
Conversational cue: "What do you want me to do?"
Imitation cue: "Say 'Throw ball.'"
Conversational cue: "What do you want me to do?"

Other cues are illustrated in Figure 54, from the recording form.

The author emphasizes the flexibility of the ELI administration procedure. The child may be seated at the table, or test materials may be arranged on the floor. Assessment can be completed in a single 30-minute session with a cooperative child or in several sessions, if needed. Examiners are encouraged to adapt the ELI content (linguistic and nonlinguistic cues) to include items relevant to an individual child's experiences. Family members or teachers may bring toys or objects for use as part of the testing materials.

In addition to the conversational task, a free-production language sample containing approximately 50 utterances is gathered. Using a natural "play" environment, imitative, conversational, and spontaneous productions are recorded. Contextual cues, as well as verbal utterances, should be indicated.

For both sections, the examiner records all the child's responses, intelligible or unintelligible. Different notations are used for recording unintelligible word units (a dash) and unintelligible utterances of undeterminable word length (a wavy line ~). The ELI provides several indices of expressive language in each production mode: imitation, conversation, and free play. The frequencies, rank order, and proportions of semantic-grammatical rules can be calculated. The mean length of utterance (MLU) can be computed for all words combined and intelligible words only. In addition, the proportion of intelligible words and frequency of unintelligible multiple-word utterances can be calculated.

By employing a parallel testing and training strategy, the ELI yields information on "trainability" as well as on responsiveness to static test items. To apply the ELI to treatment, an environmentally based model for therapy at home and in the classroom is provided (*Ready, Set, Go: Talk to Me*, Horstmeier and MacDonald 1978). Teaching begins with the child's current rule usage in imitation and generalizes it to conversation and play situations.

STRENGTHS OF THE ELI

- The ELI provides a unique and flexible system for assessing the "natural" language of individuals with limited expressive skills. It is applicable for young children as well as for a wide range of older individuals who have not established adequate social use of language, including the moderately or severely retarded, cerebral palsied, autistic, aphasic, or language-delayed populations. Furthermore, the ELI has been adapted to a variety of production modes, such as sign language, total communication, symbol systems, and a range of nonvocal communication systems.

- The ELI is one of the few formal language sampling procedures that consider both the semantic and grammatical aspects of early language development. Excellent, extensive

Nonlinguistic Cue	Conversational Cue		Imitation Cue		Conversational Cue	
B. Action + Object (AO)			"Say . . ."			
1. Pretend to throw ball to child.	"What do you want me to do?"		". . . 'Throw ball.' "		"What do you want me to do?"	
2. Kick large ball.	"What am I doing?"		". . . 'Kick big ball.' "		"What am I doing?"	
3. Put doll in chair.	"What did I do?"		". . . 'Put baby in chair.' "		"What did I do?"	
C. Agent + Object (AgO)			"Say . . ."			
1. Put car on examiner's head.	"What do you see?"		". . . 'Car head.' "		"What do you see?"	
2. Push car to child, then gesture for return.	"What should I do?"		". . . 'You push car.' "		"What should I do?"	
3. Roll ball to child, then gesture for return.	"Tell me what you did."		". . . 'I push ball there.' "		"Tell me what you did."	
Modifier + Head			"Say . . ."			
1. (Possession) Point to child's pants/dress.	"Tell me about this."		". . . 'My pants/dress.' "		"Tell me about this."	

Figure 54. ELI Recording Form

information is provided in the accompanying book for extending the ELI into the treatment of pragmatic and higher-level syntactic disorders.

• An experienced examiner can obtain a wealth of information from the ELI. Specific semantic-grammatical rules, utterance lengths, situational cues and modes (imitative, conversational, play) for use in beginning therapy are provided by this instrument.

• According to the author, ELI assessment and training procedures have been extensively used in a variety of programs serving handicapped individuals. Interested speech/language clinicians may want to consult the *Journal of Speech and Hearing Disorders* (MacDonald, Blott, Gordon, Spiegel, and Hartmann 1974) for a description of one model program ("Experimental Parent-Assisted Treatment Program for Preschool Language-Delayed Children").

• Extensive validity and reliability information is described in the ELI book. For example, the production of semantic-grammatical rules were analyzed by comparing spontaneous speech and ELI samples from preschool and mentally retarded subjects. The ELI procedure elicited the same relative distribution of rules as in free speech for both populations. With several language-delayed students, in fact, the ELI yielded longer MLUs than free speech. In additional studies, excellent interexaminer and test-retest reliability is reported.

LIMITING FACTORS OF THE ELI

- Examiners may find it difficult to structure nonlinguistic cues to elicit semantic-grammatical rules in all stimulus sets. Therefore, a child may actually use a particular rule, but the contrived ELI cues may not elicit a desired response in some cases. For these children, analysis of a spontaneous speech sample may provide this additional information.

- To use the ELI, clinicians will need to invest a substantial amount of time in studying the semantic-grammatical rules and the administration and scoring procedures.

- The imitative cues provided by the examiner are ungrammatical in that morphological markers, auxiliary verbs, and articles are omitted. The author discusses this, suggesting that the goal of this model is spontaneous, social use of language rather than correct grammar.

Multilevel Informal Language Inventory (MILI)

Candace Goldsworthy, Ph.D.
Charles E. Merrill Publishing Company, 1982
1300 Alum Creek Dr., Columbus, OH 43216

Purpose	To measure oral production of critical semantic relations and syntactic constructions
Major Areas Tested	Expressive language
Age or Grade Range	Preschool–grade 7
Usually Given By	Speech/language clinician
Type of Test	Informal Individual Criterion-referenced
Scores Obtained	None
Student Performance Timed?	No
Testing Time	Varies with purpose of testing
Scoring/Interpretation Time	Varies
Normed On	45 children between the ages of 4 and 12 years, including 15 normal children and 30 children diagnosed as language-delayed and/or language-disordered
Alternate Forms Available?	No

FORMAT

The Multilevel Informal Language Inventory (MILI) was designed to provide speech and language clinicians with an efficient means of assessing a student's syntactic development. The purpose of the MILI is to obtain quickly the quality of information usually accessible only through a time-consuming spontaneous language sample analysis.

The materials for the MILI include an examiner's manual, an easel-style picture manual, and record forms. The test manual contains background information, instructions for administration and scoring, guidelines for recording and interpreting responses, and intervention suggestions.

The MILI involves three distinct levels of oral language assessment:

1. *Survey Scenes*. These are used to elicit a short, spontaneous language sample and provide a general idea of a student's overall oral language functioning. Based on the child's age, previous test data, and/or other informal observations, the child is asked to describe a simple picture (for example, a construction site) or a more complex picture (for example, a fire scene). The student's oral responses may be recorded verbatim, or the presence or absence of key syntactic constructions may be noted. The record form provides a checklist of critical semantic relations and syntactic constructions likely to be produced for each scene.

2. *Survey Stories*. These are used to elicit more complex language structures and to determine the semantic relations and syntactic constructions that should be investigated by specific target probes. The examiner reads a simple story or a more complex story and asks the student to "tell it back." The record form contains a copy of the story script along with space to transcribe the student's paraphrasing frame by frame. A checklist of critical features likely to be elicited by the stories is also provided.

3. *Specific Probes*. These are used to elicit all constructions not produced spontaneously by the student on the scenes or stories. If the student does not produce the target construction automatically in response to a picture ("evoked spontaneous" level), the clinician models the structure by describing one part of the stimulus picture and asking the student to tell about another ("indirect imitation"). If neither of these techniques elicits the target structure, the clinician assesses the student's understanding of the construction by asking him or her to point to a specific picture ("receptive" level). A different picture is presented for each probe, and the examiner records whether each target was elicited and the level of probing at which it occurred (Ⓢ—spontaneous; Ⓔ—elicited; Ⓡ—receptive).

Following the administration of these three sections, the student's total performance is plotted on the syntax and semantic relations profile. The student's semantic and syntactic competency is viewed along a continuum from "absent" to "emerging" to "mastered."

The semantic and syntactic items included in the MILI were selected and sequenced based on current research in normal language acquisition. The eight broad semantic-syntactic categories include verbs, nouns, modifiers, interrogatives, negations, combinations of prepositions, adverbs and prepositions, and word meanings in associative language.

STRENGTHS OF THE MILI

- The MILI is an efficient and valuable tool for the speech and language clinician as part of the remediation process. Flexible and informal instruments, such as the MILI, allow clinicians to obtain a more spontaneous and natural sampling of a student's oral language than more formal, standardized measures. Since individual sections of the MILI can be administered independently, it is useful in documenting progress in specific areas and targeting new goals for therapy.

- The MILI is a well-designed instrument with several unique features. For example, the assessment of a student's verbal productions in a series of different environments from least structured (describing a survey scene) to highly structured (responding to a picture that elicits a specific construction) cannot be duplicated with other available diagnostic tools. Observing the way a student uses a language model (indirect imitation) also provides valuable information for remediation. Finally, viewing features of a student's oral language performance along a *continuum*, rather than simply as absent or present, relates directly to the natural language-acquisition process.

- The MILI's content validity is well established. The semantic relations and syntactic constructions included in the MILI have been found to be critical aspects of language acquisition among children with mean lengths of utterance (MLUs) from 1.5 to 6.0 words. The associative-language targets were included because these items appear frequently in intervention programs for older language-learning-disabled students.

- The target probes were field-tested with groups of normal and language-disordered students and were modified accordingly. The probes contained in the final version of the MILI easily elicit the target structures.

LIMITING FACTORS OF THE MILI

- The picture stimuli contained in the MILI are generally clear and appealing to students. However, the survey scenes are often too visually overwhelming for impaired students. Rather than responding with a variety of verbalizations, students tend to simply label objects in the pictures.

Expressive One-Word Picture Vocabulary Test (EOWPVT)

Morrison F. Gardner
Academic Therapy Publications, 1979
20 Commercial Blvd., Novato, CA 94947

Purpose	To obtain an estimate of a child's verbal intelligence and the quality and quantity of vocabulary
Major Areas Tested	Expressive vocabulary
Age or Grade Range	2–12 years
Usually Given By	Speech/language clinician Psychologist Special education teacher
Type of Test	Individual Standardized Norm-referenced
Scores Obtained	Mental age IQ Percentile Stanine
Student Performance Timed?	No
Testing Time	10–15 minutes
Scoring/Interpretation Time	10 minutes
Normed On	1,607 children in the San Francisco Bay Area from 2 to 12 years of age, with intellectual levels and racial-cultural backgrounds representative of total United States population
Alternate Forms Available?	No

FORMAT

The Expressive One-Word Picture Vocabulary Test (EOWPVT) was developed to provide an estimate of the vocabulary a student has learned from the home environment and formal education. The author felt that an expressive format provided more valuable diagnostic information than a receptive test. The materials for the EOWPVT include an examiner's manual, picture book, and score forms.

The EOWPVT is individually administered. The student names a series of individual black and white line drawings presented by the examiner. A table included in the manual indicates the starting point for testing, as determined by the student's age. Items are sequenced in order of difficulty, and basal and ceiling levels are provided. Two demonstration items are presented to familiarize the student with the task. All of the student's responses are recorded for analysis purposes.

Stimulus words for the EOWPVT were chosen based on questionnaires sent to parents about the words children commonly used up to 2 years of age and vocabulary presented in educational settings in selected areas of the United States. Test items represent four language categories, including general or concrete concepts, groupings, abstract concepts, and descriptive concepts.

Raw scores are determined by the number of pictures appropriately named by the student. Scoring criteria is presented in the manual. Raw scores can be converted to mental ages, intelligence quotients, stanines, and percentiles for students between the ages of 2 years and 11 years, 11 months at six-month and one-year intervals.

STRENGTHS OF THE EOWPVT

- The primary value of the EOWPVT lies in its uniqueness. While there are several standardized measures of receptive vocabulary available to diagnosticians, few tests assess single-word knowledge through the expressive mode. In addition to vocabulary level, examiners can obtain quickly and easily information about a student's word recall and retrieval abilities, speech articulation, and general developmental functioning.

- Since the EOWPVT can be administered so rapidly, it is useful as a screening of expressive language functioning. In addition, when given as part of a comprehensive test battery, the EOWPVT can provide valuable information for contrasting a student's expressive and receptive vocabulary skills.

- Adequate split-half reliability data is reported in the manual.

- Content validity for the EOWPVT was well established through the procedures employed in the test development. Only stimulus items that yielded a greater precentage of students passing at successive age levels were retained.

LIMITING FACTORS OF THE EOWPVT

- The EOWPVT is a measure of expressive, single-word vocabulary only and should never be used as an indicator of general intellectual functioning. In fact, a study (Burgemeister, Blum, and Lorge 1972) comparing performance on the EOWPVT with the Columbia Mental Maturity Scale (a measure of general cognitive ability) yielded poor correlations of .29 to .59.

- Knowledge of vocabulary, perhaps more than most other acquired skills, is closely linked with a student's cultural and education experiences. Therefore, culturally different students can be expected to perform more poorly on such a measure as the EOWPVT when compared with students from the mainstream. In addition, a student might have an excellent fund of vocabulary but perform poorly on the EOWPVT because of severe word recall and retrieval difficulties. The possibility of visual-perceptual problems should also be considered when interpreting a student's performance on this test.

- There is a Spanish version of the EOWPVT, which utilizes the same administration and scoring procedures as the English edition. However, only one set of standardized scores is available for both languages, and it was normed on an English-speaking population. Therefore, examiners can use this Spanish version to obtain descriptive information about a student's expressive Spanish vocabulary, but scores should not be reported.

- Examiners should be aware that the EOWPVT does not discriminate well between certain age groups. Scores vary insignificantly between some six-month age intervals, but discriminate better at one-year intervals (6 years–11 years, 11 months).

- Test-retest reliability information is not reported in the manual.

The Word Test

Carol Jorgensen, Mark Barrett, Rosemary Huisingh, and Linda Zachman
Linguisystems, Inc., 1981
1630 Fifth Ave., Suite 806, Moline, IL 61265

Purpose	To assess the expressive vocabulary and semantic abilities of school-age children
Major Areas Tested	Expressive language
Age or Grade Range	7–12 years
Usually Given By	Speech/language clinician Special education teacher Psychologist
Type of Test	Individual Standardized Norm-referenced
Scores Obtained	Age level Percentile Standard
Student Performance Timed?	No
Testing Time	20–30 minutes
Scoring/Interpretation Time	15 minutes
Normed On	476 students with normal development enrolled in the Milwaukee Public Schools; attempt made to insure adequate representation of minority populations
Alternate Forms Available?	No

FORMAT

The Word Test is a relatively new assessment instrument in the area of expressive language and semantics.

The materials consist of an examiner's manual and score forms. All tasks are administered orally, and the student responds verbally. Vocabulary used in The Word Test was selected from the general reading curricula of various elementary schools in Iowa. The test consists of the following six subtests:

1. *Associations*. The student chooses the one word that does not belong in a group of four words. The student must then explain this choice in terms of the relationship between the other three words. Credit is given separately for a correct word choice and a correct explanation.

2. *Synonyms*. The student expresses a one-word synonym for each stimulus word.

3. *Semantic Absurdities*. The student explains what is wrong with each stimulus sentence (for example, *The mother fed the lullaby to the baby.*).

4. *Antonyms*. The student expresses a one-word opposite for each stimulus word.

5. *Definitions*. The student explains the meaning of each stimulus word.

6. *Multiple Definitions*. The student demonstrates or explains two meanings for each stimulus word. Credit is given only if both meanings are expressed.

Each subtest is administered individually to the student. Demonstration items are provided with the subtests and should be presented to insure that the student understands each task. The examiner begins testing with the first item and continues until each subtest is completed or the student makes three consecutive errors. Stimulus items may be repeated. The manual provides specific question probes for use when an appropriate type of response is not obtained from the student. Although the score form contains a sampling of acceptable responses, during the first few times the test is administered, the examiner should refer to the complete list of correct and incorrect or incomplete responses provided in the scoring standards section of the test manual.

Correct responses on all subtests receive one point. Raw scores can be converted to age equivalents, percentiles, and standard scores for each subtest and for the total test.

STRENGTHS OF THE WORD TEST

• The Word Test is a well-organized diagnostic instrument that is quick and easy to administer. The manual is clearly written and contains all the necessary information for administration and interpretation of the test. Since the manual provides several examples of acceptable and unacceptable responses for test items, scoring judgments are usually easy to make.

• Clinicians will find The Word Test an excellent adjunct to standardized measures of receptive vocabulary, such as the Peabody Picture Vocabulary Test—Revised (p. 155). When the level of a student's lexicon is known, judgments about word recall and retrieval abilities can be aptly made with use of this test. Furthermore, it goes beyond the assessment of vocabulary by providing information about a student's ability to *use* words in the context of categorizing, reasoning, and judging appropriate word usage. These are important linguistic skills to assess, particularly with older students, and the test results can be important in planning both oral and written language-remediation programs.

• The vocabulary words used on The Word Test are well selected. Although vocabulary is always affected by cultural experience, the items chosen for this test appear to be familiar to students from a variety of ethnic and geographical backgrounds in the United States.

• The authors report excellent split-half reliability data for the total Word Test, averaging .95.

LIMITING FACTORS OF THE WORD TEST

• The authors state that stimulus items for each subtest increase in difficulty sequentially. However, this increase appears inconsistent on some subtests. For example, on the Synonyms subtest, many students seem unfamiliar with the vocabulary word *chef* (item 1) but can demonstrate knowledge of *enormous* (item 5) or *quarrel* (item 12).

• For the most part, scoring criteria on The Word Test is clear. However, differences between responses that are considered correct and those judged incomplete on the Definitions subtest are often vague. When defining the word *invent*, a student would receive credit for stating the idea "make something original" or "create something new," but definitions such as "create" or "discover" or "think of something new" are considered incomplete. This is a subtle difference that may be difficult to judge with some students, particularly those with oral language problems.

• Examiners should be cautious about reporting age equivalents for students above the upper limits of the test norms (11 years, 11 months). For example, a 15-year-old student could make only one error on the Antonyms subtest and receive an age score of 12 years, 4 months in this area. Since this language skill may increase insignificantly after approximately 12 years of age, it is meaningless to state that this student is deficient in this ability. At any age level, percentiles or standard scores allow a better comparison between a student and his or her peer group.

• The norms for The Word Test consist of separate scores for individual subtests as well as for the total test. However, since this instrument cannot be viewed as a test battery assessing different facets of a single skill, the total score provides less useful diagnostic information.

- Additional information on the reliability and validity of The Word Test is needed. Test-retest reliability and concurrent validity studies are not reported in the manual. The authors discuss the content validity of The Word Test as indicated by the fact that test scores do increase with age and the discriminative nature of the tasks. Further studies would certainly enhance the value of this instrument.
- Examiners should be cautious about using norms based on such a limited standardization as that reported for The Word Test. No attempt was made to obtain a representative national sampling of subjects. The number of subjects at each age interval was quite small, ranging from only 44 to 52 students.

Test of Language Development (TOLD)
Phyllis L. Newcomer and Donald D. Hammill
Pro-Ed, 1977; 1982
5341 Industrial Oaks Blvd., Austin, TX 78735

Purpose	To identify children below their peers in language proficiency, to identify specific strengths and weaknesses, to document progress, and to provide a measuring device in research
Major Areas Tested	Receptive and expressive language
Age or Grade Range	4–9 years (Primary) 8½–13 years (Intermediate)
Usually Given By	Classroom teacher Counselor Psychologist Special education teacher Speech/language clinician
Type of Test	Standardized Individual Norm-referenced
Scores Obtained	Language age Percentile Standard
Student Performance Timed?	No
Testing Time	30–60 minutes
Scoring/Interpretation Time	15–20 minutes
Normed On	1,836 children (Primary) and 871 children (Intermediate), balanced for age, sex, race, geographical location, and socioeconomic level
Alternate Forms Available?	No

FORMAT

The Test of Language Development (TOLD) is an individually administered formal test for assessing language proficiency, both receptive and expressive. TOLD has two forms: the Primary (TOLD-P), for ages 4 years to 8 years, 11 months; and the Intermediate (TOLD-I), for ages 8 years, 6 months to 12 years, 11 months. Both forms are based on the same theoretical model, but they have some differences in subtest content.

TOLD-P

The materials for the TOLD-P are a test manual, answer sheets, and a picture book, which contains picture stimuli for four subtests. The TOLD-P has seven subtests, all of which are identical or similar to other language tests. The subtests are:

I. *Picture Vocabulary* (25 items). The student selects the picture, from four alternatives, that best illustrates the meaning of a word pronounced by examiner (see Peabody Picture Vocabulary Test—Revised, p. 155).

II. *Oral Vocabulary* (20 words). The student defines each word (see Wechsler Intelligence Scale for Children—Revised, Vocabulary subtest, p. 265).

III. *Grammatic Understanding* (25 items). From three pictures, the student selects one that represents a spoken sentence (see Test for Auditory Comprehension of Language, p. 159).

IV. *Sentence Imitation* (30 sentences). The student repeats each sentence, which emphasizes appropriate word order and morphology (see Detroit Tests of Learning Aptitude, p. 93).

V. *Grammatic Completion* (30 items). The student fills in the morphologically correct word for each item in picture form (see Illinois Test of Psycholinguistic Abilities, p. 141).

VI. *Word Discrimination* (20 word pairs). The student identifies each word pair, pronounced by examiner, as the same or different (see Wepman Auditory Discrimination Test, p. 110).

VII. *Word Articulation* (20 items). The student pronounces each pictured item, which contains key sounds (see Appendix E, The Templin-Darley Tests of Articulation, p. 325).

The first five subtests should be administered to each student individually in the order outlined. The two phonology subtests, Word Discrimination and Word Articulation, are supplementary tests, intended primarily for children 6 years of age or younger.

Directions for administration, including procedures for determining basals and ceilings, are described in the manual. The number of correct responses on each subtest is converted into language-age scores, percentiles, and standard scores with a mean of 10 and a standard deviation of 3. Subtests are then combined into composite quotients with a mean of 100 and a standard deviation of 15. The spoken language quotient (SLQ) combines all five subtests and represents the student's overall language ability. Tables 21 and 22 illustrate the organization of the TOLD-P subtests and the combining of subtest scores into composite quotients reflecting the theoretical basis of the instrument.

TOLD-I

The intermediate form of the TOLD is for students aged 8 years, 6 months to 12 years, 11 months. The materials for

Table 21. TOLD-P Subtest Organization

Linguistic Features	Linguistic Systems	
	Listening Subtests	Speaking Subtests
Semantics	Picture Vocabulary	Oral Vocabulary Sentence Imitation
Syntax	Grammatic Understanding	Grammatic Completion
Phonology	Word Discrimination	Word Articulation

Table 22. TOLD-P Subtests Combined into Composite Quotients

Composite Quotient	Subtests
Spoken Language (SLQ)	Sum of all subtest standard scores
Listening (LiQ)	Picture Vocabulary Grammatic Understanding
Speaking (SpQ)	Oral Vocabulary Sentence Imitation Grammatic Completion
Semantics (SeQ)	Picture Vocabulary Oral Vocabulary
Syntax (SyQ)	Grammatic Understanding Sentence Imitation Grammatic Completion

the TOLD-I consist of the manual and answer sheets. There are no picture materials. While the theoretical model for the TOLD-I is the same as for the TOLD-P, five different subtests have been devised to assess receptive and expressive linguistic features. No phonology tests are included, since children over 6 years old have already incorporated most phonological abilities into their language.

The subtests are:

I. *Sentence Combining* (25 items). The examiner reads two short sentences orally and the student combines them into one sentence (for example: *Bill played the game. He got 10 points.*).

II. *Characteristics* (50 items). The examiner reads a four-word sentence, which the student identifies as true or false (for example: *All meat is beef.*).

III. *Word Ordering* (20 series of random words). The examiner reads each series, and the student reorders the words into complete and correct sentences (for example: *spilled the Dad paint was by*).

IV. *Generals* (25 items). The student gives the categorical name for groups of three words (for example: *triangle, rectangle, semicircle*).

V. *Grammatic Comprehension* (40 sentences). The examiner reads each sentence, and the student identifies it as grammatically correct or incorrect (for example: *She ate quick.*).

All five subtests are given in the order outlined, following the directions in the manual. A basal/ceiling format is used so that students are tested only over a critical range of items. The number of correct responses on each subtest is converted to percentiles and standard scores. The subtest standard scores are then combined into composite quotients. Tables 23 and 24 illustrate the organization of the TOLD-I subtests and the combining of the scores into composite quotients. There are no language-age scores provided on the TOLD-I.

Table 23. TOLD-I Subtest Organization

Linguistic Features	Linguistic Systems	
	Listening Subtests	Speaking Subtests
Semantics	Characteristics	Generals
Syntax	Grammatic Comprehension	Sentence Combining Word Ordering

Table 24. TOLD-I Subtests Combined into Composite Quotients

Composite Quotient	Subtests
Spoken Language (SLQ)	Sum of all subtest standard scores
Listening (LiQ)	Characteristics Grammatic Comprehension
Speaking (SpQ)	Sentence Combining Word Ordering Generals
Semantics (SeQ)	Characteristics Generals
Syntax (SyQ)	Sentence Combining Word Ordering Grammatic Comprehension

STRENGTHS OF THE TOLD-P AND TOLD-I

• The TOLD-P combines into one instrument a variety of well-known language assessment tools. These instruments are the criterion tests upon which the TOLD-P was validated.

• Language-age scores on the TOLD-P are included. This is appropriate, since we do have research documenting normal speech and language development for the 4- to 8-year-old age range. The TOLD-I does not include language-age scores, as they are not appropriate at that age level.

• Both the TOLD-P and TOLD-I organize individual subtests into composite scores to assess concepts such as reception, expression, syntax, or semantics. This approach leads to a broader analysis of strengths and weaknesses.

LIMITING FACTORS OF THE TOLD-P AND TOLD-I

• While the TOLD-P uses subtests similar to many other language-assessment tools, the TOLD-I includes all new subtest formats. In contrast to other tests by this author, the manual does not include discussions of the development of these subtests. It is questionable that certain subtests measure the skill they were developed to measure. For example: the Characteristics subtest contains so many "tricky" questions, one wonders if it is a valid measure of the listening vocabulary construct.

• Both tests include a small standardization sample—especially the TOLD-I.

- Validity of the TOLD-I is only compared with other tests by this author. Some of the validity studies have an extremely small number of students.
- The TOLD authors attempted to design a quick, efficient instrument for assessing language skills. The clinical information obtained regarding an individual student is much less valuable than that from several other language tests available. The TOLD should be viewed as a screening test; it should not be used as a measure to determine eligibility for language programs.

Test of Adolescent Language (TOAL)

Donald D. Hammill, Virginia L. Brown, Stephen C. Larsen, and J. Lee Wiederholt
Pro-Ed, 1980
5341 Industrial Oaks Blvd., Austin, TX 78735

Purpose	To provide a norm-referenced measure of language proficiency in adolescent students
Major Areas Tested	Receptive and expressive language, spoken and written
Age or Grade Range	11–18½ years
Usually Given By	Classroom teacher Special education teacher Speech/language clinician Any trained person
Type of Test	Group Individual Standardized Norm-referenced
Scores Obtained	Scaled Percentile Stanine
Student Performance Timed?	No
Testing Time	1½–2 hours
Scoring/Interpretation Time	20–30 minutes
Normed On	2,723 students in 17 states and 3 Canadian provinces, balanced for sex and urban/rural residence
Alternate Forms Available?	No

FORMAT

The Test of Adolescent Language (TOAL) is a standardized test for assessing adolescent language proficiency. The materials consist of a manual, reusable student booklets of test materials, student answer booklets, and individual student profile sheets. Using a three-dimensional model, Figure 55, the authors have developed eight subtests to measure semantic and syntactic features of receptive and expressive language in spoken and written form:

1. *Listening/Vocabulary* (28 items). The student selects two pictures that are related to a stimulus picture (for example: both *tree* and *part of the hand* are related to *palm*). This is a variation on the Peabody Picture Vocabulary Test—Revised (p. 155) and the Test of Language Development—Primary (p. 187) that reduces successful guessing and taps a student's knowledge of more than one meaning for a word.

2. *Listening/Grammar* (35 items). The examiner reads three statements, and the student selects two with essentially the same meaning. For example:
   A. *Ask Jack to bring it here.*
   B. *Tell Jack to bring it here.*
   C. *Ask Jack what to bring here.*

3. *Speaking/Vocabulary* (20 words). The student uses each vocabulary word in a meaningful sentence. Since the student responds orally, this subtest must be individually administered.

4. *Speaking/Grammar* (25 sentences). The student repeats each sentence orally. This subtest must be administered individually.

5. *Reading/Vocabulary* (25 items). The student reads three stimulus words that are related in some way (*red, green, blue*) and then selects from a group of four (*yellow, circle, orange, light*) the two words that are related to the stimulus words. Both responses must be correct. (See Test of Reading Comprehension, p. 59).

6. *Reading/Grammar* (20 items). The student reads five sentences and selects the two that are most nearly alike in meaning. For example:
   A. *Sam plays.*
   B. *Sam will not play.*
   C. *Sam played.*
   D. *Sam is playing.*
   E. *Sam is going to play.*
Both responses must be correct. (See Test of Reading Comprehension, p. 59.)

7. *Writing/Vocabulary* (24 words). The student uses each word in a written sentence.

8. *Writing/Grammar* (25 items). The student reads three sentences and combines them into a single written sentence. For example:
   Jack will ice skate next winter.
   The rink opens in November.
   His brother will be there too.

Typically, all eight subtests are administered to an individual student using the basal/ceiling procedures described in the manual. Alternately, groups of students may be given all subtests except Speaking/Vocabulary and Speaking/Grammar, which are given individually. Upon completion of the test, raw scores for each subtest are converted to scaled scores with a mean of 10 and a standard deviation of 3. This information is plotted on the subtest profile, shown in Figure 56. Subtests are then combined into composite scaled scores with a mean of 100 and a standard deviation of 15. The adolescent language quotient is the sum of all eight subtests and represents a student's overall

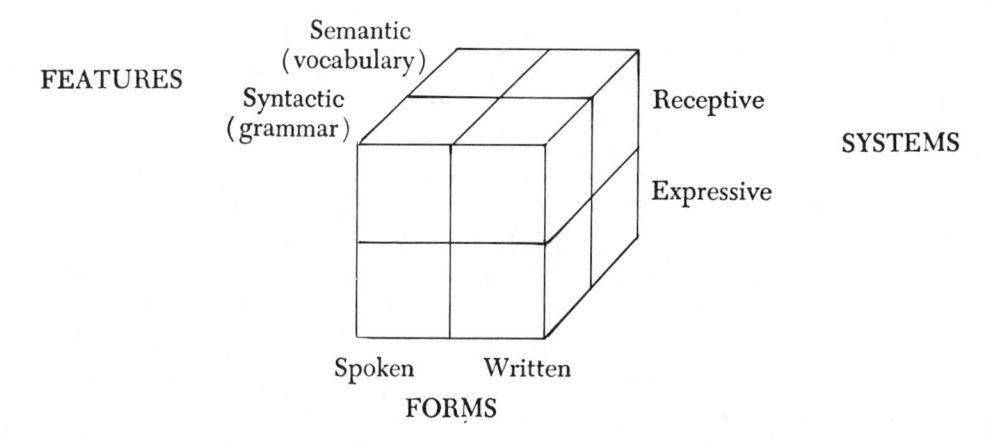

Figure 55. TOAL Three-Dimensional Model

Speech and Language Tests 193

SECTION II TOAL SUBTEST PROFILE

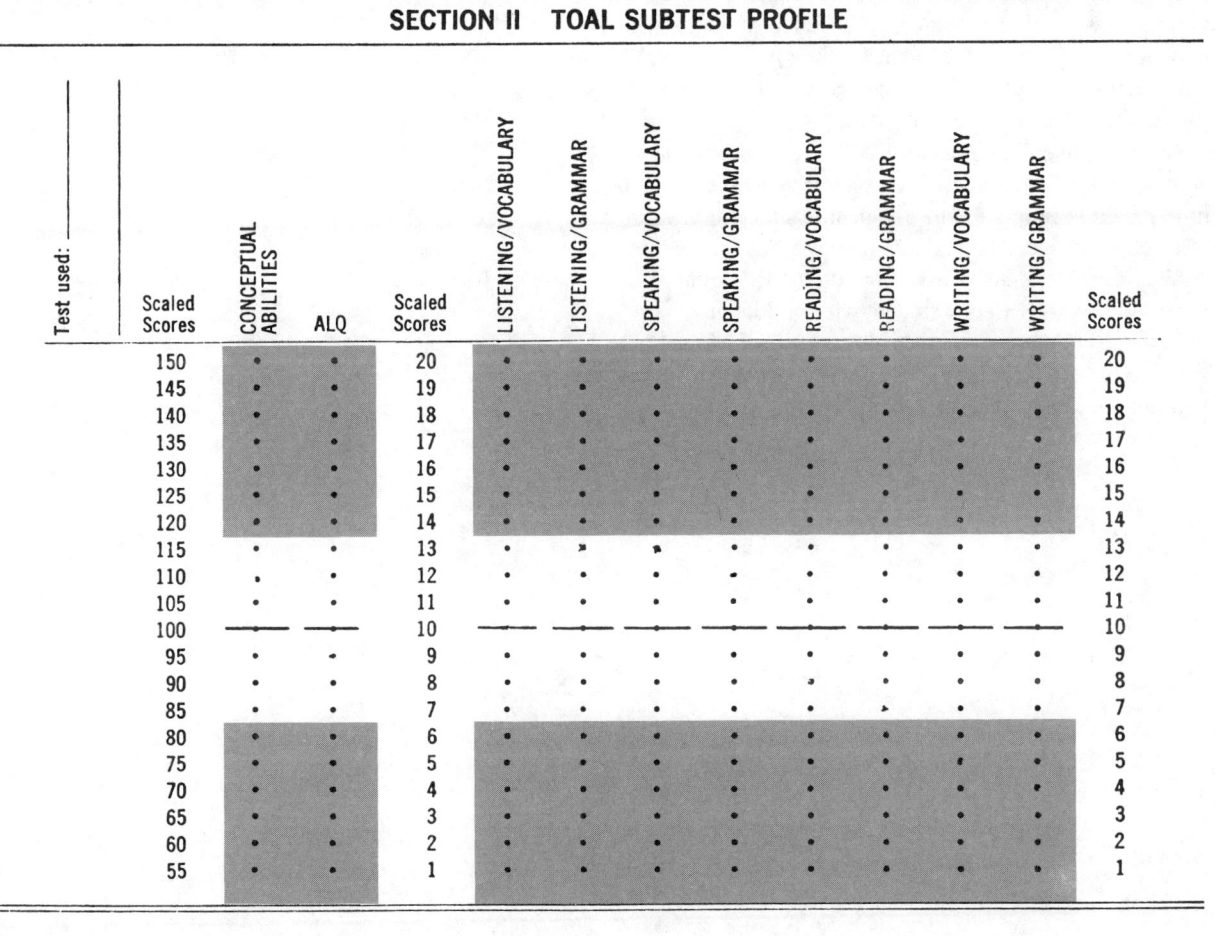

Figure 56. TOAL Subtest Profile

language proficiency. A table in the manual allows the conversion of scaled scores to percentiles, stanines, and several types of standard scores.

No grade or age equivalents are provided, because the skills assessed on the TOAL are not grade- or age-specific.

STRENGTHS OF THE TOAL
- There are few adequately normed language-assessment tools for adolescents; as such, the TOAL is a needed addition to the field.
- By combining subtests from the Test of Reading Comprehension (p. 59) and the Test of Language Development (p. 187) with some new ones, the TOAL authors have created a comprehensive and interesting instrument. The vocabulary tests, in combination, provide a more complete assessment of a student's vocabulary proficiency than the other individual tests alone. The grammar tests seem less helpful in the information they provide, with the exception of Writing/Grammar. This sentence-combining task is quite relevant to written language skills.
- The provision of a chart for converting scaled scores to percentiles is helpful. As with all Pro-Ed tests, the standardization of scaled scores to a mean of 10 and a standard deviation of 3, and of composites to a mean of 100 and a standard deviation of 15, allows easy comparison with other tests.
- Extensive reliability data are published in the manual. Provision of the "scoring exercises" in the manual's appendix demonstrates the authors' attention to statistical reliability.

LIMITING FACTORS OF THE TOAL
- The TOAL is a lengthy, difficult test for students with language deficiencies. Several subtests are difficult to explain, especially Listening/Grammar, Reading/Grammar,

and Writing/Grammar. Group administration is not recommended for learning- or language-disabled students, who may not receive enough explanation in a group. Also, a basal/ceiling process can be done individually, considerably shortening the administration time.

• The eight subtests of the TOAL seem somewhat contrived to fit the model. The composite scores may have little meaning in relation to a student's actual abilities or instructional needs. For example, does a high score on the reading composite and a low score on the listening composite really reflect a student with oral language weaknesses that are strengthened by reading? More extensive use by examiners in the field and more validity studies will help define the usefulness of the composite scores.

Chapter Four
Bilingual (Spanish-English) Language Tests

The major function of testing should be to improve instruction, that is, to diagnose learning and language difficulties and prescribe activities appropriate to individual learning needs. Unfortunately, tests often are used to label and classify students into discrete groupings to meet administrative needs. As a result of the civil rights movement in this country, examiners have become more aware of the discriminatory nature of some assessment practices. Testing students in their native languages or dialects, accounting for cultural biases in test content, and providing appropriate representation for minority groups in normative samples have all become important considerations in the assessment process.

This is particularly true in the area of language testing. Bilingual testing should be carried out with two types of students: those whose first language is other than English, and those for whom the language most often spoken in the home is not English. For a student having difficulty acquiring English as a second language, competency in both linguistic systems must be evaluated and compared. If the student's performance in both languages is below the expectations for his or her age and cultural group, a pervasive language disorder may exist. However, if the student's native language skills are intact, the difficulty in English proficiency probably represents a normal stage in the second-language acquisition process.

Over the past few years, many assessment tools have been developed for use with Spanish speakers. Some of these are direct translations of existing English language tests, often without separate normative data. These translations are listed in Appendix F.

As bilingual language assessment became more sophisticated, diagnostic tests were developed that reflected the abilities and characteristics of native Spanish speakers more adequately. Some of these instruments are adaptations of widely used English language tests. Two of these measures are reviewed in this chapter: the Screening Test of Spanish Grammar, an adaptation of the Northwestern Syntax Screening Test (p. 167), and the Prueba Illinois de Habilidades Psicolingüísticas, the Spanish version of the Illinois Test of Psycholinguistic Abilities (p. 141). Other assessment tools were independently developed using the Spanish linguistic system. The Ber-Sil Spanish Test assesses vocabulary, direction-following, and visual-motor skills. The Dos Amigos Verbal Language Scales and the Del Rio Language Screening Test assess receptive and expressive language through the use of analogous subtests in English and Spanish.

For admission to bilingual education programs, educators are required to assess a student's fluency in both his or her first and second languages. Two instruments reviewed in this chapter are designed to determine oral language proficiency, or fluency level, in English and Spanish. These include the Bilingual Syntax Measure and the Language Assessment Scales. The Woodcock Language Proficiency Battery—Spanish, a new test, evaluates proficiency not only in oral language but in reading and spelling as well.

Screening Test of Spanish Grammar   196
Prueba Illinois de Habilidades Psicolingüísticas   198
Ber-Sil Spanish Test   203
Dos Amigos Verbal Language Scales   205
Del Rio Language Screening Test   207
Bilingual Syntax Measure   209
Language Assessment Scales   212
Woodcock Language Proficiency Battery—Spanish   215

Screening Test of Spanish Grammar (STSG)

Allen S. Toronto
Northwestern University Press, 1973
1735 Benson Ave., Evanston, IL 60201

Purpose	To identify quickly those Spanish-speaking children who do not demonstrate native syntactic proficiency commensurate with their age
Major Areas Tested	Receptive and expressive language
Age or Grade Range	3–7 years
Usually Given By	Speech/language clinician
Type of Test	Individual Standardized Norm-referenced
Scores Obtained	Percentile
Student Performance Timed?	No
Testing Time	20 minutes
Scoring/Interpretation Time	10 minutes
Normed On	192 normally developing children, including 96 Mexican-Americans and 96 Puerto Rican–Americans, between the ages of 3 and 7 years, in Chicago
Alternate Forms Available?	No

FORMAT

The Screening Test of Spanish Grammar (STSG) employs the same format and methods as the widely used Northwestern Syntax Screening Test (p. 167). However, this instrument is not a direct translation, since test items are based on knowledge of the acquisition of Spanish syntax by Spanish-speaking children.

The STSG materials consist of a manual and score forms. The examiner's manual contains clear instructions for administration, scoring, and interpretation of the test, as well as the stimulus pictures. Test directions in the manual are presented in Spanish and English.

The STSG contains receptive and expressive subtests, each assessing 23 syntactic structures in Spanish. Identical structures are used in both subtests and are presented in paired sentences that generally differ in only one syntactic element. Items are presented in ascending order of difficulty. Demonstration items are included at the beginning of each subtest.

The examiner administers the receptive subtest first. On each test item, the examiner reads both stimulus sentences, repeats one, and requests the student to point to the picture illustrating the repeated sentence. To maintain a randomized order, the sentence marked with an asterisk is repeated. Four black-and-white pictures are presented with each item, two corresponding to the test sentences and two decoys.

On the expressive subtest, the examiner reads both sentences and then points to the stimulus picture corresponding to the sentence marked with an asterisk. Two stimulus pictures are presented with every expressive item, each corresponding to one of the sentences. The student is required to produce from memory the stimulus sentence represented by each picture. Credit is withheld if the student makes any grammatical error reproducing a sentence or if he or she alters the target structure in the stimulus, even if the sentence is grammatically correct. If the student modifies the stimulus sentence so that the target structure or grammatical rule is not affected, credit is received. English nouns may be substituted for Spanish nouns if these terms are generally used by that student's bilingual community. The test manual contains guidelines for noun substitutions and dialectal differences for both Mexican-American and Puerto Rican–American groups, as well as the target structures and acceptable and unacceptable responses for each expressive item.

The entire test is administered, unless the student misses all of the items in the first half of a subtest. In that case, testing on that section is discontinued. Each correct response receives one point. Raw scores for the receptive and expressive subtests are calculated independently and can be converted to percentile scores at one-year age intervals. Separate tables are provided for Mexican-American and Puerto Rican–American students. Scores between the tenth percentile and the second standard deviation below the mean are considered "low normal" and indicate the need for further assessment. Scores at or below the second standard deviation probably indicate the need for language remediation.

STRENGTHS OF THE STSG

- The STSG is a well-organized screening test that is relatively quick and easy to administer and score. It enables the clinician to isolate a group of Spanish-speaking students who need further language assessment.
- The STSG provides separate administration guidelines and norming data for two groups of Spanish-speaking students, Mexican-Americans and Puerto Rican–Americans.
- Careful investigation of a student's performance on the STSG can provide valuable information about his or her syntactic skills. Receptive and expressive abilities can be compared, and specific problem areas, such as verb tense, can be pinpointed. Sentence formulation on a formal task such as this can be contrasted with a spontaneous language sample to help determine a student's ability to use structure and adult language models.

LIMITING FACTORS OF THE STSG

- Although the author states that this test is *not* a direct translation of the Northwestern Syntax Screening Test (p. 167), there are a large number of parallel target structures and translated items. Some aspects of the STSG do not reflect common usage of Spanish by certain groups. For example, several test items involve sentence structures not frequently used by Spanish speakers, such as passive tense constructions. Furthermore, a student's response is considered incorrect on certain expressive items if the pronoun is omitted, although this is acceptable in Spanish.
- The standardization group used in the STSG represents only one geographical area of the United States and, therefore, norms should not be used with Spanish-speaking students from other areas. The norming population was quite limited in number, with only 24 subjects in each age interval for either Mexican-American or Puerto Rican–American students. Low reliability coefficients are reported for the STSG, particularly for the receptive subtest. Information on test validity is sparse and needs to be expanded.

Prueba Illinois de Habilidades Psicolinguísticas (SITPA)
(Spanish Version of the Illinois Test of Psycholinguistic Abilities)
Aldine von Isser and Winifred Kirk
University of Arizona, 1980
Tucson, AZ 85721

Purpose	To evaluate psycholinguistic abilities of Spanish-speaking children and to help develop appropriate remediation programs
Major Areas Tested	Auditory-vocal and visual-motor skills
Age or Grade Range	3–9 years
Usually Given By	Speech/language clinician Psychologist
Type of Test	Individual Standardized Norm-referenced
Scores Obtained	Stanine
Student Performance Timed?	Yes (some subtests)
Testing Time	1½ hours
Scoring/Interpretation Time	30–40 minutes
Normed On	436 children between the ages of 3 and 9 years from Mexico, Colombia, Peru, Chile, and Puerto Rico
Alternate Forms Available?	No

FORMAT

The Prueba Illinois de Habilidades Psicolinguísticas (SITPA) is a Spanish adaptation of the widely used Illinois Test of Psycholinguistic Abilities (ITPA) (p. 141). The materials include an instruction manual written in Spanish, several picture books, and test protocols. The clearly written manual contains information on test development, a description of the subtests, administration and scoring instructions, and guidelines for recording, profiling, and interpreting test results. The SITPA is based on the same model as the English version. For a description of the 10 SITPA subtests, see Table 25.

The examiner administers the 10 subtests in the order presented on the protocol. Since vocabulary terms vary from country to country, some word substitutions are listed in parentheses. Responses presented in a language other than Spanish can be accepted. All 10 subtests include demonstration items, and 7 subtests contain basal and ceiling levels.

The final page of the test protocol contains a summary of abilities (see Figure 57), where raw scores and stanines for each subtest, as well as other statistical data, are recorded. This profile is arranged according to communication channels and organizational levels. The test manual provides several examples of test profiles and interpretations.

Statistical tables contained in the test manual enable the examiner to convert raw scores to stanines. In addition, means, standard deviations, and standard errors of measurement and dependency are provided for 3, 5, 7, and 9 years of age.

STRENGTHS OF THE SITPA

- Although the ITPA has been subject to increasing criticism over the past few years, it is still a commonly used and respected assessment instrument. This Spanish adaptation, therefore, makes an important contribution to the diagnosis of language disorders in non-English-speaking

RESUMEN DE LAS HABILIDADES

PRUEBAS		NIVEL SEMANTICO				NIVEL AUTOMATICO			
		AUDITIVA/VOCAL		VISOMOTORA		AUDITIVA/VOCAL		VISOMOTORA	
NUMERO	NOMBRE	PUNT.	STANINE	PUNT.	STANINE	PUNT.	STANINE	PUNT.	STANINE
4	ASOCIACION VISUAL								
3	ASOCIACION AUDITIVA								
2	COMPRENSION VISUAL								
1	COMPRENSION AUDITIVA								
5	FLUIDEZ LEXICA								
6	EXPRESION MOTORA								
7	INTEGRACION AUDITIVA								
8	INTEGRACION VISUAL								
9	MEMORIA SECUENCIAL AUDITIVA								
10	MEMORIA SECUENCIAL VISOMOTORA								

NORMA TOTAL (Suma de los stanines dividida entre 10) _____

NORMA SEMANTICA (Suma de los stanines dividida entre 6) _____

NORMA AUTOMATICA (Suma de los stanines dividida entre 4) _____

NORMA AUDITIVA/VOCAL (Suma de los stanines dividida entre 5) _____   Fecha de la prueba _____

NORMA VISOMOTORA (Suma de los stanines dividida entre 5) _____   Edad cronológica _____

Figure 57. SITPA Summary of Abilities

Table 25. SITPA Subtests

Subtest	Description	Psycholinguistic Process	Channel of Communication	Comments
Semantic Level (Representational):				
1. Comprensión Auditiva (Auditory Comprehension)	Assesses the understanding of verbally presented material. The student answers a series of questions about each of three episodes of a single oral narrative by pointing to one of four pictures. Each episode increases in length and complexity.	Reception	Auditory-Vocal	This subtest has a unique format and is *not* a Spanish adaptation of the ITPA Auditory Reception subtest. The format of this subtest enables the clinician to assess nonverbal students.
2. Comprensión Visual (Visual Comprehension)	Assesses the ability to match pictures representing a similar concept. After the presentation of a single stimulus picture for three seconds, the student selects a match from four choices on the following page.	Reception	Visual-Motor	Since the student does not view all stimulus pictures simultaneously, visual memory deficits can hinder performance on this task.
3. Asociación Auditiva (Auditory Association)	Assesses the ability to relate concepts presented orally. The student completes increasingly difficult verbal analogies.	Organization (Association)	Auditory-Vocal	Vocabulary deficits and word-recall and -retrieval difficulties may affect task performance.
4. Asociación Visual (Visual Association)	Assesses the ability to relate concepts presented visually. At the lower level, the student selects one of four stimulus pictures that goes with another. At a higher level, the student selects a picture to complete a visual analogy.	Organization (Association)	Visual-Motor	At the higher level, students can sometimes choose a correct item without processing the two-part analogy.
5. Fluidez Léxica (Word Fluency)	Assesses the ability to express concepts orally. In the first section, the student states all the words he or she can think of in one minute. In the following sections, the student produces words in specific categories, such as animals, parts of the body, and things seen outside the house. Performance is measured by the total number of words produced in all sections.	Expression	Auditory-Vocal	This subtest is *not* a Spanish adaptation of the ITPA Verbal Expression subtest. This subtest provides a good measure of vocabulary and word recall and retrieval.
6. Expresión Motora (Motor Expression)	Assesses the ability to express meaning through the use of pantomime. The student demonstrates the use of a variety of objects, gesturally, after each stimulus picture representing the item is presented. Performance is measured by the number of appropriate gestures used by the student.	Expression	Visual-Motor	This subtest is an improvement over the ITPA Manual Expression subtest since more objects familiar to culturally different students were included. Shy or inhibited students may be penalized on this task.

Table 25.—Continued

Subtest	Description	Psycholinguistic Process	Channel of Communication	Comments
Automatic Level:				
7. Integración Auditiva (Auditory Integration)	Assesses the ability to perceive a complete word after an incomplete verbal presentation (for example, *muñe-muñeca*). On the first four items, the student points to a picture that represents the whole word. On the remaining items, the student must verbally produce an entire word.	Integration (Closure)	Auditory-Vocal	On some items, such sparse phonemic information is presented that a vast number of responses are appropriate. Performance on this task is affected by the vocabulary level of the student.
8. Integración Visual (Visual Integration)	Assesses the ability to recognize a pictured object when partially obscured in a scene. The student is instructed to rapidly point to every example of a specific object that he or she can find in 20 seconds. Four picture strips are presented.	Integration (Closure)	Visual-Motor	This task requires visual closure, visual scanning, figure-ground discrimination, and task persistence. Some students are overwhelmed by the amount of visual information presented and by the time pressure.
9. Memoria Secuencial Auditiva (Auditory Sequential Memory)	Assesses the ability to verbally reproduce a series of digits presented orally. The student is instructed to repeat sequences of two to eight digits presented at a rate of two per second.	Sequential Memory	Auditory-Vocal	This subtest differs from the ITPA Auditory Memory subtest in that two trials to repeat the digits are not permitted.
10. Memoria Secuencial Visomotora (Visual-Motor Sequential Memory)	Assesses the ability to reproduce a sequence of vertical and horizontal lines and circles by drawing them from memory. The student draws sequences of two to eight figures after viewing them for three seconds.	Sequential Memory	Visual-Motor	This subtest differs from the ITPA Visual Memory subtest, which does not have a drawing component. The SITPA manual states that rudimentary forms were chosen for this subtest to minimize the effects of visual-motor coordination difficulties.

students. The modifications of the format and materials in some of the Spanish subtests are an improvement over the original version.

• The SITPA, like its English counterpart, is a comprehensive test battery that provides valuable information about a student's strengths and weaknesses. Performance can be measured in terms of modality preference (auditory-vocal versus visual-motor) and levels of organization (automatic versus semantic or representational), and various psycholinguistic processes can be compared.

• The materials for the SITPA include a guide for the remediation of psycholinguistic deficits, a translation and adaptation of the English version.

LIMITING FACTORS OF THE SITPA

• The authors of the SITPA stress that the current norms are based on a very small sample and should be considered tentative. They stress that other areas with Hispanic populations should develop their own local norms. The SITPA standardization group was gathered only from Latin American countries. Examiners should be cautious about using this information for interpreting the performance of Spanish-speaking students in the United States.

- Like the English version, the SITPA is a lengthy and complicated test to administer. Even if examiners are familiar with the English test, a significant commitment of time is needed to learn the Spanish adaptation. The authors suggest administering no less than 10 experimental tests before formally assessing a Spanish-speaking student.
- The use of the term "psycholinguistic abilities" in this test, as well as in the ITPA, is misleading. Examiners should be aware that this test actually assesses cognitive, as well as linguistic, functioning in a variety of areas, both verbal and nonverbal.
- Since this test is still in the experimental stage, reliability and validity studies are not yet reported.

Ber-Sil Spanish Test (Ber-Sil)
Marjorie L. Beringer
The Ber-Sil Company, 1972; revised 1976
3412 Seaglen Dr., Rancho Palos Verdes, CA 90274

Purpose	To screen the vocabulary, direction-following, and visual-motor abilities of Spanish-speaking children
Major Areas Tested	Receptive language and visual-motor integration
Age or Grade Range	4–12 years
Usually Given By	Speech/language clinician Psychologist Paraprofessional
Type of Test	Individual Standardized Norm-referenced
Scores Obtained	Percentile
Student Performance Timed?	No
Testing Time	20–25 minutes
Scoring/Interpretation Time	10 minutes
Normed On	343 Spanish-speaking children in the Los Angeles Unified School District, half of whom were born in Spanish-speaking countries in the Americas and almost half of whom were born in the United States
Alternate Forms Available?	No

FORMAT

The Ber-Sil Spanish Test (Ber-Sil) was developed to meet the need for a standardized Spanish instrument that could be compared to the Peabody Picture Vocabulary Test—Revised (p. 155). It was devised as a screening test for use with Spanish-speaking children residing in southern California. The Ber-Sil consists of three sections:

1. *Vocabulary*. Assesses knowledge of single-word vocabulary (nouns and verbs) in Spanish. The student selects one of three pictures that represents the word spoken on an audiotape; vocabulary items that are home-related (*ball, drum, skirt*) and community-related (*cow, clown, teacher*) are indicated on the protocol.

2. *Response to Directions*. Assesses the ability to carry out verbal directions motorically. The tasks include gross motor activities, pointing to body parts, and others. The examiner judges whether the student executes the task correctly and the speed in which it is completed ("immediately," "in time," "not in time").

3. *Handwriting, Geometric Figures, and Draw a Boy or a Girl*. Assesses visual-motor coordination through writing and drawing activities. The student is requested to write his or her name, copy a series of geometric forms, and draw a person.

The materials necessary for administering the Ber-Sil include the manual, the picture book, the test booklet, a tape recorder and cassette tape, a card with a hole punched in the center, and a ball. All test instructions and stimulus items for the vocabulary and direction-following subtests are presented in Spanish on the audiotape. All three test sections in their entirety are presented to each student on an individual basis.

A student's raw score on the vocabulary section can be converted to a percentile score. The student's Spanish vocabulary level is then judged to be "low" (below the twenty-fifth percentile), "middle" (between the twenty-fifth percentile and the seventy-fifth percentile), or "high" (above the seventy-fifth percentile). For the second and third test sections, the manual provides guidelines and scoring criteria for various age groups. The student's performance in these areas is judged to be at, above, or below the expectancy level for his or her age. Suggestions for remediation and/or further assessment in various areas are also provided in the manual.

STRENGTHS OF THE BER-SIL

- The Ber-Sil appears to be a useful screening instrument, particularly for young Spanish-speaking children. It is quick and easy to administer and score. The inclusion of an audiotape enables trained bilingual paraprofessionals, as well as special educators, to administer the Ber-Sil.

- The division of the vocabulary items into home- and community-related words is particularly useful for the assessment of bilingual students. If a student demonstrates poor knowledge of Spanish vocabulary in a specific environment, the student's performance may reflect bilingual experience rather than a pervasive receptive language deficit.

- Adequate test-retest reliability is reported.

LIMITING FACTORS OF THE BER-SIL

- The Ber-Sil standardization population is limited in number and geographical location. Since norms were established only for Spanish-speaking students residing in southern California, examiners should be cautious about interpreting test results for students in other areas. In addition, the test developers did not control for the length of time that norming subjects had resided in the United States, the subjects' birthplaces, or their home language environments. Criteria of normal functioning for these subjects were not reported.

- The author states that the dominant language of a student can be determined by comparing his or her mental age on the Peabody Picture Vocabulary Test—Revised with his or her functioning age on the Ber-Sil Vocabulary section. She suggests that a two-year difference in scores indicates that a particular language is dominant. Examiners should be aware that language dominance is a complex issue and cannot be determined solely on the basis of receptive vocabulary. Furthermore, mental age scores based on the nonrevised version of the Peabody Picture Vocabulary Test—Revised may be difficult to obtain.

- Validity of the Ber-Sil was measured by a sampling of expert opinions, item analysis, and comparison with other tests. Solicitation of expert opinions from Los Angeles special educators cannot be considered an objective measure of test validity. Correlation of the Ber-Sil with the Wechsler Intelligence Scale for Children—Revised (p. 265), the Leiter International Performance Scale and the Arthur Adaptation (p. 282), and the Stanford-Binet Intelligence Scale (p. 276) was not significant. Further validity studies would enhance the usefulness of this instrument.

# Dos Amigos Verbal Language Scales (Dos Amigos)
Donald C. Critchlow
Academic Therapy Publications, 1973
20 Commercial Blvd., Novato, CA 94947

Purpose	To measure language dominance and define developmental levels in Spanish and English
Major Areas Tested	Expressive vocabulary
Age or Grade Range	5–13½ years
Usually Given By	Speech/language clinician Paraprofessional Bilingual teacher
Type of Test	Individual Standardized Norm-referenced
Scores Obtained	Percentile Standard
Student Performance Timed?	No
Testing Time	10 minutes (for each scale)
Scoring/Interpretation Time	5 minutes (for each scale)
Normed On	1,224 children of Mexican-American ancestry who resided in southern Texas and spoke Spanish as their first language
Alternate Forms Available?	No

FORMAT

The purposes of the Dos Amigos Verbal Language Scales (Dos Amigos) are to determine the language in which a student is best equipped to learn and to provide a comparative analysis of English and Spanish lexical development.

The Dos Amigos consists of separate English and Spanish scales, each containing 85 stimulus words. Either scale or both scales may be administered to an individual student. Test materials consist of an examiner's manual and a single protocol for the English and Spanish scales.

Both language versions require the student to verbally produce an antonym for a stimulus word. The examiner should determine that the student understands what an opposite is and can demonstrate this knowledge before beginning the test. The examiner starts testing with the first item and continues until the scale is completed or the student makes five consecutive errors. Credit is given only for responses indicated on the test protocol. Raw scores are determined by the number of correct responses on each scale and can be converted to percentiles. If a student scores below the fiftieth percentile in English and/or Spanish, further evaluation is recommended. A bilingual student who scores below the mean on the English scale only may require intensive oral language instruction before learning to read in English.

The English and Spanish scales are not direct translations. Selection of test items in both languages was based on commonly used vocabulary in oral language activities in kindergarten to sixth-grade classrooms. Although test items are arranged in ascending order of difficulty, English and Spanish concepts don't occupy the same relative positions on their respective scales. For example, field testing revealed that the verbal concept *dead-alive* was acquired sooner by Spanish-speaking students (*muerto-vivo*) than by English-speaking students.

STRENGTHS OF THE DOS AMIGOS

- The Dos Amigos is quick and easy to administer, score, and interpret. With a minimum of training, a paraprofessional who is bilingual in Spanish and English could successfully administer this test.

- Comparison of a student's performance on the English and Spanish scales can provide information about the student's dominant or stronger language. Word recall and retrieval difficulties can indicate loss of proficiency in a first language after a second language is introduced.

LIMITING FACTORS OF THE DOS AMIGOS

- The Dos Amigos is essentially a vocabulary test, and its diagnostic information should be considered as part of a comprehensive assessment battery. However, the author purports that this task involves associative and integrative decoding and encoding processes, since it elicits meaningful responses at the "comprehension or conceptual level in both languages." Conclusions about a student's language dominance or level of language development should not be based on this assessment instrument alone.

- Information about the distribution of sex, socio-economic level, home environment, and development of overall language ability in the norming population is not provided. Standardization is based on students residing in southern Texas, and examiners should be cautious about interpreting test results for bilingual students in other areas.

- Examiners are instructed only to credit responses listed on the test protocol. Although a few alternate responses are provided for the Spanish and English scales, students often produce seemingly appropriate antonyms that are not listed. For example, a student receives credit for producing *cheap* in response to the stimulus *costly,* but *inexpensive* is not credited.

- No reliability or validity studies are reported for this test.

Del Rio Language Screening Test (Del Rio)

A. Toronto, D. Leverman, C. Hanna, P. Rosenzweig, and A. Maldonado
National Educational Laboratory Publishers, Inc., 1975
P.O. Box 1003, Austin, TX 78767

Purpose	To identify children with deviant language performance in English and/or Spanish who need further evaluation
Major Areas Tested	Receptive and expressive language and auditory memory
Age or Grade Range	3–7 years
Usually Given By	Speech/language clinician Special education teacher Bilingual teacher
Type of Test	Standardized Individual Norm-referenced
Scores Obtained	Percentile
Student Performance Timed?	No
Testing Time	12–15 minutes
Scoring/Interpretation Time	10 minutes
Normed On	384 children from Del Rio, Texas, between the ages of 3 and 7 years, with equal numbers of Anglo-Americans, English-speaking Mexican-Americans, and Spanish-speaking Mexican-Americans
Alternate Forms Available?	No

FORMAT

The Del Rio Language Screening Test (Del Rio) consists of five subtests, which may be administered separately or in combination with other subtests. There are analogous versions in English and Spanish; they are not direct translations. The five subtests are:

1. *Receptive Vocabulary*. Assesses understanding of 25 single nouns and verbs in a picture recognition task. Items are presented in order of difficulty, ranging from concrete words that are frequently used to more abstract words that are used less often.
2. *Sentence Repetition—Length*. Assesses memory for sentences of gradually increasing length. An attempt was made to control the syntactic complexity of the stimulus sentences.
3. *Sentence Repetition—Complexity*. Assesses the ability to repeat relatively short sentences that gradually increase in grammatical complexity. The syntactic hierarchies were chosen for the English version based on Lee and Koenigsknecht's research (1974), and the Spanish sentences were selected on the basis of Allen Toronto's research (1972).
4. *Oral Commands*. Assesses memory for increasing numbers of oral directions. The student executes one to four simple tasks, which are presented orally. Performance is measured by the total number of directions correctly executed, regardless of order.
5. *Story Comprehension*. Assesses memory for information presented in brief oral narratives. The student verbally answers a set of factual questions based on a series of increasingly lengthy oral stories.

The Del Rio is quick and easy to administer in either language. The test manual contains background information and clear directions for administration, scoring, and interpretation, as well as stimulus pictures for the English and Spanish Receptive Vocabulary subtests. Separate test protocols are provided for the English and Spanish versions.

Normative information is available for three distinct groups: Anglo-Americans, predominantly English-speaking Mexican-Americans, and predominantly Spanish-speaking Mexican-Americans. The authors report significant differences between the test performances of these three groups, as arranged in one-year age intervals. Raw scores for individual subtests can be converted into percentiles. Scores between the second and third percentile (two standard deviations below the mean) are used as the cutoff point for deviant performance. Scores below the tenth percentile indicate the need for further assessment.

STRENGTHS OF THE DEL RIO

- The Del Rio is a widely used screening instrument for English- and Spanish-speaking students. Clinicians will find it to be efficient and highly flexible. Since norms are provided for each subtest, portions of the Del Rio may be administered as part of a quick screening. If only one or two subtests are used, the Receptive Vocabulary and Story Comprehension tasks provide the most valuable diagnostic information. The inclusion of two distinct sentence repetition tasks enables the clinician to compare the effects of length and syntactic complexity on auditory memory skills.
- Although the formats for the two language versions are identical, they are not direct translations. Therefore, both the English and Spanish forms may be administered to an individual student to help determine the degree of bilingualism. By comparing performance on specific tasks in both languages, overall strengths and weaknesses in language functioning can be determined. The Del Rio is one of the only standardized tests available that provides separate norms for two groups of Mexican-American students—predominantly English- and Spanish-speaking. Adequate test-retest reliability is reported for both language versions. The highest reliability for all three norming groups was obtained for the Receptive Vocabulary subtest.

LIMITING FACTORS OF THE DEL RIO

- Examiners are cautioned to use the Del Rio only with the Spanish-speaking group on which it was normed. Test items are consistent with the culture and language of the southwestern United States, and dialectal differences of Mexican-Americans from other areas are not considered. If substitutions in test vocabulary or syntactic structure are made to reflect a different linguistic or cultural group, norms should not be reported.
- The standardization groups used in the Del Rio are quite limited in number. Only 38 students, representing each language group, were used within a single age interval.
- The Del Rio does not discriminate well between older age groups for some subtests. For example, expected performance on the Sentence Repetition—Complexity and Story Comprehension subtests varies insignificantly for 5- and 6-year-old Anglo-American students.
- Some test items, on each of the five subtests, are identical in English and Spanish. In fact, four out of the five oral narratives on the Story Comprehension subtest are direct translations. If both versions are given to a single student, they should be administered in separate sessions to minimize any learning effect.
- Few validity studies on the Del Rio are reported. Content validity was suggested, since the subtest scores increase significantly with age. Intertest validity has not been explored.

Bilingual Syntax Measure (BSM)

Marina K. Burt, Heidi C. Dulay, and Eduardo Hernández Chávez
Harcourt Brace Jovanovich, Inc., 1978
The Psychological Corporation
7500 Old Oak Blvd., Middleburg Heights, OH 44130

Purpose	To measure children's oral proficiency in English and/or Spanish grammatical structures through natural speech
Major Areas Tested	Expressive syntax in English and Spanish
Age or Grade Range	Grades K–12
Usually Given By	Speech/language clinician Bilingual teacher Paraprofessional
Type of Test	Individual
Scores Obtained	Language proficiency level
Student Performance Timed?	No
Testing Time	10–15 minutes (each language version)
Scoring/Interpretation Time	5–10 minutes (each language version)
Normed On	4,000 students from 10 states and Mexico with approximately equal numbers of English- and Spanish-speaking subjects
Alternate Forms Available?	No

FORMAT

The Bilingual Syntax Measure (BSM) assesses expressive syntax in English and Spanish. BSM Level I is appropriate for children from 4 to 9 years old (grades K–2), and BSM Level II is appropriate for students from 10 to 18 years old (grades 3–12). The materials for each level consist of test manuals in English and Spanish, a picture booklet, student response booklets in English and Spanish, supplementary material (*Rationale and Technical Report*, Burt, Dulay, Chávez 1975), and class record forms.

The purpose of the BSM is to elicit "natural speech." Simple verbal questions are used with cartoon-type pictures to provide the framework for a conversation with the student. The analysis of the student's speech yields a numerical indicator and qualitative description of the student's structural language proficiency. Therefore, the BSM can be used to determine the "degree" of bilingualism, structural proficiency in English or Spanish as a second language, and maintenance or loss of basic Spanish structures.

Administration of the BSM begins with a preliminary screening. An initial set of questions about the stimulus pictures is presented to put the student at ease. If the student is able to respond verbally to only two or fewer of these and the first five test questions, testing is discontinued. For responsive students, 25 test questions are presented while the examiner refers to the appropriate picture. The test protocols contain the stimulus questions and spaces for recording the student's responses verbatim. The examiner is reminded to try to maintain a natural flow of conversation throughout the administration of the BSM. If both the English and Spanish versions are presented to a single student, they should be administered in separate sessions.

Scoring criteria and examples of responses are provided in the test manuals. The primary criterion for scoring is grammar in conversation. Therefore, grammatically correct responses with inappropriate content, incomplete sentences considered acceptable in conversation, and colloquial conversational forms (for example, *would'a*) are credited. The correctness of a student's response is always judged in the context of the stimulus question. Thus, a response such as "*He's* sleeping" is considered incorrect for the question "Why do you think *their* eyes are closed?" Only responses verbalized in the test language are credited. Overall scoring is based on the successive evaluation of the student's responses to certain groups of test questions. Instructions provided in the student response booklet include minimal criteria for assigning the student to one of the five following proficiency levels:

Level I. No English/Spanish.
Level II. Receptive English/Spanish. The student can produce some verbal routines and repeat short sentences or questions in either English or Spanish but cannot use that language to communicate thoughts and opinions.
Level III. Survival English/Spanish. The student usually can make himself or herself understood by using a combination of simple speech, gestures, and an occasional word from his or her native language. When verbalizing in the second language, the student may omit words or word endings.
Level IV. Intermediate English/Spanish. The student has little difficulty communicating ideas in either English or Spanish and demonstrates control of a number of basic grammatical structures.
Level V. Proficient English/Spanish. The student exhibits native or near-native control in either English or Spanish.

The BSM provides instructional suggestions for each proficiency level in the areas of receptive and expressive language, reading, and other academic subjects. Also included are categories of language dominance (see Figure 58) defined by English and Spanish proficiency levels and equivalent Lau categories (*Lau vs Nichols* 1975). The English-speaking designations consist of NES (non-English-speaking), LES (limited English-speaking), and FES (fluent English-speaking) categories, used for qualification for bilingual education programs in many states.

STRENGTHS OF THE BSM

• The BSM is a language proficiency instrument whose format and materials are appealing to most students. The stimulus pictures are attractive, brightly colored, and durable. The content of the pictures is interesting to students, holds their attention easily, and is familiar to many diverse cultural groups. Scoring does not rely on a student's cultural experience or knowledge, since answers contrary to fact can be credited.

• The BSM is simple to administer. Paraprofessionals who read and write in English and Spanish can be trained to administer this test. However, speech/language clinicians should judge the grammar of a student's responses.

• The BSM has several uses. It is helpful in diagnosis of expressive language difficulties and placement of students in second-language instruction programs. Furthermore, gain or loss of structural proficiency in English and Spanish can be determined by administration of the BSM at the beginning and end of a specific time interval.

• The authors present detailed information in support of the content validity of the BSM. They cite psycholinguistic research indicating that students of diverse language backgrounds follow a similar pattern in acquiring a second language, and they suggest that this research has resulted in the production of the BSM scoring system. In addition, they

Categories of Language Dominance Defined by English and Spanish Proficiency Levels, and Equivalent Lau Categories

BSM Language Dominance Category	BSM Proficiency Levels English[a]	Spanish	Lau Category[b]
Spanish Monolingual	1 or 2 (NES)	4 or 5	A: Monolingual speaker of the language other than English
Spanish Dominant	3 4 (LES)[c]	4 or 5 5	B: Predominantly speaks the language other than English
FOR KINDERGARTEN AND GRADE 1 ONLY			
Balanced Bilingual: Proficient	4 (FES)	4	C: Bilingual
Balanced Bilingual: Intermediate	4 (LES)[c]	4	C: Bilingual
Balanced Bilingual: Proficient	5 (FES)	5	C: Bilingual
English Dominant	4 or 5 (LES)[c] (FES) 5 (FES)	3 4	D: Predominantly speaks English
English Monolingual	4 or 5 (LES)[c] (FES)	1 or 2	E: Monolingual speaker of English
Special Diagnosis	Any combination where neither the English nor the Spanish Proficiency Level is higher than 3.		

[a]The English-speaking designations, printed in parentheses below the numerical levels, are defined as follows:
  NES—non-English-speaking
  LES—limited English-speaking
  FES—fluent English-speaking

[b]From *Task force findings specifying remedies available for eliminating past educational practices ruled unlawful under Lau v. Nichols.* Washington, D.C.: Department of Health, Education, and Welfare: Office for Civil Rights Summer 1975.

[c]English Proficiency Level 4 is LES only for Grades 2 and above. For Kindergarten and Grade 1, Level 4 is FES.

Figure 58. BSM Categories of Language Dominance

provide evidence that BSM proficiency classifications reflect expected relationships between the first and second acquired language of bilingual children.

LIMITING FACTORS OF THE BSM

- The BSM should be considered solely a measure of language proficiency. It is not an appropriate instrument for identification of a language disorder, since students who perform poorly on both language versions are classified as requiring special diagnosis. Students who misinterpret stimulus questions still receive credit if they produce grammatically correct responses. Furthermore, the BSM assesses only standard English syntax and is not appropriate for use with students who use Black English.

- Test-retest reliability of the BSM is low. The authors defend these figures by suggesting that they reflect characteristic changes in a student's acquisition of grammatical structures.

- Although a description of content validity is provided by the authors, formal validity studies are not reported.

Language Assessment Scales (LAS)

Edward A. DeAvila and Sharon E. Duncan
Linguametrics Group, 1981
P.O. Box 3495, San Rafael, CA 94912

Purpose	To identify children with oral English language difficulties and to ascertain linguistic proficiency in English and Spanish
Major Areas Tested	Receptive and expressive language, articulation, and auditory discrimination
Age or Grade Range	Grades K–12
Usually Given By	Speech/language clinician Bilingual teacher Paraprofessional
Type of Test	Individual Standardized Criterion-referenced
Scores Obtained	Language proficiency level
Student Performance Timed?	No
Testing Time	15–25 minutes
Scoring/Interpretation Time	20 minutes
Normed On	Not reported
Alternate Forms Available?	Yes (English version only)

FORMAT

The Language Assessment Scales (LAS) were designed to diagnose oral language problems in English- and Spanish-speaking students. Level I is appropriate for kindergarten through grade 5, and Level II is appropriate for grades 6 through 12. The formats for the English and Spanish versions are identical, although they are not direct translations. The LAS materials include an administration manual, a scoring and interpretation manual, an audio cassette with test items and two alternate stories, and student test forms and booklets with stimulus pictures.

The LAS consists of the following subscales:

1. *Minimal Sound Pairs*. Assesses the ability to distinguish between minimal sound pairs. The student listens to word pairs on the audiotape and indicates whether they are the same or different.

2. *Lexical*. Assesses single-word expressive vocabulary. The student is presented with 20 pictures to label. The student's response is judged correct if the noun is "commonly used in the area and of the approximate level of complexity" as the label tested in the manual. For example, a label of *chicken* for *rooster* would receive credit, while *animal* for *dog* would be judged incorrect.

3. *Phonemes*. Assesses phoneme production through a word and sentence repetition task presented on the audiotape. The student's production is judged correct if he or she repeats the item in a manner that would preclude any misunderstanding or ridicule.

4. *Comprehension*. Assesses understanding of various syntactic structures found to be difficult for students acquiring English or Spanish as a second language. The student hears a description on the tape and points to the drawing that best illustrates the stimulus sentence.

5. *Oral Production*. Assesses the ability to retell a brief story presented on the tape. A story is played while four drawings are presented to the student. The student is then asked to retell the narrative exactly the way it was heard. If the student doesn't produce at least 50 words, probe questions listed on the test form are presented. The student's response is recorded verbatim and is rated according to a five-point oral production scale. Samples are provided in the manual for various age groupings and language proficiency levels (nonspeaker, limited speaker, fluent speaker) to aid the examiner in assigning an oral production rating in English or Spanish.

6. *Written Production* (Level II—Optional). Assesses the ability to reproduce in writing the story presented in subscale 5. After the student retells the story, he or she is instructed to write what happened as closely as can be remembered. This writing sample is scored according to the same criteria used for the Oral Production section.

7. *Pragmatic Language* (Optional). Consists of an observational rating scale of language usage. The scale is not part of the total test calculations. The information about pragmatic skills in English or Spanish is used to reduce errors in classification of students and is usually completed by the classroom teacher or another adult familiar with the student.

The examiner may administer these subscales in any order. Test directions may be given in either language; however, only responses produced in the specific language being assessed are credited. Raw scores are entered in the box provided at the end of each subscale. Tables are then used to derive converted scores (from 0 to 100), which are summed to obtain a total score. The total score is multiplied by 100 and, finally, a language proficiency level (from 1 to 5) can be assigned for English and Spanish.

STRENGTHS OF THE LAS

- The LAS provides a more diverse set of language tasks than those provided by most other bilingual assessment instruments. Rather than using a measure of expressive syntax (Bilingual Syntax Measure, p. 209) or vocabulary (Dos Amigos Verbal Language Scales, p. 205) to determine language dominance or proficiency, the LAS provides information about the phonemic, lexical, syntactic, and pragmatic aspects of language. Inclusion of an observational checklist of language usage outside of the testing situation is a unique and valuable feature of the LAS.

- The use of an audiotape for administration of the LAS makes it possible for a bilingual paraprofessional to be trained to give this test. However, due to the complexity of the scoring system, a speech/language clinician should evaluate the student's oral or written production samples.

- The LAS has a language arts remediation program associated with it, named the Linguametrics Language Arts Series. Spanish and English test items are cross-indexed with portions of the series that contain a wide variety of language arts games and activities for school-age children.

- Adequate test-retest and split-half reliability is reported for the LAS.

- There is a great deal of statistical information available on the LAS. Discriminant, convergent, content, and construct validity are discussed in depth in the authors' book, *A Convergent Approach to Language Assessment: Theoretical and Technical Specifications on the Language Assessment Scales* (DeAvila and Duncan 1981).

LIMITING FACTORS OF THE LAS

- The LAS is a complex assessment instrument and, unfortunately, the test manuals are disorganized and confusing. There are two separate manuals—one on administration and one on scoring and interpretation—each providing bits of information needed to use the LAS. Not only are there separate tests for two levels and two languages, the English Level I test is available in two equivalent forms, A and B. In addition, the scoring procedure, which involves changing raw scores to converted scores to a total score and then to a language proficiency level, seems needlessly complicated.

- Although numerous examples are provided in the manual, assigning oral production levels is a difficult task. Many of the criteria used seem subjective, and establishing interrater reliability is a time-consuming process.

Woodcock Language Proficiency Battery—Spanish (WLPB-S)

Richard W. Woodcock
Teaching Resources Corporation, 1981
50 Pond Park Rd., Hingham, MA 02043

Purpose	To measure proficiency in oral language, reading, and writing in Spanish
Major Areas Tested	Oral language, written language, and reading
Age or Grade Range	Grades K–12
Usually Given By	Speech/language clinician Special education teacher Bilingual teacher
Type of Test	Individual Standardized Norm-referenced Criterion-referenced
Scores Obtained	Age level Grade level Percentile Relative mastery Standard
Student Performance Timed?	No
Testing Time	45 minutes (all subtests)
Scoring/Interpretation Time	20–30 minutes
Normed On	802 children in grades K, 1, 3, 5, 8, and 11 from urbanized areas in Costa Rica, Mexico, Peru, Puerto Rico, and Spain and 4,732 subjects from a wide distribution of communities in the United States, balanced for sex, race, occupation, geographic location, and type of community
Alternate Forms Available?	No

FORMAT

The Woodcock Language Proficiency Battery—Spanish (WLPB-S) consists of eight subtests that assess oral language, written language, and reading in Spanish. This battery is a translation and modification of selected subtests from the English form, the Woodcock-Johnson Psycho-Educational Battery (p. 293), and contains a separate set of norms.

The WLPB-S materials include an examiner's manual, an easel-style test book, and a response booklet for recording responses, summarizing results, and interpreting test performance.

The subtests include:

A. *Picture Vocabulary*. The student identifies pictured objects and actions.

B. *Antonyms-Synonyms*. In part A, the student states the opposite of a stimulus word; in part B, the student states the word whose meaning approximates the stimulus word.

C. *Analogies*. The student completes verbal analogies.

D. *Letter-Word Identification*. The student identifies isolated letters and words printed in the test book. To receive credit, the student must correctly identify the letter by name or phonetic sound and must correctly read the word in 4 to 5 seconds.

E. *Word Attack*. The student reads nonsense words, which range from consonant-vowel digrams to multisyllable items. Almost all Spanish phonemes are represented by at least one major spelling pattern.

F. *Passage Comprehension*. The student identifies key words missing from a reading passage.

G. *Dictation*. The student responds in writing to questions involving knowledge of letter forms, spelling, punctuation, capitalization, and usage.

H. *Proofing*. The student identifies mistakes in typewritten passages and indicates how to correct each error. The errors include punctuation, capitalization, spelling, and inappropriate word forms.

The WLPB-S enables the examiner to combine selected items from the above subtests to obtain additional measures of performance. These three composite subtests include Punctuation and Capitalization, Spelling, and Usage.

The entire battery or individual subtest or groups of subtests may be administered. For each subtest, items are arranged in order of difficulty, and basal and ceiling levels are provided. Although starting-point tables are included to assist the examiner in beginning subtests at an appropriate level, examiners are encouraged to use an estimate of the student's ability rather than the student's actual age or grade level.

Clusters of subtests provide the primary basis for interpretation of the WLPB-S. The Oral Language cluster consists of a combination of the Picture Vocabulary, Antonyms-Synonyms, and Analogies subtests. The Reading cluster combines the Letter-Word Identification, Word Attack, and Passage Comprehension subtests, and the Written Language cluster includes Dictation and Proofing. Furthermore, a general index of overall language functioning (Broad Language Ability) can be obtained by combining these three clusters.

A broad range of scores is provided to interpret a student's performance on the WLPB-S. Raw scores can be converted to grade scores, age scores, and percentiles. Other types of scores include an extended grade scale, extended age scale, and relative performance index. Refer to the Woodcock Reading Mastery Tests (p. 53) and the Woodcock-Johnson Psycho-Educational Battery (p. 293) for discussion of these newer scores.

STRENGTHS OF THE WLPB-S

- There are few Spanish assessment instruments that evaluate reading or written language skills. The WLPB-S makes an important contribution by providing a flexible, organized, and well-normed diagnostic tool. The examiner is able to evaluate a student's performance on clusters of subtests, a single subtest, or the entire test battery. If both the English and Spanish versions are administered to an individual student, relative language proficiency in the areas of oral and written linguistic skills and reading can be determined. This information about language proficiency is essential in deciding whether to provide a reading instruction program in English or Spanish for bilingual students.

- The WLPB-S is useful for identifying specific language disorders as well as for determining language proficiency. Subtests A, B, and C can provide information about a student's word recall and retrieval abilities, knowledge of vocabulary, and verbal reasoning skills. Subtest F, which consists of a cloze procedure, evaluates the student's ability to use the language context to provide an appropriate word.

- The test manual for the WLPB-S is exceptionally complete and well organized. Practice exercises are provided to acquaint the examiner with administration procedures. The clever design of the test book is also an asset.

- A student's performance on the WLPB-S can be compared with norms from two separate standardization populations. One set of norms was gathered from urbanized areas in several Spanish-speaking countries. The equated United States norms provide data for converting scores on the WLPB-S into equivalent proficiency scores on the English version. That is, these scores indicate the level of English proficiency that corresponds with the student's demonstrated Spanish proficiency. This information is quite useful for planning instructional programs for Spanish-speaking students in the United States.

LIMITING FACTORS OF THE WLPB-S

- There are several methods of analyzing a student's performance on the WLPB-S that are time-consuming and complicated. Although valuable diagnostic information can be obtained, it requires a substantial time commitment on the part of the examiner to study the test manual, practice administering the battery, and understand the scoring procedures.

- Reliability and validity information is not reported or referred to in the test materials.

Chapter Five

Gross Motor Tests

Relatively few standardized tests of gross motor skills are available. More often, informal rating scales are devised by the special education teacher interested in perceptual motor training. In addition to the usual skills emphasized in physical education—running, catching, throwing, and total body coordination—basic skills such as balance and posture have often been found to be underdeveloped in children with learning and language disabilities. Special education theorists such as Newell Kephart (1960) and A. Jean Ayres (1973) have hypothesized that adequate motor development is prerequisite to developing higher-level perceptual and cognitive skills. Although recent research (Hallahan and Cruickshank 1973; Cratty 1970) has shown no direct connection between motor skills and academic performance, no one disputes the fact that many special education students have delayed motor skills for which they need specific teaching. Although training in balance, posture, rhythm, and ball skills may not improve spelling, it often leads to improvement in the equally important areas of playground activities and social skills.

For this reason, it is important to be familiar with some tests of gross motor ability. In this chapter, two test batteries are reviewed. The Bruininks-Oseretsky Test of Motor Proficiency is a recent modification of the earlier Oseretsky scales familiar to many special education teachers. The Southern California Sensory Integration Tests is a highly technical battery administered by occupational and physical therapists to assess not only gross motor skills but also tactile and kinesthetic perception systems. Both tests reviewed here include gross and fine motor skills, attesting to the close relationship between the two areas.

Developmental delays in motor skills and coordination are often one of the first signs of possible learning disorders. As a result, many of the tests for preschool children include assessments of gross motor skills. In Part II: Preschool and Kindergarten Tests, four of the six tests reviewed have sections on gross motor skills. Readers interested in the assessment of motor skills in very young children are referred to this section.

Bruininks-Oseretsky Test of Motor Proficiency   220
Southern California Sensory Integration Tests   223

Bruininks-Oseretsky Test of Motor Proficiency
(Bruininks-Oseretsky Test)

Robert H. Bruininks
American Guidance Service, 1978
Publishers' Bldg., Circle Pines, MN 55014

Purpose	To assess motor skills, to develop and evaluate motor training programs, and to assess serious motor dysfunctions and developmental delays in children
Major Areas Tested	Motor proficiency and gross and fine motor skills
Age or Grade Range	4½–14½ years
Usually Given By	Special education teacher Occupational therapist Physical education teacher Motor therapist
Type of Test	Standardized Individual
Scores Obtained	Age level Standard Percentile Stanine
Student Performance Timed?	Yes (some subtests)
Testing Time	45–60 minutes (complete battery); 15–20 minutes (short form)
Scoring/Interpretation Time	15–20 minutes
Normed On	765 students from north central, southern, and western states and Canada, balanced for age, sex, race, and community size according to the 1970 census
Alternate Forms Available?	No

FORMAT

The materials for the Bruininks-Oseretsky Test of Motor Proficiency (Bruininks-Oseretsky Test) consist of the examiner's manual, individual record forms for recording responses and scores, student booklets that include materials for pencil-and-paper and cutting tasks, and a variety of manipulative materials for use with the various subtests. All of the materials are packaged in a specially designed metal carrying case.

The test is designed to yield three estimates of motor proficiency: a gross motor score, a fine motor score, and a battery composite score. The 46 items are divided into 8 subtests:

Gross Motor Skills

1. *Running Speed and Agility* (1 item). Running speed during a shuttle run is measured.

2. *Balance* (8 items). Static balance and walking balance on a taped line and a balance beam are assessed.

3. *Bilateral Coordination* (8 items). Simultaneous coordination of upper and lower limbs is measured by asking the student to reproduce such rhythmic patterns as tapping alternate feet and hands or jumping and clapping hands.

4. *Strength* (3 items). Shoulder and arm, abdominal, and leg strength are measured by tasks that include the broad jump, situps, and pushups.

Gross and Fine Motor Skills

5. *Upper-Limb Coordination* (9 items). Coordination of visual tracking with arm and hand movements and precise movements of the arms and hands is assessed by throwing and catching a ball, fingers-to-nose and thumb touching, and others.

Fine Motor Skills

6. *Response Speed* (1 item). Quick response to a moving visual target is measured by catching a sliding stick on the wall.

7. *Visual-Motor Control* (8 items). Coordination of precise visual and hand movements is assessed by such tasks as cutting, copying designs, and following mazes.

8. *Upper-Limb Speed and Dexterity* (8 items). Hand and finger dexterity and hand and arm speed are assessed by such tasks as placing pennies in a box, stringing beads, and rapidly drawing lines and dots.

Raw scores for individual items are converted to a point score using the conversion tables printed directly below each item on the individual record form. Item scores are totaled to obtain subtest scores, which are in turn totaled to make the three composite scores:

1. Gross motor composite score (total of subtests 1 to 4)
2. Fine motor composite score (total of subtests 6 to 8)
3. Total battery composite score (total of subtests 1 to 8)

The three composite scores are converted to normalized standard scores with a mean of 50 and a standard deviation of 10. Percentile ranks and stanines are provided for the composite scores; age-equivalent scores are available for each subtest. Standard error of measurement is provided for the three composite scores.

A short form of the Bruininks-Oseretsky Test is also described in the manual. Fourteen items have been selected from the 46 items comprising the total test. Each of the 14 items was selected because of its high correlation with the subtest and total test scores, the range of ages for which it was useful, the short amount of time needed to administer the item, and the ease of scoring. The short-form items are clearly marked in the manual and on the individual record form. A standard score, percentile, stanine, and standard error of measurement are provided for the short form.

STRENGTHS OF THE BRUININKS-OSERETSKY TEST

• The Bruininks-Oseretsky Test is a modification of the Oseretsky motor tests developed in Russia in the 1920s. The most-used form of the Oseretsky tests for children was the Lincoln-Oseretsky Development Scale. Bruininks's carefully constructed test reflects advances in content and technical quality. Extensive efforts were made to secure a balanced norming sample, and validity figures indicate that the test provides a good estimate of developmental changes in motor proficiency.

• The wide variety of items included in the eight subtests, together with well-designed manipulative materials, makes the test interesting and challenging for students with a wide range of ages and abilities.

• The administration procedures include several good features: a pretest for determining the preferred hand and leg, more than one trial on most subtests, and demonstration of items by the examiner.

• The short form of the test is particularly helpful when large numbers of students need to be screened. Because the short form is embedded in the full test, the short form items can be used for reevaluation purposes.

• The manual is clearly written and gives not only directions for administration and scoring but also information on test construction, norming, reliability, and validity.

LIMITING FACTORS OF THE BRUININKS-OSERETSKY TEST

• The Bruininks-Oseretsky Test requires a skilled examiner. Many items require setting up equipment in a specific manner and timing the student's responses precisely. Several items need to be demonstrated to the student, so the examiner must also be coordinated. This test is difficult to administer and score. Inexperienced persons should not administer it without careful study of the manual and several practice tests.

- The Bruininks-Oseretsky Test requires space. A running area of 15 meters is necessary, so a playground or multipurpose room will be needed. If many students are to be tested, it is most convenient to set up the physical equipment and leave it in place for the duration of the testing.

- The scoring system for the test is complex. Each item has very specific and different scoring techniques—some record time, others number of correct responses, others pass-fail. Once each item receives a point score, the translation into standard scores, percentiles, stanines, and age-equivalent scores is a many-stepped process. The examiner is urged to doublecheck all scoring for accuracy.

- Test-retest reliability on the individual subtests is somewhat low and makes interpretation of results somewhat questionable. Professionals using this test should be aware of the low reliability factor and not use the test alone to diagnose motor problems.

- Although the author claims that the test can be used to determine "whether a student should enter school early" or be placed in a higher grade, such usage of a motor test is highly questionable. Although some research studies using mentally retarded and learning-disabled students are reported in the manual, it reports little data on the relationship between the disabilities and the lack of motor proficiency.

- The manual does not present any information on how to use the Bruininks-Oseretsky Test results to plan individual or small-group motor programs. Presumably the eight subtests would serve as guidelines for the components of a motor training program; more information in this area would be helpful to the user.

Southern California Sensory Integration Tests (SCSIT)

A. Jean Ayres
Western Psychological Services, 1972
12031 Wilshire Blvd., Los Angeles, CA 90025

Purpose	To assess sensory integrative functioning
Major Areas Tested	Visual, tactile, kinesthetic, and vestibular functioning; motor planning ability; postural mechanisms; bilateral integration; and coordination of gross and fine motor skills
Age or Grade Range	4–9 years
Usually Given By	Occupational therapist Physical therapist
Type of Test	Standardized Individual
Scores Obtained	Standard
Student Performance Timed?	Yes (some subtests)
Testing Time	1½ hours
Scoring/Interpretation Time	1 hour
Normed On	Heterogeneous population of children from public and private schools, organizations, and children's centers from metropolitan Los Angeles, California, and surrounding areas
Alternate Forms Available?	No

FORMAT

The Southern California Sensory Integration Tests (SCSIT) consist of 18 standardized tests and a series of informal clinical observations. The format of each of the standardized tests is described in Table 26. The clinical observation items include a variety of motor tasks designed to provide supplementary information about postural mechanisms, praxis, bilateral integration, muscle tone, and other aspects of motor functioning.

The materials consist of a test manual, an interpretation manual, scoring forms, profile sheets, and picture and manipulative materials for the 18 tests. The materials for the total SCSIT can be purchased in one kit; most of the test materials can also be purchased separately.

STRENGTHS OF THE SCSIT

* The SCSIT is designed to assess the student's ability to interpret and use meaningfully certain kinds of sensory information from the environment and from the student's own body. Visual, tactile, kinesthetic, and vestibular functioning are assessed, as well as motor planning skill (praxis), postural mechanisms, bilateral integration, and coordination for basic gross and fine motor skills. The skills assessed are automatic rather than cognitive functions.

* The SCSIT is, therefore, a comprehensive battery of tests that provides information about a broad range of motor functioning. Through the use of 18 short tests, a balance is achieved between the need to maintain student interest and the need to include sufficient numbers of test items to gain meaningful information.

* The test battery is useful not only in determining which students are experiencing difficulty in the sensorimotor areas, but also in defining the nature of those difficulties. Through the use of factor-analytic studies, several areas of sensory integrative functioning have been identified, and the SCSIT provides information necessary for this differential diagnosis. For example, an apraxic student may score poorly in the tactile tests and on the motor-involved tests but may achieve average or above-average scores on tests of form and space perception, which do not require precise motor responses. In this example, the SCSIT not only would indicate that this student is experiencing difficulties in the sensorimotor areas but would also identify the area of dysfunction, providing information necessary for planning an appropriate intervention program.

* The SCSIT is a useful tool for evaluating sensorimotor development in language-impaired students. Expressive language requirements are minimal. The student is required to respond orally (one-word answers are sufficient) on two items on Right-Left Discrimination; no other tests in the battery require oral responses. The understanding of language required of the student is somewhat more demanding. However, directions are simple, they can be repeated and reexplained on most tests, and all tests include trial items with additional explanations as indicated. In addition, a great deal of imitation is used in the administration of the tests.

* Although most of the tests in the battery cannot be used in isolation, the tests of Motor Accuracy and Design Copying have adequate reliability to be used independently. These two tests may provide useful information regarding a child's progress in fine motor coordination and visual-motor integration skills. The Motor Accuracy test is particularly sensitive for measuring small skill changes in younger students.

* The student's scores are presented on a profile that graphically illustrates how his or her scores compare to those of the normative population, as well as how scores in one area of functioning compare to scores in another area (see Figure 59). This profile is a clear and accurate means of reporting scores to parents and other professionals.

* The test manual provides, for the most part, thorough statistical information, including coefficients of test-retest reliability, standard errors of measurement, size and sex distribution of the normative sample, means, standard deviations, and standard scores for each age group on each test. With the exception of Motor Accuracy, the size of the standardization sample was adequate for each age group, ranging from 60 to 125 students. The manual also provides basic information about test interpretation and validity studies, including analyses of the relationship between SCSIT scores and other established measures of perceptual-motor skills, as well as the relationship between SCSIT scores and various aspects of sensory integrative functioning. The author cautions, quite appropriately, that meaningful interpretations of the SCSIT are still in the early stages.

LIMITING FACTORS OF THE SCSIT

* The standardization sample of the SCSIT is poorly defined. "Geographic and socioeconomic levels of metropolitan Los Angeles and surrounding areas" gives little information. The intellectual levels of the sample were not controlled. There were no learning-disabled students in the sample. In addition, the numbers of students tested at each age level were sometimes quite small (Evans and Peham 1981).

* The reliability of the SCSIT is quite poor, with coefficients ranging from .01 to .94 with a mean of .53 (Gaines 1972; Landis 1972). The author cautions that the test must be administered in its entirety, and cluster scores should be used for interpretation, rather than individual subtest scores.

* It is difficult to obtain validity information on the SCSIT. Information is scattered through the manuals. Data substantiating the relationship between the SCSIT and either

neurological criteria or educational criteria is not provided (Reed 1978).

- When a student obtains low scores on the SCSIT, a course of sensory integration therapy is often recommended. Given the poor reliability of the test, its questionable validity, and the lack of data supporting its relationship to academic skills, such recommendations should be made with great caution.
- The SCSIT is a complex battery to administer and interpret, and it requires a highly trained examiner. A workable system exists for training and certifying professionals (usually occupational and physical therapists), but there is no requirement that an individual be certified before purchasing and administering the tests. The subtleties of administration and interpretation leave the SCSIT highly vulnerable to misuse by untrained examiners.
- The tests are time-consuming to administer, score, and interpret.
- The test scores are sometimes used to hypothesize about suspected areas of brain dysfunction (for example, right or left cortical hemisphere, brainstem). This interpretation is highly controversial.
- Owing to the nature of the tasks, it is often difficult to determine the student's degree of attentiveness. This is particularly true of the tactile tests.
- The tests were designed to assess automatic rather than highly cognitive functions, but a bright, motivated student may be able to respond adequately on some tests through cognitive skills, thus obscuring some deficits in automatic functioning. A trained examiner is alert to this possibility, but observation of it is subjective at best.

Table 26. SCSIT Tests

Test	Task	Functions
Space Visualization	The student is given a simple formboard (one shape), with a peg in it, and two blocks, each with a hole. Without manipulating the blocks, the student must select the block that fits onto the formboard with the hole correctly aligned over the peg. He or she then indicates the choice by placing one block onto the formboard. The item is scored for time and accuracy from the moment the student first moves (or points to) a block. Early items require only discrimination by shape, but more complex, later items require mental manipulation of the blocks.	Visual perception
Figure-Ground Perception	The student is shown a test plate of several superimposed figures and a response plate of six separate figures. The student must select the three figures embedded in the test plate. Figure-ground discrimination is required. Both common objects and geometric forms are used.	Visual perception
Position in Space	This test is in three parts. For parts 1 and 2, the student is shown a stimulus figure (a geometric form or a sequence of forms) and two to four response figures from which to choose a match. This may require discriminating among reversed or rotated forms or matching sequences of forms. A complex procedure minimizes the effect of chance, and considerable instruction is permitted. For part 3, the stimulus is removed, requiring the student to rely on visual memory.	Visual perception, visual memory
Design Copying	The student copies patterns on dot grids. The responses are scored according to the ability to connect the correct dots and the precision with which the lines are drawn.	Visual perception, visual motor integration, fine motor coordination
Motor Accuracy	With one hand, then the other, the student traces a curved line about 51 inches long, printed on paper 17 by 11 inches. This requires fine finger movements, as well as shoulder girdle and elbow adjustments on a horizontal surface. In scoring, the examiner measures the length of the line the student traced inaccurately and the distance strayed from the correct line. The scores achieved with the more-accurate hand and the less-accurate hand are compared with those of the normative sample.	Praxis, other aspects of upper-extremity coordination
Kinesthesia	A shield occludes the student's vision throughout. The examiner places the student's index finger at a spot on the kinesthesia chart, then says that it is the student's "pretend house," from which he or she will visit a "pretend friend's house." The examiner moves the student's finger to a second spot ("Bob's house"), then back to the original spot. The student attempts to return to "Bob's house" without guidance, and the examiner measures the distance from it to the student's finger. The process is repeated for each "friend's house."	Perception of joint position and movement
Manual Form Perception	With a shield occluding the student's vision, the examiner places a geometric form in the student's hand. The student feels the form and then points to the picture that he or she thinks shows that form.	Tactile discrimination, form and space perception
Finger Identification	With a shield occluding the student's vision, the examiner touches one or two of the student's fingers, and the student attempts to point to the designated finger(s) on a paper chart.	Tactile discrimination

Gross Motor Tests

Mode of Presentation	Mode of Response	Significant Motor Component?	Timed?	Notes
Visual, three-dimensional	Pointing to and/or moving blocks	No	Yes—separate accuracy scores, timed and untimed	The test discriminates well in younger age groups. It is less effective in discriminating between average and above-average performance in older age groups. The large chance factor in selecting answers requires cautious interpretation of scores.
Visual, two-dimensional	Pointing to figures in a plate (multiple choice)	No	Not precisely—a time limit is set for each item	Test performance is particularly vulnerable to anxiety. The large chance factor in selecting answers requires cautious interpretation of scores.
Visual, two-dimensional	Pointing or saying yes/no to figures (multiple choice)	No	Part 2 only	This test does not discriminate well among 4-year-olds with severe perceptual handicaps.
Visual, two-dimensional	Dot-to-dot drawing with pencil	Yes	No	Students experienced in exercises of this kind may achieve unrealistically high scores. The test does not discriminate well among 4-year-olds with perceptual deficits.
Visual	Tracing with pencil	Yes	Yes—separate accuracy scores, timed and untimed	The test does not discriminate well among well-coordinated 8-year-olds. It does provide a precise tool for measuring subtle changes in accuracy with a pencil in younger children, particularly poorly coordinated ones.
Kinesthetic, vision occluded (examiner moves student's arm)	Moving arm, vision occluded	Yes	No	The test provides the opportunity to observe automatic postural adjustments.
Tactile, vision occluded	Pointing to pictures, vision permitted	No	Yes	These five tactile discrimination tests must be given in one sitting and in the correct order. The scores must also be viewed as a constellation if interpretation is to be accurate. A score on any one of the tests should not be taken in
Tactile, vision occluded	Pointing to fingers, vision permitted	No	No	

Table 26.—*Continued*

Test	Task	Functions
Graphesthesia	With a shield occluding the student's vision, the examiner traces a simple design with a pencil eraser on the back of the student's hand. The examiner then removes the shield, and the student attempts to retrace the design with a fingertip on his or her own hand.	Tactile discrimination, form and space perception, fine motor coordination
Localization of Tactile Stimuli	A shield occludes the student's vision throughout the test. First, the examiner touches a spot on the student's hand or arm with the tip of a pen; then the student attempts to touch the spot with a fingertip. The examiner measures the distance from the spot to the student's finger.	Tactile discrimination
Double Tactile Stimuli Perception	Standing behind the student, the examiner uses two pencil erasers simultaneously to touch the student's hands, cheeks, or one hand and one cheek. The student then attempts to point to the places where he or she felt the erasers. The response that is scored is touching the correct cheek or hand.	Tactile discrimination
Imitation of Postures	The examiner quickly assumes positions requiring precise placement of hands and arms and, on some items, of trunk and/or legs. The student then attempts to copy these postures.	Praxis, postural mechanisms, bilateral integration
Crossing the Midline of the Body	The examiner points to his or her ear or eye, and the student copies in mirror image. Explicit instructions and trial items establish whether the student understands the concept of mirror image. The examiner scores according to whether the student crosses the body midline in responding. For example, does the student consistently use the right hand to point to the right ear or eye, even when the correct imitation requires using the left hand?	Bilateral integration, praxis
Bilateral Motor Coordination	The examiner demonstrates a rhythmic pattern of light slaps against his or her thighs, and the student imitates in mirror image. The student's ability to coordinate arm movements enters into the scoring.	Bilateral integration, praxis
Right-Left Discrimination	The examiner asks the student to indicate the right or left hand, foot, ear, and so on. Two items also require the student to distinguish between right and left on the examiner.	Bilateral integration
Standing Balance, Eyes Open	With eyes open, the student folds his or her arms and balances as long as possible first on the right foot, then on the left foot.	Postural mechanisms
Standing Balance, Eyes Closed	With eyes closed, the student repeats the procedure above.	Postural mechanisms
Postrotary Nystagmus	The student sits on a PNT board (a board that rotates on ball bearings) and is turned in the same direction 10 times in 20 seconds. The student then stares at a blank wall, and the examiner observes his or her eyes for nystagmus. The examiner also watches for postural changes and dizziness. This procedure is repeated with turns in the opposite direction.	One component of vestibular function, namely selected aspects of response to rotation

Gross Motor Tests

Mode of Presentation	Mode of Response	Significant Motor Component?	Timed?	Notes
				isolation, because each is highly subject to testing error. These tests also provide an opportunity to observe the presence or lack of tactile defensiveness.
Tactile, vision occluded	Retracing designs with a fingertip, vision permitted	Yes	No	
Tactile, vision occluded	Touching designated spots on hands and arms, vision occluded	No	No	
Tactile, vision occluded	Pointing to hands and cheeks	No	No	
Visual	Motor—whole body	Yes	Not precisely—a time limit is set on each item for full and partial credit	This and the five tests that follow must be administered in one sitting and in the correct sequence.
Visual	Pointing to ears and eyes	Yes, although precise movements are not required	No	
Visual	Motor—hands and arms used in clapping pattern	Yes	No	Scoring coordination on this test is more subjective than on the other tests in the battery.
Oral	Pointing to body parts and saying "right" and "left"	No	Not precisely—a time limit is set on each item for full credit	This test includes the only two items in the battery that require oral responses.
Oral	Motor	Yes	Yes	
Oral	Motor	Yes	Yes	
Vestibular input	No voluntary response required	No	Yes	This test is discontinued if the student becomes fearful, excessively dizzy, or uncomfortable in any way. It may be contraindicated for seizure-prone children.

Southern California Sensory Integration Tests

Profile of Standard Scores
by A. Jean Ayres, Ph.D.

Published by

WPS — WESTERN PSYCHOLOGICAL SERVICES
PUBLISHERS AND DISTRIBUTORS
12031 WILSHIRE BOULEVARD
LOS ANGELES, CALIFORNIA 90025
A DIVISION OF MANSON WESTERN CORPORATION

Name _____   Test Date   Yr. ____ Mo. ____ Dy. ____
Examiner _____   Birth Date Yr. ____ Mo. ____ Dy. ____
Preferred Hand: L (R); Preferred Eye: L (R) _____   Chron. Age Yr. 7 Mo. 5 Dy. 3

- Double Tactile Stimuli Perception −2.4
- Localization of Tactile Stimuli −1.9
- Motor Accuracy, Right Hand −1.8 (raw score 443)
- Standing Balance, Eyes Open −1.7
- Motor Accuracy, Left Hand −1.6 (raw score 420)
- Graphesthesia −1.5
- Standing Balance, Eyes Closed −1.4
- Manual Form Perception −1.3
- Crossing the Midline of the Body −1.3
- Imitation of Postures −1.1
- Kinesthesia −1.0
- Bilateral Motor Coordination −1.0
- Design Copying −0.5
- Postrotary Nystagmus −0.2
- Space Visualization 0.0
- Finger Identification +0.2
- Right-Left Discrimination +0.4
- Position in Space +0.5
- Figure-Ground Perception +1.3

Figure 59. SCSIT Profile

PART II
Preschool and Kindergarten Tests

Early identification of children with learning disabilities has been a major topic of discussion in special education for the past 15 years. The early detection of any type of handicap receives wide support from the fields of medicine, psychology, and education; the recognition and diagnosis of a specific condition leads directly to treatment.

The process becomes a little less clear, however, when the condition being identified is predicted rather than currently present. In other words, assessing preschool children's performance on test items believed to be related to academic success may result in a prediction of academic failure when the actual academic failure has not occurred—and may not occur. It is one thing to assess learning disabilities in the third grader who has not learned to read; it is another to assess potential learning disabilities in a 5-year-old. Everyone agrees that the earlier a child gets help, the better. But many professionals are afraid that the identification of potential problems may create in parents and teachers an expectation set that will increase the likelihood that the problem will occur.

The concerns regarding early identification procedures are well outlined by Keogh and Becker (1973, pp. 5–11). They divide the problems of early identification into three main areas: (1) the predictive validity of the tests, (2) the implications of the diagnostic information for placement and remediation, and (3) the weighing of the benefits of early detection with the possible negative effects of such recognition.

In order to validate early identification measures, the students tested during their preschool and kindergarten years must be followed to determine their actual academic success in the primary and intermediate years. Longitudinal research can help to show whether the predictive tool did, in fact, predict academic success or failure with a high degree of accuracy. The best-known longitudinal research was reported by de Hirsch, Jansky, and Langford (1966) in *Predicting Reading Failure*. A wide variety of standardized and informal tests were administered to over 400 kindergarten students, who were then followed for two years. This study resulted in a predictive index of five tests that could be administered in 15 to 20 minutes. The predictive index identified three out of four students with reading failure in second grade. Longitudinal research is currently in progress using other instruments and student populations (Satz *et al*. 1975; Morrissey 1979). Because the decisions about placement and program that result from early identification procedures are crucial, the use of assessment measures with high predictive validity is imperative.

Preschool and kindergarten tests can be classified in various ways: group versus individual, single content area versus multiple areas, standardized versus informal, and screening instruments versus diagnostic tools. The eight tests reviewed in Part II are arranged in order from the general to the specific: The first four assess developmental delays in young children; the last four assess delays in specific content areas (language, mathematics, and reading) and are used with older children.

The first test reviewed, the Denver Developmental Screening Test, has been widely used in medical and educational settings for several years as a quick individual screening test to identify high-risk infants and preschool children. The Brigance Diagnostic Inventory of Early Development is a comprehensive assessment instrument.

It lowers the age range of the criterion-referenced format of the Brigance Diagnostic Inventories (p. 29) from kindergarten to birth. The Brigance® K and 1 Screen pulls together items from the kindergarten and first-grade levels into a screening instrument. The Miller Assessment for Preschoolers screens children from 2½ to 5 years of age in motor, cognitive, and language skills. The well-known Meeting Street School Screening Test is reviewed, as well as the new Basic School Skills Inventory.

Of the tests measuring a single content area, the Preschool Language Scale is a quick method of screening children from 1 to 7 years old for language problems. The Kraner Preschool Math Inventory assesses math skills at the readiness level and also provides an assessment of language in the areas of spatial and quantitative concepts. The Slingerland Pre-Reading Screening Procedures is the kindergarten-level test of the Slingerland Screening Tests for Identifying Children with Specific Language Disability (p. 102). It is designed to identify children who are at high risk for reading failure.

Many tests reviewed in other chapters of this book are appropriate for preschool and kindergarten children. Appendix G lists these tests.

**DENVER DEVELOPMENTAL SCREENING
  TEST 233
BRIGANCE DIAGNOSTIC INVENTORY OF EARLY
  DEVELOPMENT 237
MILLER ASSESSMENT FOR PRESCHOOLERS 241
THE MEETING STREET SCHOOL SCREENING
  TEST 244
BASIC SCHOOL SKILLS INVENTORY 248
PRESCHOOL LANGUAGE SCALE 251
KRANER PRESCHOOL MATH INVENTORY 254
SLINGERLAND PRE-READING SCREENING
  PROCEDURES 257**

Denver Developmental Screening Test (DDST)

William Frankenburg and Josiah Dodds
Ladoca Project and Publishing Foundation, Inc., 1970
East 51st Ave. and Lincoln St., Denver, CO 80216

Purpose	To detect developmental delays
Major Areas Tested	Social, fine motor, gross motor, and language skills
Age or Grade Range	Birth–6 years
Usually Given By	Special education teacher Speech/language clinician Occupational therapist Doctor/nurse Psychologist
Type of Test	Standardized Individual
Scores Obtained	Age level
Student Performance Timed?	No
Testing Time	20 minutes
Scoring/Interpretation Time	10 minutes
Normed On	1,000 children from Denver, Colorado, with race, ethnic, and occupational group characteristics of the 1960 Denver census; children with atypical birth histories or known handicaps excluded
Alternate Forms Available?	No

FORMAT

The Denver Developmental Screening Test (DDST) consists of an examiner's manual and individual scoring sheets. A few simple materials, such as red wool, one-inch colored blocks, and a tennis ball, are included in the kit. The 105 test items are arranged in four sections as shown in Table 27.

The individual scoring sheets are arranged with age scales across the top and bottom, as shown in Figure 60. Ages are given in monthly intervals from 1 to 24 months and in three-month intervals from 2 to 6 years. Each of the 105 items is represented on the form by a bar that indicates at what age 25, 50, 75, and 90 percent of the children in the standardization sample passed the item. A vertical line is drawn on the scoring sheet to represent the child's chronological age.

Every effort is made to make the young child comfortable with the testing situation. A parent or other familiar person is always present, and the infant or young child often sits on that person's lap. Items in the Personal-Social sector are administered first, because many of the items can be passed by parent report. In other sectors, the examiner begins with items slightly below the child's chronological age and continues downward until three items are passed; then the examiner proceeds to items at the child's age level or above until three items are failed. Items are scored Pass, Fail,

Table 27. DDST Sectors

Sector	Description of Tasks	Age	Sample Tasks Task Name	Task
Personal-Social	Tasks that indicate the child's ability to get along with people and to take care of himself or herself	5½ mo.	Resists Toy Pull	Resists having toy taken away
		2½ yr.	Dresses with Supervision	Puts on any article of own clothing
Fine Motor-Adaptive	Tasks that indicate the child's ability to see, to use hands to pick up objects, and to draw	3½ mo.	Reaches for Object	Reaches for toy placed in front of him or her
		2 yr.	Tower of Eight Cubes	Balances eight cubes on top of each other
Language	Tasks that indicate the child's ability to hear, to carry out commands, and to speak	1 yr.	Three Words Other Than Ma-ma, Da-da	Uses at least three specific words for three objects
		4½ yr.	Defines Words	Defines six out of nine words by use, shape, composition, or category (words are *ball, lake, desk, house, banana, curtain, ceiling, hedge, pavement*)
Gross Motor	Tasks that indicate the child's ability to sit, walk, and jump	11 mo.	Stoops and Recovers	Bends over, picks up a toy, and stands up again without holding on or touching the floor
		2½ yr.	Broad Jump	Jumps with both feet together over an 8½-inch paper placed flat on the floor

Part II Preschool and Kindergarten Tests   235

Refusal, or No Opportunity. If a child refuses to try an item, the examiner instructs the parent on how to administer it. All items are allowed three trials before being scored as failed.

The DDST attempts to discover delays in development. A *delay* is defined as any failed item that is completely below the chronological age line; that is, the child fails an item that 90 percent of the children pass at a younger age. Test results are determined *abnormal* when (1) two sectors have two or more delays or (2) one sector has two delays and another sector has one delay and no passes at age level. Test results are determined *questionable* when (1) one sector has two delays or (2) one sector has one delay and no passes at age level. Children whose tests are determined abnormal or questionable should be retested in two or three weeks. If test results are still abnormal, the child should be referred to a doctor.

STRENGTHS OF THE DDST

- The Denver Developmental Screening Test is clearly a screening test, designed to give quick but reliable and valid information on children's performance in the major areas of early development. Designed to be administered by persons unfamiliar with psychological testing, it is concise, clear, and relatively simple to administer and interpret.

- The manual is well written and gives explicit directions for each test item, as well as for such basic procedures as what to tell parents and how to calculate chronological age.

- The scoring sheet is well designed, and the scoring procedures are as explicit as possible. Although the

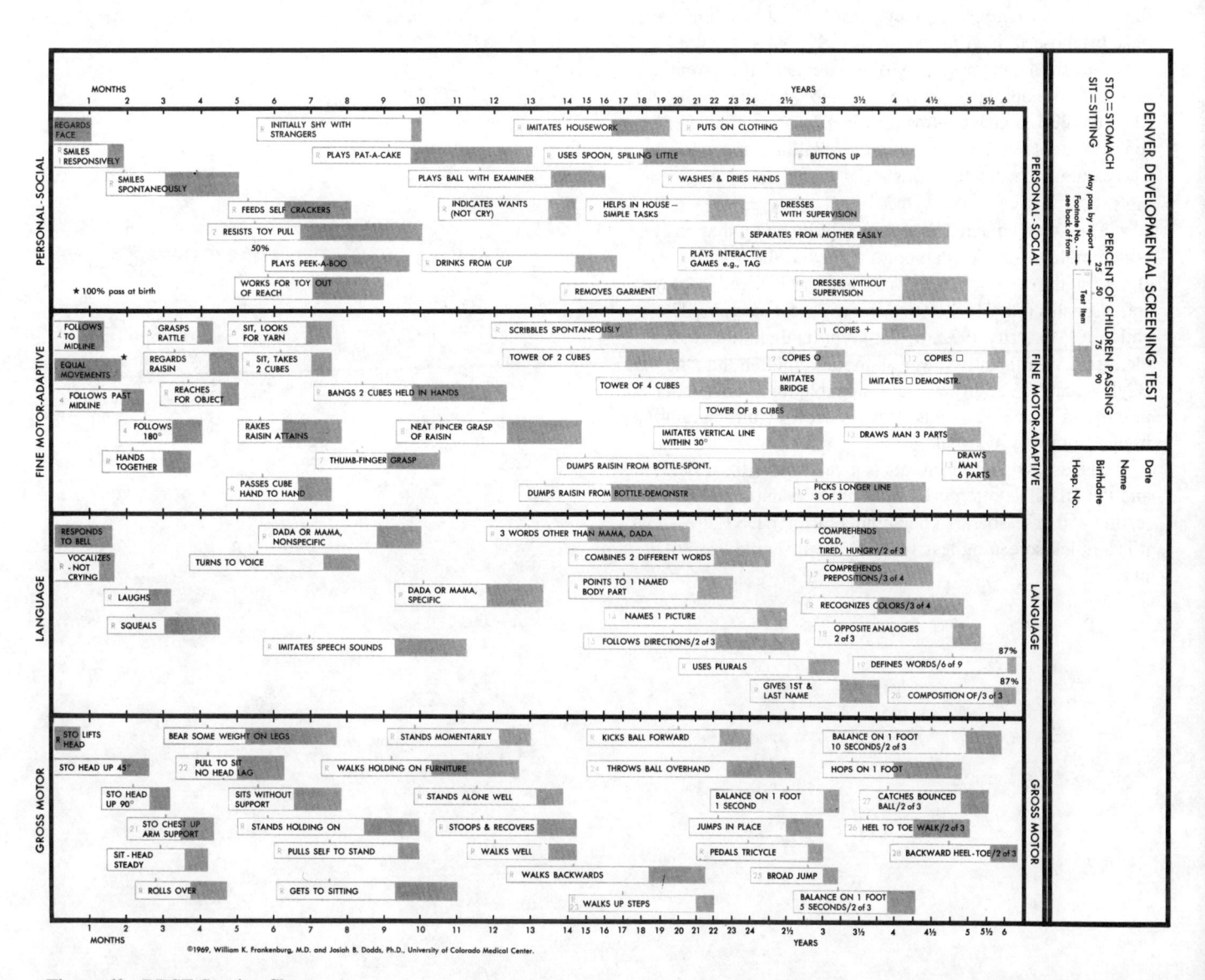

Figure 60. DDST Scoring Sheet

standardization sample was limited in size and region and included few minority-group children, the DDST has been used successfully in medical and psychological research and seems to hold up well as a tool for the early detection of developmental problems (Wallace and Larsen 1978, p. 165).

LIMITING FACTORS OF THE DDST

- The DDST was developed primarily by doctors for use in medical settings. The examples given in the manual reflect this orientation, suggesting physical causes for developmental delays. The term *abnormal* applied to test results also reflects the medical model. However, as a screening tool the DDST is useful in both infant and preschool educational programs.

- Although the examiner's manual states that the test may be given by persons unfamiliar with psychological testing, the authors strongly recommend that the test be administered only by those trained in its use.

- The child can pass many of the items by the parent's report. For example, 17 of the 23 Personal-Social items and 12 of the 20 Language items may be passed by the parent's report. Parents vary greatly in their reliability as reporters. The examiner needs to be aware of this even on a screening test.

- The DDST manual reports a validity study that obtained high correlations among the DDST, the Stanford-Binet Intelligence Scale (p. 276), and the Revised Bayley Infant Scales (Bayley 1969). A more recent study of 236 children (Moriarity 1972, p. 733) reports that the DDST identified significantly fewer abnormal children than the Bayley Scales. Validity was questionable for infants under 30 months and for 3-year-olds. It was best for children ranging in age from 4 to 4½ years.

- The assessment of infants is a very specialized field, and the DDST is often used by examiners untrained in testing and assessment. The authors of the DDST stress that it is a quick screening test; all who use it should keep that in mind.

Brigance Diagnostic Inventory of Early Development

Albert H. Brigance
Curriculum Associates, Inc., 1978
5 Esquire Rd., North Billerica, MA 01862

Purpose	To assess developmental or performance levels in children, to identify appropriate instructional objectives, and to provide a systematic record-keeping tool
Major Areas Tested	Psychomotor, self-help, speech and language, general comprehension, and preacademic skills
Age or Grade Range	Birth–6 years
Usually Given By	Classroom teacher Administrator Special education teacher Paraprofessional Psychologist
Type of Test	Informal Individual Criterion-referenced
Scores Obtained	Age level
Student Performance Timed?	No
Testing Time	30–60 minutes (depending on purpose of testing)
Scoring/Interpretation Time	15–30 minutes
Normed On	Literature review; field-tested in a wide variety of programs in 16 states
Alternate Forms Available?	No

FORMAT

The Brigance Diagnostic Inventory of Early Development consists of 98 subtests (skill sequences) organized into the following categories:

A. Pre-Ambulatory Motor Skills and Behaviors (4 subtests, including sitting, standing)

B. Gross Motor Skills and Behaviors (13 subtests, including running, hopping, balance, wheel toys)

C. Fine Motor Skills and Behaviors (9 subtests, including blocks, puzzles, clay)

D. Self-Help Skills (11 subtests, including eating, dressing, household chores)

E. Pre-Speech (3 subtests, including receptive language, gestures, vocalization)

F. Speech and Language Skills (10 subtests, including syntax, vocabulary, articulation)

G. General Knowledge and Comprehension (13 subtests, including body parts, colors, weather)

H. Readiness (5 subtests, including visual discrimination, letter recognition)

I. Basic Reading Skills (11 subtests, including auditory discrimination, initial sounds, beginning reading)

J. Manuscript Writing (7 subtests, including printing from copying and dictation)

K. Math (12 subtests, including rote counting, ordering numerals, beginning computation)

The materials consist of the examiner's notebook and individual developmental record books. The examiner's notebook opens flat between the examiner and the child. The examiner's page includes a statement of the skill being assessed, directions for administration and scoring, and instructional objectives for each skill. The child's page includes the test items. The author gives permission for the child's pages to be reproduced. Some pages have been designed to be cut apart so that items can be presented separately, as in Figure 61. (In this example, the bottom row of geometric shapes is cut out, and the child is asked to match them with the appropriate shapes above.)

A variety of assessment procedures can be used, specifically, parent interview, observation of the infant or child, and the child's performance on structured tasks. If using the test as an informal inventory, the examiner is

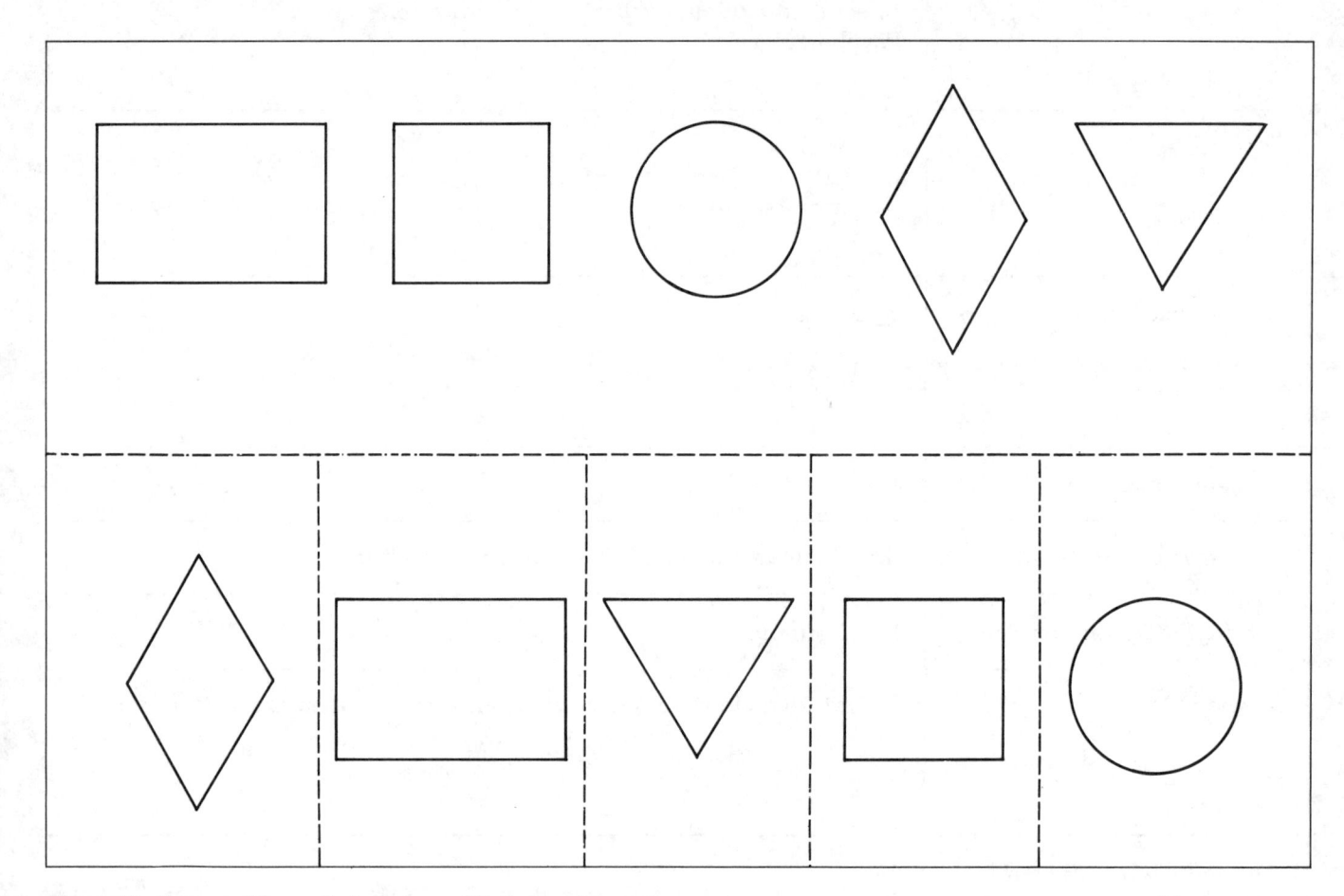

Figure 61. Brigance Diagnostic Inventory of Early Development

encouraged to modify the material to give the child the best opportunity to demonstrate his or her skill. Some tasks require verbal responses, others require pointing, and still others are pencil-and-paper tasks. The child's performance, observation report, or parent interview information is recorded in the individual developmental record book. Different colored pens are used to record the data each time the test is administered, to provide an ongoing record of progress. Each skill the child has achieved is circled; some items have an optional bar graph that can be colored to denote developmental level. A group developmental record book is also available.

The Brigance Diagnostic Inventory of Early Development is an informal assessment tool. It covers a wide age range, so no child would be assessed in all of the 98 skill sequences. The examiner selects only those skills that are appropriate for each child, depending on age and purpose of the testing. Because each skill sequence covers several years, the examiner also selects an approximate developmental level to begin the assessment. Developmental levels are printed on both the examiner's page and the developmental record book (see Figure 62).

The examiner's notebook also includes references to the literature that was used to validate the skill sequences and developmental ages, as well as information on field testing of the test.

STRENGTHS OF THE BRIGANCE DIAGNOSTIC INVENTORY OF EARLY DEVELOPMENT

- The Brigance Diagnostic Inventory of Early Development is a comprehensive instrument assessing a wide range of skills over the critical infant and preschool period. Although it is primarily a criterion-referenced tool, developmental ages are also provided for key skills. Many skills not usually assessed are included, such as use of wheel toys, brush painting, and knowledge of weather and

Developmental Record Book

B. GROSS MOTOR

Test Page				
B-1 24-26	**STANDING:** 1-0 1. *Standing with broad stance. 2. Standing with normal stance. 1-6 3. Standing on one foot with one hand held. 4. Standing on either foot with one hand held. 5. *Squats to pick up object from floor and re-erects. 6. Standing with heels together. 2-0 7. Standing on tiptoes momentarily—1 second.	2-6 8. Bends at waist to pick up object from floor. 9. Attempts to stand on 1 foot—no assistance. 3-0 10. Stands on 1 foot momentarily—1 second. 11. Stands on either foot momentarily—1 second. 4-0 12. Stands on one foot 5 seconds.	13. Stands on either foot 5 seconds. 5-0 14. Stands on one foot 10 seconds. 15. Stands on either foot 10 seconds. 6-0 16. Stands on one foot momentarily with eyes closed. 17. Stands on either foot momentarily with eyes closed. 18. Stands heel and toe 5 seconds.⁷⁻⁰	
	1 year　　2　　3　　4　　5　　6　　7			
	NOTES:			
B-2 28-30	**WALKING:** 1-0 1. *Walks with broad stance. 2. *Walks with knees slightly bent and shoulders slightly hunched. 3. *Walks holding hands out for balance rather than at side. 4. Walks with hands swinging at side. 5. Walks sideways. 1-6 6. Walks well and rarely falls.	7. Walks fast. 8. Walks stepping over 2"x4" (5 cm x10cm) board without difficulty. 2-0 9. Walks backwards three steps. 10. Walks backward distance of 6'8" (2 m). 11. Walks on tiptoes 3 steps. 3-0 12. Walks forward heel and toe three steps. 13. Walks on tip toes a distance of 6'8" (2 m).	14. Walks on straight line. 4-0 15. Walks circular 1" (25 mm) line. 16. Walks forward on line heel and toe a distance of 6'8" (2 m). 17. Walks scissor steps across 1" (25 mm) wide line a distance of 6'8" (2 m). 5-0 18. Walks backward toe and heel six steps. 19. Walks backward toe and heel a distance of 6'8" (2 m).⁷⁻⁰	
	1 year　　2　　3　　4　　5　　6　　7			
	NOTES:			
B-3 30-31	**STAIRS AND CLIMBING:** 1-0 1. Creeps up stairs. 2. Creeps down stairs backward. 3. Climbs on/in low furniture such as a low couch. 4. Climbs in and out of adult chair. 1-6 5. Walks up stairs with one hand held. 6. Walks down stairs with one hand held. 7. Walks up stairs alone holding rail.	2-0 8. Walks down stairs alone holding rail. 9. Walks up stairs using alternate feet with one hand held. 3-0 10. Walks down stairs using alternate feet with one hand held. 11. Climbs ladder of low play equipment. 12. Walks up stairs using alternate feet, holding rail.	4-0 13. Walks down stairs using alternate feet, holding rail. 14. Walks up stairs carrying object in one hand, not holding rail. 15. Walks down stairs carrying object and not holding rail. 5-6 16. Walks up and down stairs carrying object(s) with both hands.⁷⁻⁰	
	1 year　　2　　3　　4　　5　　6　　7			
	NOTES:			

Figure 62. Brigance Diagnostic Inventory of Early Development, Developmental Record Book

time concepts. Because these skills represent curriculum areas common in many preschool programs, they are useful for many teachers. The inclusion of instructional objectives also increases the usefulness of the instrument for teachers who need to plan individual educational programs. The built-in record-keeping system is also very helpful.

- The Brigance Diagnostic Inventory of Early Development is easy to administer and can be used by well-trained paraprofessionals. The materials are compact, well organized, and reasonably priced.

- The nature of the tool allows such variety in assessment procedures that it can be used with older low-functioning children.

LIMITING FACTORS OF THE BRIGANCE DIAGNOSTIC INVENTORY OF EARLY DEVELOPMENT

- The Brigance Diagnostic Inventory of Early Development is very new to the market. Although the test has had extensive field testing, no validity or reliability data is available at this time. Studies comparing this instrument with other preschool screening devices, such as the Denver Developmental Screening Test (p. 233), are needed, as are test-retest reliability data.

- The grouping of the 98 skill sequences into 11 categories is somewhat haphazard. For example, colors and body parts are grouped under General Knowledge and Comprehension; most tests describe them as readiness skills. Readiness, in this inventory, includes only five subtests, four of which deal with the alphabet; these subtests would seem more appropriately placed under Basic Reading Skills. Examiners should study all the subtests carefully, rather than relying on category headings, to ensure that all areas appropriate for the child are included in the assessment.

- The examiner's page includes so much information in addition to the directions for administration that the examiner needs to become quite familiar with the instrument before using it with infants and young children. The developmental record books are also quite complex in format—they include extensive information all on one page. If they are to be used effectively as a communication tool with parents, the examiner will need a good deal of practice in explaining the record form. It may well be necessary to transfer the assessment information to a summary sheet for parents.

- The inventory uses parent report as the data for tasks that are not easily observed during a school program. As with all assessments using parent reports to determine the skill levels of a child, the examiner needs to help parents become reliable reporters. When in doubt about a parent's accuracy, tasks and situations should be established at school to observe the child's performance.

THE BRIGANCE® K AND 1 SCREEN

The Brigance® K and 1 Screen for kindergarten and first grade (1982) has been added to the Brigance array of inventories. The screening can be completed in 10 to 20 minutes and provides a quick view of a child's development in key areas. Kindergarten tasks are presented in the following 13 areas: personal data, color recognition, picture vocabulary, visual discrimination, visual-motor skills, gross motor skills, rote counting, body parts, verbal directions, numeral comprehension, printing, syntax, and fluency. For first graders, draw-a-person, alphabet, auditory discrimination, and numerical sequence are added. Several advanced assessments in speech and language, reading, and numbers are included.

The materials consist of the examiner's loose-leaf notebook and the student data sheets. Generally, children are tested individually by one examiner, but procedures for screening a large number of children using a station method are described in the examiner's notebook. Paraprofessionals may be trained to administer the screening tests.

The number of correct answers in each skill area are multiplied by a point value reflecting the number of items in the skill area (one point for each item in a group of 10; two points for each item in a group of 5). A total score of 100 points is possible. Students are compared with other students in the screening and are rated higher, average, or lower. Behavioral observations and recommendations complete the student data sheet.

The Brigance® K and 1 Screen attempts neither to label children as high risk nor to identify a cutoff score. It simply provides a quick screening measure for students in a given group—entering kindergarteners in a specific school, all first graders in a district, and so forth. Its purpose is to provide a means for grouping children and planning individualized programs.

Miller Assessment for Preschoolers (MAP)

Lucy J. Miller
The Foundation for Knowledge in Development, 1982
1901 W. Littleton Blvd., Littleton, CO 80120

Purpose	To provide a brief screening tool for identifying preschool children in need of further evaluation, to identify children with moderate preacademic problems that may affect development, and to provide profiles of strengths and weaknesses of individual children
Major Areas Tested	Sensory and motor abilities and verbal and nonverbal cognitive abilities
Age or Grade Range	3–6 years
Usually Given By	Classroom teacher Speech/language therapist Psychologist Nurse Occupational therapist Paraprofessional
Type of Test	Standardized Individual Norm-referenced
Scores Obtained	Percentile
Student Performance Timed?	Yes (selected items)
Testing Time	20–30 minutes
Scoring/Interpretation Time	15 minutes
Normed On	1,200 preschoolers in nine U.S. Census Bureau Regions, randomly selected, stratified, and balanced by age, sex, race, urban/rural, and socioeconomic levels
Alternate Forms Available?	No

FORMAT

The materials for the Miller Assessment for Preschoolers (MAP) consist of the following:
- An examiner's manual including a description of the test, related literature, technical data, administration and scoring procedures, norms, and interpretation
- Cue sheets for each of six age groups, including specific administration directions
- Item score sheets for each age group for recording each child's performance and behavior
- Record booklets for summarizing each child's performance, family history, developmental background, and supplemental observations
- Drawing booklets for drawing and writing items
- Scoring transparencies
- Test kit materials, such as blocks, pennies, puzzles, and other manipulative items

The materials are packaged in a sturdy, well-designed test kit, divided notebook, and briefcase-style portfolio.

The MAP consists of 27 items grouped into five performance indices and three classifications. The organization of the test is shown in Table 28. The entire test is usually given in the order described in the manual. The order of tests can be changed to meet an individual child's needs.

Three scoring procedures are included. Each child's performance is recorded on the four-color item score sheet appropriate for his or her age. Since the raw score on each item is recorded, the examiner can observe the child's performance in relation to other children of that age group. The performance is color-coded as described below.

A percentile score for the total test is derived by calculating the number of reds and yellows a child obtained on the 27 items. In addition, nine areas of behavior are rated by the examiner on a seven-point scale and recorded on the back of the item score sheet. Although behavior does not affect the child's score, the author feels that the behavioral observations are critical in determining the reliability of the test as well as in indicating areas in which the child may have difficulty.

Color	Performance Indication
Red	Stop—This child appears to need help (fifth percentile or below).*
Yellow	Caution—This child should be watched (fifth to twenty-fifth percentile).*
Green	Go—This child is performing within normal limits (twenty-fifth to one-hundredth percentile).*

*Percentiles vary somewhat from item to item.

For those clinicians who wish to use the MAP not only as a screening instrument but also to portray strengths and weaknesses of an individual child, several optional supplemental scoring procedures are outlined. Percentile scores for each performance index, as well as for each item, are included, but caution is advised in the interpretation of individual items.

A unique feature of the MAP is the supplemental observations sheet. This procedure is designed to be used by clinicians who wish to report more subjective information, such as quality of language or quality of movement. It is recommended that only examiners trained in an accredited MAP workshop utilize these assessment procedures.

STRENGTHS OF THE MAP

- The extensive MAP manual discusses in detail the theoretical background of the test, test construction procedures, data on the norming process, and reliability and

Table 28. MAP Organization

Classification	Performance Index	Number of Items	Functions
Sensory and Motor Abilities	Foundation	10	Kinesthesia, tactile discrimination, postural mechanisms, and motor coordination
	Coordination	7*	Gross, fine, and oral motor abilities
Cognitive Abilities	Verbal	4	Receptive and expressive language
	Non-Verbal	5	Visual-memory and sequencing
Combined Abilities	Complex Tasks	4	Combined sensory, motor, and cognitive abilities

*Three items are also in the Foundation Index.

validity studies. In addition, cautions to the examiner in terms of administration and interpretation are explicitly spelled out. All examiners should read this important information.

- Most instruments for preschool screening identify only those children with severe developmental delays; the MAP was designed to detect subtle, moderate delays that often affect school performance.
- The author's experience with preschool children is demonstrated through the recognition of the need for flexible testing procedures with young children. Changes in testing order, inclusion of practice items, and positive reinforcement are part of the standardized procedures.
- A primary requisite of a screening test is that it be quick and reliable, as well as cost efficient. Through meticulous attention to test construction and the use of either single clinicians or trained paraprofessionals, the MAP author seems to have achieved these goals. Extensive information on test construction and standardization is included in the manual. Children with preacademic difficulties were included in the sample.
- The attention to behavioral observation and quality of performance are strong features, reflecting the author's understanding of preschool children.

LIMITING FACTORS OF THE MAP

- Testing preschool children requires the examiner to know the materials and procedures well. The MAP is a complex test with many materials. The examiner must take the time necessary to become proficient in administration and interpretation.
- Several of the subtests of the MAP involve sensory and motor abilities. Since the author is an occupational therapist, she has drawn upon her background and has included tests of stereognosis, motor accuracy, finger localization, balance, reflexes, imitation of postures, and others. Although extensive research is cited in the manual, other authors would feel that such tests are not predictive of later school difficulties (see Southern California Sensory Integration Tests, p. 223).
- The MAP includes tests usually given by a teacher, a speech therapist, and an occupational therapist. Only one examiner is present so that he or she can maintain rapport with the child. This means the examiner will need to prepare especially well to administer the tests in areas that are unfamiliar.
- As a new test, the MAP has not been subjected to long-term validity studies. Time will tell whether or not it does indeed identify at-risk preschoolers.

The Meeting Street School Screening Test (MSSST)

Peter K. Hainsworth and Marian L. Siqueland
Crippled Children and Adults of Rhode Island, Inc., 1969
Meeting Street School, 333 Grotto Ave., Providence, RI 02906

Purpose	To identify children with potential learning disabilities
Major Areas Tested	Gross motor skills, fine motor skills, visual perception, and language
Age or Grade Range	5—7½ years
Usually Given By	Classroom teacher Special education teacher Psychologist Paraprofessional
Type of Test	Standardized Individual Norm-referenced
Scores Obtained	Age level Standard
Student Performance Timed?	No
Testing Time	15–20 minutes
Scoring/Interpretation Time	15 minutes
Normed On	500 students, including 50 girls and 50 boys at each six-month age interval
Alternate Forms Available?	No

FORMAT

The materials for The Meeting Street School Screening Test (MSSST) consist of a record form for each student and the manual, which includes nine test administration cards. The manual is contained within a monograph, *Early Identification of Children with Learning Disabilities: The Meeting Street School Screening Test*. In addition to administration and scoring procedures and statistical information related to the MSSST, the monograph includes extensive information on screening programs for young and high-risk children and a discussion of the information processing model on which this test is theoretically based.

The MSSST is composed of three subtests, each covering a skill area and comprising several tasks. The organization of the test is shown in Table 29.

Scores are recorded on the record form as the tasks are performed, according to the scoring directions in the manual. Four raw score totals are obtained: motor patterning, visual-perceptual-motor, language, and MSSST total.

For kindergarten children, a MSSST total raw score of 39 points or below indicates that the child is at high risk for learning disabilities. For first-grade children, a raw score of 55 points or below is the cutoff score. These scores were selected for children tested about four months into the school year.

The raw scores are converted to scale scores using a table that corresponds to the student's chronological age. The scaled scores are then plotted on the profile of scores on the record form. This gives a graphic summary of the child's strengths and weaknesses.

The record form also provides a behavior rating scale that rates each child on the following dimensions:

Test cooperation
Attention
Concentration
Use of feedback
Motor control
Pencil skills
Eye control
Speech
Language
Overall efficiency

These dimensions were selected because they have been found to be important indicators of learning disabilities. Each of the dimensions is discussed in depth in the manual.

STRENGTHS OF THE MSSST

• The MSSST is a well-designed, theoretically based screening instrument for kindergarten and first-grade children. The Meeting Street School in Providence, Rhode Island, has long been known for its diagnosis and treatment of children with cerebral palsy. The multidisciplinary staff turned to the evaluation of children with learning disabilities, and the MSSST is the result of their expertise. The manual (p. 49) defines the "learning disability child" as one "whose information processing inefficiencies in the language, visual-perceptual-motor, and motor patterning modalities interfere with learning."

The authors suggest that the MSSST be used as part of a program of progressive levels of screening:

1. Gross screening of all children by teacher rating and group tests
2. Finer individual screening of selected children with instruments such as the MSSST
3. Intensive individual diagnostic assessment for a few children

The authors stress that the MSSST scores alone should not be used to label a child as "learning disabled."

In addition to the sound background of the MSSST, the test has several other strengths:

• The sections of the manual on interpretation of test results, including the graphic profile and the behavioral rating scale, are excellent. Case studies are used to illustrate test interpretation.

• Studies related to content and predictive validity of the MSSST are reported in the manual, and although they are poorly reported and somewhat incomplete, they show a moderate degree of predictability.

• The MSSST has good test-retest reliability and interscorer reliability over a two- to four-week period.

• The MSSST is designed so that it can be given by trained paraprofessionals.

• The three subtests are constructed so that they have equal numbers of items and the same scaled score mean (10) and standard deviation (3).

LIMITING FACTORS OF THE MSSST

• Strangely, in such a complete monograph, there is no description of the norming sample. Extensive research is reported that gives the numbers of children in different schools and their IQs and achievement levels, but there is no information on such variables as age, sex, racial background, or socioeconomic class. This is a serious deficit if one attempts to use the mean scaled scores for interpretation or the cutoff point for identification of children at risk.

• The cutoff score of 39 points or below for kindergarteners is not well substantiated by research. The cutoff score of 55 for first graders was not validated at all.

• The Language subtest is the weakest of the three subtests. It does not include any measure of receptive or expressive vocabulary or articulation. The placement of counting tasks in the Language subtest is questionable, and there is no task assessing auditory discrimination. Although

Table 29. MSSST Subtests

Subtest	Purpose	Tasks	Task Points (total: 87½)	Skills
1. Motor Patterning	To survey bilateral sequential movement patterns and spatial awareness	Gait Patterns	5	Unilateral and bilateral body movement patterns, such as hopping and skipping
		Clap Hands	6	Unlearned sequential spatial patterns
		Hand Patterns	6	Unlearned sequential spatial patterns
		Follow Directions I	6	Comprehension, memory, and translation of verbal directions involving spatial concepts
		Touch Fingers	6	Coordination of hands and fingers in rapid bilateral patterned movements
		Total: 29		
2. Visual-Perceptual-Motor	To survey visual discrimination, visual memory, design copying, and comprehension of spatial and directional concepts on paper	Block Tapping	6	Memory for spatial sequences
		Visual Matching	5	Discrimination of form and spatial orientation
		Visual Memory	6	Short-term memory for geometric and letter forms
		Copy Forms	8	Eye-hand coordination
		Follow Directions II	5	Spatial and directional concepts through drawing
		Total: 30		
3. Language	To survey listening comprehension, auditory memory, and language formulation	Repeat Words	5½	Discrimination and repetition of speech sound sequences
		Repeat Sentences	5	Auditory memory for words
		Counting	7	Ability to sequence numbers
		Tell-a-Story	5	Ability to formulate and express thoughts
		Language Sequencing	6	Comprehension of time concepts
		Total: 28½		

the skilled examiner can pick up information on both articulation and discrimination throughout the test administration, there is no place to record this critical information, and it is not included in the score. Both Follow Directions tasks include a large component of language comprehension, but these scores are not included in the Language subtest.

• The authors state that the cutoff scores of 39 and 55 points "identify those children whose information processing skills are not sufficient to allow them to meet the curriculum demands of the grade" (manual, p. 15). Obviously, this depends somewhat on the curriculum being offered. More information is needed regarding the relationship between MSSST subtest scores and curriculum areas (reading, spelling, writing, and math) and instructional techniques.

Basic School Skills Inventory (BSSI)

Donald D. Hammill and James E. Leigh
Pro-Ed, 1976; revised, 1983
5341 Industrial Oaks Blvd., Austin, TX 78735

Purpose	To identify young children significantly below their peers in activities related to classroom learning, to determine specific strengths and weaknesses in individual children, to document progress related to remediation, and to provide a measurement instrument for research involving young children
Major Areas Tested	Daily living skills, language, reading, writing, mathematics, and classroom behaviors
Age or Grade Range	4–6 years
Usually Given By	Classroom teacher Special education teacher Paraprofessional
Type of Test	Standardized Individual Norm-referenced
Scores Obtained	Percentile Standard
Student Performance Timed?	No
Testing Time	30 minutes
Scoring/Interpretation Time	15 minutes
Normed On	376 children between the ages of 4 and 7 years from 15 states
Alternate Forms Available?	No

FORMAT

The Basic School Skills Inventory (BSSI) has two forms: the Diagnostic (BSSI-D) and the Screening (BSSI-S).

BSSI-D

The materials for the BSSI-D consist of the examiner's manual, student record forms for each student, and the picture book containing materials for direct testing of certain items.

The BSSI-D is based on two major assumptions. The first is that assessments of readiness skills, in order to be helpful for teachers and predictive of a child's school success, must include measurement of a child's skills on classroom instructional tasks. In other words, the more "classroomlike" the assessment procedure, the more valid are the results. The second assumption logically follows; that is, assessment should be done by classroom teachers, aides, or other school personnel who work with the child on a daily instructional basis. The instrument combines the format of a teacher rating scale with a more formalized testing procedure.

The BSSI-D is composed of the following subtests:

1. *Daily Living Skills*. The 20 items assess basic knowledge and skills related to daily school activities. For example:
   Is the child responsible for his or her own belongings?
   Can the child identify the penny, the nickel, and the dime?
2. *Spoken Language*. The 20 items assess oral communication. For example:
   Is the child's speech reasonably free of "baby talk"?
   Does the child use some sentences exceeding six words in length?
3. *Reading*. The 20 items measure a child's knowledge of written symbols and book-handling skills. For example:
   Does the child hold the book in the proper orientation for reading?
   Can the child recognize letters when letter names are provided?
   Can the child answer questions pertaining to events in a story he or she has just read?
4. *Writing*. The 15 items measure skills in written expression. For example:
   Can the child write his or her last name?
   Can the child write a three-sentence story?
5. *Mathematics*. The 15 items assess numerical concepts and arithmetic computation. For example:
   Can the child name a number smaller than 3?
   Can the child print the numerals 1 to 10 in proper sequence?
6. *Classroom Behavior*. The 20 items relate to attentiveness, cooperation, attitude, participation, and socialization. For example:
   Can the child wait his or her turn?
   Can the child understand and accept the consequences of his or her behavior?
   Can the child refrain from excessive talking?

The teacher or aide indicates which items a child has mastered by crediting the child with one point for each on the student record form. Skills that the child does not possess or that the child is inconsistent in demonstrating are scored as 0. When the teacher or aide is unclear about whether the child has the skill, further observation or direct testing is done and a 1 or a 0 is recorded.

Raw scores for each subtest are totaled and converted to percentiles and standard scores with a mean of 10 and a standard deviation of 3. The six subtest totals are then converted to a total test percentile and standard score with a mean of 100 and a standard deviation of 15. This composite skill quotient provides a general index of the child's overall skill performance. To aid in the presentation of results, a profile of standard scores is provided, as are categories of performance (average, below average) for each subtest and the composite skills quotient.

BSSI-S

The BSSI-S is a quick screening device to identify children who are "high risk" for school failure. Twenty items that correlated well with the BSSI-D total were selected to locate children who need referrals for more complete testing or remedial services. Standard scores and percentiles are also available for the BSSI-S; children with standard scores of 85 or lower or percentile scores below 16 are considered high risk. The authors recommend that when large numbers of children are to be screened, the BSSI-S should be used first; the high-risk students should then be given the BSSI-D.

STRENGTHS OF THE BSSI

- The 110 items of the BSSI-D survey a wide range of preacademic, academic, and behavior skills. Recognition of the relationship between behavior and academic success is a good feature of the instrument.
- The manual includes extensive discussion of test construction, standardization, reliability, and validity information.
- The manuals of Pro-Ed tests always include excellent discussions of the purpose of testing, of theoretical assumptions underlying the instrument, and of cautions of test interpretation, which should be read by every examiner.

LIMITING FACTORS OF THE BSSI

- The use of national norms for assessing readiness skills of preschool and kindergarten children is of questionable value. The skill levels of entering kindergarteners and first graders vary dramatically from community to community depending upon socioeconomic factors. The real question behind a screening is often "Is this child ready for kindergarten (or first grade or reading)?" Local expectations are a more critical factor than national norms. The authors address this issue on the last page of the manual. It deserves more prominence.

- The age range of 4 years to 6 years, 11 months encompasses a very diverse population of children. It includes children in nursery school programs, children entering and completing kindergarten, and children entering and completing first grade. The skills of, and expectations for, children in these different developmental stages are very different. Including all of them in one screening instrument seems unwise. In addition, despite their extensive statistical data, the authors given no information on the number of students at each age level. The norms are based on one-year increments (4 years to 4 years, 11 months; 5 years to 5 years, 11 months; and 6 years to 6 years, 11 months), which is questionable.

- The transforming of a teacher rating scale into a standardized instrument is an interesting process. In order to obtain standardized scores, data that is usually scored on a three- or five-point scale is transformed into a 1 or 0 rating, indicating mastery or nonmastery. Much information about emerging or inconsistent skills is lost in this process. The combining of observational data with direct testing by teachers has a very nonstandardized feeling, and directions to the teachers do little to change this. For example, the directions to the teacher for scoring a test item that requires the child to describe the contents of a picture are as follows:

> To pass this item, the child must meet your expectations for satisfactory performance; this task cannot be standardized from one classroom to another. As a general guide, you might expect the child to produce at least three different relevant ideas. (BSSI-D Manual, pp. 27–28)

Many of the items included cannot be standardized from one classroom to another, yet national norms are provided.

- When an instrument uses a basal/ceiling procedure, the ordering of items within a subtest is critical. The ordering of items on several BSSI-D subtests seems questionable, particularly in Classroom Behavior. For example, the item on whether the child understands and accepts the consequences of his or her own behavior precedes the item on whether the child follows classroom rules.

Preschool Language Scale (PLS)

I. L. Zimmerman, V. G. Steiner, and R. E. Pond
Charles E. Merrill Publishing Company, 1969; revised 1979
1300 Alum Creek Dr., Columbus, OH 43216

Purpose	To systematically appraise the early stages of language development
Major Areas Tested	Receptive language and expressive language articulation
Age or Grade Range	1–7 years
Usually Given By	Speech/language clinician Special education teacher Psychologist
Type of Test	Individual Criterion-referenced
Scores Obtained	Age level Language quotient
Student Performance Timed?	Yes (some tasks)
Testing Time	20 minutes
Scoring/Interpretation Time	5–20 minutes
Normed On	Large numbers of Head Start children and children enrolled in a variety of other early childhood education programs
Alternate Forms Available?	No

FORMAT

The revised Preschool Language Scale (PLS) materials consist of a manual, a picture book, individual record forms, and the following items supplied by the examiner:

- 12 one-inch colored blocks in a box (red, yellow, blue, green, orange, and purple)
- A small piece of coarse sandpaper
- A set of coins, including a half dollar, a quarter, a dime, a nickel, and a penny
- A watch or clock with a second hand

The PLS is a developmental inventory with two separate scales: Auditory Comprehension and Verbal Ability. Each scale is administered independently and contains 10 sections spanning the ages of 1 to 7 years. These sections cover six-month intervals from ages 1 to 5 years and two one-year intervals from ages 5 to 7 years. Each interval contains four different items that assess sensory discrimination, logical thinking, grammar and vocabulary, memory and attention span, temporal/spatial relations, or self-image. Consonant articulation is evaluated by word and sentence repetition tasks. References that follow the descriptions of items in the test manual indicate the sources from which these language tasks are drawn. Developmental age-level placement of test items was determined from language research and experience with the original version of the PLS.

The Auditory Comprehension scale is administered first. Testing begins at the point where the child is most apt to succeed, approximately six months below the child's assumed language functioning level. A basal age is obtained when all items within an age interval are passed. Testing proceeds until the child fails all items within a single age interval (ceiling age). The Verbal Ability scale is subsequently administered in the same manner, with testing beginning at the basal age obtained on the Auditory Comprehension scale.

A convenient feature of the PLS is the inclusion of identical items at different age levels with varying criteria for passing. For example, in the Verbal Ability section, the child has to correctly repeat a single four-digit series to pass item 25 at the 4-year to 4-year-6-month level but must reproduce two series to pass item 33 at the 5-year to 6-year level. Therefore, item 25 is administered in its entirety only once, and pass or fail is assigned in both age intervals.

Age levels are obtained by adding 1½ months of credit for each item passed beyond the basal age and 3 months of credit for items from the age range of 5 to 7 years. A more complicated point-credit system may also be used for determining age levels. Auditory Comprehension (AC) and Verbal Ability (VA) ages are calculated separately and can be averaged to obtain an overall language age. Furthermore, quotients may be obtained by applying the formula:

$$\frac{\text{AC (or VA) Age}}{\text{Chronological Age}} \times 100$$

A composite language quotient is calculated by averaging the two quotients.

The authors suggest that any child who scores below age level on the PLS is "at risk" for language problems. Careful examination of response patterns and comparison of performances on the Auditory Comprehension and the Verbal Ability scales provides a more detailed picture of a child's strengths and weaknesses.

STRENGTHS OF THE PLS

- The PLS is a valuable screening tool for young children. The tasks and materials are appealing to most children, the test protocol is simple to use, and responses are easily elicited. The diversity of items enables the examiner to obtain a sampling of performance in several developmental areas in a short time.

- The 1979 edition of the PLS is a revision of the original 1969 form. Modifications in the current version include clearer administration instructions, a simplified scoring system, and the repositioning of some test items to reflect increased knowledge of language acquisition stages. A valuable addition to the PLS is a Spanish translation, contained in Appendix A of the test manual, and Spanish protocols. The examiner may administer the PLS in both English and Spanish to obtain information about language dominance in receptive and expressive areas.

- The "Preschool Language Scale" is a deceptive name. In addition to language, this instrument evaluates areas more commonly considered as "school readiness," such as color recognition, counting, and numerical concepts.

- Various studies reported by the authors demonstrate adequate to excellent reliability and validity. Three studies in which PLS scores were compared with later school success suggest strong predictive validity, an important quality for a preschool screening instrument.

LIMITING FACTORS OF THE PLS

- Effective administration of the PLS requires practice by the examiner—materials vary from task to task, and the manipulation of pictures, objects, and the test protocol can be difficult. Maintenance of a rapid test pace can be important in sustaining the attention of young children.

- Recording a child's performance in chart form can provide useful diagnostic information. However, the value of such a profile on the PLS is diluted significantly by the misrepresentation of several test items. For example: Articulation items are listed as tasks assessing memory and attention span; a task involving the discrimination of pictures of a dog and a wagon (1 year, 6 months to 2 years) is considered "logical thinking," while a subsequent item involving the discrimination of playing, washing, and blowing in pictures (2 years, 6 months to 3 years) is omitted from this category.

- Speech and language clinicians should be aware of the limitations of assessing articulatory proficiency only through imitation of single words rather than through a sampling of connected speech. On the PLS, a child may be able to imitate words that he or she does not articulate correctly on a spontaneous basis.
- The authors acknowledge that further normative studies of the PLS are needed. Establishment of means and standard deviations for age intervals covered on the English and Spanish versions would enhance the value of the PLS as a diagnostic tool.

Kraner Preschool Math Inventory (KPMI)

Robert E. Kraner
Learning Concepts, Inc., 1976
2501 N. Lamar Blvd., Austin, TX 78705

Purpose	To determine the acquisition age of quantitative concepts of young children and to provide practical information for planning early childhood learning programs
Major Areas Tested	Mathematics
Age or Grade Range	3–6½ years
Usually Given By	Classroom teacher Speech/language clinician Special education teacher Paraprofessional Psychologist
Type of Test	Standardized Individual Criterion-referenced
Scores Obtained	Age level Receptive age Mastery age
Student Performance Timed?	No
Testing Time	30–40 minutes
Scoring/Interpretation Time	15–20 minutes
Normed On	273 suburban, middle-class children from one south central state
Alternate Forms Available?	No

FORMAT

Both the manual and test items for the Kraner Preschool Math Inventory (KPMI) are contained in a three-ring vinyl binder. The binder has a flip-page arrangement for presentation, with the examiner's instructions on one side, and the test materials on the side facing the student. The student responds verbally or by pointing to the test items, which are presented in conjunction with pictorial material using common shapes and animals. The animals are black-and-white, cartoonlike figures. The majority of the KPMI test items have a multiple-choice format.

The KPMI is an untimed test administered on an individual basis. The examiner uses a separate scoring form to record individual responses. To facilitate the use of test data, a classroom record form and an individual record form are also provided.

The KPMI evaluates mathematics skills and concepts in seven areas: Set Comparison, Counting, Cardinal Numbers, Sequence, Position, Direction, and Geometry/Measurement. Three performance exercises are provided for each of the test items. If successful performance is achieved on Trial A and B of an item, credit is given. If the student fails one trial and succeeds on the other, the Optional trial is given to determine if credit is allowed.

Because the KPMI is a criterion-referenced inventory, testing sessions do not demand the rigid constraints of norm-referenced tests. No required testing sequence must be followed; that is, the seven areas may be given in any order. However, to avoid confusing the student, the items within an area should be given in order.

Before testing begins, the warm-up exercises should be administered to the student. These exercises contain the key words and symbols used throughout the test and help to make certain that the student will understand the test directions and material.

STRENGTHS OF THE KPMI

• Many features of the KPMI are advantageous. The test is easy to administer, is applicable for very young students, and permits evaluation of a student's comprehension of such mathematical concepts as quantity, number, and space (dimension, direction, location, and orientation). No specific training is needed to administer the KPMI, which extends its use to paraprofessionals.

• The test items consist of familiar pictures and shapes, selected because of their inclusion in most preschool instructional materials. Each test plate is clear and uncluttered; numerals are printed in large-sized type, appropriate for young students. The multiple-choice format for most items reduces the demands on memory and recall, because the correct answer can be identified by recognition.

• Requiring the student to give two correct responses out of three trials is an especially good feature. Young students often respond inconsistently in testing situations because their attention may wander. Giving a student a second chance assures the examiner of a more valid estimate of the student's abilities. The warm-up exercises are also helpful because they familiarize the student with the test demands.

• Although the KPMI is not intended for use with students beyond age 6½, it does have value as a clinical evaluation tool for older students who are having difficulty in arithmetic. The KPMI is useful for assessing the concept formation of slow learners and learning-disabled, mentally retarded, and language-impaired students.

• Comparing a student's performance in the seven skill and concept areas provides important diagnostic information. A pattern of errors at times gives information regarding the nature of specific vocabulary and concept-formation problems. For example, the student may fail most items that have a spatial reference but correctly answer items that have a quantitative reference. The analysis of error patterns may suggest areas for instructional emphasis, especially if the concept is within a student's mastery age.

Mastery age refers to the earliest age interval at which 80 percent of the students in the norming sample responded correctly to an item. The mastery age indicates the age level at which students can be expected to know the skill or concept. Individual instruction is warranted for the student who fails a mastery-age item.

Receptive age, on the other hand, represents the earliest age level at which 50 percent of the students responded correctly to an item. The receptive age represents the age level at which the skill or concept may be appropriately included in the instructional program for normal learners. The manual presents forms for receptive and mastery ages at six-month intervals between the ages of 3 and 6½ years.

• The KPMI, built on the criterion-referenced model, identifies specific skills and concepts required for learning mathematics. When the test has been completed, the examiner can clearly see what the student knows and needs to learn. Thus the test can aid in curriculum planning, diagnostic teaching, and program evaluations.

LIMITING FACTORS OF THE KPMI

• Although the KPMI is a criterion-referenced measure, the inventory contains some normative data. The test was normed on a middle-class suburban population from only one state. The sample size was quite small (273), with several age intervals represented by less than 15 students. Evidently, students from different ethnic groups are not represented in the sample. Caution must be used when applying the norms to students from low socioeconomic and minority groups. Students from a culturally different background may receive low scores on the test because they have not had adequate language stimulation and experience at home. Measures of validity and reliability are not available for the KPMI.

- The quantitative concepts behind the test items were selected from research studies, curriculum guides, national study reports, and other sources. The concepts were included because they are required by entering first-grade students. However, no specific information is provided that describes how all entries into the item pool were screened and ultimately accepted or rejected for the final version of the test.
- The aesthetic quality of the black-and-white line drawings is mediocre, and the shapes (hearts, balls, and stars) are used repeatedly throughout the test. Although there are advantages in using familiar shapes, after a while many students find the items uninteresting. The inclusion of colorful and stimulating materials would help to sustain students' interest in the KPMI.
- The KPMI requires the student to give the correct response on two out of three performance exercises. This is a good test feature. However, the drawback from the student's viewpoint is a long, repetitious testing session. The bright student, especially, may become bored quickly.
- The basic concepts tested in the KPMI are assessed at the receptive level only. An example of an item: "Show me the star on top." Understanding a word and pointing to the correct picture is a very different task from following such directions as "Sit on top of the box." If a student performs poorly on the KPMI, the examiner may want to examine mastery of spatial prepositions through direct physical experience. This can be accomplished by having the student act out verbal commands to place an object or position himself or herself in different locations in space ("Sit on/under/behind the desk.").

Slingerland Pre-Reading Screening Procedures

Beth H. Slingerland
Educators Publishing Service, Inc., 1968; revised 1976, 1977
75 Moulton St., Cambridge, MA 02188

Purpose	To identify bright children with difficulties in the auditory, visual, and kinesthetic modalities that may indicate specific language disability
Major Areas Tested	Auditory, visual, and kinesthetic skills related to beginning reading
Age or Grade Range	Grades K–1
Usually Given By	Classroom teacher Special education teacher Psychologist Administrator
Type of Test	Informal Group
Scores Obtained	Rating scale (guidelines for evaluating test performance)
Student Performance Timed?	Yes
Testing Time	20–25 minutes each for three test sessions
Scoring/Interpretation Time	15–20 minutes
Normed On	Not normed
Alternate Forms Available?	No

FORMAT

The materials for the Slingerland Pre-Reading Screening Procedures consist of student booklets, cards and charts for three subtests, and a teacher's manual. Practice pages and markers are also provided. The tests are designed to be used with groups of kindergarten children who have not yet been introduced to formal reading. The recommended group size is 15 children. At least one monitor is needed to help the children locate the right page and to prohibit them from copying each other's work. The students use pencils without erasers and are taught to bracket their errors so that self-corrections can be noted.

The recently revised Slingerland Pre-Reading Screening Procedures contain 12 subtests to be given to the group and a set of individual auditory tests. The 12 subtests are:

1. *Visual Perception* requires matching single-letter and two-letter combinations (Figure 63).

2. *Visual Perception* requires visual matching of three-letter combinations (Figure 64).

3. *Visual Perception and Memory* requires visual memory of geometric and letter forms (Figure 65).

4. *Near-Point Copying* requires copying geometric and letter forms (Figure 66). Space is provided on both sides of the geometric and letter forms for left-handed and right-handed students.

5. *Auditory-Visual Perception* requires listening to a spoken direction and marking the appropriate picture. In Figure 67 the examiner says, "Mark the picture of the bird flying to its nest."

6. *Letter Recognition* requires marking the visual symbol of the letter name pronounced by the examiner. In Figure 68 the examiner says, "Mark the *f*."

7. *Visual-Kinesthetic Memory* requires visual perception and memory of geometric forms. The student draws the forms from memory after being shown a model (Figure 69).

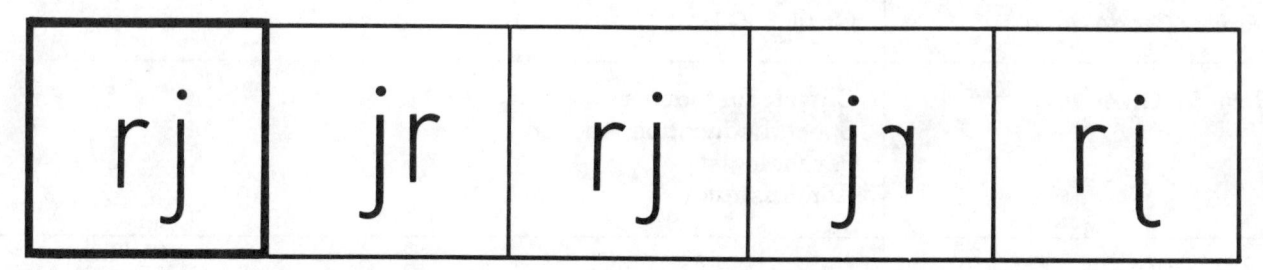

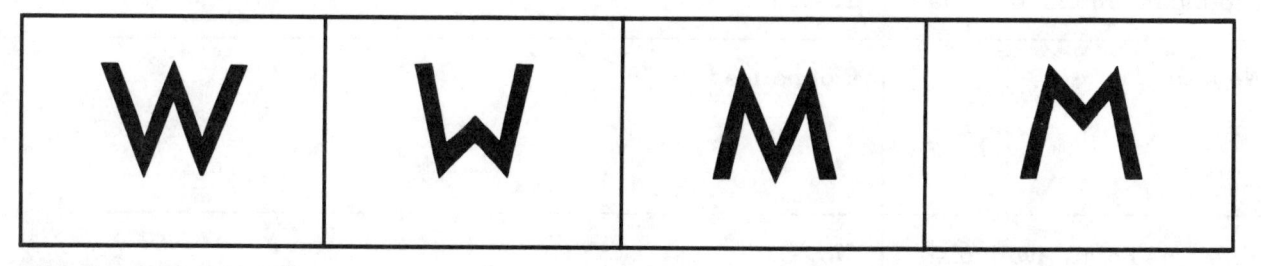

Figure 63. Slingerland Pre-Reading Screening Procedures, Procedure 1, Visual Perception

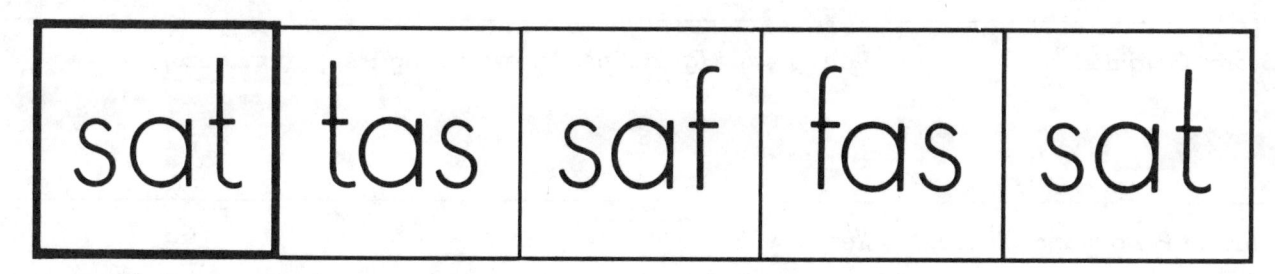

Figure 64. Slingerland Pre-Reading Screening Procedures, Procedure 2, Visual Perception

Figure 65. Slingerland Pre-Reading Screening Procedures, Procedure 3, Visual Perception and Memory

Part II   Preschool and Kindergarten Tests   259

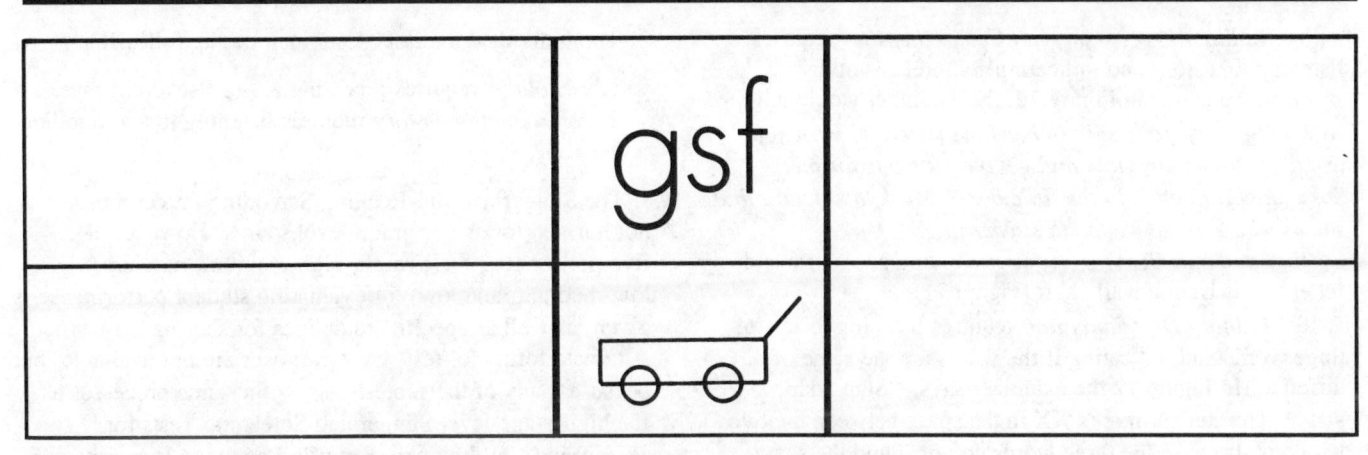

Figure 66. Slingerland Pre-Reading Screening Procedures, Procedure 4, Near-Point Copying

Figure 67. Slingerland Pre-Reading Screening Procedures, Procedure 5, Auditory-Visual Perception

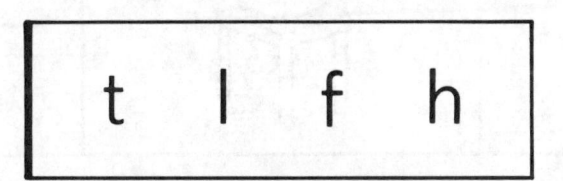

Figure 68. Slingerland Pre-Reading Screening
Procedures, Procedure 6, Letter Recognition

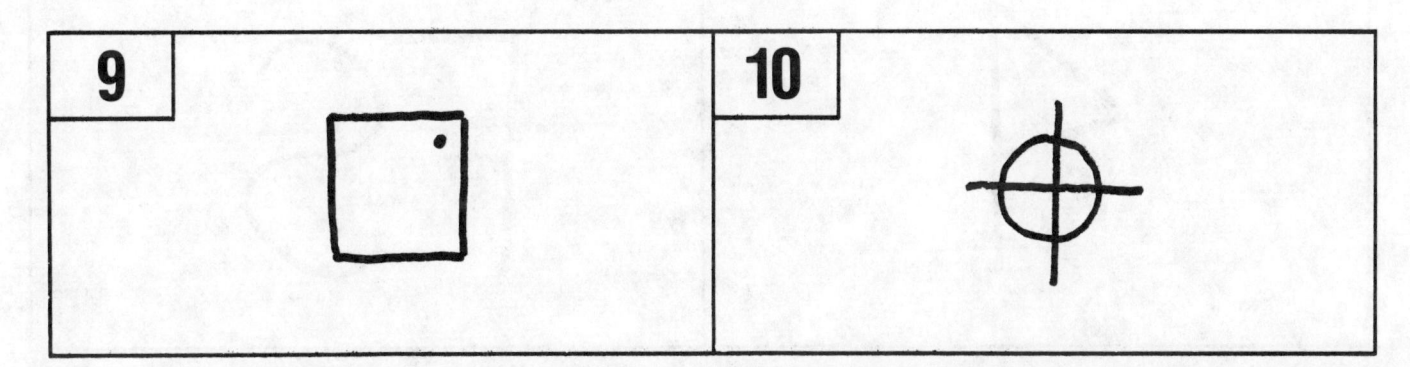

Figure 69. Slingerland Pre-Reading Screening Procedures, Procedure 7, Visual-Kinesthetic Memory

8. *Auditory Perception with Comprehension* requires listening to a story and indicating comprehension by marking a picture. In Figure 70, the examiner would tell the following story: *Jane said to her little sister, "I wish you would go to the big table and get the little box for me. Something for you is in the little box."* Mark the picture that shows where Jane wanted her sister to go.

9. *Far-Point Copying* requires copying geometric and letter forms from a wall chart (Figure 71).

10. *Auditory Discrimination* requires listening to sets of three words and indicating if the words are the same or different. In Figure 72 the examiner says, "Slap, slap, slab." The student marks XX in the space between the two balloons, because the three words do not sound the same. When the words all sound the same, the student marks / / in the space.

11. *Auditory-Visual-Kinesthetic Integration* requires listening to the name of a letter, selecting it from three printed letters, and copying it. In Figure 73 the examiner says, "Copy the letter *B* in the last box in the row."

12. *Auditory-Visual Association* requires identifying pictures that begin with a specific sound pronounced by the examiner. In Figure 74 the examiner says, "You see a book, a pencil, and a table. Mark the picture of the one that begins with the sound *t*."

The individual auditory tests include the following:

1. *Echolalia* requires repeating a word several times.
2. *Reproducing a Story* requires listening to and retelling a story.

The Slingerland Pre-Reading Screening Procedures are not normed for age or grade-level scores. However, a five-point rating scale (high, high-medium, medium, low-medium, and low) for evaluating student performance is given, as well as specific guidelines for scoring the tests. Alternate forms for test-retest purposes are not available, but because many of the subtests assess the same processes as the higher-age-level Slingerland Screening Tests for Identifying Children with Specific Language Disability (p. 102), the series of tests can be used as a measure of progress.

STRENGTHS OF THE SLINGERLAND PRE-READING SCREENING PROCEDURES

• The Slingerland Pre-Reading Screening Procedures are a well-planned battery of readiness tests. They have been carefully designed to include tasks that assess a student's skills in all modalities: auditory, visual, and kinesthetic, alone and in combination. The teacher's manual is well organized, and the directions are very clear. The idea of

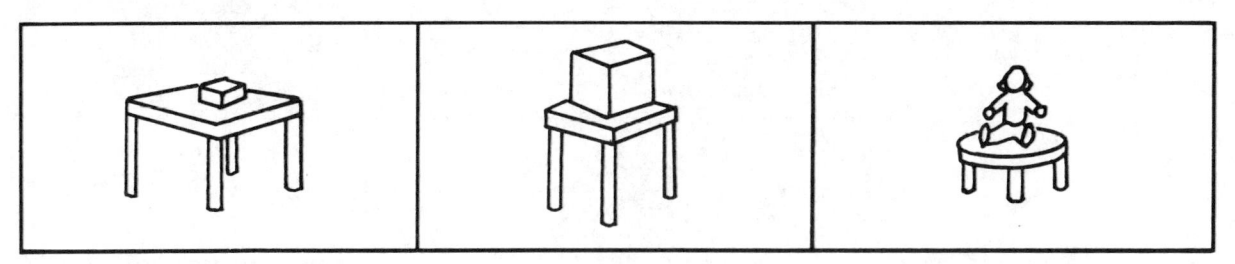

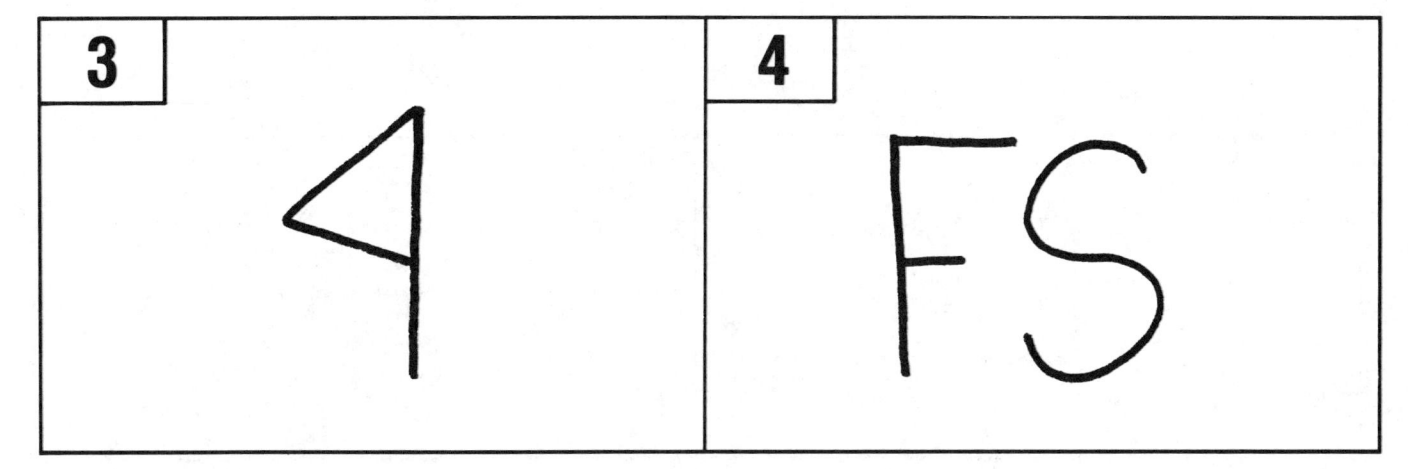

Figure 70. Slingerland Pre-Reading Screening Procedures, Procedure 8, Auditory Perception with Comprehension

Figure 71. Slingerland Pre-Reading Screening Procedures, Procedure 9, Far-Point Copying

using practice pages to train the students in the proper procedures is excellent. One part of the practice pages is a "This is Me" picture, which yields a great deal of information about the student's readiness skills. Although the subtests are timed, this is primarily to keep the group testing moving along and does not put serious constraints on the students. The teacher's manual gives excellent discussions of the subtests and the skills being measured by each. The Slingerland Pre-Reading Screening Procedures are an excellent contribution to the field when used as a group screening measure (1) to give the first-grade teacher extensive information on the modality strengths and weaknesses of a class of beginning readers and (2) to identify children who may need further individual testing.

LIMITING FACTORS OF THE SLINGERLAND PRE-READING SCREENING PROCEDURES

- The Slingerland Pre-Reading Screening Procedures must be considered informal tests at this time. No age or grade norms are provided. The five-point rating scale is based on the test results of several hundred children just entering first grade in school districts throughout the United States, but no further information about the sample is given.
- The Slingerland Pre-Reading Screening Procedures were designed to identify children who would enter first grade using the Slingerland adaptation of Orton-Gillingham (Gillingham and Stillman 1960) techniques as a curriculum. The teacher's manual interprets student test performance from the Orton-Gillingham point of view. This is not a serious problem in using the tests, but the teacher should be aware that such statements as "The brighter the child, the more opportunities there have been for language learning" is an opinion, not a statement of fact.
- The author suggests that the Slingerland Pre-Reading Screening Procedures be used with the Pintner-Cunningham Primary Test of general intelligence (1966). This suggestion points up the need to be cautious about diagnosing any child's learning disabilities on the basis of one test.

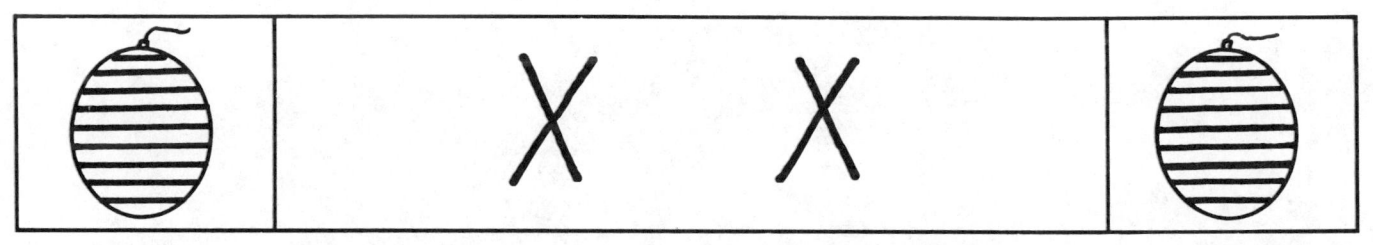

Figure 72. Slingerland Pre-Reading Screening Procedures, Procedure 10, Auditory Discrimination

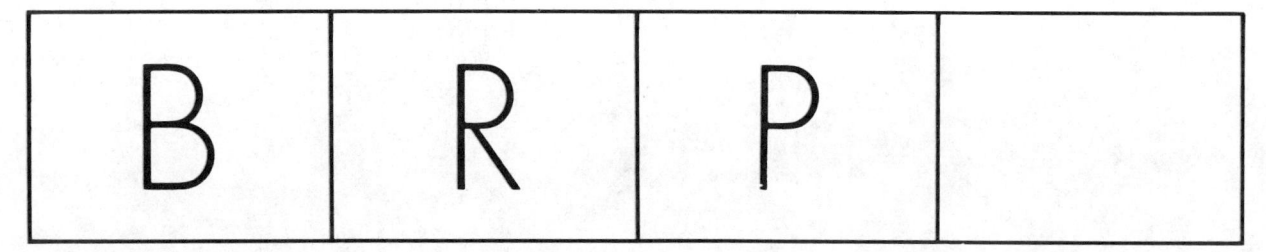

Figure 73. Slingerland Pre-Reading Screening Procedures, Procedure 11, Auditory-Visual-Kinesthetic Integration

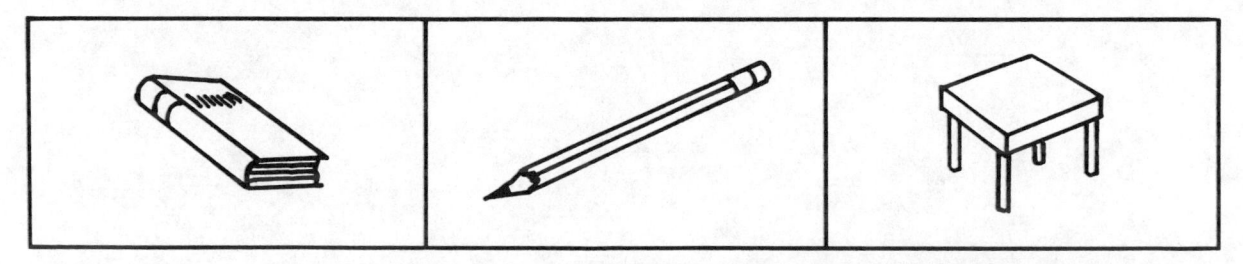

Figure 74. Slingerland Pre-Reading Screening Procedures, Procedure 12, Auditory-Visual Association

PART III
General Intelligence Tests and Developmental Scales

No other area of assessment has caused so much controversy as the area of intelligence testing, or IQ tests. Debates rage over such topics as the meaning of intelligence, the use of IQ tests as predictors of school achievement, the cultural biases of standard IQ tests, and the interpretation (or misinterpretation) of IQ scores. There may never be any widespread agreement about whether IQ tests should be given, what they measure, or what they mean, but they continue to be used regularly in the field of special education.

In this section, individual IQ tests are viewed as another source of information about a student that may be used in planning an instructional program. Teachers who are familiar with the format and content of general intelligence tests can use information about the student's performance to plan a curriculum.

The most commonly used individual test of general intelligence, the Wechsler Intelligence Scale for Children—Revised, is reviewed in depth and contrasted with the Wechsler Preschool and Primary Scale of Intelligence and the Wechsler Adult Intelligence Scale. The oldest and best-known intelligence test, the Stanford-Binet Intelligence Scale, is also reviewed. Four less-familiar tests are included: The Slosson Intelligence Test for Children and Adults, a short screening test patterned after the Stanford-Binet Intelligence Scale; the Leiter International Performance Scale and the Arthur Adaptation, for language-impaired students; the Coloured Progressive Matrices, another test for nonverbal intelligence; and the McCarthy Scales of Children's Abilities, a new test for preschool and primary students.

Two new tests, which include the aptitude measure and the achievement measure in the same instrument, are reviewed. The Woodcock-Johnson Psycho-Educational Battery is becoming widely used in special education, and the Kaufman Assessment Battery for Children, not released at the time of this publication, promises to be an interesting addition to the field. The System of Multicultural Pluristic Assessment is a comprehensive measure of the whole child designed for minority populations. It is reviewed in this chapter because it includes the Wechsler Intelligence Scale for Children—Revised as a major component.

Developmental scales are measures of a particular process in a maturing child. Language and visual perception are examples of processes that mature without specific teaching. Because they are age-related, developmental scales are often indicators of advanced development or immaturity. The Goodenough-Harris Drawing Test is reviewed in this section because it is most often used as a test of cognitive development and intellectual maturity. Several other tests in the book can be considered developmental in nature. Because of the specific nature of their content, the Marianne Frostig Developmental Test of Visual Perception (p. 118) and the Beery-Buktenica Developmental Test of Visual-Motor Integration (p. 134) are reviewed in Part I, Chapter Two: Perception and Memory Tests. For the same reason, the Developmental Sentence Scoring system (p. 172) is included in Part I, Chapter Three: Speech and Language Tests, and the Denver Developmental Screening Test (p. 233) and the Brigance Diagnostic Inventory of Early Development (p. 237) are reviewed in Part II: Preschool and Kindergarten Tests.

WECHSLER INTELLIGENCE SCALE FOR
   CHILDREN—REVISED 265
STANFORD-BINET INTELLIGENCE SCALE 276
SLOSSON INTELLIGENCE TEST FOR CHILDREN
   AND ADULTS 279
LEITER INTERNATIONAL PERFORMANCE SCALE
   AND THE ARTHUR ADAPTATION 282
COLOURED PROGRESSIVE MATRICES 286
McCARTHY SCALES OF CHILDREN'S
   ABILITIES 290
WOODCOCK-JOHNSON PSYCHO-EDUCATIONAL
   BATTERY 293
KAUFMAN ASSESSMENT BATTERY FOR
   CHILDREN 300
SYSTEM OF MULTICULTURAL PLURISTIC
   ASSESSMENT 303
GOODENOUGH-HARRIS DRAWING TEST 311

Wechsler Intelligence Scale for Children— Revised (WISC-R)

David Wechsler
The Psychological Corporation, 1974
7500 Old Oak Blvd., Middleburg Heights, OH 44130

Purpose	To measure specific mental abilities and processes
Major Areas Tested	General intelligence
Age or Grade Range	6–17 years
Usually Given By	Psychologist
Type of Test	Standardized Individual
Scores Obtained	Verbal IQ Scaled Performance IQ Test age Full-scale IQ
Student Performance Timed?	Yes (7 subtests)
Testing Time	50–75 minutes (10 subtests)
Scoring/Interpretation Time	30–40 minutes
Normed On	2,200 children, including 100 boys and 100 girls at each age level, balanced for race, geographic regions, urban and rural residence, and occupation of the head of household, conforming to the 1970 census
Alternate Forms Available?	No

FORMAT

The Wechsler Intelligence Scale for Children—Revised (WISC-R) is an individually administered test designed to assess the global aspects of general intelligence. To probe intelligence in as many different ways as possible, the WISC-R includes 12 subtests that emphasize various types of ability. These subtests, by representing different ways in which intelligence may manifest itself, contribute to a composite view of intellectual functioning.

The WISC-R is divided into two main parts, a verbal scale and a performance scale, each having five mandatory subtests and one subtest usable as a supplement or an alternate. IQs are calculated on the basis of the five verbal and five performance tests listed below. The numbers indicate the order in which the tests are given. Most examiners find it convenient to give the tests in the following order; however, the examiner is free to change the prescribed order to meet the needs of the testing situation.

Verbal Scale	Performance Scale
1. Information	2. Picture Completion
3. Similarities	4. Picture Arrangement
5. Arithmetic	6. Block Design
7. Vocabulary	8. Object Assembly
9. Comprehension	10. Coding (or Mazes)
11. Digit Span (supplement or alternate)	12. Mazes (supplement or alternate)

Digit Span on the verbal scale and Mazes on the performance scale have been retained as supplementary tests to be given when time allows or as substitutes if a regularly administered test is invalidated or cannot properly be administered. It is always permissible to administer all 12 subtests. The supplementary tests add useful qualitative and diagnostic information.

Because the WISC-R is appropriate for students from 6 to 17 years of age, different starting points for each subtest have been specified, depending on the student's age and estimated level of ability. The directions for starting and discontinuing each subtest are conveniently indicated on the record form as well as in the WISC-R manual. Rules for establishing a basal level on each subtest are given in the manual. A basal must be established in order to assume credit for easier items not given.

Test materials for the WISC-R are packaged in a briefcase-sized kit. They include the manual, individual record forms, and the cards, blocks, puzzles, and booklets necessary for the various subtests. The examiner must supply a stopwatch.

The specific items within each subtest on the WISC-R are arranged in order of increasing difficulty. A general idea of the kinds of abilities assessed by each subtest, along with other descriptive information, is given in Table 30. The examples given in the table are similar, but not identical, to those found on the WISC-R.

In scoring the WISC-R, raw scores on each subtest are first transmitted into scaled scores within the student's age group. Tables of such scores are given for every four-month interval between the ages of 6 years and 16 years, 11 months. The subtest scaled scores are expressed in terms of a distribution with a mean of 10 and a standard deviation of 3. Thus, if Bobby obtains a score of 10 on a subtest, he is average for his age. If Joey obtains a scaled score of 7 on a subtest, he is 1 standard deviation below the mean for his age.

After obtaining the subtest scaled scores, the next step is to add these scores together to produce an overall verbal score, an overall performance score, and a full scale score. Finally, using the norm tables, the scores are converted into verbal, performance, and full scale IQs; each IQ has a mean of 100 and a standard deviation of 15. Thus, an IQ of 100 on any of the scales defines the performance of the average student of a given age on that scale. An IQ of 130 on any of the scales defines the performance of the very superior student, falling 2 standard deviations above the mean for that age group. With equal standard deviations, IQs are directly comparable for various ages—a particular advantage of the test.

It is also possible to obtain test ages on the WISC-R. This allows comparison of WISC-R scores with age norms of other scales and facilitates the interpretation of scores from a developmental viewpoint.

STRENGTHS OF THE WISC-R

- The WISC-R is a convenient, reliable instrument that is modern in construction and contains materials intrinsically interesting to students. The test materials are compact and very accessible. The WISC-R manual is efficiently arranged and contains clear directions and tables. An improvement in the WISC-R manual that facilitates administration is the use of brown boldface type for the test directions to students and black boldface type for the examiner's instructions.

- The WISC-R record form gives adequate space for recording answers. Some minor improvements in the record form ease administration. For instance, the directions for starting and discontinuing each subtest are printed directly on the form. The front of the form also contains a profile (see Figure 83) that can be filled in to show graphically a student's strengths and weaknesses on the WISC-R subtests.

- Changes made in the WISC-R over the original edition have strengthened the test. One principal change involves the age range of the battery: The WISC-R spans the age range 6 through 17 years, whereas the 1949 WISC was appropriate for students aged 5 through 15 years. Another change involves the sequence in which the tests are given. The verbal and performance tests are now administered in alternating order, as in the Wechsler Preschool and Primary Scale of Intelligence. Alternating verbal and performance tasks helps to maintain a student's interest in the test.

Another change allows the examiner to demonstrate the solution to a problem or to provide the correct answer to a question when a student fails the first item of any test. Giving the correct response to at least the first item helps ensure that the student understands the nature of each test. This modification is especially important for young students and for those who are mentally deficient.

Other important changes in the WISC-R involve modifying or eliminating ambiguous or obsolete test items and dropping items that were allegedly unfair to minority populations. For example, in the Information subtest, such questions as "What does COD mean?" were eliminated. To strengthen the reliability of each test, some new items were added. In Picture Completion, additional items include more pictures of female and black subjects. But overall, an effort was made to retain as much of the 1949 WISC as possible because of its widespread use and established credibility as a clinical and diagnostic tool.

In terms of reliability, the coefficients for the WISC-R are quite high across the entire age range. Split-half coefficients in the .90s have been reported for the verbal, performance, and full scale IQs. The reliabilities for the individual subtests are generally satisfactory, with the average coefficients ranging from .77 to .86 for the verbal subtests and from .70 to .85 for the performance subtests.

Special studies have indicated good correlations between the WISC-R and other individually administered intelligence tests. The Stanford-Binet Intelligence Scale and the WISC-R tend to be highly correlated despite the differences in test items. As might be anticipated, the verbal and full scale IQs on the WISC-R generally correlate higher with the Stanford-Binet Intelligence Scale than do the performance IQs (.71, .73, and .60 respectively).

The correlation between the full scale IQs of the WISC-R and the Wechsler Preschool and Primary Scale of Intelligence is .82. The WISC-R and Wechsler Adult Intelligence Scale full scale IQs show a .95 correlation coefficient.

• The WISC-R is a particularly well standardized test. The 1974 revision used the data from the 1970 census. The test was carefully normed on 2,200 boys and girls of wide geographic distribution, and the procedures were fully reported. Attention was given to including race as a variable, which makes the WISC-R one of the better standardized tests for current use with nonwhite students. There is also a Spanish-language adaptation of the WISC (*Escala de Intelligencia Wechsler Para Niños* 1951), also available from The Psychological Corporation.

• One of the primary strengths of the WISC-R is the wealth of diagnostic information it provides. For example, analysis of the size of the difference between the verbal IQ and the performance IQ may be of clinical significance. Wechsler claims that a discrepancy of 15 points or more is important and warrants further investigation. Generally, a student's verbal and performance IQs do not differ significantly. A large difference between them suggests a true difference in ability. On the WISC-R record form shown in Figure 82, one can easily see how low verbal scores have depressed this particular student's full scale IQ. Thus, a student's differential ability in verbal and nonverbal tasks can be assessed objectively on the WISC-R.

It is important for an examiner to know how large a difference there must be between a student's scaled scores on two separate subtests for that difference to be considered meaningful. As a general rule, Wechsler states that a difference of three or more scaled-score points between any pair of tests may be considered significant at the 15-percent level of confidence. It is thus possible to analyze inter-subtest scatter to determine a student's strengths and weaknesses and to help answer such questions as "What particular educational deficits are handicapping Mary?" In the WISC-R profile shown in Figure 83, one can readily see a significant imbalance between verbal and performance skills and the great degree of intersubtest scatter suggestive of specific disabilities. The low Coding score, for example, may indicate poor visual-motor coordination; the depressed verbal scores probably indicate a language disability. On the plus side are the near-average Comprehension score and the superior Picture Arrangement score; these scores reflect strengths in commonsense knowledge and social competence.

• In addition to analyzing scores and subtest patterns of the WISC-R, the examiner can consider the quality of a student's responses. By observing the student's behavior in the test situation, the examiner may gain valuable insights that may explain the student's difficulty. Why are some items passed and others failed? If, for example, a student fails questions dealing with temporal-sequential and spatial relationships on the Information subtest, the examiner will want to investigate more thoroughly the student's mastery of such concepts. If a student begins a story in Picture Arrangement at the right instead of beginning at the left, other tasks requiring left-to-right progression should be investigated. If a student performs poorly on Mazes, the reason may be extremely slow working speed or perhaps a lack of foresight and planning ability.

The examiner will also need to assess a whole range of behavioral factors during testing. What is the student's relationship with the examiner: Cooperative? Self-reliant? Confident? Fearful? Negative? What is the student's reaction to tasks: Motivated? Persistent? Attentive? Impulsive? Reliant on trial and error? The testing situation can provide the examiner with clinical observations that may be more significant in many cases than the actual test scores.

Table 30. WISC-R Subtests

Verbal Scale
Requires auditory-verbal input and verbal output. Questions are read aloud by the examiner; the student responds orally.

Subtest	Description	Sample Test Items
Information	30 basic fact questions	"Name the month that comes after June." "Why does the moon look larger than the stars?" "On what continent is Argentina?"
Comprehension	17 questions requiring the practical knowledge needed to make judgments about social situations	"What are some reasons why we need an army?" "What is the thing to do if you have a bloody nose?"
Arithmetic	18 arithmetic word problems requiring mental computation	"Tommy had three pennies and his mother gave him two more. How many pennies did he have altogether?" "A salesperson earned $35; she was paid $5 an hour. How many hours did she work?"
Similarities	17 pairs of words requiring recognition of likenesses (critical or superficial) between concrete objects, substances, facts, or ideas	"In what way are a *sweater* and a *coat* alike?" "In what way are *happiness* and *sadness* alike?"
Vocabulary	32 words (20 nouns, 7 verbs, and 5 adjectives) requiring definition; the list progresses from concrete words representing objects to more abstract words	"What is a *wagon*?" "What does *isolate* mean?"
Digit Span	14 series of numbers: numbers are given at a rate of one per second; no digits are repeated within a series; digit series must be repeated without error and in correct sequence after a single presentation	
Digit Forward	7 series of unrelated digits requiring the student to repeat three to nine digits in two trials	Trial 1: 4-3-1-7 Trial 2: 5-8-1-6
Digit Backward	7 series of unrelated digits requiring the student to repeat backward two to eight digits in two trials	Trial 1: 7-5-3-1-4 Trial 2: 2-5-8-7-9

- Although considerable research has been carried out regarding the diagnostic significance of particular subtest patterns on the WISC (1949 version), the results are inconclusive. Nevertheless, certain generalizations seem warranted, because several studies have reported finding certain subtest patterns with some degree of regularity. For example:

1. Many mentally deficient students are likely to score higher on the performance than on the verbal section.
2. Many brain-damaged students are likely to score higher on the verbal than on the performance scale. They also show the most difficulty with Coding and Block Design.
3. Students classified as poor readers are likely to score higher on subtests not directly related to the school curriculum (Picture Arrangement, Object Assembly, and Block Design). They often score lowest on subtests related to school instruction (Information, Arithmetic, and Digit Span).
4. Students with specific language disability (dyslexia) are more likely to score lower on the verbal scale than on the performance scale. Frequently the verbal IQ is significantly lower than the performance IQ.

Part III General Intelligence Tests and Developmental Scales   269

Timed?	Areas Measured	Notes
No	General information acquired from experience and education, remote verbal memory, understanding, associative thinking	The socioeconomic background and reading ability of the student may influence the subtest score.
No	Social judgment, commonsense reasoning based on past experience, practical intelligence	Compare with Picture Arrangement subtest.
Yes	Mental alertness, concentration, attention, arithmetic reasoning, reaction to time pressure, practical knowledge of computational facts	This is the only subtest directly related to the school curriculum.
No	Abstract and concrete reasoning, logical thought processes, associative thinking, remote memory	
No	Understanding of spoken words, learning ability, general range of ideas, verbal information acquired from experience and education, kind and quality of expressive language	This subtest is relatively unaffected by emotional disturbance, but it is highly susceptible to cultural background and level of education. It is also the best single measure of intelligence in the entire battery.
No	Attention, concentration, immediate auditory memory, auditory attention, behavior in a learning situation	This subtest correlates poorly with general intelligence.

• Finally, particular mention should be made regarding the usefulness of the WISC-R for the evaluation of the student suspected of having a learning disability. The dichotomy between verbal and performance skills is only one of the several ways the tests could be grouped. Other groupings have included:

1. *Meaningfulness versus Nonmeaningfulness of the Subtests*. In this grouping, all the verbal subtests, with the exception of Digit Span, are considered meaningful tasks. The meaningful nonverbal tests are Object Assembly, Picture Arrangement, and Picture Completion. The performance tests considered nonmeaningful (Block Design, Coding, and Mazes) are categorized as such because they deal with material that is not generally within the typical experience of the student. Analyzing WISC-R subtests within this framework may show a student's ability to process meaningful information successfully and inability to deal with nonmeaningful material (or vice versa).

2. *Social versus Nonsocial Tasks*. The verbal subtests all involve social perception, with the exception of Digit Span and Similarities. Only the Picture Arrangement subtest of the performance tests entails this ability. The division into Social versus Nonsocial may be another useful way of

Table 30.—*Continued*

Performance Scale
Presented visually; requires motor, nonverbal output. Although brief verbal directions for each task are given by the examiner, the student receives the information visually and nonverbally, and the motor response demands no verbalization.

Subtest	Description	Sample Test Items
Picture Completion	26 line drawings on cards (15 objects, 7 human figures, 4 animals) each requiring the student, after a 20-second exposure, to identify verbally or by pointing to a missing element	"What is missing in this picture?" (see Figure 75 on p. 272)
Picture Arrangement	12 comic-strip picture sequences of three to five pictures requiring logical rearrangement	"Put these pictures in the right order." (see Figure 76 on p. 272)
Block Design	11 two-color block designs requiring reproduction either from an actual block model or from a picture	"Make a block design like this one." (see Figure 77 on p. 273)
Object Assembly	5 puzzle pictures of four to eight pieces depicting familiar objects; the name of the object is given on the first two pictures only	"Put these pieces together to make a star." (see Figure 78 on p. 273)
Coding		
Coding A (under 8 years)	45 symbols in the test booklet requiring the student to match shapes and write the proper symbols inside	"Put the right mark inside each of these shapes." (see Figure 79 on p. 273)
Coding B (8 years and above)	93 symbols with numerals in the test booklet requiring the student to match numerals and write the symbols below	"Put the right mark in the box below each number." (see Figure 80 on p. 273)
Mazes	9 mazes to be followed by the student without lifting the pencil	"Draw a line from the circle to the X without lifting your pencil." (see Figure 81 on p. 273)

viewing a student's WISC-R patterns in relation to learning disabilities.

3. *Spatial versus Conceptual versus Sequential Tasks.* Bannatyne (1968) has offered another way to analyze WISC-R subtest patterns, by categorizing them as follows:

Conceptual Score. Sum of scaled scores of Comprehension, Similarities, and Vocabulary. Language ability is required by these subtests.

Spatial Score. Sum of scaled scores of Block Design, Picture Completion, and Object Assembly. These subtests require the ability to manipulate objects in multidimensional space, either directly or symbolically.

Sequential Score. Sum of scaled scores of Digit Span, Coding, and Picture Arrangement. These subtests demand short-term memory of visual and auditory sequences.

The composite scaled score for each of these three groupings should average 30. Bannatyne compares a student's scores in the three areas to obtain information about particular strengths and weaknesses. Recently Bannatyne (1974) added a fourth category, *Acquired Knowledge,* composed of Information, Arithmetic, and Vocabulary.

In summary, the WISC-R is a high-quality general-purpose intelligence test that compares favorably with

Timed?	Areas Measured	Notes
Yes	Visual alertness to surroundings, remote visual memory, attention to detail, visual perception (closure ability), ability to isolate essential from nonessential detail, perceptual and conceptual skills	This subtest may indicate word recall problems or inadequate vocabulary if the student points to the missing part but is unable to give the word.
Yes	Visual perception, comprehension, and synthesis of environmental experiences used to anticipate and size up a total situation; logical sequencing of events; attention to detail; ability to see cause-effect relationships	This is considered a test of social intelligence. Compare with Comprehension subtest.
Yes (bonus points given for quick perfect performance at the higher levels)	Ability to perceive, analyze, synthesize, and reproduce abstract forms; visual perception; nonverbal concept formation; capacity for sustained concentration; visual-motor coordination; abstract and concrete reasoning applied to spatial relationships; general ability to plan and organize	This is considered the best single non-verbal measure of general intelligence in the battery, because it is little influenced by cultural factors.
Yes (bonus points given for quick perfect performance)	Immediate perception of a total configuration; understanding the relationship of individual parts; visual perception and anticipation of part-whole relationships; visual synthesis abilities; visual-motor-spatial coordination; simple assembly skills; ability to work flexibly toward a goal	This subtest does not correlate highly with general intelligence.
Yes (bonus points given for perfect score)	Ability to associate meaning with symbol, visual-motor dexterity (pencil manipulation), flexibility and speed in learning tasks when stimuli are visual and kinesthetic, ability to memorize rapidly	This subtest does not correlate highly with general intelligence.
Yes	Ability to shift attention and visual focus quickly and accurately, ability to use left-right progression	
Yes	Ability to formulate and execute a visual-motor plan, pencil control and visual-motor coordination, speed and accuracy, planning capability, foresight	

other individual scales and will likely remain the most commonly used measure of intelligence within the school system. It is a reliable and well-known instrument that usually provides scores correlating highly with school achievement.

LIMITING FACTORS OF THE WISC-R

• Caution must be exercised in interpreting WISC-R scores. The level of intellectual ability achieved on the test indicates only a small sample of the student's performance at one moment in time. An IQ is not immutable; it reflects the present capacity of the student and shows what can be expected if current conditions remain the same. Furthermore, the test may or may not be an adequate sample of a student's potential intellectual abilities. All tests give only a limited measure of a student's assets. The significance of an IQ score for a particular student can accurately be assessed only when it is compared to other data: the student's social-emotional maturity level, the amount of schooling, achievement levels, and cultural or language background. The testing situation itself is important, because emotional reactions such as anxiety can significantly diminish a student's performance. Thus, the examiner must weigh a number of factors and check for discrepancies and

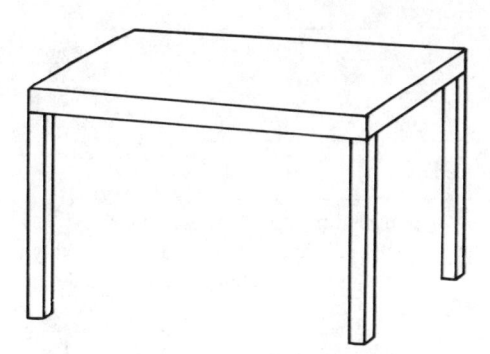

Figure 75. WISC-R Picture Completion

Figure 76. WISC-R Picture Arrangement

congruencies in order to better understand the meaning of the IQ results and test scatter obtained.

- It is clear that the verbal scale is more closely related to academic achievement than the performance scale. The verbal score also predicts much more accurately than the performance score how successful an individual is likely to be in future school situations. This fact should be borne in mind when evaluating the protocols of students showing high nonverbal scores but poor verbal facility. Although the performance score may reflect average intellectual functioning, this score alone cannot be taken at face value when assessing a student's chances for future school success.

- The WISC-R shows limits for the tabled IQs. Verbal and performance IQs range from 45 to 155; the full scale IQ ranges from 40 to 160. There is also no breakdown or diagnostic classification of mental deficiency in terms of severity (mild, moderate, severe). All IQs below 69 are simply classified as "mentally deficient." The WISC-R is not a particularly sensitive instrument for students at either end of the intelligence distribution.

- Of concern to many investigators is that most of the WISC-R's content was based on a test for adults, the Wechsler-Bellevue Intelligence Scale (1947). The question researchers pose is, Should a children's intelligence scale simply be a downward extension of an adult scale? Wechsler himself comments that we cannot assume that similar tests tap identical skills at all ages.

- Several of the WISC-R subtests have limitations that the examiner should be aware of.

Vocabulary. Scoring of vocabulary items contains some subjectivity, although the revised manual includes expanded sample answers. If a student fails to express a definition of a word, there is no procedure the examiner can follow to find out if the student has at least a passive familiarity or understanding of the word.

Picture Completion. The difficulty level of this subtest increases unevenly, because success is influenced by the student's familiarity with the objects pictured.

Digit Span. Digit Span is the only test of short-term memory on the WISC-R. Serial presentation of such items as the repetition of digits forward and backward tires

Part III General Intelligence Tests and Developmental Scales 273

Figure 77. WISC-R Block Design

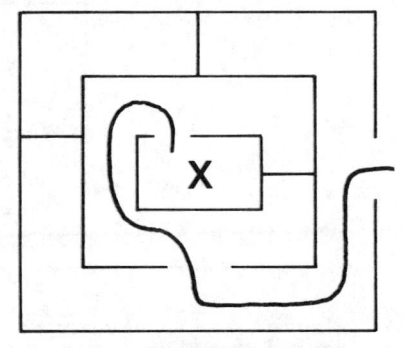

Figure 81. WISC-R Mazes

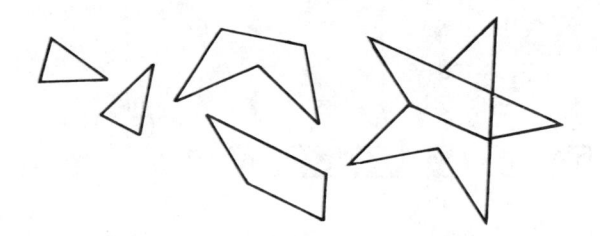

Figure 78. WISC-R Object Assembly

Figure 79. WISC-R Coding A

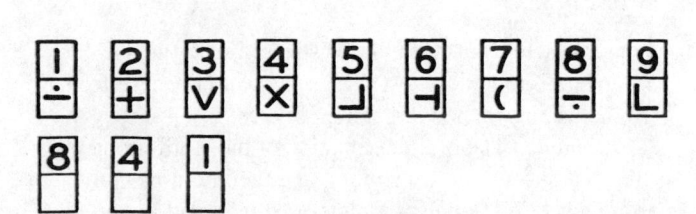

Figure 80. WISC-R Coding B

	Year	Month	Day
Date Tested	77	11	9
Date of Birth	64	6	30
Age	13	4	

	Raw Score	Scaled Score
VERBAL TESTS		
Information	11	4
Similarities	15	8
Arithmetic	12	8
Vocabulary	30	7
Comprehension	14	5
(Digit Span)	(8)	(5)
Verbal Score		32
PERFORMANCE TESTS		
Picture Completion	22	11
Picture Arrangement	31	10
Block Design	38	10
Object Assembly	27	12
Coding	57	11
(Mazes)	( )	( )
Performance Score		54

	Scaled Score	IQ
Verbal Score	32	* 78
Performance Score	54	* 105
Full Scale Score	86	89

*Prorated from 4 tests, if necessary.

Figure 82. WISC-R Record Form

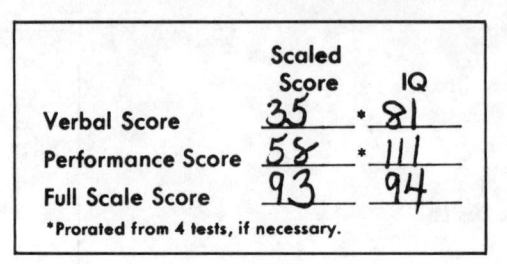

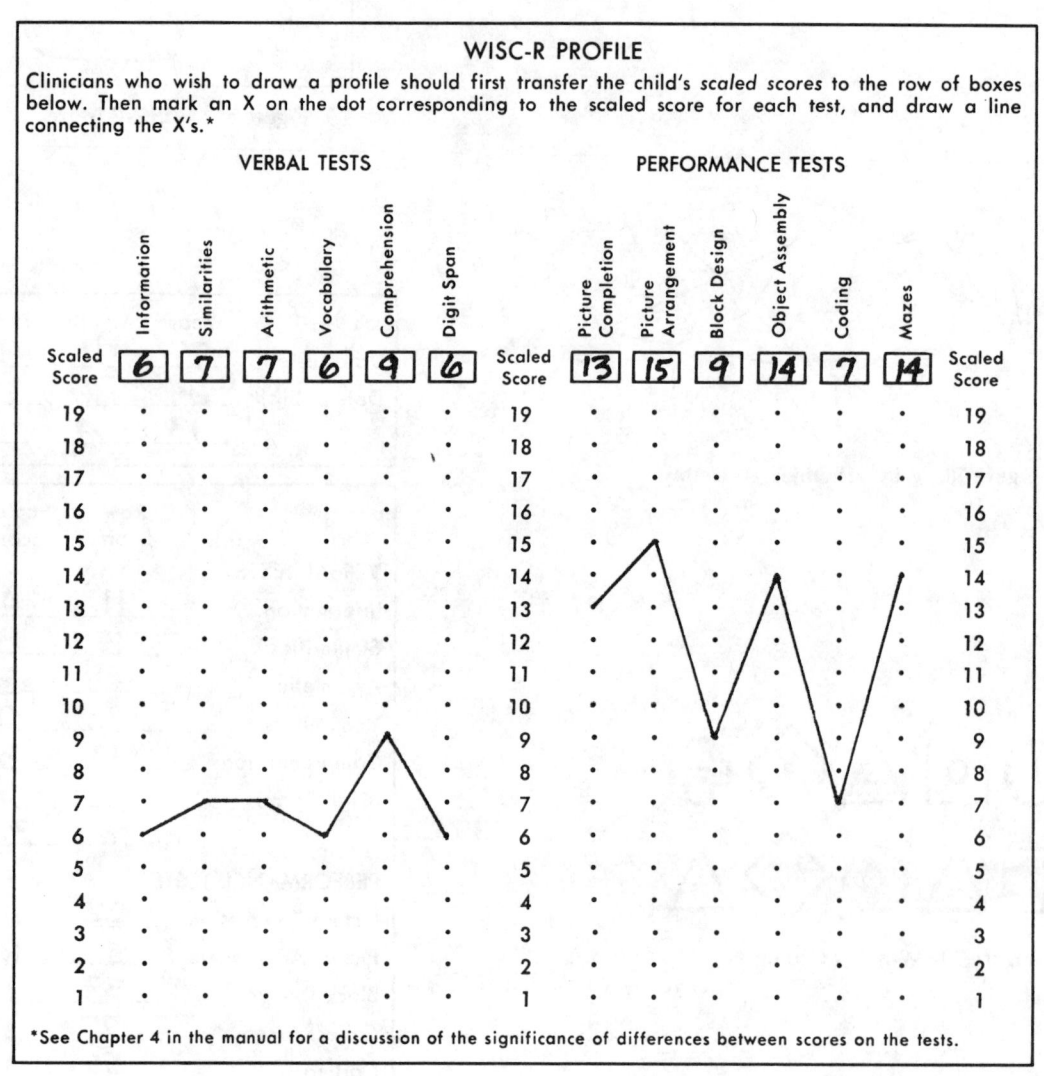

Figure 83. WISC-R Profile

children. The fatigue factor is increased on the WISC-R because both trials of each of the items must be administered. Furthermore, Digit Span is the least reliable of the verbal subtests. It may be more useful to include a meaningful verbal memory test, such as sentence, phrase, or story repetition, in a diagnostic evaluation.

Coding. This subtest is frequently purported to reflect a memory factor, but it should be stressed that it is not designed as a memory test. The scale would benefit from the inclusion of a nonverbal memory test.

Arithmetic. The oral presentation of the word problems stresses concentration, memory, and facility in mental arithmetic. This subtest should not be regarded as an index of a student's achievement level in arithmetic.

WECHSLER PRESCHOOL AND PRIMARY SCALE OF INTELLIGENCE (WPPSI)

The WPPSI is intended for use with children between the ages of 4 and 6½ years. There are 11 subtests, but only 10 are used in computing the IQ. Verbal and performance subtests are alternated during administration to provide variety, which is helpful in holding the young child's attention.

The subtests are listed below in order of administration:

Verbal Scale	Performance Scale
1. Information	2. Picture Completion
3. Comprehension	4. Block Design
5. Arithmetic	6. Animal House
7. Similarities	8. Mazes
9. Vocabulary	10. Geometric Design
11. Sentences (alternate)	

The verbal scale is essentially the same as the WISC-R. Sentences is a new subtest, replacing Digit Span. The student listens to sentences read by the examiner and repeats them. Although both tasks assess rote automatic auditory memory, the memory for words in a sentence appears to be less abstract and less demanding of the student's attention. The Sentences subtest is used only as an alternate to another verbal subtest.

On the performance scale, Picture Arrangement, Coding, and Object Assembly from the WISC-R have been dropped; Mazes has been made a required subtest, and two new subtests have been added—Animal House and Geometric Design. Animal House, like Coding, is an associative learning task. The student places a particular colored peg in the board under the picture of one of four animals. For example, the student is asked to place all the red pegs under the picture of the pig, the blue pegs under the horse, and so forth. Attention and concentration are enhanced by the gamelike quality of this subtest, which is more appropriate for preschoolers than is the pencil-and-paper task, Coding. Visual-motor coordination is measured by the Geometric Design subtest. Geometric Design requires the child to copy 10 designs made up of circles and straight lines.

As on the WISC-R and the Wechsler Adult Intelligence Scale, verbal, performance, and full scale IQs are obtained, with a mean of 100 and a standard deviation of 15.

WECHSLER ADULT INTELLIGENCE SCALE (WAIS)

The WAIS is almost identical in organization, administration, and scoring to the WISC-R. It may be used with students from age 16 to adult. The verbal scale consists of six required subtests, and the performance scale has five required subtests. There are no alternate or supplemental subtests. The subtests are given in the following order:

Verbal Scale	Performance Scale
1. Information	7. Digit Symbol (equivalent to WISC-R, Coding)
2. Comprehension	
3. Arithmetic	8. Picture Completion
4. Similarities	9. Block Design
5. Digit Span	10. Picture Arrangement
6. Vocabulary	11. Object Assembly

Verbal, performance, and full scale IQs with a mean of 100 and a standard deviation of 15 are obtained, as on the WISC-R.

Stanford-Binet Intelligence Scale (Stanford-Binet)

Lewis M. Terman and Maud A. Merrill
Houghton Mifflin Company, third revision (Form L-M), 1960; renorming 1972
Test Department, Box 1970, Iowa City, IA 52240

Purpose	To measure general intellectual ability
Major Areas Tested	General intelligence
Age or Grade Range	2 years–adult
Usually Given By	Psychologist
Type of Test	Standardized Individual Norm-referenced
Scores Obtained	Mental age IQ
Student Performance Timed?	Yes (some items)
Testing Time	30–90 minutes (depending on age and ability)
Scoring/Interpretation Time	30–45 minutes
Normed On	2,100 urban and rural students from various geographic locations, with a wide range of intellectual abilities; 100 individuals at each age level
Alternate Forms Available?	No

FORMAT

The materials for the Stanford-Binet Intelligence Scale (Stanford-Binet) consist of an examiner's manual, individual record booklets, and a variety of pictures and manipulative materials necessary for administration of the individual test items. All of the materials are packaged in a suitcase-style carrying case.

The test items are arranged by age level. At each age level, six tests are administered. They assess a variety of abilities, such as vocabulary, memory, abstract reasoning, numerical concepts, visual-motor skills, and social competence. Testing begins at an age level where the examiner thinks the student will be challenged but successful, usually about one year below age level. The manual defines the basal age as "that level at which all tests are passed which just precedes the level where the first failure occurs" (p. 60). Testing is discontinued when the student fails all of the tests at a given age level. One alternate test is available at each age level, to be substituted when a test is invalidated by examiner error.

Table 31 gives examples at different age levels that illustrate the types of test items. (These items are similar but not identical to test items.) Often an item such as Vocabulary is listed at several age levels. The item is administered once, the first time it is listed. Scoring criteria differ, and more correct answers are required to pass the item at each higher age level. For example, in the Vocabulary section, the criteria change as follows:

Year	Correct Answers Required to Pass
6	6
8	8
10	11
12	15
14	17
AA (Average Adult)	20
SA, I (Superior Adult, I)	23
SA, II (Superior Adult, II)	26
SA, III (Superior Adult, III)	30

Each item is scored pass or fail according to the specific instructions in the manual. A specified number of months' credit is given for each item passed. All items below the basal are assumed passed; all items above the ceiling are assumed failed. The number of months credited is totaled to get a mental age. Tables are used to convert mental age to IQ.

STRENGTHS OF THE STANFORD-BINET

• The Stanford-Binet is the grandfather of individual intelligence tests. The original Binet scales were developed in 1905; in 1916 they were revised and extended for use in the United States. They were revised again in 1937 and 1960. The current 1972 edition is a renorming of the 1960 edition.

• The Stanford-Binet is the only intelligence scale available for the age range between 30 months, when the Bayley Scales (1969) end, and 48 months, when the Wechsler Preschool and Primary Scale of Intelligence begins. It remains the favored test for assessing the preschool child because of its better coverage at the lower end of the scale. Because of its emphasis on verbal skills and its greater reliability at the extremes of IQ, the Stanford-Binet also continues to be a favorite of psychologists for testing students with very high intellectual ability.

LIMITING FACTORS OF THE STANFORD-BINET

• The Stanford-Binet was designed as a test of general intellectual ability, not as a differential measure of several aspects of mental ability. It is based on a unitary concept of intelligence. With the gain in popularity of the Wechsler Scales (WISC-R, WAIS, WPPSI) and other tests yielding profiles of subtest performances, the Stanford-Binet has become less frequently used. Several attempts (Meeker 1969; Sattler 1965; Valett 1964) have been made to develop systems for classifying the kinds of items on the Stanford-Binet. These classification systems have had little agreement and no attempts at validation. The Stanford-Binet was not designed as a test of differential skills and any attempt to use it in that way yields questionable results. However, the teacher benefits when the psychologist lists the tests that were passed and failed at each level with some description of their content. Because the Stanford-Binet yields a single score, the Wechsler Intelligence Scale for Children—Revised is usually selected for exceptional children when knowledge of their particular pattern of skill development is essential for proper placement and program planning.

• Salvia, Ysseldyke, and Lee (1975) demonstrated that the 1972 edition does not have items placed appropriately for the age levels. In earlier editions, an item was placed at the 8-year-old level because a majority of 8-year-olds answered it correctly. When the test was renormed, items were not changed in relationship to new data. The result is that students must perform above age level to earn average IQs.

• Reliability and validity for the 1972 edition are not reported. The assumption is that, because earlier editions were reliable and valid, this one is too.

• The Stanford-Binet is a difficult test to learn to administer correctly. The variety in items and materials requires the psychologist to practice the test many times

Table 31. Stanford-Binet Sample Test Items

Age Level	Test	Materials	Procedure
2.6	Identifying Objects by Use	Card with small objects attached (bed, boat, pencil, hat, stove)	Present the card and say: "Show me what... a. we sleep on." b. goes in the water." c. we can write with." d. we can cook on."
3	Copying a Triangle	Printed triangle in the record booklet	Give the child a pencil and point to the triangle and say: "Make one like this."
4.6	Three Commissions	Any available book	Say: "Here is a book. I want you to put it under the desk, touch the window curtain, and sit down in that chair."
6	Vocabulary	Vocabulary card	Say: "When I say a word, you tell me what it means." a. "tomato" b. "hay" c. "acrobat" d. "abundance"
8	Similarities and Differences	None	Say: "Tell me how these two things are alike and how they are different." a. "tennis ball and a tire" b. "fish and a submarine" c. "mountains and desert"
10	Abstract Words	None	Say: "What do we mean by... a. suffering?" b. astonishment?" c. patriotism?"
11	Memory for Designs	Card with two designs	Show the card to the student for 10 seconds. Take it away and have the student draw the designs.
13	Copying a Bead Chain from Memory	48 kindergarten beads	Make this bead chain while the student watches: ○ ○ □ ○ ○ □ ○ ○ □ Show it to the student for five seconds, then remove it. Say: "Make one just like it."

on individuals of various ages and types before assuming that a test is valid. One feature that increases the difficulty of test administration is the placement of the scoring standards at the back of the manual. The examiner needs to check almost every response to determine when a basal and ceiling level have been reached.

Slosson Intelligence Test for Children and Adults (SIT)

Richard L. Slosson
Slosson Educational Publications, Inc., 1961; reprinted 1975; renorming 1981
140 Pine St., East Aurora, NY 14052

Purpose	To evaluate mental ability
Major Areas Tested	Mental ability
Age or Grade Range	5 months–adult
Usually Given By	Classroom teacher Counselor Special education teacher Principal Psychologist Nurse
Type of Test	Standardized Individual Norm-referenced
Scores Obtained	Mental age IQ Percentile Stanine
Student Performance Timed?	No
Testing Time	15–30 minutes
Scoring/Interpretation Time	10 minutes
Normed On	1,109 persons from New England ranging in age from 2 to 18 years with a wide range of mental ages; scores equated with the Stanford-Binet Intelligence Scale by an equating method
Alternate Forms Available?	No

FORMAT

The materials for the Slosson Intelligence Test for Children and Adults (SIT) consist of the examiner's manual containing the test questions, directions for administration and scoring, and SIT score sheets. The SIT technical manual includes detailed information on test construction and norming reliability and validity. The *Slosson Intelligence Test, 1981 Norms Tables: Application and Development* (Armstrong and Jensen 1981) is also available. No other materials except a pencil are needed to administer the test with preschool students through adults. For infant testing, some simple toys (rattle, ball) are needed.

The SIT is a question-and-answer test; no reading or writing is required. The examiner asks the student a series of short-answer questions. The items are very similar to those on the Stanford-Binet tests. The following questions illustrate the types of content areas assessed. (These questions are similar but not identical to test items.)

Math Reasoning: A boy was carrying a box of four dozen eggs. He dropped the box and broke a third of them. How many eggs did he break?

Vocabulary: If you heard that the old man was *frugal*, what would that mean?

Auditory Memory: Say these letters backwards for me. For example, if I should say *a, b, c,* you would say *c, b, a*. Say these letters backwards: *m, r, b, v, t.*

Information: Name the three months of the summer season.

The testing usually begins with a question at the student's chronological age and continues forward until the student answers 10 consecutive questions correctly. This constitutes the basal age. If necessary, the examiner goes backward, asking easier questions, until the basal age is obtained. Testing continues until a ceiling level of 10 consecutive errors in a row is achieved.

The answers to each item are printed immediately following the item; all correct items are marked + on the score sheet, and all incorrect items are marked √ or −. In this way, scoring is completed as the test is administered. In field testing by teachers and others inexperienced in intellectual testing, all items that were difficult to administer or score were eliminated.

After the test is completed, the examiner finds the mental age by multiplying the number of correct answers above the basal age by a specific number of month's credit; that is, 0 to 2 years equals .5 month's credit per item, 2 to 5 years equals 1 month credit per item, and so forth. The total months are added to the basal age to obtain the mental age.

This procedure is well described in the manual and indicated on the score sheet. For example:

Basal age = 6 years, 8 months = 80 months
Credit for items over basal = 30 months
110 months or
Mental age = 9 years, 2 months

IQ is then calculated by looking up the chronological and mental ages in the appropriate table in the 1981 norms. Since the SIT is equated to the Stanford-Binet Intelligence Scale (p. 276), the average IQ is 100, with a standard deviation of 16.

Because this is a screening test, the examiner is directed to encourage and support the student and to repeat items as many times as needed to obtain as accurate an indication of the student's ability as possible. No time limits are imposed.

Items for the infant section of the test were taken from the *Gesell Developmental Schedules* (1949). The items require observation of the infant sitting, playing, walking, and "talking." (Obviously the question-answer format is not appropriate for an infant.) The author cautions the examiner about overinterpretation of infant IQ scores, which have questionable reliability.

STRENGTHS OF THE SIT

• The SIT is a brief individual test of intellectual ability. It was designed as a screening test to be used by professionals relatively untrained in individual testing. It can be administered and scored in 30 minutes. As a quick screening device, it can provide useful information about a student's probable level of mental ability and can identify students in need of more intensive intellectual assessment.

• The format and test items were selected because they were unambiguous to administer and score. Test-retest reliability is high. The printing of the correct answers next to each question allows the scoring to be accomplished during the administration. The fact that the test is individually administered and untimed allows the very distracted or deliberate student more opportunity to demonstrate knowledge and ability than a group test does. Also, group intelligence tests often require reading and writing, which the SIT does not. The wide age range of items allows even the young or very disabled student an opportunity to experience success.

• Although the SIT was not intended to give a profile of a student's strengths and weaknesses, it is possible to identify areas that need further assessment by analyzing the student's error pattern. Some students, for example, make errors on most of the math reasoning problems, whereas others have particular difficulty with vocabulary. Such information can be used to plan further diagnostic procedures.

- The norming sample for the SIT is described by Armstrong and Jensen (1981). Although all of the sample is taken from New England, the method used to equate scores with the Stanford-Binet Intelligence Scale gives the SIT the same generalizability as if a stratified random sample had been used.

LIMITING FACTORS OF THE SIT

- The author reports validity studies correlating SIT scores with the Stanford-Binet Intelligence Scales. High correlations are to be expected, because many of the items are the same. However, on the SIT, standard deviations are very large (ranging from 16.7 at age 17 to 31.2 at ages 18 and above). Validity studies on the Wechsler Scales (p. 265) are on very small numbers of students. Because the SIT is a screening instrument, comparisons with group IQ tests would be interesting.
- The author mentions the lack of reliability and validity for infant intellectual assessment. His criticism includes the SIT. Many items in the infant section would be difficult to observe during a brief testing session. No provision is made for parent report or for correcting the scoring for items not observed. For infants, other screening tests, such as the Denver Developmental Screening Test (p. 233), would be more appropriate.
- The SIT for preschoolers also has serious limitations. The items are too verbal for children with delayed language or with language problems due to cultural or physical factors.
- The SIT manual states that it can be used with blind and deaf students, yet for the blind, the only advice given is to eliminate the items the student needs to see. No procedure is given for correcting the scoring for the omitted items, and no data is provided on the validity of the test with blind students. If the deaf student cannot read, it is recommended that another test be given.
- The content of the SIT is limited to items that can be presented in a question-and-answer format. No performance tasks are included, other than a few design-copying items. Thus, students with excellent visual-spatial skills have no opportunity to demonstrate them, and students with deficits in these areas will go unidentified. In terms of content and type of test, the SIT is more clearly a substitute for the Stanford-Binet Intelligence Scale than for the Wechsler Scales.
- The SIT is a screening test, and under no circumstances should it be substituted for the in-depth intellectual assessment needed for such critical educational decisions as special education class placement or termination, retention, or acceleration.

Leiter International Performance Scale and the Arthur Adaptation (Leiter Scale)

Russell Leiter and Grace Arthur
C. H. Stoelting Company, 1948; revised 1969; Arthur Adaptation, 1950
424 North Homan Ave., Chicago, IL 60624

Purpose	To assess nonverbal intellectual functioning in children with difficulties in verbal expression
Major Areas Tested	Nonverbal intellectual functioning
Age or Grade Range	2–18 years
Usually Given By	Psychologist
Type of Test	Standardized Individual Norm-referenced
Scores Obtained	Mental age IQ
Student Performance Timed?	No
Testing Time	30—60 minutes
Scoring/Interpretation Time	30 minutes
Normed On	289 students from a homogeneous middle-class, midwestern, metropolitan background (Arthur Adaptation)
Alternate Forms Available?	No

FORMAT

The history of the Leiter International Performance Scale (Leiter Scale) is long and complex. Constructed in 1929 by Russell Leiter for the purpose of assessing deaf and non-English-speaking students, the test was revised several times. In 1950, Grace Arthur published an adapted version of the test for children between the ages of 2 and 12 years. Only minor changes in instructions were made in the Arthur Adaptation, and the test materials remained almost identical. Because it seemed impractical to manufacture two sets of materials, one for the Leiter Scale and one for the Arthur Adaptation, the five additional response blocks necessary for the Arthur Adaptation were added to the Leiter Scale materials. As a result, the examiner ordering either the Leiter Scale or the Arthur Adaptation receives the same materials for children from 2 to 12 years old.

The following materials are available: (1) wooden response form with adjustable card holder (see Figure 84); (2) trays of response blocks with corresponding stimulus cards (two trays for the 2- to 12-year-olds and an additional tray for the 13- to 18-year-olds); (3) individual record cards for recording scores; and (4) a carrying case.

The Leiter Scale manual is organized into two parts. Part I contains general instructions for the Leiter Scale, including directions for obtaining basal age, ceiling, mental age, and IQ scores. Part II is the examiner's manual, which includes directions for administering and scoring test items. The Arthur Adaptation manual includes directions for administering and scoring the test and some information on test construction.

The Leiter Scale consists of 68 items arranged in order of increasing difficulty. There are four items at each year level from ages 2 to 18 years. Each item is administered in the same manner. The examiner places the stimulus card in the adjustable card holder on top of the wooden response form. The blocks for the item are placed in front of the student in the manner described in the manual. The student places each block in the correct slot in the wooden response form.

The items range from simple tasks of color and form matching to more complex tasks that require an understanding of spatial relationships, sequencing, and numerical and verbal reasoning. Most of the items require visual discrimination and perceptual organization.

The following illustrates the types of items used at various age levels (these examples are similar but not identical to the test items):

Year Level	Task
3	*Number Discrimination* (Figure 85). A card with the top design is placed on the card holder. The student places each block in the holder under the picture with the same number of objects.
6	*Analogous Progression* (Figure 86). The student arranges the blocks in descending order, analogous to the arrangement of the triangles.
10	*Block Design* (Figure 87). The student arranges four triangular blocks to make a square identical to the one on the picture card and places them in the corresponding slot in the card holder.

Because the test was devised for language-impaired students, all directions are given in pantomime. The examiner is instructed to keep busy with clerical work rather than to watch the child's performance. No time limits are imposed (except on the block-design items). When the student is finished, the examiner scores the item and puts the blocks away. Last-minute corrections are allowed.

Testing begins with the first item at an age level two years below the student's estimated mental age. There are no verbal directions, so the task must be simple enough for the student to understand what to do. If that item or any other in that age level is missed, the examiner goes back to the first item at the next-lower age level. Testing continues in this manner until a basal age is reached; that is, until all items at a given age level are passed. Once the basal age is obtained, the examiner moves forward again, repeating items failed during the establishment of the basal age. Before the basal age is established, it is not certain whether the student fails an item because he or she does not understand what to do or because the student does not have the ability to do it. But

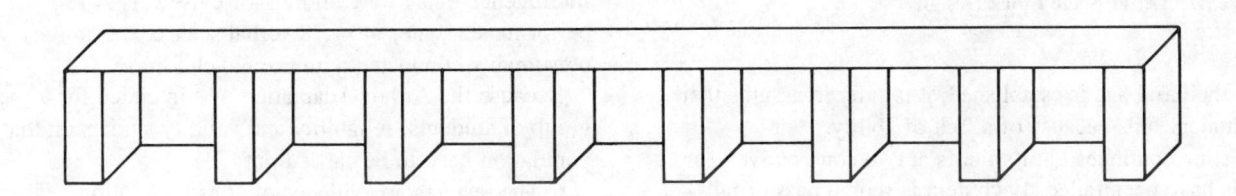

Figure 84. Leiter Scale Card Holder

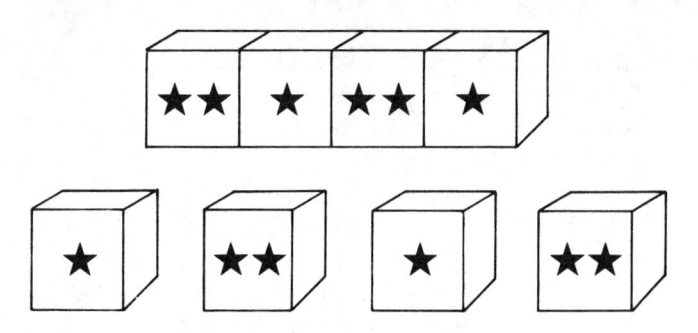

Figure 85. Leiter Scale Number Discrimination

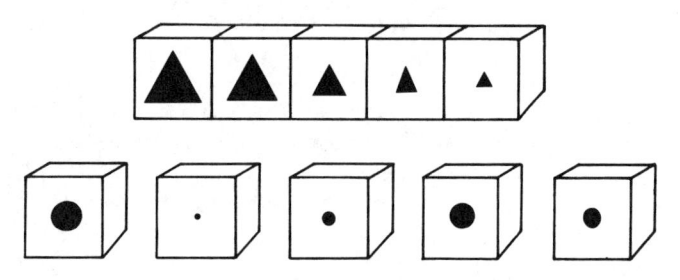

Figure 86. Leiter Scale Analogous Progression

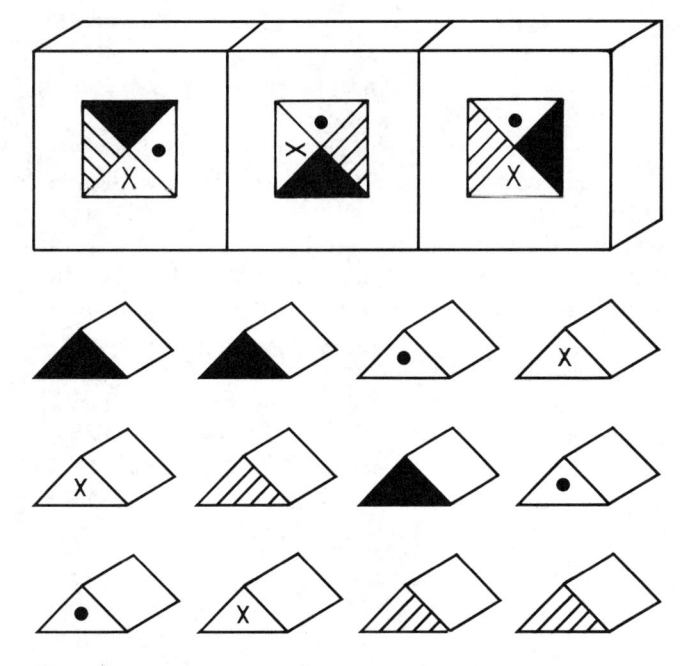

Figure 87. Leiter Scale Block Design

after the basal age is established, it is safer to assume that the student fails because of a lack of ability.

Testing continues until all tests at two consecutive year levels have been failed. Each item is scored pass or fail before the blocks are put away. The mental age is found in the same manner as on the Stanford-Binet Intelligence Scale (p. 276). A specified number of months' credit is given each item passed. All items below the basal are assumed passed; all items above the ceiling are presumed failed. The total number of months credited yields a mental age. The formula

$$\frac{\text{Mental age}}{\text{Chronological age}} \times 100$$

is used to calculate IQ.

The mean IQ on the Leiter Scale is 95; the standard deviation is 16. In order to compare the IQ of the Leiter Scale with the Stanford-Binet Intelligence Scale or the Wechsler Scales, which have a mean of 100, 5 points are added to the Leiter IQ. This adjusted IQ is always the IQ reported from the Leiter Scale. Tables are used to adjust the mental-age score.

STRENGTHS OF THE LEITER SCALE

• The Leiter Scale is unique because it enables intellectual assessment of students with difficulties in verbal expression, such as hearing-impaired and non-English-speaking students. The pantomimed instructions and nonverbal response format is also very useful in evaluating students with language disorders such as aphasia, students with delayed language due to retardation or emotional disturbance, and bilingual students. The materials are highly interesting to young children and older students alike. The test is designed for children as young as 2, and the beginning items seem to allow them to learn the process as they take the test.

LIMITING FACTORS OF THE LEITER SCALE

• It is difficult to find information on standardization, reliability, and validity of the Leiter Scale. Leiter published this information in the 1952 manual, but it is not available in either the 1969 manual or in the Arthur Adaptation manual.

Arthur's standardization was based on only 289 students from a middle-class midwestern urban background. No exceptional children, for whom the test was designed, were in the sample.

No reliability data is published in either the 1969 manual or Arthur's manual. Such data is seriously lacking. Validity studies indicate moderate correlations with the Stanford-Binet Intelligence Scale (169–193) and the Wechsler Intelligence Scale for Children—Revised (179–180 performance scale, .40–.78 verbal scale). The studies were presumably conducted with normal children.

Because the Arthur Adaptation was intended for a specific group of students, reliability and validity studies on that population need to be carried out.

• The test has no evidence of construct validity. There is no information explaining how the test items were selected. The level of difficulty of the items seems uneven, and this makes the process of obtaining a basal age and a ceiling difficult and lengthy.

- Some of the Leiter Scale items are outdated. For example, on Year V, Test 3, Clothing, many students make errors because they do not recognize the styles. Because there are only four items at each age level, poor items can seriously affect scores.

- Fine visual discrimination is needed to do many of the items. Children with organically based hearing or language deficiencies often have problems with visual perception as well. Thus, a low score on the Leiter Scale may be the result of inadequate visual perception.

- The manuals are very confusing. Because only black-and-white pictures are used, the examiner must read the full description of each item to determine how to set up the blocks. Colored illustrations would facilitate this process.

- No answers are given to the test items. The examiner must go through the test, performing each task and coding the blocks, to facilitate efficient scoring.

- Although the test manual states that the Leiter Scale extends to age 18, Leiter sets 13.0 years as the maximum chronological age for determining mental age and IQ. This is based on the questionable assumption that the ability to visually organize new materials does not increase after age 13, as verbal learning does.

- Items on the scale are scored pass or fail; credit is all or none. This penalizes the child who understands the concept but does not complete the whole item correctly. Partial credit would seem to reflect many students' abilities more fairly.

Coloured Progressive Matrices (CPM)

J. C. Raven
A. P. Watt and Son, 1947; revised 1956
Distributed by The Psychological Corporation
7500 Old Oak Blvd., Middleburg Heights, OH 44130

Purpose	To provide a quick assessment of mental development in children under the age of 11 years
Major Areas Tested	Visual perception and analogous reasoning
Age or Grade Range	5½–11 years
Usually Given By	Psychologist Speech/language clinician Educational diagnostician
Type of Test	Standardized Individual Norm-referenced
Scores Obtained	Percentile
Student Performance Timed?	No
Testing Time	10–40 minutes
Scoring/Interpretation Time	10 minutes
Normed On	627 children in the Burgh of Dumfries, Scotland, whose names began with letters E through L
Alternate Forms Available?	No

Part III General Intelligence Tests and Developmental Scales   287

FORMAT
The Coloured Progressive Matrices (CPM) is a test of nonverbal intelligence designed for use with children and older people. The materials consist of an examiner's manual, a book of colored illustrations, a set of puzzle boards and moveable pieces, and scoring forms. The test may be administered as either a series of form boards or in book form.

The CPM is composed of three sets of matrices, each with 12 items. In book form, the designs are printed on brightly colored background. Each item consists of a pattern with a missing piece. The student selects from six visual patterns the one that completes the puzzle. At early levels, visual matching is used. At higher levels, the student must perceive changes in two or three pattern variables. Each student begins with the first item and continues through the 12 items of Set A. Figures 88 and 89 illustrate two items in Set A. By working through the items in standard order, the student learns to solve the progressively more difficult puzzles. Set AB contains 12 items beginning with the least difficult and progressing through the more difficult items. A third set of 12 items, Set B, allows the student a third

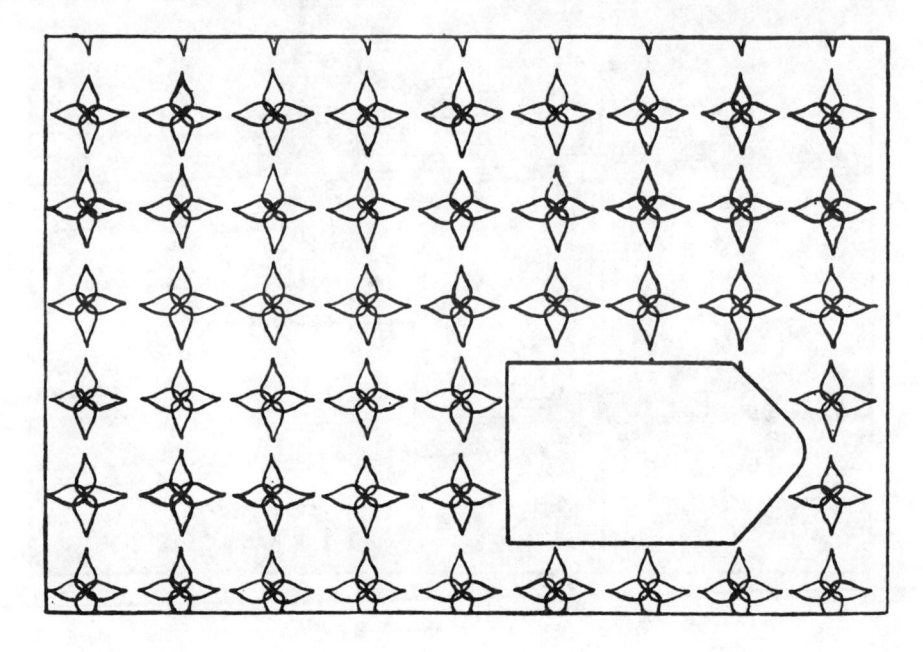

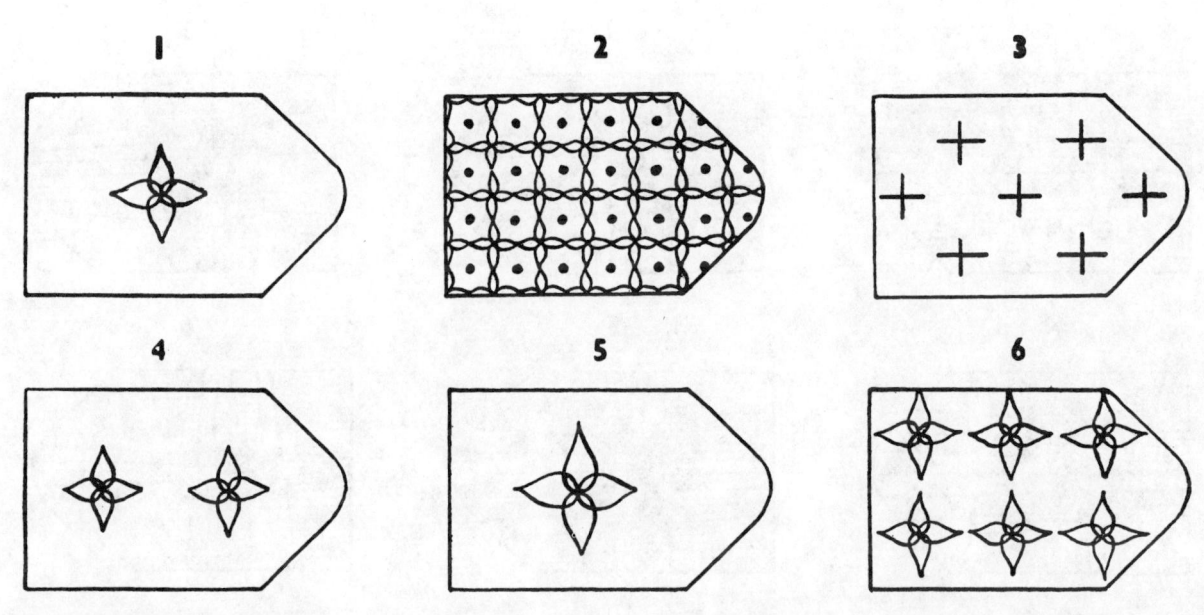

Figure 88. CPM, Item 5, Set A

opportunity to work through the progression. The board form of the test allows the student to select from six puzzle pieces the one necessary to complete the pattern. In either format, one point is given for each correct response and the total score is converted into a percentile rank using the tables in the examiner's manual.

If the student does very well on Sets A, AB, and B, the examiner should continue with the Standard Progressive Matrices.

STRENGTHS OF THE CPM

- The CPM has minimal verbal instructions and requires no verbal response. It can be used satisfactorily with students who exhibit severe language disorders, physical disabilities, deafness, or limited English.
- The CPM is designed to assess analogous reasoning. Students are allowed ample instruction and demonstration to learn the task. The sets of items are arranged to facilitate learning during the test.

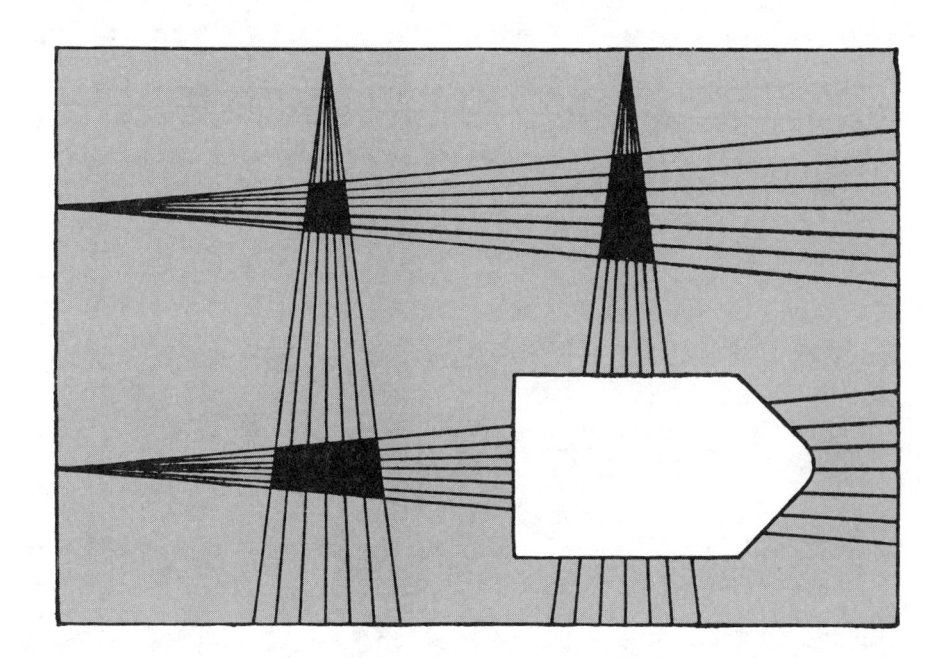

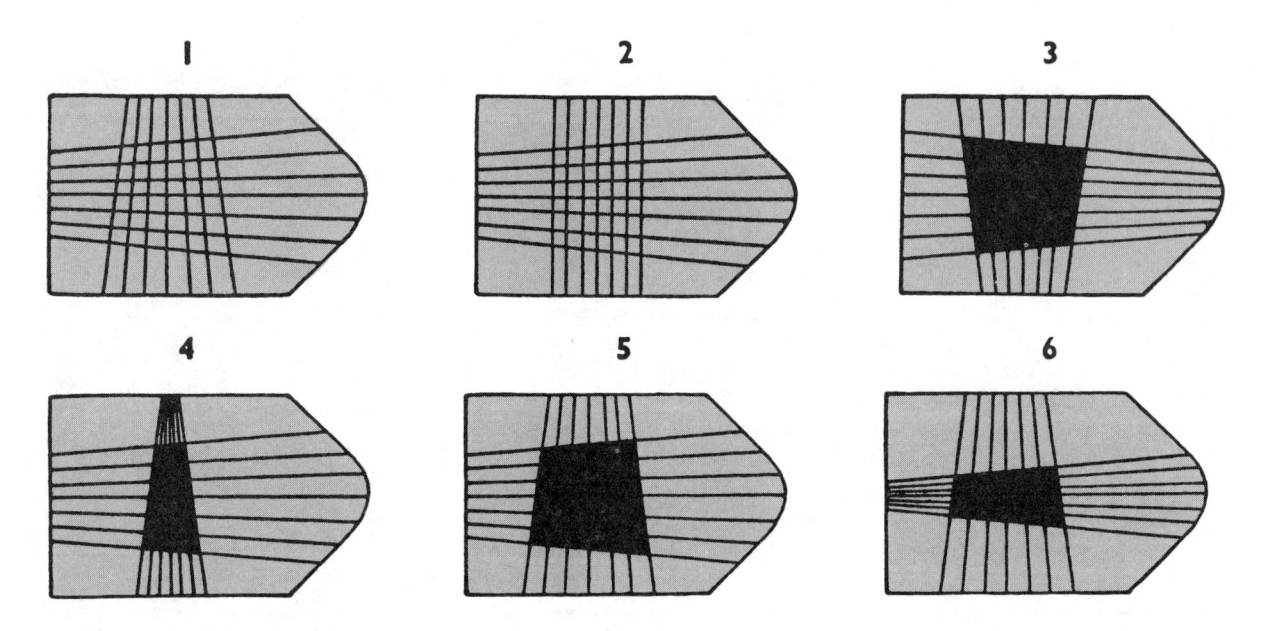

Figure 89. CPM, Item 12, Set A

- The book and the board form of the test give practically the same results in children over 6 years of age.
- The colorful format and self-paced nature of the CPM make it very interesting to students.
- The Advanced Progressive Matrices, a 10-minute screening test taken from the Standardized Progressive Matrices, is also available.

LIMITING FACTORS OF THE CPM
- While the CPM is a test of mental development or nonverbal intelligence, the author cautions against using it as a general test of mental deficiency. Inadequate norms for United States populations make it inappropriate for use in placement decisions.
- Although norms are provided for children between the ages of 3 and 6 years, the author demonstrates no evidence of their prognostic value.
- The CPM is a multiple-choice test; students must be cautioned and monitored to discourage impulsive selection of the answers. Although the manual states that "bright children" or those over 8 years old can work on their own and record their own answers, it is not recommended for students suspected of learning disabilities or other handicapping conditions.
- No norms for United States populations are available. Reliability is adequate above the age of 9 years but not for younger students.
- No validity studies are reported in the examiner's manual. Many claims are made about the measurement of mental development, but no correlating data with other tests of mental development are reported in the manual.
- The information obtained from a student's performance on the CPM is interesting but is not related to long-term goals or behavioral objectives.

McCarthy Scales of Children's Abilities
(McCarthy Scales)

Dorothea McCarthy
The Psychological Corporation, 1972
7500 Old Oak Blvd., Middleburg Heights, OH 44130

Purpose	To measure intelligence and to identify children with possible learning disabilities
Major Areas Tested	General intellectual ability
Age or Grade Range	2½–8½ years
Usually Given By	Special education teacher Psychologist
Type of Test	Standardized Individual Norm-referenced
Scores Obtained	Mental age Standard Percentile
Student Performance Timed?	Yes (some subtests)
Testing Time	1 hour
Scoring/Interpretation Time	30 minutes
Normed On	1,032 urban and rural children stratified by age, sex, race, father's occupation, and geographic region
Alternate Forms Available?	No

FORMAT

The materials for the McCarthy Scales of Children's Abilities (McCarthy Scales) consist of an examiner's manual, individual scoring sheets, and a kit of attractive manipulative materials (ball, blocks, puzzles, xylophone, and others).

The McCarthy Scales consist of 18 subtests grouped into six scales. The organization and content of the test is shown in Table 32. The sequence of subtests has been carefully organized to facilitate and maintain the interest and attention of the young child. The test begins with two manipulative tests and then gradually increases the demand for a verbal response. The three motor tests are grouped in the middle of the sequence to provide a natural activity break. The drawing tests come next to refocus attention, and the battery ends with three tests requiring minimal verbal response. Examples are given on most subtests, and in many cases "second chances" secure the child's best performance.

Using an eight-step process clearly outlined in the manual, the following scores are obtained and recorded on the individual scoring sheet:

- The general cognitive scale raw score is converted into a standard score with a mean of 100 and a standard deviation of 16. This score is called the general cognitive index and is the equivalent of an IQ score.
- Separate scale indexes on each of the other five scales have a mean of 50 and a standard deviation of 10.
- Percentile ranks for each of the scaled scores.
- An estimated mental-age score for the general cognitive index.

STRENGTHS OF THE McCARTHY SCALES

- The McCarthy Scales are a well-designed, theoretically based instrument to assess the intellectual functioning of preschool and primary-age children. The tasks include a variety of different activities of interest to young children, and the colorful and interesting materials naturally engage the children in the tasks. Particular attention has been given to the sequence of the subtests and to procedures for providing feedback and support to the child during the testing situation. The well-written manual explains the test administration and scoring procedures very clearly.
- The McCarthy Scales include a number of subtests particularly appropriate for children with suspected learning disabilities. The Motor Scale includes an assessment of gross motor ability, which is not included on any other individual IQ test. The subtests that measure verbal and nonverbal short-term memory are also good.
- The McCarthy Scales were normed on a representative standardization sample stratified by age, sex, race, father's occupation, and urban or rural residence. Good test-retest reliability is reported, and although more validity studies are needed, those reported by Kaufman and Kaufman in *Clinical Evaluation of Young Children with the McCarthy Scales* (1977) show promise. The Kaufman and Kaufman book contains an excellent critique of the McCarthy Scales as well as helpful information on administration, scoring, and interpretation.
- The field of assessment is greatly in need of valid instruments for assessing Black children. The McCarthy Scales were constructed with this in mind, and the items were selected to avoid cultural bias. Kaufman and Kaufman report studies of good construct validity of the McCarthy Scales for both racial groups. Kaufman also reports that the Black preschool children did not differ significantly from the white children on mean general cognitive index; but for school-age children, the Black children obtained a lower mean general cognitive index.

LIMITING FACTORS OF THE McCARTHY SCALES

- The McCarthy Scales should be administered by examiners experienced in the clinical assessment of young children. The test may only be given by psychologists, learning-disabilities specialists, or other professionals well trained in individual testing. The test requires a fair amount of time to administer, score, and interpret. The computational process for scoring is long and offers many opportunities for error.
- The McCarthy Scales cover a very limited age range. The tasks and materials are clearly designed for young children; there is no test form for older children. This presents some problems for using the test with children who require periodic reevaluations. The ceiling is too low for most children older than 7 years.
- The McCarthy Scales are lacking in items that assess social and practical judgment as well as abstract problem-solving skills. This is another reason why the McCarthy Scales are more appropriate for preschool children.
- More studies of predictive and concurrent validity are needed, particularly with exceptional children. No exceptional children were included in the sample, and no research has been done on the validity of the test for retarded or learning-disabled children.
- Research reported by Kaufman and Kaufman (1974) indicated that learning-disabled children obtained general cognitive index scores about 15 points lower than their IQ scores on the Wechsler Preschool and Primary Scale of Intelligence (p. 275) and the Stanford-Binet Intelligence Scale (p. 276). Given the rigid criteria for qualifying a child for a learning-disability program in some schools, the McCarthy Scales may need to be supplemented with another IQ test or an adaptive-behavior scale to document a significant discrepancy between ability and achievement.

Table 32. McCarthy Scales Subtests

Scale	Content/Process	Response	Subtests	Task
Verbal	Words	Verbal	3. Pictorial Memory	Recalling pictured objects
			4. Word Knowledge	Identifying and naming objects; defining words
			7. Verbal Memory	Repeating words, sentences, and story
			15. Verbal Fluency	Naming things within four categories
			17. Opposite Analogies	Completing verbal analogies
Perceptual-Performance	Concrete materials	Nonverbal	1. Block Building	Copying block structures
			2. Puzzle Solving	Assembling two- to six-piece puzzles
			6. Tapping Sequence	Repeating sequences of three to six notes on xylophone
			8. Right-Left Orientation	Recognizing right and left on self and on picture
			12. Draw-a-Design	Copying geometric designs
			13. Draw-a-Child	Drawing a child of the same sex
			18. Conceptual Grouping	Demonstrating concepts of size, color, and shape; discovering rules
Quantitative	Digits	Verbal and Nonverbal	5. Number Questions	Answering questions about number facts and quantitative concepts
			14. Numerical Memory	Recalling sequences of digits, forward and backward
			16. Counting and Sorting	Counting and sorting blocks into groups using concepts such as *equal*
Motor	Motor coordination	Nonverbal	9. Leg Coordination	Walking, tiptoeing, and hopping
			10. Arm Coordination	Bouncing, catching, and throwing
			11. Imitative Action	Performing three tasks of eye and hand preference
			Subtests 12 and 13	
Memory	Short-term memory	Verbal and nonverbal	Composite of subtests 3, 6, 7, and 14	
General Cognitive			Composite of Verbal, Perceptual-Performance, and Quantitative scales	

Woodcock-Johnson Psycho-Educational Battery (WJPEB)

Richard W. Woodcock and M. Bonner Johnson
Teaching Resources Corporation, 1977
50 Pond Park Rd., Hingham, MA 02043

Purpose	To provide a comprehensive instrument to assess cognitive abilities, scholastic aptitudes, achievement, and interests over a wide age range
Major Areas Tested	Cognitive ability, academic achievement, interests
Age or Grade Range	3 years–adult
Usually Given By	Psychologist Educational diagnostician
Type of Test	Individual Standardized Norm-referenced
Scores Obtained	Grade level Relative performance index Age level Functional level Percentile Standard
Student Performance Timed?	Yes (some subtests)
Testing Time	1½–2 hours
Scoring/Interpretation Time	30–40 minutes
Normed On	4,734 subjects ranging from 3 to 9 years of age, from 49 communities in the United States, sample balanced for sex, race, occupational status, geographic regions, and urban and rural communities
Alternate Forms Available?	No

FORMAT

The Woodcock-Johnson Psycho-Educational Battery (WJPEB) is composed of 27 subtests that measure cognitive abilities, scholastic aptitude, achievement, and interests. The instrument is organized into three parts. Part One: Tests of Cognitive Ability includes 12 pencil-and-paper subtests. The manuals, scoring tables, cassette tape, and individual response booklets for Part One are organized into one 10-inch-square easel book. The materials for Part Two: Tests of Achievement (10 subtests) and Part Three: Tests of Interest Level (5 subtests) are organized into a second easel book. Table 33 illustrates the subtest organization and content.

Each subtest is administered according to explicit directions, which are printed directly on the examiner's pages of the easel book. Basal and ceiling procedures are used to limit testing to items appropriate for a student's age and ability. The entire test may be given, or subtests may be selected, to measure particular skills or abilities. The charts in Figure 90 illustrate the way in which the examiner selects subtests to measure particular skills. This selective testing dramatically reduces testing time.

Table 33. WJPEB Subtests

Subtest	Task	Description
Part One: Tests of Cognitive Ability		
1. Picture Vocabulary	Naming pictured objects	Student names pictured objects (*apple, printing press, gondola*)
2. Spatial Relations	Selection of component shapes to make a whole	Student selects two of three shapes that together would match the stimulus shape (see Figure 91)
3. Memory for Sentences	Auditory recall of meaningful material	Student repeats sentences pronounced by the examiner ("Hardware stores sell many kinds of tools.")
4. Visual-Auditory Learning	Paired-associates learning task	Student associates symbols with words (see Figure 92)
5. Blending	Auditory synthesis of syllables or phonemes	Student blends syllables or phonemes pronounced by the examiner ("*m-e-t—meet*")
6. Quantitative Concepts	Knowledge of math concepts and vocabulary	Student answers questions involving math concepts and vocabulary (*Which is larger: 3^2 or 3×2?*)
7. Visual Matching	Rapid matching of numbers	Student selects two of four numbers that are alike (*142, 241, 142, 214*)
8. Antonyms-Synonyms	Knowledge of word meanings	Student names antonyms ("Tell me the opposite of *safe*.") and synonyms ("Tell me another word for *abolish*.")
9. Analysis-Synthesis	Analysis of an equivalency statement	Student studies a symbolic equation and supplies the answer to a related equation (see Figure 93)
10. Numbers Reversed	Perceptual reorganization of a numerical series	Student repeats backwards numerals pronounced by the examiner
11. Concept Formation	Categorical reasoning	Student is given several rules based on the size, shape, color and/or number of simple drawings and selects the correct rule to solve a reasoning problem. (In Figure 94, the examiner asks, "What is different about the drawing inside the box?")
12. Analogies	Verbal reasoning	Student completes a verbal analogy (*Rome is to Italy as Moscow is to _____ .*)

Table 33.—Continued

Subtest	Task	Description
Part Two: Tests of Achievement		
13. Letter-Word Identification	Naming letters and words	Student names letters and words presented visually (*O*, *Q*, *yacht*, *schism*)
14. Word Attack	Reading nonsense words	Student reads visually presented nonsense words (*piff*, *traunch*, *mepdontill*)
15. Passage Comprehension	Silent reading comprehension	Student completes a sentence with a meaningfully correct word (*Please _____ the enclosed notice carefully.*)
16. Calculation	Performing mathematical operations	Student adds, subtracts, multiplies, and divides whole numbers, fractions, and decimals
17. Applied Problems	Solving practical problems	Student solves applied problems read by the examiner ("How many cubic feet of water are in a pool 80 feet long, 8 feet wide, and 6 feet deep?")
18. Dictation	Writing words and numbers	Student writes words and phrases as directed by the examiner ("Write the word that means *more than one child*.")
19. Proofing	Identifying errors in grammar, punctuation, and capitalization	Student reads sentences and corrects errors (*She read a knew book.*)
20. Science	Knowledge of biological and physical science	Student answers questions read by the examiner ("What is meant by *evaporation*?")
21. Social Studies	Knowledge of geography, government, economics, and history	Student answers questions read by examiner ("What is *social security*?")
22. Humanities	Knowledge of art, music, and literature	Student answers questions read by examiner ("Who wrote *Romeo and Juliet*?")
Part Three: Tests of Interest Level		
23. Reading Interest	Preference for reading activities	Student identifies preferred activity (*going to the library* or *playing video games*)
24. Mathematics Interest	Preference for mathematical activities	Student identifies preferred activity (*going to the ball game* or *playing "baseball" with number facts*)
25. Written Language Interest	Preference for activities involving writing	Student identifies preferred activity (*watching a mystery on television* or *writing a mystery story*)
26. Physical Interest	Preference for physical activities	Student identifies preferred activity (*hiking* or *reading a book*)
27. Social Interest	Preference for activities involving other people	Student identifies preferred activity (*having a party* or *watching television*)

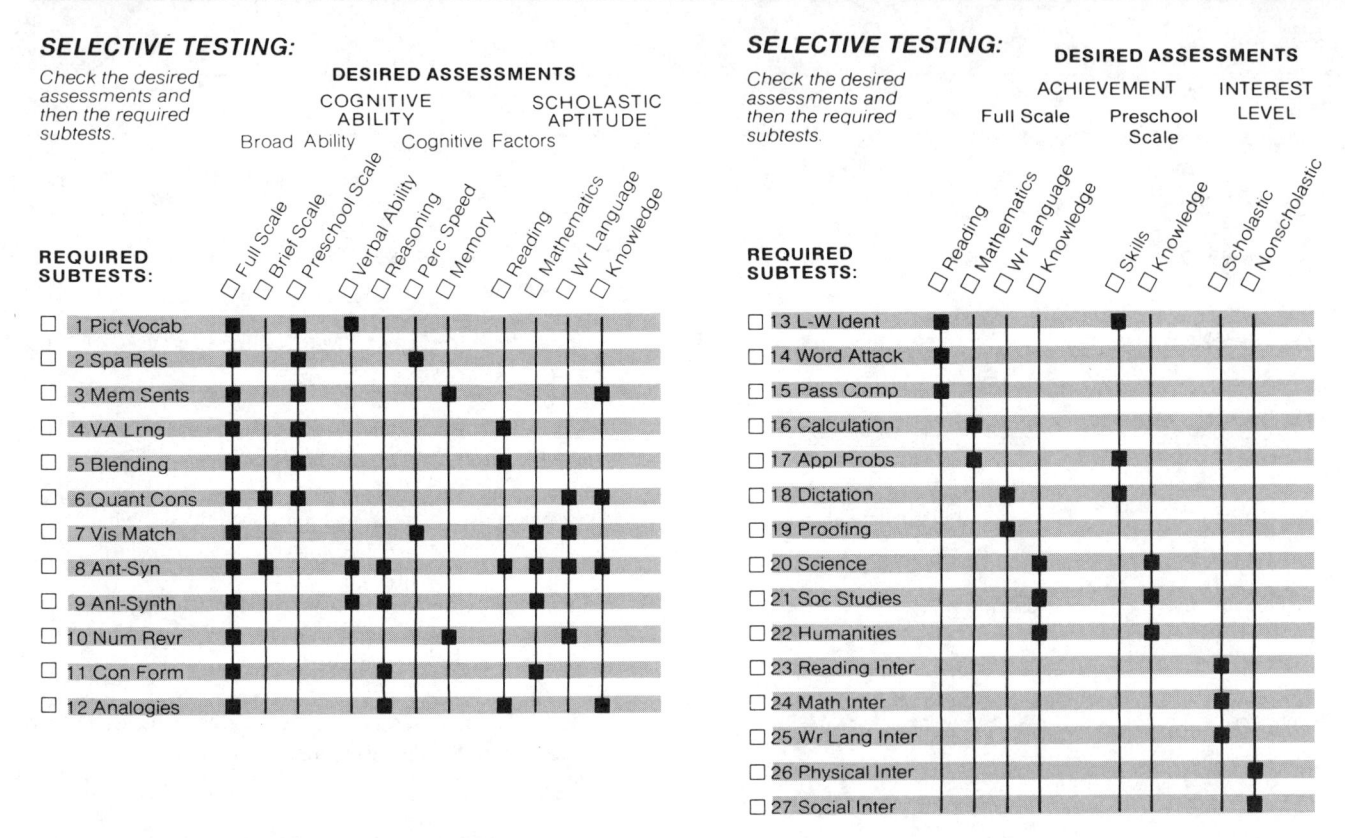

Figure 90. WJPEB Selective Testing Procedure

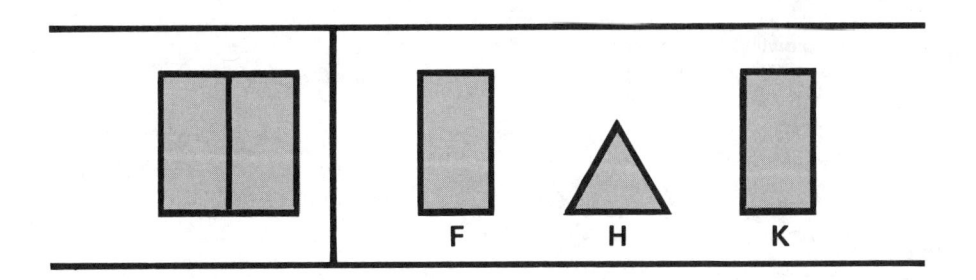

Figure 91. WJPEB Spatial Relations

Figure 92. WJPEB Visual-Auditory Learning

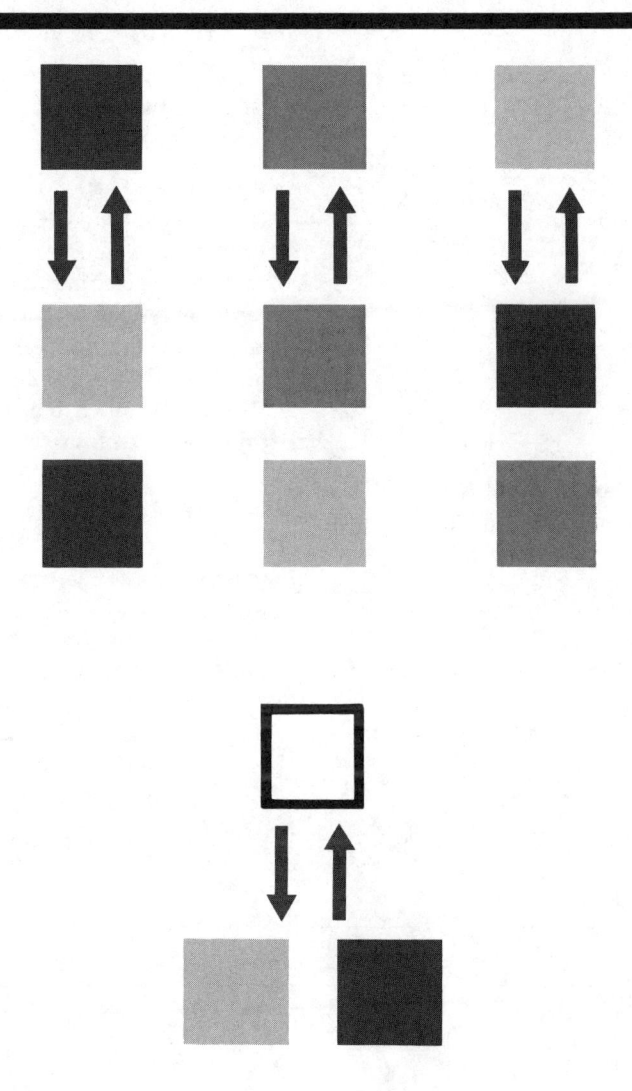

Part III General Intelligence Tests and Developmental Scales 297

Figure 93. WJPEB Analysis-Synthesis

Figure 94. WJPEB Concept Formation

Rather than individual subtests, clusters of subtests provide the primary analysis of the WJPEB. The Reading cluster, for example, is composed of the Letter-Word Identification, Word Attack, and Passage Comprehension subtests. The Perceptual Speed cluster combines the Spatial Relations and Visual Matching subtests. Norms are provided for 18 clusters. Table 34 outlines the clusters and lists the subtests included in each cluster.

Following administration, subtests are scored, and cluster scores for broad cognitive ability, cognitive factors, scholastic aptitude, and achievement are calculated. A variety of scores are obtained, including age and grade scores, percentiles, instructional ranges, a relative performance index, functioning level ratings, and standard scores.

The scores are plotted on four profiles to aid in interpretation:

1. *Subtest Profile* allows quick visual presentation of subtest performance.
2. *Percentile Rank Profile* allows visual presentation of cluster performance related to age or grade placement.
3. *Instructional Implications Profile* relates instructional range to grade placement and provides useful information on grouping for instructional needs.

4. *Achievement-Aptitude Profile* allows direct comparison of a student's expected achievement and actual achievement.

A unique feature of the WJPEB is the direct comparison of a student's cognitive skills with achievement. By comparing a student's actual Reading cluster score in Part Two with his or her Reading Aptitude score in Part One, the examiner can determine if there is a discrepancy between ability and achievement. Since this discrepancy concept is the basis for the definition of learning disabilities, the WJPEB promises to be a widely used test in the assessment of students with suspected learning disabilities.

STRENGTHS OF THE WJPEB

- The WJPEB contains some unique subtests. Visual-Auditory Learning, Concept Formation, and Analysis-Synthesis are interesting measures of cognitive abilities. Picture Vocabulary is one of the few expressive vocabulary tests available.
- The WJPEB provides an array of scores and profiles to highlight a student's strengths and weaknesses.
- The WJPEB achievement clusters can be used for screening academic skills. For example, the Mathematics

Table 34. WJPEB Cluster Analysis

Category	Clusters	Subtests Included
Part One: Tests of Cognitive Ability		
Broad Cognitive Ability	Full Scale	1–12
	Preschool Scale	1–6
	Brief Scale	6, 8
Cognitive Factors	Verbal Ability	1, 8, 9
	Reasoning	8, 9
	Perceptual Speed	2, 7
	Memory	3, 10
Scholastic Aptitude	Reading Aptitude	4, 5, 8, 12
	Math Aptitude	7, 8, 9, 11
	Written Language Aptitude	6, 7, 8, 10
	Knowledge Aptitude	3, 6, 8, 12
Part Two: Tests of Achievement		
	Reading	13, 14, 15
	Mathematics	16, 17
	Written Language	18, 19
	Knowledge	20, 21, 22
	Preschool Skills	13, 17, 18
Part Three: Tests of Interest Level		
	Scholastic	23, 24, 25
	Nonscholastic	26, 27

cluster, Calculation and Applied Problems, is a quick assessment of basic math. The three reading subtests are quicker to administer than the entire Woodcock Reading Mastery Tests (see p. 53).

• Several features are provided for decreasing testing time. These include selective testing procedures, clear basal and ceiling levels, and suggested starting points for each subtest.

• Standardization information, reliability data, and validity studies are reported in *Development and Standardization of the WJPEB*, a comprehensive book available from the publisher.

• A variety of additional information and services are available to the WJPEB user. These include workshops and seminars on test administration and interpretation, and computerized test analysis and reports.

LIMITING FACTORS OF THE WJPEB

• The WJPEB is an extremely complicated test to administer and interpret. The examiner must make a serious commitment of time and training to use the battery effectively. The examiner's manual has an extensive section on examiner preparation, and the authors also provide a test tape. In addition, a new publication, *Use and Interpretation of the WJPEB* (Hessler 1982) is strongly recommended.

• The WJPEB has extremely complicated scoring procedures. Since the numbers involved have no meaning (464, 532, etc.), it is very easy to make errors. Examiners must develop an understanding of the test that allows them to monitor the scoring. Even then, extreme caution must be exercised and double checking must be standard procedure.

• The basic concept of the WJPEB is the assessment of cognitive abilities and academic achievement in the same battery. The cognitive abilities are grouped into scholastic aptitude clusters. When these are compared with the academic achievement clusters, one can presumably determine whether or not a student is achieving to his or her ability. Determination of this ability-achievement discrepancy is the heart of the diagnosis of learning disabilities. The crucial question is: Are the scholastic aptitude clusters reliable and valid measures of reading, math, written language, and knowledge aptitude? The composition of some of the aptitude clusters is questionable on the surface. For example, the Written Language Aptitude cluster is composed of the Quantitative Concepts, Visual Matching, Antonyms-Synonyms, and Numbers Reversed subtests. How is this cluster of subtests—three of which deal with numerical concepts, perception, and memory—related to written language? Discussion of the formation of the scholastic aptitude clusters is found in *Development and Standardization of the Woodcock-Johnson Psycho-Educational Battery* (Woodcock 1975). Extensive studies of reliability and validity are reported in the same volume. The WJPEB is a relatively new test. Extensive research will be needed to validate this and other critical constructs. Meanwhile, examiners should be cautious about drawing conclusions about individual students' test results.

• Since the cluster scores are the primary analysis of the WJPEB, individual subtests are not analyzed except on the subtest profile. If an examiner omits a subtest in a cluster, no scores for the individual subtests given are available in the manual. Users should be aware that a separate handbook, *Derived Subtest Scores for the WJPEB* (Marston and Ysseldyke 1980) is available; it contains grade and age equivalents, percentile ranks, and normal curve equivalents for individual subtests.

Kaufman Assessment Battery for Children (K-ABC)

Alan S. Kaufman and Nadeen L. Kaufman
American Guidance Service, Inc., 1983
Publishers' Bldg., Circle Pines, MN 55014

Purpose	Psychological, clinical, and psychoeducational assessment of learning-disabled and other exceptional children, including minority groups and preschoolers
Major Areas Tested	Intelligence and achievement
Age or Grade Range	2½–12½ years
Usually Given By	Psychologist Reading diagnostician Educational diagnostician Counselor Learning disability specialist Any trained person
Type of Test	Individual Standardized Norm-referenced
Scores Obtained	Age level Scaled Standard Grade level Percentile
Student Performance Timed?	Yes (some subtests)
Testing Time	30–90 minutes
Scoring/Interpretation Time	30–45 minutes
Normed On	2,000 children, 100 at each half-year age interval between 2 years, 6 months and 12 years, 5 months, stratified for sex, parent education, race or ethnic group, geographical region, community size, and grade level; additional sample of 496 Black and 119 low-socioeconomic-status children added to norms
Alternate Forms Available?	No

Part III General Intelligence Tests and Developmental Scales

FORMAT

The Kaufman Assessment Battery for Children (K-ABC) is an individually administered test of mental processes and achievement. The materials consist of three easel-kits of test items, an administration and scoring manual, an interpretive manual, individual test records, and manipulative materials for four subtests. All of the materials are included in one materials box or plastic carrying case.

Intellectual functioning is defined as problem-solving ability, that is, the ability to be flexible and adaptable when faced with unfamiliar problems. The K-ABC divides intellectual functioning into two ways of processing information: sequential processing and simultaneous processing. Sequential processing focuses on serial or temporal order, while simultaneous processing requires a gestalt approach or spatial integration. In contrast to these problem-solving skills, academic achievement is a set of acquired skills or knowledge of facts. These three dimensions—sequential processing, simultaneous processing, and achievement—are assessed through 16 subtests on the K-ABC:

Sequential Processing Scale

1. *Hand Movements*. Performing a series of hand movements in the same sequence as the examiner
2. *Number Recall*. Repeating a series of digits in the same sequential order as given by the examiner
3. *Word Order*. Touching a series of pictures in the same order as named by the examiner

Simultaneous Processing Scale

4. *Magic Window*. Identifying a picture exposed slowly behind a narrow window
5. *Face Recognition*. Selecting from a group photograph one or two faces previously seen (see Figures 95 and 96)
6. *Gestalt Closure*. Naming a partially completed pictured object (see Figure 97)
7. *Triangles*. Arranging several identical triangles into an abstract pattern to match a model
8. *Matrix Analogies*. Selecting a picture or geometric form to complete a visual analogy
9. *Spatial Memory*. Recalling the placement of pictures on a page after brief exposure
10. *Photo Series*. Placing photographs of an event in chronological order

Achievement Scale

11. *Expressive Vocabulary*. Naming pictured objects
12. *Faces and Places*. Naming the well-known person, fictional character, or place pictured
13. *Arithmetic*. Demonstrating knowledge of numbers and math concepts, counting, and computation
14. *Riddles*. Inferring the name of a concept, given a list of its characteristics
15. *Reading/Decoding*. Identifying letters and reading words
16. *Reading/Understanding*. Following commands printed in sentences

The student's scores on each of the three sequential processing subtests and the seven simultaneous processing subtests are converted to a scaled score with a mean of 10 and a standard deviation of 3; the six achievement subtests each convert to a standard score with a mean of 100 and a standard deviation of 15.

Four global scales are computed:

• Sequential processing scale, emphasizing temporal order
• Simultaneous processing scale, using a gestalt or holistic approach
• Mental processing composite, a combination of sequential and simultaneous processing, yielding a global estimate of intellectual functioning
• Achievement scale, assessing knowledge of facts, language concepts, and school-related skills

A special Nonverbal Scale is also provided, including those subtests which may be administered totally in pantomime and require nonverbal responses. Each of these five scales has a mean of 100 and a standard deviation of 15. Scores are recorded on the individual test record, designed to highlight a comparison of the global scales.

Figure 95. K-ABC Face Recognition

Figure 96. K-ABC Face Recognition

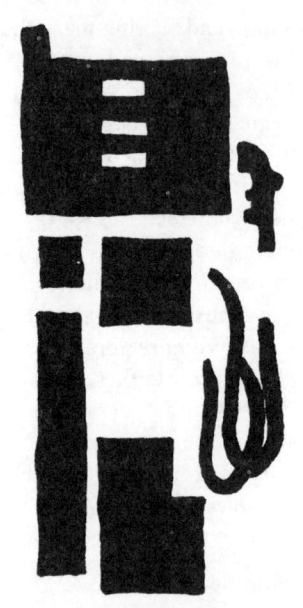

Figure 97. K-ABC Gestalt Closure

NOTE
Only prepublication materials were available for this review. Therefore, all strengths and limiting factors are based on reading the materials rather than on actual clinical experience with the K-ABC.

STRENGTHS OF THE K-ABC
- The K-ABC is similar to the Woodcock-Johnson Psycho-Educational Battery (p. 293) in that it combines measures of intellectual ability and achievement in the same test; therefore, the norms are based on the same population.
- The K-ABC was designed to evaluate three hard-to-assess groups of students: handicapped students, minority students, and preschoolers. The standardization sample includes a good representation of each group.
- Despite the newness of the test, extensive reliability and validity studies have been completed and are reported in the interpretive manual.
- The nonverbal scale provides a means of assessing hearing-impaired, speech- and language-disordered, and non-English-speaking children.
- The uniqueness of the subtests aids in motivating the student.
- Each subtest includes three teaching items that permit the examiner to use alternate wording, gestures, and other methods to ensure that the student understands the nature of the task. This is especially important, given the uniqueness of the K-ABC subtests.
- The interpretive manual offers extensive guidelines to interpretation of scores and educational planning.

LIMITING FACTORS OF THE K-ABC
- The K-ABC draws upon the theories of neuropsychologists and cognitive psychologists, most especially upon the research of cerebral specialists who deal with differing functions of the right and left hemispheres. Whether or not a test based on these theories will yield useful educational theories is as yet unknown.
- The K-ABC omits the assessments of many skills usually included in mental abilities testing, especially visual-motor and expressive language skills.
- The K-ABC is a complicated test—complicated in theory, in administration, and in interpretation. The authors urge the examiners to take training courses to ensure proper use of the instrument.

System of Multicultural Pluristic Assessment (SOMPA)

Jane R. Mercer and June F. Lewis
The Psychological Corporation, 1977
7500 Old Oak Blvd., Middleburg Heights, OH 44130

Purpose	To provide schools and agencies with a basis for reaching educational decisions that take sociocultural differences into account
Major Areas Tested	Cognitive abilities, sensory-motor skills, and adaptive behavior
Age or Grade Range	5–11 years
Usually Given By	Psychologist (student assessment) Educational diagnostician (parent interview) Counselor (parent interview) Paraprofessional (parent interview)
Type of Test	Standardized Individual Norm-referenced
Scores Obtained	Percentile Scaled
Student Performance Timed?	Yes (some items)
Testing Time	1½–2 hours (student assessment) 1 hour (parent interview)
Scoring/Interpretation Time	1 hour
Normed On	2,085 public school children in California, aged 5 to 11 years, carefully selected for equal proportions of Black, Anglo, and Hispanic students
Alternate Forms Available?	No

FORMAT

The System of Multicultural Pluristic Assessment (SOMPA) is a unique instrument in the field of educational assessment. The purpose of the SOMPA is to assess the whole child, including medical status, sociocultural environment, and functioning in academic and social situations. The SOMPA incorporates three assessment models: the medical model, the social system model, and the pluristic model. Concepts of abnormality are treated differently in the three models. The medical model looks for organic abnormality. The social system model looks at role performance, while the pluristic model compares students of the same age from a similar sociocultural background.

The SOMPA is composed of nine instruments, divided into the student assessment instruments and the parent interview instruments. Table 35 outlines the SOMPA student assessment instruments and the materials needed for each. Table 36 describes the SOMPA parent interview instruments. While the student assessment instruments are intended for individual examination of the student, the parent interview instruments are designed to obtain information about the student and the student's environment. All of the parent interview instruments may be administered in Spanish, as may most of the student assessment instruments.

The SOMPA includes many materials for administration and recording results. These include:

- Student assessment manual
- Parent interview manual
- Technical manual
- Student assessment record forms
- Parent interview record forms in English
- Parent interview record forms in Spanish
- SOMPA profile folders
- Adaptive Behavior Inventory for Children (ABIC)—Spanish Edition
- ABIC transparencies for scoring

In addition to the materials provided in the SOMPA kit, examiners will need the administration and scoring materials for The Bender Visual Motor Gestalt Test (Bender) (p. 130) and the Wechsler Intelligence Scale for Children—Revised (WISC-R) (p. 265). After completing the student assessment and parent interview forms, all of the information is transferred to the SOMPA profile folder for a permanent record (see Figure 98). The profile folder is printed in two

Table 35. SOMPA Student Assessment Instruments

Instrument	Tasks	Time	Language of Directions

Physical Dexterity Tests	29 tasks divided into six scales:
	    Ambulation
	    Equilibrium
	    Placement
	    Fine Motor Sequencing
	    Finger Tongue Dexterity
	    Involuntary Movement
		20 minutes	English or Spanish

The Bender Visual Motor Gestalt Test (see p. 130)	9 design-copying tasks	10–15 minutes	English or Spanish
Weight by Height Visual Acuity Auditory Acuity	Measurement of height and weight Snellen eye test Audiometric screening	10–15 minutes	English or Spanish
Wechsler Intelligence Scale for Children—Revised (see p. 265)	Verbal Scale (see Table 30, pp. 268–269) Performance Scale (see Table 30, pp. 270–271)	50–75 minutes	English only

colors; scores that fall in the red areas (black areas in Figure 98) indicate students "at risk" in the skills or information assessed in that scale. "At risk" means that the student is in need of special or immediate attention by the school authorities.

Extensive information is provided in the SOMPA manuals to interpret the student assessment and parent interview data. A unique aspect of the SOMPA is a comparison of the student's school functioning level (SFL) and his or her estimated learning protential (ELP). The SFL is the student's WISC-R score, since the WISC-R is an instrument useful in identifying children at risk for school failure. However, the WISC-R is best at predicting the success of students with similar learning experiences, encouragement, reward systems, and test-taking opportunities. The ELP score combines the raw scores on the SOMPA Sociocultural Scales instrument with raw scores from the WISC-R for each of the three ethnic groups—Anglo, Black, and Hispanic. ELP represents the degree to which a child is likely to progress in an educational program that takes into account the child's sociocultural background. It does not predict the child's success in a mainstreamed program.

STRENGTHS OF THE SOMPA

- The SOMPA is the most recent attempt in a series of efforts over the years to produce a nondiscriminatory assessment procedure. The comprehensive nature of the test, developed to view the total child, is a definite strength and supports the need for multicultural educational programs. The use of previously normed instruments (the WISC-R and the Bender) is commendable. The development of parent interview scales of family situations, behavior, and health history is an excellent feature of the test.

- The norming sample of the SOMPA is the largest, best-balanced sample ever formed for a tool of nonbiased assessment. The SOMPA looks at each child in relation to his or her own ethnic group and to the Anglo middle class. The ELP is the key measure in a nondiscriminatory assessment.

- The materials, interview forms, and manuals of the SOMPA are clear and easily followed. Recording of data is systematically done, and the profile folder provides a convenient, easily read, permanent record. Important cautions are made to assessment personnel regarding interpretation. For example, it is a serious error to overlook a problem

Materials	Scoring	Comments
Stopwatch Student assessment manual Record form	Error score is obtained for each of the six scales and transformed into a scaled score and percentile rank. The six scales are then averaged to obtain a physical dexterity average scaled score and percentile.	Includes measures of balance, reflexes, and other measures usually included in a neurodevelopmental examination
Bender cards Paper and pencil Student assessment manual Record form *The Bender-Gestalt Test for Young Children* (Koppitz 1963)	Total error score is calculated using the Koppitz scoring criteria and is transformed into a SOMPA scaled score and percentile rank.	A standard, familiar measure of visual-motor integration in children
Physicians' scale with height bar Snellen chart Audiometer Record form	Using charts by sex, a scaled score is derived representing a height-by-weight ratio. No conversion necessary for visual or auditory acuity.	Weight of the child, controlled for height and sex, is an overall indicator of health.
WISC-R materials Record forms Stopwatch	WISC-R standard scoring procedures	Must be given by a trained psychologist in the standard manner

Table 36. SOMPA Parent Interview Instruments

Instrument	Areas Measured	Description
Sociocultural Scales	Four scales: 　Family Size 　Family Structure 　Socioeconomic Status 　Urban Acculturation	11 questions covering the four scales; a rating of the respondent's use of standard English is included.
Adaptive Behavior Inventory for Children (ABIC)	Six scales of social adaptation: 　Family 　Community 　Peer Relations 　Nonacademic School Roles 　Earner/Consumer 　Self-Maintenance	242 questions; the first 35 are asked of all respondents; of the remaining 207, only those for the appropriate age range are asked.
Health History Inventories	Health History	45 questions grouped into prenatal/postnatal, trauma, disease and illness, and vision and hearing inventories

Examples

Family Size:
"How many people live in the household, including your child and you?"

Family Structure:
"What is your child's relation to the head of the household?"

Socioeconomic Status:
"What is the chief source of income for the family?"

Urban Acculturation:
"About how often do you go to get-togethers or social groups where people meet because they enjoy doing things together, not counting church or religious groups?"

General Question:
"How does your child get along with the children in the neighborhood?"
0) not so well
1) fairly well
2) very well

Age 5:
"Does your child handle sharp or hot objects carefully?"
0) only when being watched
1) only when reminded
2) most of the time without being reminded

Age 8:
"How often does your child make plans with friends about what they will do after school or on a weekend?"
0) never
1) sometimes
2) all of the time

Age 11:
"Does your child become afraid if left alone for an hour or so during the weekend?"
0) usually
1) sometimes
2) never

Prenatal/Postnatal:
"Was your child born earlier than expected? If so, how many weeks early?"

Trauma:
"Has your child ever been knocked unconscious? If so, how long was he or she unconscious?"
"How long was it before he or she recovered and was able to go back to school or play?"

Disease and Illness:
"As you think about your child's health, how often would you say he or she has been sick?"
0) not much at all
1) fairly often
2) a lot of the time

Vision and Hearing:
"Has your child ever had an operation on his or her eyes or ears?"

Scoring

Each question is given a score; weighted totals within each scale are obtained, yielding a total score for each scale; these scores are converted to scaled scores using charts appropriate for the student's ethnic background (Black, Hispanic, or Anglo) and scaled scores appropriate for the school culture (Anglo). Scores for each of the four scales are converted into percentile ranks.

Each ABIC item is given one of five scores:
- 0 = Latent role (child has not engaged in activity)
- 1 = Emergent role (child is just beginning to perform activity; needs supervision)
- 2 = Mastered role (child performs activity frequently with little or no experience)
- N = No opportunity, or not allowed
- DK = Don't know

ABIC also contains a veracity score designed to provide information on the validity of the interviewer. Raw scores are determined for each of the six scales; these are converted to scaled scores based on the age of the child.

Individual items are scored and totaled to obtain a score for each inventory; no scaled score conversion is needed to determine at risk scores. The results are not plotted if too many responses are "don't know."

308 Part III General Intelligence Tests and Developmental Scales

MEDICAL MODEL

Color Coding: ▓ At Risk

Physical Dexterity Tasks

Scaled Score

Percentile: 1 3 5 10 20 30 40 50 over 50

- Ambulation ____
- Equilibrium ____
- Placement ____
- Fine Motor Sequencing ____
- Finger-Tongue Dexterity ____
- Involuntary Movement ____
- Physical Dexterity Average Scaled Score ____

Scaled Score: 10 20 30 40 50 over 50

Bender Visual Motor Gestalt Test

Scaled Score ____

Percentile: 1 3 5 10 20 30 40 50 over 50
Scaled Score: 10 20 30 40 50 over 50

Weight by Height

Scaled Score ____

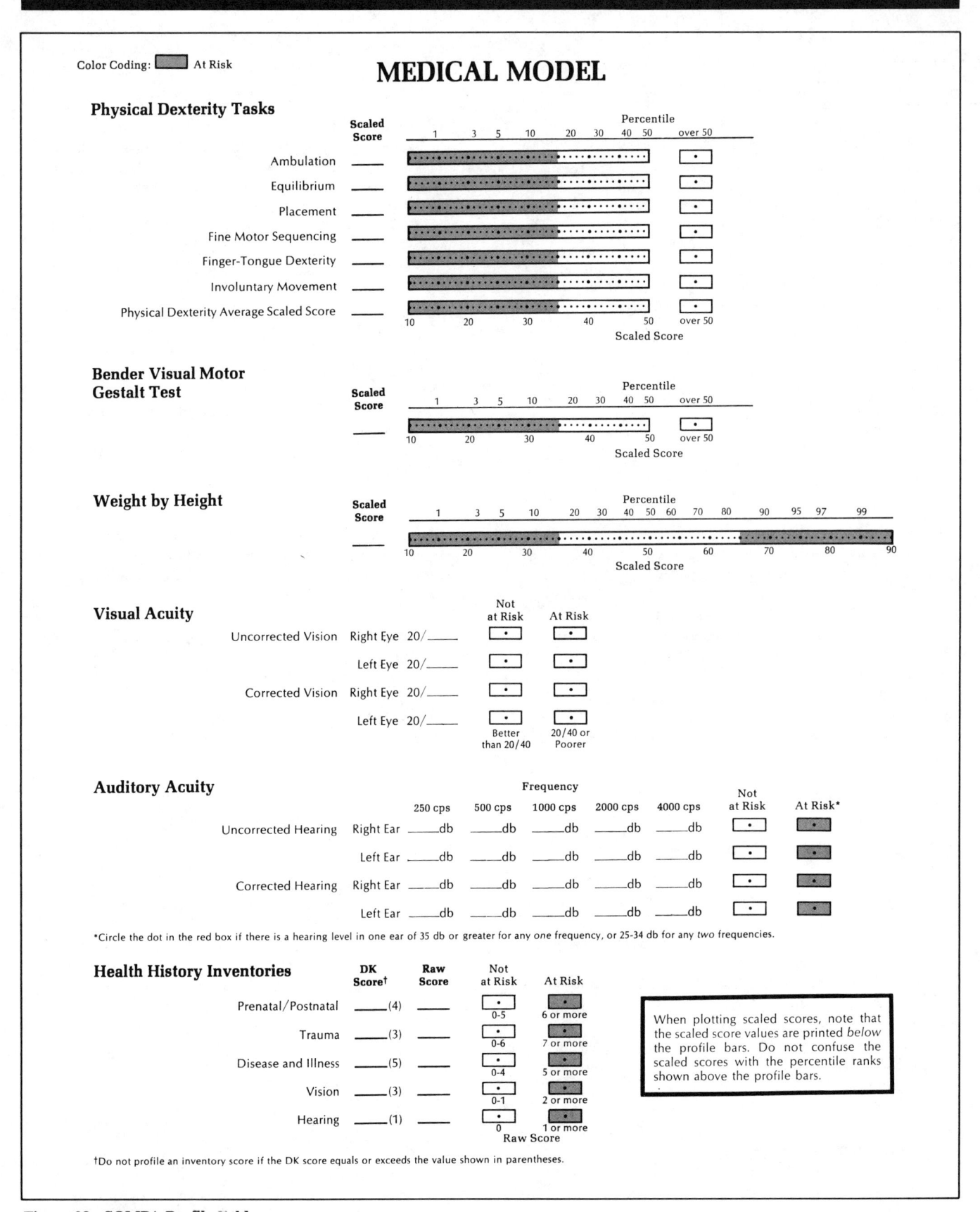

Percentile: 1 3 5 10 20 30 40 50 60 70 80 90 95 97 99
Scaled Score: 10 20 30 40 50 60 70 80 90

Visual Acuity

		Not at Risk	At Risk
Uncorrected Vision	Right Eye 20/____	·	·
	Left Eye 20/____	·	·
Corrected Vision	Right Eye 20/____	·	·
	Left Eye 20/____	·	·
		Better than 20/40	20/40 or Poorer

Auditory Acuity

Frequency

		250 cps	500 cps	1000 cps	2000 cps	4000 cps	Not at Risk	At Risk*
Uncorrected Hearing	Right Ear	___db	___db	___db	___db	___db	·	·
	Left Ear	___db	___db	___db	___db	___db	·	·
Corrected Hearing	Right Ear	___db	___db	___db	___db	___db	·	·
	Left Ear	___db	___db	___db	___db	___db	·	·

*Circle the dot in the red box if there is a hearing level in one ear of 35 db or greater for any *one* frequency, or 25-34 db for any *two* frequencies.

Health History Inventories

	DK Score†	Raw Score	Not at Risk	At Risk
Prenatal/Postnatal	____(4)	____	0-5	6 or more
Trauma	____(3)	____	0-6	7 or more
Disease and Illness	____(5)	____	0-4	5 or more
Vision	____(3)	____	0-1	2 or more
Hearing	____(1)	____	0	1 or more

Raw Score

> When plotting scaled scores, note that the scaled score values are printed *below* the profile bars. Do not confuse the scaled scores with the percentile ranks shown above the profile bars.

†Do not profile an inventory score if the DK score equals or exceeds the value shown in parentheses.

Figure 98. SOMPA Profile Folder

Part III General Intelligence Tests and Developmental Scales

SOCIAL SYSTEM MODEL

Adaptive Behavior Inventory for Children (ABIC)

Scaled Score / Percentile (1, 3, 5, 10, 20, 30, 40, 50, 60, 70, 80, 90, 95, 97, 99)

- Family (F) ____
- Community (C) ____
- Peer Relations (P) ____
- Nonacademic School Roles (S) ____
- Earner/Consumer (E) ____
- Self-Maintenance (M) ____
- ABIC Average Scaled Score ____

Scaled Score: 10, 20, 30, 40, 50, 60, 70, 80, 90

School Functioning Level (SFL)

WISC-R IQ* / Percentile (1, 3, 5, 10, 20, 30, 40, 50, 60, 70, 80, 90, 95, 97, 99)

- Verbal ____
- Performance ____
- Full Scale ____

WISC-R IQ*: 60, 70, 80, 90, 100, 110, 120, 130, 140

*WPPSI for children under 6 years of age. IQs below 60 should be plotted as 60; IQs above 140 should be plotted as 140.

PLURALISTIC MODEL

Estimated Learning Potential (ELP)

Scaled Score† / Percentile (1, 3, 5, 10, 20, 30, 40, 50, 60, 70, 80, 90, 95, 97, 99)

- Verbal ____
- Performance ____
- Full Scale ____

Scaled Score†: 60, 70, 80, 90, 100, 110, 120, 130, 140

†Scaled scores below 60 should be plotted as 60; scaled scores above 140 should be plotted as 140.

Sociocultural Scales

Own Ethnic Group
Check one: ___Black ___Hispanic ___White ___Other (specify:_____)

Scaled Score / Percentile (1, 3, 5, 10, 20, 30, 40, 50, 60, 70, 80, 90, 95, 97, 99)

- Family Size ____
- Family Structure ____
- Socioeconomic Status ____
- Urban Acculturation ____

Scaled Score: 10, 20, 30, 40, 50, 60, 70, 80, 90

School Culture

Scaled Score / Percentile (1, 3, 5, 10, 20, 30, 40, 50, 60, 70, 80, 90, 95, 97, 99)

- Family Size ____
- Family Structure ____
- Socioeconomic Status ____
- Urban Acculturation ____

Scaled Score: 10, 20, 30, 40, 50, 60, 70, 80, 90

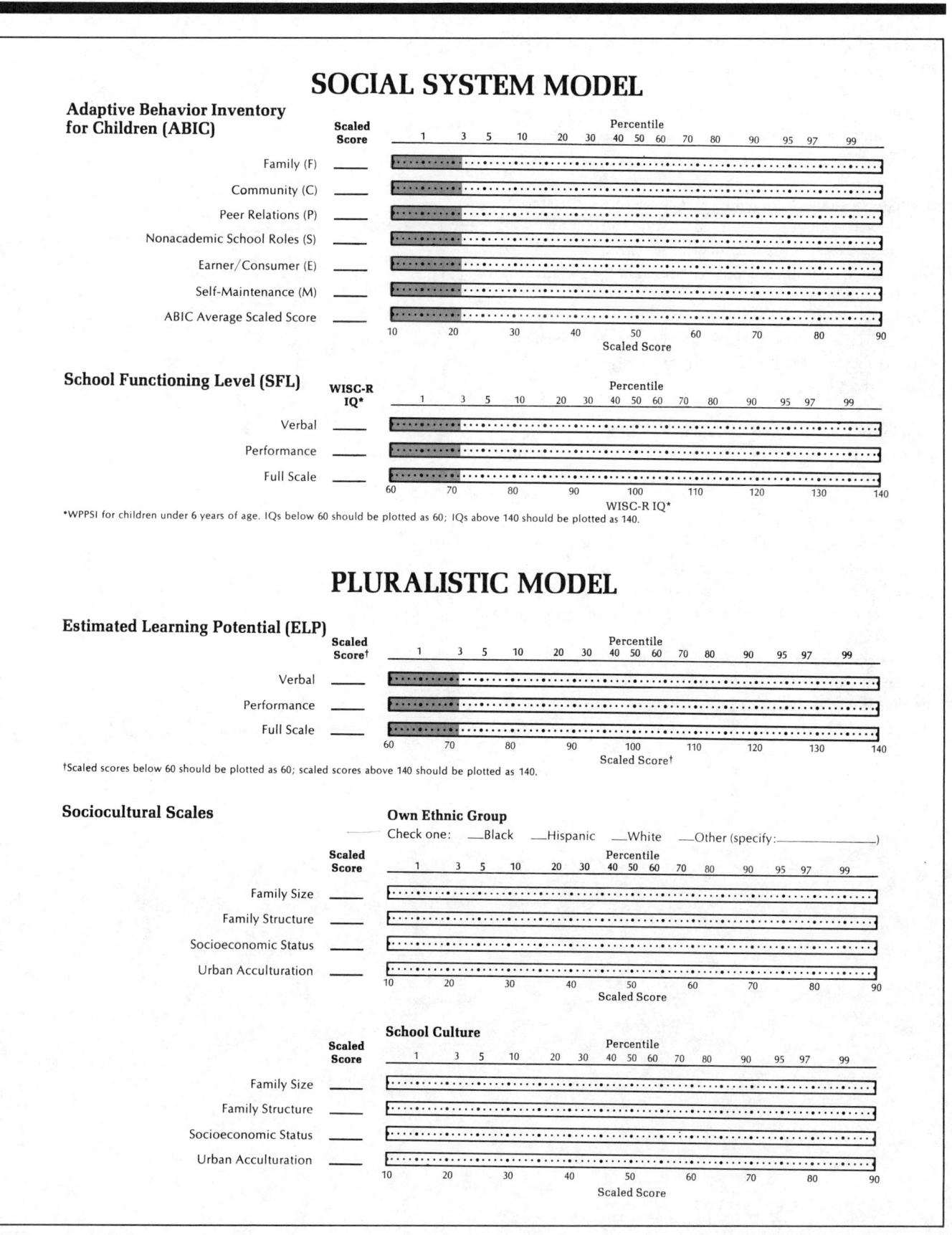

Figure 98.—*Continued*

in the medical model and to overinterpret behavior in the social system model.

• The technical material provided in the manuals is extensive and provides necessary theoretical and research background on the development of this complex test.

• The SOMPA recognizes the need to use paraprofessionals in parent interviewing procedures. Among the strengths of the test are the techniques described for training interviewers. Suggestions regarding style and communication, as well as specific information gathering, are provided.

• The ABIC is an excellent behavioral rating scale, with uses beyond the population usually assessed by the SOMPA. The veracity score, which provides information on the validity of the interviewer, and the wide range of behaviors covered increase the ABIC's utility in many special education settings.

LIMITING FACTORS OF THE SOMPA

• The ABIC provides for excellent information from the parents, but it allows for no input from sources outside the home. Provisions should be made for observing the child in school, interviewing the child's teacher, or both.

• The SOMPA claims to be very useful in providing recommendations regarding a student's placement in special education, yet no educational assessments are provided. Measures of academic functioning are needed to supplement the SOMPA.

• The Sociocultural Scales instrument is seriously lacking in items regarding the use of language in the home. Since the SOMPA was designed for use with families of Hispanic background, this is a serious omission.

Goodenough-Harris Drawing Test (Goodenough-Harris)

Dale B. Harris
Harcourt Brace Jovanovich, Inc., 1963 (revised extension of the Goodenough Draw-A-Man Test by Florence Goodenough, 1926)
The Psychological Corporation
7500 Old Oak Blvd., Middleburg Heights, OH 44130

Purpose	To assess cognitive development and intellectual maturity
Major Areas Tested	Conceptual and intellectual maturity and personality characteristics
Age or Grade Range	3–15 years
Usually Given By	Special education teacher Psychologist
Type of Test	Standardized Individual Group
Scores Obtained	Standard Percentile Quality scale
Student Performance Timed?	No
Testing Time	10–15 minutes
Scoring/Interpretation Time	10–15 minutes
Normed On	275 urban and rural children from the South, West Coast, Upper Midwest, Middle Atlantic, and New England; sample representative of 1950 United States population in regard to father's occupation
Alternate Forms Available?	No

FORMAT

Materials needed for the Goodenough-Harris Drawing Test (Goodenough-Harris) consist of a test booklet, with separate pages for three drawings, and a pencil. Plain white typing paper may be used in lieu of a test booklet, but crayons should not be substituted for a pencil. Very simple oral instructions are required. The student instructions read, "Make a picture of a man. Make the very best picture that you can. Be sure to make the whole man, not just his head and shoulders." After drawing a picture of a man, the student is instructed in a similar fashion to draw a picture of a woman. The student's final drawing is a self-portrait.

The Goodenough-Harris is administered with no time limit, but most students rarely take more than 15 minutes to complete all three drawings. The test can be given individually or in groups. Individual administration is necessary for preschool children and for students being examined clinically. Group administration requires an assistant to help proctor the test. Erasing, redrawing some features of a figure, or starting completely over again is allowed on the Goodenough-Harris. If given individually, the examiner may question the student about any unclear aspects of the drawings. Responses are recorded on the drawing itself. The examiner may encourage the students with praise. However, the examiner must refrain from offering any suggestions that might influence the nature of the drawing.

No alternate, equivalent forms of the test are available. However, because the correlation of the man and woman scoring scales is about as high as the split-half reliability of the man scale, Harris suggests that the two drawings be considered alternate forms.

The test manual for the Goodenough-Harris contains detailed, exact scoring instructions, with examples of items marked for credit or no credit. Illustrative scored drawings are also provided. There is a total of 73 scorable items, chosen on the basis of age differentiation, relation to total scores on the test, and relation to group intelligence scores. Credit is given for such features as the inclusion of individual body parts, clothing detail, proportion, and perspective.

After carefully studying the instructions, scoring may be accomplished by teachers or paraprofessionals. Separate sections for scoring the man and woman scales are provided. In addition, separate norms for boys and girls and for the man and woman scales are given.

A short scoring guide for both the man and woman point scales is contained in the manual. This guide should only be used by experienced scorers, however.

The total raw score for each drawing is obtained first. The raw score, representing the total points earned, is then converted into a standard score with a mean score of 100 and a standard deviation of 15. The standard score is particularly useful, because it expresses a student's relative standing on the test in relation to the student's own age and sex group. Thus a standard score of 130 indicates that the student's performance is two standard deviations above the average of his or her age and sex group.

Another advantage of standard scores is that they can be averaged. Averaging the standard scores on the man and woman drawings results in a more reliable estimate of maturity than is found when using the scores on either test alone. To score the self-drawing, the examiner uses the point scale of the appropriate sex.

An alternative method of evaluating performance on the Goodenough-Harris is the use of the quality scale. The examiner selects one of 12 sample drawings that most closely resemble the student's drawing and then assigns the scale value of that sample to the drawing. The quality scale value is converted into a standard score, which can ultimately be converted into a percentile score. The quality scale is advantageous for school psychologists who wish to screen large groups of students efficiently. Separate quality scales are provided for man and woman drawings.

STRENGTHS OF THE GOODENOUGH-HARRIS

- The Goodenough-Harris is an easy-to-administer test that is generally nonthreatening and appealing to students. It is valuable as a measure of intellectual maturity, providing indications of development in the areas of self-perception and body concept.

- The results of extensive reliability studies with the original Goodenough Draw-A-Man Test have been encouraging. Both interscorer and same-scorer correlations were found to be high. The effect of art instruction on test scores was found to be negligible, as was examiner effect. The majority of correlations with other intelligence tests are adequate. In addition, the Goodenough-Harris has been used in many studies of different cultures and ethnic groups.

- The results of the Goodenough-Harris give the classroom teacher some information about the intellectual maturity of students. The psychologist may use the test as a screening device to gain a quick impression of a student's general ability level. The test identifies students needing further clinical evaluation.

- If administered individually by an experienced examiner, the Goodenough-Harris may provide valuable clinical information from observations of the student's behavior. For example, spontaneous comments made while drawing, excessive erasing, the sequence of drawing the figure, or using the examiner or self as a model are all important diagnostic indicators. Although the test is not designed to be a measure of visual-motor integration per se, comparisons of the drawings with other tests measuring visual-motor skills is often useful.

- Helpful to the examiner who uses the Goodenough-

Harris is Harris's *Children's Drawings as Measures of Intellectual Maturity* (1963). It contains a comprehensive survey of literature dealing with the psychology of children's drawings, as well as a wealth of other information.

LIMITING FACTORS OF THE GOODENOUGH-HARRIS

- Any adult can learn to reliably score the Goodenough-Harris, but psychological training is necessary to adequately interpret the test results. Clinical observations of the student, together with the score, lead to valuable diagnostic insights.

- Although the author does not recommend using the Goodenough-Harris as a personality or projective test, it is often used in this way by psychologists. The student's self-portrait is used for projective purposes. Harris includes an experimental qualitative checklist for evaluating the self-drawing by comparing it with the other two drawings. The self-drawing is not standardized and is therefore regarded as a tentative measure of intellectual maturity. To date, the projective uses of the self-drawing have been disappointing. Thus, one should be cautious in making generalizations about the usefulness of drawings in personality assessment.

- Neither the 1926 nor the 1963 versions of the Goodenough-Harris report any correlation studies with academic achievement.

- The Goodenough-Harris is most useful for assessing the conceptual maturity of the elementary-age student. Beyond grade school, the test has only limited applicability. The mean raw scores increase sharply between the ages of 5 and 14. Above 14 years, however, the scores level off for both sexes on both the man and woman scales. For older students, the point scale is a better scoring method than the quality scale, because the latter shows less age differentiation at the upper ages. The test can also be given to 3- and 4-year-olds. Harris provides tentative guides for interpretation.

- The manual, which is Part 2 of Harris's book, is reproduced in its entirety and published separately. It contains, however, only the instructions for administration and scoring. For specific information on construction and technical properties of the Goodenough-Harris, the examiner must consult the book.

Appendix A

A GUIDE TO SPECIFIC TESTS FOR ASSESSING ACADEMIC SKILL AREAS

Skill Area	Tests

Reading
Decoding
  Phonic skills

                                Brigance Diagnostic Inventories
                                Spache Diagnostic Reading Scales
                                Durrell Analysis of Reading Difficulty
                                Gates-McKillop-Horowitz Reading Diagnostic Tests
                                McCarthy Individualized Diagnostic Reading Inventory
                                Woodcock-Johnson Psycho-Educational Battery

  Sight-word recognition

                                Wide Range Achievement Test
                                Peabody Individual Achievement Test
                                Brigance Diagnostic Inventories
                                Spache Diagnostic Reading Scales
                                Durrell Analysis of Reading Difficulty
                                Gates-McKillop-Horowitz Reading Diagnostic Tests
                                McCarthy Individualized Diagnostic Reading Inventory
                                Woodcock Reading Mastery Tests
                                Diagnostic Spelling Potential Test
                                Woodcock-Johnson Psycho-Educational Battery

  Oral paragraph reading

                                Basic Achievement Skills Individual Screener
                                Brigance Diagnostic Inventories
                                Gray Oral Reading Tests
                                Gilmore Oral Reading Test
                                Spache Diagnostic Reading Scales
                                Durrell Analysis of Reading Difficulty
                                Gates-McKillop-Horowitz Reading Diagnostic Tests
                                McCarthy Individualized Diagnostic Reading Inventory

Comprehension
  Oral reading

                                Basic Achievement Skills Individual Screener
                                Brigance Diagnostic Inventories
                                Gray Oral Reading Tests
                                Gilmore Oral Reading Test
                                Spache Diagnostic Reading Scales
                                Durrell Analysis of Reading Difficulty
                                Gates-McKillop-Horowitz Reading Diagnostic Tests
                                McCarthy Individualized Diagnostic Reading Inventory

  Silent reading

                                Peabody Individual Achievement Test
                                Spache Diagnostic Reading Scales
                                Durrell Analysis of Reading Difficulty
                                Woodcock Reading Mastery Tests
                                Gates-MacGinitie Silent Reading Tests
                                Test of Reading Comprehension
                                Test of Adolescent Language
                                Woodcock-Johnson Psycho-Educational Battery

A GUIDE TO SPECIFIC TESTS FOR ASSESSING ACADEMIC SKILL AREAS —*Continued*

Skill Area	Tests
Listening	Brigance Diagnostic Inventories Spache Diagnostic Reading Scales Durrell Analysis of Reading Difficulty Test of Language Development Test of Adolescent Language
Comprehension in specific content areas	Test of Reading Comprehension

Writing

Penmanship (Manuscript, Cursive)	Brigance Diagnostic Inventories Durrell Analysis of Reading Difficulty Test of Written Language Slingerland Screening Tests for Identifying Children with Specific Language Disability Malcomesius Specific Language Disability Test
Written Expression (Fluency, Syntax, Mechanics, Content)	Basic Achievement Skills Individual Screener Gates-McKillop-Horowitz Reading Diagnostic Tests Myklebust Picture Story Language Test Test of Written Language

Spelling

Written (Phonic words, Irregular words)	Wide Range Achievement Test Basic Achievement Skills Individual Screener Brigance Diagnostic Inventories Larsen-Hammill Test of Written Spelling Diagnostic Achievement Test in Spelling Diagnostic Spelling Potential Test Test of Written Language Woodcock-Johnson Psycho-Educational Battery
Recognition of Sight Words	Peabody Individual Achievement Test Diagnostic Analysis of Reading Errors Diagnostic Spelling Potential Test Woodcock-Johnson Psycho-Educational Battery
Oral	Gates-McKillop-Horowitz Reading Diagnostic Tests

Arithmetic

Concepts	Peabody Individual Achievement Test Brigance Diagnostic Inventories KeyMath Diagnostic Arithmetic Test Woodcock-Johnson Psycho-Educational Battery
Computation (Addition, Subtraction, Multiplication, Division)	Wide Range Achievement Test Basic Achievement Skills Individual Screener Brigance Diagnostic Inventories KeyMath Diagnostic Arithmetic Test Enright™ Diagnostic Inventory of Basic Arithmetic Skills Woodcock-Johnson Psycho-Educational Battery

A GUIDE TO SPECIFIC TESTS FOR ASSESSING ACADEMIC SKILL AREAS—*Continued*

Skill Area	Tests
Word Problems (Oral, Written)	Peabody Individual Achievement Test Basic Achievement Skills Individual Screener Brigance Diagnostic Inventories KeyMath Diagnostic Arithmetic Test Woodcock-Johnson Psycho-Educational Battery
Oral Language Receptive Vocabulary	Peabody Picture Vocabulary Test—Revised Assessment of Children's Language Comprehension Test of Language Development
Listening comprehension	Spache Diagnostic Reading Scales Durrell Analysis of Reading Difficulty Illinois Test of Psycholinguistic Abilities Clinical Evaluation of Language Functions Assessment of Children's Language Comprehension Test for Auditory Comprehension of Language Boehm Test of Basic Concepts Token Test for Children Northwestern Syntax Screening Test Sequenced Inventory of Communication Development Test of Language Development Test of Adolescent Language
Expressive Articulation	The Word Test Test of Language Development
Language (Morphology, Syntax, Semantics, Pragmatics)	Illinois Test of Psycholinguistic Abilities Clinical Evaluation of Language Functions Northwestern Syntax Screening Test Developmental Sentence Scoring Environmental Language Inventory Multilevel Informal Language Inventory Expressive One-Word Picture Vocabulary Test Test of Language Development Test of Adolescent Language Woodcock-Johnson Psycho-Educational Battery

Appendix B

PROCESS-MODALITY CHART

Modality	Process				
	Reception (initial receiving of information)	**Perception** (initial organizing of information)	**Association** (relating new information to other information)	**Memory** (short-term, sequential memory)	**Expression** (output)
Auditory (primary stimuli are auditory)	ACLC Boehm Brigance Inventories CELF Detroit ITPA NSST PPVT-R SICD TACL TOAL TOLD	CELF Detroit GFW ITPA LAC Malcomesius Test Slingerland Tests TOLD Wepman WJPEB	CELF Detroit ITPA Malcomesius Test Slingerland Tests WJPEB Word Test	CELF Detroit ITPA K-ABC LAC Malcomesius Test Slingerland Tests Token Test TOLD WJPEB	**Verbal expression** CELF Detroit DSS ELI EOWPVT ITPA K-ABC MILI NSST Slingerland Tests TACL TOAL TOLD WJPEB Word Test
Visual (primary stimuli are visual)	Detroit ITPA PPVT-R	CPM Detroit DTVP ITPA K-ABC Malcomesius Test MVPT SCSIT Slingerland Tests WJPEB	CPM Detroit ITPA K-ABC Malcomesius Test Slingerland Tests WJPEB	DARE Detroit DSPT ITPA K-ABC Malcomesius Test MVPT Slingerland Tests WJPEB	**Written expression** BASIS Bender Brigance Inventories Detroit DTVP Malcomesius Test PSLT Slingerland Tests TOAL TOWL VMI
Tactile/ Kinesthetic (primary stimuli accompanied by motoric output)	SCSIT	SCSIT		K-ABC Malcomesius Test SCSIT Slingerland Tests	**Motoric expression other than written or verbal** ITPA K-ABC SCSIT

Key
ACLC: Assessment of Children's Language Comprehension
BASIS: Basic Achievement Skills Individual Screener
Bender: The Bender Visual Motor Gestalt Test
Boehm: Boehm Test of Basic Concepts
Brigance Inventories: Brigance Diagnostic Inventories
CELF: Clinical Evaluation of Language Functions
CPM: Coloured Progressive Matrices
DARE: Diagnostic Analysis of Reading Errors
Detroit: Detroit Tests of Learning Aptitude
DSPT: Diagnostic Spelling Potential Test
DSS: Developmental Sentence Scoring
DTVP: Marianne Frostig Developmental Test of Visual Perception
ELI: Environmental Language Inventory
EOWPVT: Expressive One-Word Picture Vocabulary Test
GFW: Goldman-Fristoe-Woodcock Test of Auditory Discrimination
ITPA: Illinois Test of Psycholinguistic Abilities
K-ABC: Kaufman Assessment Battery for Children
LAC: Lindamood Auditory Conceptualization Test
Malcomesius Test: Malcomesius Specific Language Disability Test
MILI: Multilevel Informal Language Inventory
MVPT: Motor-Free Visual Perception Test
NSST: Northwestern Syntax Screening Test
PPVT-R: Peabody Picture Vocabulary Test—Revised
PSLT: Myklebust Picture Story Language Test
SCSIT: Southern California Sensory Integration Tests
SICD: Sequenced Inventory of Communication Development
Slingerland Tests: Slingerland Screening Tests for Identifying Children with Specific Language Disability
TACL: Test for Auditory Comprehension of Language
TOAL: Test of Adolescent Language
Token Test: Token Test for Children
TOLD: Test of Language Development
TOWL: Test of Written Language
VMI: Beery-Buktenica Developmental Test of Visual-Motor Integration
Wepman: Wepman Auditory Discrimination Test
WJPEB: Woodcock-Johnson Psycho-Educational Battery
Word Test: The Word Test

Appendix C

EDUCATIONAL EVALUATION REPORT, SAMPLE 1

Student's Name: Ken　　　　　　　　　　　　Grade: 9, City High School

Birth Date: 8/24/66　　　　　　　　　　　　Chronological Age: 15 years, 5 months

Date of Testing: January, 1982

REFERRAL

Ken was referred by his father for educational testing. The purpose of the evaluation was to determine whether Ken has a learning disability and, if so, what type and extent of special educational services are needed. Ken has not done well during his first high school quarter. He has received warning notices in algebra, science, and Spanish and has received Cs in English and history. Recently, his grades have improved to As and Bs, with the exception of a C in Spanish. Ken's parents are considering sending him to a small boarding school for students with learning disabilities. Ken would like to go. Recent intellectual assessment places Ken's ability in the high-average range.

BEHAVIORAL OBSERVATIONS DURING TESTING

Ken was totally cooperative throughout all the testing sessions. He presented himself as a quiet, thoughtful boy who worked slowly and carefully on all tasks presented. When given feedback on his test performance, he was pleased and seemed satisfied. Ken offered little spontaneous conversation about his school and living situation. When questioned, he stated that he doesn't like his high school because he doesn't feel comfortable there. It is too big, and teachers are not readily available to help. He now has a few friends. He is pleased with his improved grades and thinks he'll be able to bring his Spanish grade up to get on the honor roll. He would like to go to boarding school but he did not say exactly why, except that it would be smaller, and he would be more comfortable.

TEST RESULTS

Woodcock-Johnson Psycho-Educational Battery

Subtest	Grade Score	Instructional Range	Percentile	Percentile Range
Reading cluster	12.8	8.8–12.9	81	73–88
Mathematics cluster	7.8	6.6–9.7	64	50–76

Gilmore Oral Reading Test

Skill	Grade Score	Stanine	Percentile Range
Accuracy	9.8+	9	95+
Comprehension	9.8+	9	95+

Wide Range Achievement Test

Subtest	Grade Score	Standard Score	Percentile
Spelling	8.1	100	50

Basic Achievement Skills Individual Screener

Subtest	Rating
Writing	Average

The Bender Visual Motor Gestalt Test

No errors

DISCUSSION

Ken was given nationally normed tests in reading, spelling, and math. In reading, his scores were all above average. On the Woodcock-Johnson Psycho-Educational Battery, he demonstrated good phonics and word attack skills for both meaningful and nonmeaningful words. His comprehension, as measured by the cloze procedure (filling in a missing word in a sentence or paragraph) was strong. On the Gilmore Oral Reading Test, Ken read complex paragraphs at the ninth- and tenth-grade levels fluently and accurately. His comprehension, as measured by answering oral factual questions, was very good.

In spelling on the Wide Range Achievement Test, Ken was exactly average, fiftieth percentile. He demonstrated difficulties with double letters (*ilogical, necesity*) and *tion* and *sion* word endings. Ken was given this same test in September, 1981. At that time, his grade score was 5.4 with a standard score of 86, the bottom of the average range. His score this time is a significant improvement.

Ken's math score on the Woodcock-Johnson Psycho-Educational Battery was somewhat, but not significantly, lower than his reading scores and still within the average range. He made several careless errors (misinterpreting signs, not reducing fractions) and did not know how to divide fractions. His performance on applied problems was quite erratic. He missed many problems involving fractions and solved problems involving discounts and interest. His approach to all these problems was very slow and cautious.

In the area of written language, Ken was asked to write for 10 minutes on the subject "Your Favorite Place." He chose to write about going to Europe with his friends. Using the scoring criteria described in the Basic Achievement Skills Individual Screener, Ken's paragraph would be rated average for eighth graders. The test doesn't have ninth-grade norms. His paragraph included feelings and involvement, adequate organization, low-average vocabulary, good sentence structure, and average mechanics.

Ken's handwriting is small, with some poorly formed letters. It is, however, legible and not labored. While visual-motor skills are not strong (as seen previously by a low Coding score on the Wechsler Intelligence Scale for Children—Revised), he did not display significant problems in this testing.

SUMMARY

Ken is a pleasant, cooperative adolescent who has just recently entered a new high school environment. At this time, his test performance in all academic areas is average to above average. His current school grades are the same. He has achieved this without special remedial assistance.

There are two primary characteristics of the test performance of children with learning disabilities: (1) a significant discrepancy between ability tests and achievement tests and (2) an error pattern exhibiting problems in visual perception, auditory perception, and memory.

1. From previous testing, Ken's scores on the Wechsler Intelligence Scale for Children—Revised were 111 on the verbal scale, 112 on the performance scale, and 112 on the full scale. From this, his predicted academic levels should be in the seventy-seventh to seventy-ninth percentile range. His reading scores are appropriate; his spelling and math scores slightly lower. His spelling performance has improved significantly since the last testing, and his current grade in algebra is a low A. He has obtained this improvement without remedial assistance.

2. An error analysis of Ken's test protocols does not reveal significant problems in visual or auditory perception or memory. In spelling, there is one instance of an auditory discrimination error (*sudgestion* for *suggestion*) and one visual sequencing error (*muesum* for *museum*). There were no sequencing errors in math and no memory deficits noted.

Any evaluation takes place at one point in time. At this time, Ken does not display any learning disabilities that are interfering with academic achievement. This is not to say he may not be compensating for residual learning disabilities. The goal of learning disabilities programs for adolescents is to teach them strategies for compensation. Ken is mastering these strategies and does not need special academic programing at this time. In answer to the questions posed at the beginning of this evaluation, Ken does not currently display a learning disability that requires special educational services.

Given his personality and past experiences, Ken may feel more comfortable in a smaller school. It should be clear that if such a decision is made, it is because of a preference, not because he cannot achieve academically in a regular high school program.

Appendix C

EDUCATIONAL TESTING REPORT, SAMPLE 2

Student's Name: Martha Smith Grade: 5, Kennedy School

Birth Date: 10/14/70 Chronological Age: 10 years, 4 months

Date of Testing: 2/14/81

REFERRAL
Martha was referred to the Children's Health Council by her mother. She has been participating in the Resource Specialist Program at her school for several years and is currently receiving 30 minutes of tutorial assistance in spelling and math each day. Martha's mother is concerned because Martha does not complete her assignments. Homework issues at home are very difficult. Mrs. Smith would like to know to what extent Martha's learning disabilities contribute to these problems. Martha has been participating in the Gifted Program for three years.

BEHAVIORAL OBSERVATIONS DURING TESTING
Martha was totally cooperative throughout the testing. She gave good effort to each task presented, approaching each in a thoughtful manner. She worked somewhat slowly. There was no evidence of distractibility or inattention. Task persistence was good. When given feedback about her performance, Martha demonstrated little affect. Attempts to discuss her school performance with her did not lead to much information.

TEST RESULTS AND DISCUSSION
Woodcock Reading Mastery Tests

Subtest	Reading Level Range	Percentile
Letter Identification	4.8–12.9	80
Word Identification	4.2–6.2	43
Word Attack	3.5–8.1	55
Word Comprehension	3.1–6.3	36
Passage Comprehension	4.3–7.4	46
Total Reading	4.1–7.8	50

Martha's skills in reading, as measured by the Woodcock Reading Mastery Tests, are all in the average range. Her ability to read and comprehend material is appropriate for her grade level though below expectation for her ability. Several things are important about her performance:

1. She reads slowly and responds slowly.
2. Evidences of reversals of letters and syllables are present (*blamy* for *balmy*, *penteration* for *penetration*, *meranodum* for *memorandum*).
3. She has difficulty with consonant blends (*figid* for *frigid*, *circle* for *clerical*, *satab* for *stab*).
4. She demonstrates slight word-finding problems (*transportate* for the word *move*).

Informal Writing Assessment
After great consideration, Martha chose to write a paragraph entitled "My Best Friend." She was very involved in this task and wrote without interruption for more than 15 minutes.

Martha's paragraph was long (approximately 130 words) and pursued the topic in a logical and organized way. The composition had a beginning, a middle, and an end, and all of the sentences were relevant.

The vocabulary used was quite simple, and most of the sentences were simple subject-verb sentences. A few complex sentences were included.

Martha struggled with mechanics. Indenting was haphazard, and a few periods were omitted. She has learned about the apostrophe but does not know when to use it (*play's* for *plays*, *go's* for *goes*). Spelling was satisfactory for this basic vocabulary. She had difficulty with two words: *a lot* was consistently written as one word, and *across* as two.

Martha's involvement with this task was excellent, probably related to her choice of topic. The product demonstrates adequate written language skills for a fifth grader.

Informal Math Testing
Sections of the KeyMath Diagnostic Arithmetic Test were given in an informal manner to assess Martha's math skills. Again, she worked in a thoughtful manner.

Content (computation). Martha's addition and subtraction of whole numbers was quick and accurate, but she did not know how to add or subtract fractions. Her multiplication facts above six were inconsistent; she did not know how to multiply two-place numbers. She demonstrated very minimal division skills.

Applications (understanding). Martha had a good understanding of number sequences, but she did not know how to "round off." She had some difficulty with word problems, especially when multiplication was involved.

SUMMARY
Martha is a gifted child who is currently performing in the average range of basic academic skills. There continues to be a significant discrepancy between her ability and her achievement. She works slowly, even when she is very interested in a task. Her slow approach is partly her style and partly a compensation for difficulties, such as reversals, that are still present in her reading and spelling. There may be emotional reasons for her slowness, as well.

Martha is a child who tests better than she performs and who works better individually than in a group. Intensive instruction in her skill deficits, reassurance about her skills, and training in independence are all needed.

RECOMMENDATIONS
1. Continued participation in the Resource Specialist Program, with emphasis on three specific skills: consonant blends, multiplication, and division
2. Development of a plan for parents to resolve some of the homework issues
3. Continued exploration of emotional issues in Martha's performance

Appendix D

A COMPARISON OF READING TESTS

Features of the Test

Test	Standardized	Battery	Alternate Forms Available	Student Performance Timed	Grade Range
WRAT	X				K–12
PIAT	X				K–12
BASIS	X				1–12
Brigance Inventories		X			Preschool–12
Gray Oral	X		X	X	1–12
Gilmore Oral	X		X		1–8
DRS	X	X	X		1–7
Durrell Analysis	X	X		X	1–6
Gates-McKillop-Horowitz	X	X			1–6
IDRI		X			1–9
Woodcock	X	X	X		K–12
Gates-MacGinitie	X		X	X	1–12
TORC	X	X			1–8

Skills Assessed

Test	Oral Paragraph Reading	Silent Paragraph Reading	Word Reading	Reading Subskills	Oral Comprehension	Silent Comprehension	Listening Comprehension
WRAT			X				
PIAT			X			X	
BASIS					X		
Brigance Inventories	X	X	X	X	X	X	X
Gray Oral	X				X		
Gilmore Oral	X				X		
DRS	X	X	X	X	X	X	X
Durrell Analysis	X	X	X	X	X	X	X
Gates-McKillop-Horowitz	X		X	X			
IDRI	X		X	X	X		
Woodcock		X	X	X		X	
Gates-MacGinitie		X	X	X		X	
TORC		X		X		X	

Key

BASIS: Basic Achievement Skills Individual Screener
Brigance Inventories: Brigance Diagnostic Inventories
DRS: Spache Diagnostic Reading Scales
Durrell Analysis: Durrell Analysis of Reading Difficulty
Gates-MacGinitie Tests: Gates-MacGinitie Silent Reading Tests
Gates-McKillop-Horowitz: Gates-McKillop-Horowitz Reading Diagnostic Tests
Gilmore Oral: Gilmore Oral Reading Test
Gray Oral: Gray Oral Reading Tests
IDRI: McCarthy Individualized Diagnostic Reading Inventory
PIAT: Peabody Individual Achievement Test
TORC: Test of Reading Comprehension
Woodcock: Woodcock Reading Mastery Tests
WRAT: Wide Range Achievement Test

Appendix E

THREE TESTS FOR ASSESSING ARTICULATION

As noted in Part I, Chapter Three: Speech and Language Tests, a complete speech and language evaluation includes assessment of phonology. Phonology is a sound system that constitutes spoken language. Errors in sound production are called articulation errors. The features of three articulation tests are compared in the chart below. Also, brief descriptions of the tests are provided.

	Fisher-Logemann	Goldman-Fristoe	Templin-Darley
Features of the Test			
Screening function	X		X
Diagnostic function	X	X	X
Easy-to-use manual	X	X	
Stimuli that easily elicit response	X	X	
Easy-to-record response forms	X		
Developmental norms for phoneme acquisition	X		X
Provision for geographical variants and foreign dialects	X		
Distinctive-feature analysis	X		
Skills Assessed			
Consonants, vowels, diphthongs, clusters	X	Consonants and vowels	X
Phonemes in three syllable positions	X	X	Initial, final only
Articulation in connected speech	X	X	
Coarticulation factors	X		
Imitation and stimulability		X	X

Key

Fisher-Logemann: The Fisher-Logemann Test of Articulation Competence
Goldman-Fristoe: The Goldman-Fristoe Test of Articulation
Templin-Darley: The Templin-Darley Tests of Articulation

The Fisher-Logemann Test of Articulation Competence (Fisher-Logemann)

Hilda B. Fisher and Jerilyn A. Logemann
Houghton Mifflin Company, 1971
Test Department, Box 1970, Iowa City, IA 52240

Purpose	To examine a student's phonological system in an orderly framework and to facilitate the recording and analysis of phonetic notations of articulation and the comprehensive and accurate analysis and categorization of articulation errors
Age or Grade Range	3 years–adult (Picture Test) 9 years–adult (Sentence Articulation Test)
Scores Obtained	None

The Goldman-Fristoe Test of Articulation (Goldman-Fristoe)

Ronald Goldman and Macalyne Fristoe
American Guidance Service, Inc., 1969; revised 1972
Publishers' Bldg., Circle Pines, MN 55014

Purpose	To provide systematic assessment of articulation of the consonant sounds in English
Age or Grade Range	3–16 years
Scores Obtained	Percentile

The Templin-Darley Tests of Articulation

(Templin-Darley)

Mildred C. Templin and Frederic L. Darley
The University of Iowa, 1960; revised 1969
Bureau of Educational Research and Service, The University of Iowa, Iowa City, IA 52240

Purpose	To assess general accuracy of articulation (Screening Test); to assess production of a wide range of speech sounds in a variety of word positions and phonetic contexts (Diagnostic Test); to evaluate consistency of production of various types of speech elements (Iowa Pressure Articulation Test)
Age or Grade Range	3 years–adult
Scores Obtained	Age level

Appendix F

A LIST OF TESTS THAT HAVE SPANISH TRANSLATIONS

PART I: SKILL AREA TESTS
Chapter One: Academic Tests
Brigance Diagnostic Inventories
Chapter Three: Speech and Language Tests
Assessment of Children's Language Comprehension
Test for Auditory Comprehension of Language
Boehm Test of Basic Concepts

PART II: PRESCHOOL AND KINDERGARTEN TESTS
Preschool Language Scale

PART III: GENERAL INTELLIGENCE TESTS AND DEVELOPMENTAL SCALES
Wechsler Intelligence Scale for Children—Revised
Woodcock-Johnson Psycho-Educational Battery

Appendix G

A LIST OF TESTS APPROPRIATE FOR
PRESCHOOL CHILDREN

PART I: SKILL AREA TESTS

Chapter Two: Perception and Memory Tests
Marianne Frostig Developmental Test of Visual Perception
Motor-Free Visual Perception Test
Beery-Buktenica Developmental Test of Visual-Motor Integration

Chapter Three: Speech and Language Tests
Illinois Test of Psycholinguistic Abilities
Peabody Picture Vocabulary Test—Revised
Assessment of Children's Language Comprehension
Test for Auditory Comprehension of Language
Boehm Test of Basic Concepts
Token Test for Children
Northwestern Syntax Screening Test
Sequenced Inventory of Communication Development
Developmental Sentence Scoring
Environmental Language Inventory
Multilevel Informal Language Inventory
Expressive One-Word Picture Vocabulary Test

Chapter Four: Bilingual (Spanish-English) Language Tests
Screening Test of Spanish Grammar
Ber-Sil Spanish Test
Del Rio Language Screening Test

Chapter Five: Gross Motor Tests
Bruininks-Oseretsky Test of Motor Proficiency
Southern California Sensory Integration Tests

PART II: PRESCHOOL AND KINDERGARTEN TESTS
Denver Developmental Screening Test
Brigance Diagnostic Inventory of Early Development
Miller Assessment for Preschoolers
The Meeting Street School Screening Test
Basic School Skills Inventory
Preschool Language Scale
Kraner Preschool Math Inventory
Slingerland Pre-Reading Screening Procedures

PART III: GENERAL INTELLIGENCE TESTS AND DEVELOPMENTAL SCALES
Wechsler Preschool and Primary Scale of Intelligence
Stanford-Binet Intelligence Scale
Slosson Intelligence Test for Children and Adults
Leiter International Performance Scale and the Arthur Adaptation
McCarthy Scales of Children's Abilities
Woodcock-Johnson Psycho-Educational Battery
Kaufman Assessment Battery for Children
Goodenough-Harris Drawing Test

Glossary of Testing Terms

Words set in italics are defined elsewhere in the glossary. The glossary contains six sections: General Terms, Diagnostic Categories, Academic Terms, Visual and Visual-Perceptual Motor Processing, Oral Language and Auditory Processing, and Fine and Gross Motor Skills.

GENERAL TERMS

AGE NORM (Age score). A score indicating average performance for students classified according to *chronological age.* Generally expressed in terms of *central tendency, standard score, percentile rank,* or *stanine.* In an *achievement test,* the age equivalent for grades.

AGE SCORE. See *age norm.*

ALTERNATE FORMS. See *equivalent forms.*

BASAL LEVEL. The level at which all items of a test are passed, just preceding the level where the first failure occurs. All items below the basal point are assumed correct. Contrast with *ceiling level.*

BATTERY. A group of carefully selected tests administered to a student, the results of which are of value individually, in combination, and/or totally.

CEILING LEVEL. The maximal level of a test. The highest item of a sequence in which a certain number of items has been failed. All items above the ceiling item are assumed incorrect. Contrast with *basal level.*

CENTRAL TENDENCY. A statistical measure used to describe typical values in a set or distribution of scores. The most common such measures used in educational testing are the *mean, median,* and *mode.*

CHRONOLOGICAL AGE (CA). Age from birth expressed in years and months; for example, 7 years, 6 months.

CORRELATION COEFFICIENT (r). A statistical index that measures the degree of relationship between any two variables (for example, sets of scores). It ranges in value from −1.00 (a perfect negative correlation) to +1.00 (a perfect positive correlation). An example is the high positive correlation between vocabulary and *intelligence.*

DERIVED SCORE. Any score that has been converted from a qualitative or quantitative unit on one scale into the units of another scale, thereby allowing a direct comparison of the student's performance on different tests or a comparison of his or her performance to the performance of others. Examples of derived scores are *percentile rank, age norm, standard score, T-score, Z-score,* and *normal curve equivalent score.*

DIAGNOSTIC TESTING. An intensive, in-depth evaluation process using formal, *standardized tests* and *informal tests* designed to determine the nature and severity of specific learning problems. Generally provided by an interdisciplinary team of specialists.

EQUIVALENCY METHOD. One method of standardizing a new test. Each raw score on the new test is matched with the same raw score on a test with established norms. In this way, the raw scores of the new test can be directly associated with the standard scores of the anchor test. The advantage of the equivalency method is that a smaller standardization sample is needed. A major assumption is that the new test measures the same process as the anchor test. The equivalency method was used in standardizing the Diagnostic Spelling Potential Test (using the Wide Range Achievement Test as the anchor test) and the Slosson Intelligence Test for Children and Adults (using the Stanford-Binet Intelligence Scale as the anchor test).

EQUIVALENT FORMS (Alternate forms). Two comparable or parallel forms of a test that measure the same skill or trait to the same degree and are standardized on the same population. Useful for *pretest* and *posttest* measurement.

EXTRAPOLATION. A process of estimating the scores of a test beyond the range of available data.

FREQUENCY DISTRIBUTION. A tabulation of scores from low to high that indicates the number of individuals who obtain each score.

INTELLIGENCE. A global construct or entity composed of several functions. The abilities constituting intelligence are such factors as cognitive skills or processes, abstract verbal and numerical aptitudes, comprehension and memory functions, and the abilities to learn, reason, and solve problems.

INTELLIGENCE QUOTIENT (IQ). An index of mental ability, expressing a student's performance on an intelligence test. If a student's *mental age* and *chronological age* are equal, his or her IQ is 100 (which represents average performance). Thus IQ is a *standard score* with a *mean* fixed statistically at 100 and the *standard deviation* fixed according to the test author's discretion.

DEVIATION IQ. Indicates the amount by which a student's performance on an IQ test is above or below the average performance of students of his or her age group.

RATIO IQ. A *derived score* that expresses the student's *mental age* in relation to *chronological age,* according to the formula:

$$IQ = \frac{MA}{CA} \times 100$$

INTERPOLATION. A process of estimating an intermediate value between two known points. In the example, a *raw score* value of 55, by interpolation, would be assigned a *grade norm* of 4.9.

Raw Score	Grade Norm
52	4.5
54	4.8
56	5.0
58	5.2

MEAN (M). The sum of a set of scores divided by the number of scores. The value of the mean can be strongly influenced by a few extreme scores.

MEDIAN (MD). The middle point in a set of ranked scores. The value that has the same number of scores above it and below it in the distribution. For example, the median in the following set of scores is 10: 17, 13, 11, 10, 9, 9, 8. In a distribution of scores such as 9, 8, 6, 5, the median, by *interpolation*, would be 7.

MENTAL AGE (MA). A measure of a child's level of mental development, based on performance on a test of mental ability and determined by the level of difficulty of the test items passed. If a child, no matter what age, can pass only those items passed by the average 8-year-old, the child will be assigned a mental-age score of 8.

MODE (MO). The score that occurs most frequently in a distribution. In the distribution 18, 14, 12, 11, 10, 10, 7, the mode is 10. Its value is entirely independent of extreme scores.

NONVERBAL TEST. See *performance test*.

NORMAL CURVE EQUIVALENT SCORES (NCE). A scale designed to transform percentile rankings into equal units. The NCE scale is designed so that NCEs of 150 and 99 coincide with percentile rankings of 150 and 99. However, a difference of 5 NCE units represents the same difference in achievement at any point on the NCE scale; therefore, NCEs are suitable for computing averages. The NCE that corresponds to any raw score is lower at the end of the year than at the beginning, since students learn to read better during the year. Therefore, different NCE charts are needed for different intervals of the year.

PERCENTILE RANK. A type of converted score that expresses a student's score relative to his or her group in percentile points. Indicates the percentage of students tested who made scores equal to or lower than the specified score. If a score of 82 has a percentile rank of 65, this means that 65 percent of the students who took the test had a score of 82 or lower than 82.

PERFORMANCE TEST (Nonverbal test). Designed to evaluate the general intelligence or specialized aptitudes of students. Consists primarily of motor test items or perceptual items in which verbal abilities play a minimal role. Contrast with *verbal test*.

PROJECTIVE TECHNIQUE. A test situation in which the student responds to ambiguous stimulus materials, such as pictures, inkblots, or incomplete sentences, thereby projecting personality characteristics.

PROTOCOL. The original record of the test results.

RANK ORDERING. The arrangement of scores from highest to lowest.

RAW SCORE. The basic score initially obtained by scoring a test according to the directions in the manual. Generally equal to the number of right answers—but may be the number of incorrect responses, the time required for a task, or some other criterion.

RELIABILITY. The degree to which a student would obtain the same score if the test were readministered (assuming no further learning, practice effects, or other change). Stability or consistency of scores.

ALTERNATE-FORM RELIABILITY. A method of estimating test reliability by the *correlation coefficient* between two equivalent or comparable forms of the test. The student is tested with one form on the first occasion and with another, parallel form on the second.

INTERSCORER RELIABILITY. A method that requires a sample of tests to be scored independently by two examiners. The two scores are correlated, and the resulting *correlation coefficient* is an estimate of interscorer reliability.

SPLIT-HALF RELIABILITY. A method for determining the reliability coefficient for a test by obtaining the *correlation coefficient* for two halves of the same test. Usually items are split odd-even to provide the two comparable halves.

TEST-RETEST RELIABILITY. A method of establishing reliability that involves readministering the same test to the same sample of students and then determining the degree of correlation between the two sets of test scores.

SCATTER. The extent of variation among a student's scores on all subtests of a single test or on several different tests. May indicate whether all aspects of a student's ability are developing evenly or whether the student has an unusual facility or handicap in a certain area. Wide discrepancies in a student's profile of abilities do not necessarily suggest underlying pathology.

STANDARD DEVIATION (SD). The most commonly used measure of variation. A statistic used to express the extent of the distribution's deviations from the *mean*. In the normal distribution, about 68 percent of the scores lie within one SD above or below the mean.

STANDARD ERROR OF MEASUREMENT (SE_M, Standard error, Test error). A statistic that indicates how chance errors may cause variation in the scores that a given student might obtain if he or she were to take the same test an infinite number of times. If the SE_M is 3, the chances are 2 to 1 that any given student's score will fall within a range of three points of the obtained score. For example, if Jerry gets a score of 160, his "true" score lies somewhere between 157 and 163.

STANDARDIZATION. In test construction, refers to the process of trying the test out on a group of students to determine uniform or standard scoring procedures and methods of interpretation.

STANDARDIZATION SAMPLE. Refers to the section of the reference population that is chosen for use in establishing test norms. Should be representative of the reference population in main characteristics, such as sex, race, age, grade, geographical location, socioeconomic status, and other factors.

STANDARDIZED TEST. Contains empirically selected materials, with specific directions for administration, scoring, and interpretation. Provides data on *validity* and *reliability*, and has adequately derived norms.

STANDARD SCORE. *Derived score* that transforms a *raw score* in such a manner that it has the same *mean* and the same *standard deviation*. The standard score scale is an equal-interval scale; that is, a difference of, say, five points has the same meaning throughout the scale.

STANINE. A weighted scale divided into nine equal units that represent nine levels of performance on any particular test. The stanine is a *standard score*. Thus the intervals between different points on the scale (for example, the difference between 8 and 5 and between 4 and 1 on the scale) are equal in terms of the number of correct test responses they represent. The *mean* is at stanine 5 in the example.

Stanine	1	2	3	4	5	6	7	8	9
Percent in Stanine	4	7	12	17	20	17	12	7	4

TEST ERROR. See *standard error of measurement*.

T-SCORE. A standard score with a mean of 50 and a standard deviation of 10.

VALIDITY. The extent to which a test measures what it is designed to measure. A test valid for one use may have negligible validity for another.

CONCURRENT VALIDITY. How well scores on a test correspond to performance on some criterion data available at the time of testing. For example, comparing end-of-course achievement test scores with school grades.

CONSTRUCT VALIDITY. Reports the extent to which the test measures a theoretical construct or trait. *Intelligence*, verbal fluency, and mechanical comprehension represent theoretical constructs.

CONTENT VALIDITY. How well the content of the test samples the behavior domain or subject matter about which conclusions are to be made. This concept is used principally with *achievement tests*.

FACE VALIDITY. The idea that the test appears as if it should be valid. That is, a test is assumed to be valid simply by definition. For example, a scale is a valid instrument of weight, by definition of what constitutes weight.

PREDICTIVE VALIDITY. How effectively predictions made from the test are substantiated by data obtained at a later time. An example is the correlation of intelligence test scores with school grades.

VERBAL TEST. Designed to evaluate the general *intelligence* or specialized aptitudes of students. Consists primarily of items requiring the use of language. Contrast with *performance test*.

Z-SCORE. A standard score with a mean of 0 and a standard deviation of 1.

DIAGNOSTIC CATEGORIES

A-, AN-. A prefix equivalent to un- or in- that signifies absence, lack, -less, not. Contrast with *dys-*.

ACALCULIA. See *dyscalculia*.

AGNOSIA. Lost or impaired ability to identify familiar objects or events in the absence of a defective sense organ.

AUDITORY AGNOSIA. Impairment of the ability to recognize sounds or sound combinations (for example, nonrecognition of the ring of an alarm clock).

TACTILE AGNOSIA (Astereognosis). Impaired ability to recognize objects through the sense of touch.

VISUAL AGNOSIA. Inability to recognize objects, persons, or places by sight.

AGRAPHIA. See *dysgraphia*.

ALEXIA. See *dyslexia*.

APHASIA. See *dysphasia*.

APRAXIA. See *dyspraxia*.

BRAIN DAMAGE. Any structural damage or insult to the brain, whether by accident or disease.

DYS-. In medicine, a prefix denoting difficult or painful, faulty or impaired, abnormal or morbid.

DYSCALCULIA. Disturbed or impaired ability to calculate, to manipulate number symbols, or to perform simple arithmetic.

DYSFUNCTION. Abnormal or impaired behavior of any organ.

DYSGRAPHIA. A type of *dyspraxia* affecting the visual-motor system. Results in the inability to remember the kinesthetic patterns that go into writing. That is, an inability to relate the mental image of words or symbols to the motor movements necessary for writing them.

DYSLEXIA. Partial inability to read. Generally thought to be associated with neurological dysfunction.

DYSNOMIA (Word-finding difficulty). Weakness in the ability to name objects or to recall and retrieve words. Generally the individual knows the word, recognizes it when spoken, but cannot retrieve it at will.

DYSPRAXIA. Impairment of the ability to recall and perform purposeful, skilled movements. Contrast with *praxis*.
  MOTOR DYSPRAXIA. Weakness in the ability to plan and execute unfamiliar motor tasks, even though coordination may be adequate for familiar tasks.
  ORAL DYSPRAXIA. Severe impairment in the ability to perform voluntary movements involving the speech musculature, even though automatic movements of the same musculature appear to be intact.
MINIMAL BRAIN DAMAGE. See *minimal brain dysfunction*.
MINIMAL BRAIN DYSFUNCTION (Minimal brain damage, Minimal cerebral dysfunction). A mild neurological abnormality that causes learning difficulties in the child with near-average or even above-average intellectual potential. Common behavioral characteristics may include hyperactivity, distractibility, impulsivity, and poor motor functioning.
MINIMAL CEREBRAL DYSFUNCTION. See *minimal brain dysfunction*.
NEUROSIS. Behavior disturbance characterized by emotional conflict and anxiety but not a loss of contact with reality. Represents the milder forms of mental illness. Contrast with *psychosis*.
PERSEVERATION. The tendency to continue a specific act of behavior after it is no longer appropriate (for example, repeating a word over and over again, continuing a movement such as letter writing, prolonging laughter). Related to difficulty in shifting from one activity to another.
PSYCHOSIS. The class of the more severe mental disorders, in which there is a departure from normal patterns of thinking, feeling, or acting. Commonly characterized by loss of contact with reality, distortion of perception, disruptions of cognitive and emotional processes, and abnormal mental content, including hallucinations and delusions. Contrast with *neurosis*.
SPECIFIC LANGUAGE DISABILITY (SLD). Refers to those who have great difficulty learning to read and spell but who are otherwise intelligent. Generally applies to any language deficit impeding learning (oral, visual, or auditory). Sometimes used interchangeably with *dyslexia*.
WORD-FINDING DIFFICULTY. See *dysnomia*.

ACADEMIC TERMS

ACHIEVEMENT TEST. An objective test that measures how much a student has learned or knows about a specific subject.
ACTUAL GRADE PLACEMENT. The student's grade and month-in-grade at the date of testing. A tenth of a grade-placement unit is added for every month of school finished. For example, a first-grade student tested in late October has an actual grade placement of 1.2.

CHANNEL. The sensorimotor route through which language flows (for example, visual-motor, visual-vocal, auditory-motor). Theoretically, many combinations are possible.
CLOZE FORMAT. A procedure used in teaching and testing reading comprehension in which certain words are deleted from the text, leaving blank spaces. Measurement is made by rating the number of blanks that the student can accurately fill.
CRITERION-REFERENCED TEST (CR). Objective test yielding a *ratio score* and designed to assess a student's development of certain skills in terms of absolute levels of mastery. CR devices are made up of a specified set of sequential skills (criterion behaviors) arranged in a hierarchical order. These tests provide answers to specific questions such as, "Can Billy identify the topic sentence in at least three out of four paragraphs?" Contrast with *norm-referenced test*.
DECODING. In reading, refers to the ability to translate the printed symbol into language. Entails visual perception and discrimination, preceded by auditory perception and discrimination.
DISCRIMINATION. The process of detecting differences among stimuli.
  AUDITORY DISCRIMINATION. Ability to determine whether two acoustic stimuli (either speech sounds or nonspeech sounds) are the same or different.
  TACTILE DISCRIMINATION. Central response to stimuli presented only to the tactile sense. The ability to recognize differences and similarities in shape and pattern by touch alone.
  VISUAL DISCRIMINATION. Ability to distinguish between different objects, forms, and letter symbols presented visually.
ENCODING. In writing, refers to the ability to translate verbal language into graphic symbols. The act of committing one's thoughts to the written form encompasses the ideational use of language, as well as visual, auditory, and visual-motor abilities.
FRUSTRATION READING LEVEL. The level at which a student reads orally with less than 93 percent accuracy or 70 percent comprehension. Frequent errors, repetitions, and omissions occur at this level, indicating that the material is too difficult for instruction. See *independent reading level* and *instructional reading level*.
GESTALT PSYCHOLOGY. A German school of psychology that places emphasis on a whole perceptual configuration and the interrelations of its component parts.
GRADE EQUIVALENT. See *grade norm*.
GRADE NORM (Grade equivalent, Grade score). The average test score obtained by students classified at a given grade placement. For example, a grade score of 3.4 indicates that the student performed as well on the test as an average student who has been in the third grade for four months.

GRADE SCORE. See *grade norm*.

HOLISTIC IMPRESSION. A method for overall assessment of written language. The holistic impression method requires looking at a piece of writing as a whole, not as having a series of separate, specific characteristics.

INDEPENDENT READING LEVEL. The level at which a student reads orally with 98 percent accuracy and 90 percent comprehension. Reading is fluent and expressive. Library reading, recreational reading, and homework should be assigned at the independent reading level. See *instructional reading level* and *frustration reading level*.

INFORMAL TEST. Nonstandardized test, often teacher-constructed, useful in analyzing a student's learning style and thinking processes. Indicates what the student does and how he or she does it.

INSTRUCTIONAL READING LEVEL. The level at which a student reads orally with 94 percent accuracy and 70 percent comprehension. Material is challenging and not too difficult. Classroom learning under teacher direction should be assigned at the instructional level. See *independent reading level* and *frustration reading level*.

MODALITY. A pathway for acquiring sensory information. Auditory, visual, tactile, and kinesthetic are the most common modalities through which learning occurs.

MULTISENSORY APPROACH. Generally refers to teaching methods that rely simultaneously on several sensory modalities—visual, auditory, kinesthetic, and tactile.

NORM-REFERENCED TEST. Objective test standardized on groups of individuals. Compares a student's performance to the performance of other students who are the same *chronological age*. Using norm-referenced tests, for example, Jill's reading can be assigned a grade-level score of 3.2 on a standardized reading test. In other words, the test tells how Jill is doing compared with other students. Contrast with *criterion-referenced test*.

ORTON-GILLINGHAM TECHNIQUE. A method of teaching reading that is highly structured and phonetically oriented and that stresses a *multisensory approach* (visual, auditory, and kinesthetic).

POSTTEST. A terminal evaluation of the student's status on completion of specific instruction or training. *Pretests* and posttests make it easier to measure progress in the course of remedial work.

PRETEST. A preliminary test used to establish a baseline of performance in a specified area.

RATE OF READING. A speed-of-reading score comparing the time required for a student to read a selection with standard rates obtained from cases in the standardization population. Generally expressed as the number of words read per minute.

RATIO SCORE. Refers to *criterion-referenced* testing, where the score can be expressed as a ratio. The total number of skills mastered divided by the total number of skills required:

$$\frac{\text{Number of skills mastered}}{\text{Number of skills required}} = \text{Score in percent}$$

For example, if Mary has learned 180 words out of a total of 200 words on a reading test, her score would be 180/200, or 90 percent.

SCREENING. A fast, efficient measurement for a large number of students. The purpose of screening is to identify students from the general population who need further diagnostic testing because of suspected deviance in a specific area.

SEQUENCING. A distinctive, fairly automatic function of the mind related to the serial ordering of stimuli. For example, remembering a series of movements within a skill, recalling the pattern of letters in a spelling word, or remembering the sequence of sounds within a word.

STRUCTURAL ANALYSIS. Breaking a word into its component parts, such as word families, rhyming aspects, roots, prefixes, and suffixes.

TACHISTOSCOPE. An apparatus that exposes visual material for brief, controllable periods of time. Practice with this device is designed to improve rate and span of the visual perception of words and phrases.

WORD ANALYSIS. A reading term that refers to the analysis of an unlearned word in terms of known elements for the purpose of identification.

WORD RECOGNITION. Identification of a word presented in isolation, either through the use of form configuration or skill in phonetic analysis. Indicates accurate decoding ability, but does not tap knowledge of word meaning.

VISUAL AND VISUAL-PERCEPTUAL MOTOR PROCESSING

COPY. Direct reproduction of a form with a pencil. Involves the ability to look at a figure and reproduce it without any additional clues. Contrast with *imitation*.

FAR-POINT COPYING. Copying with constant access to a model placed at a distance (for example, copying from a blackboard). Requires visual perception in association with a kinesthetic-motor response. Contrast with *near-point copying*.

IMITATION. A process used in learning copying skills by demonstration. First the student watches the examiner demonstrate how to draw the form; then the student imitates the examiner's movements. Contrast with *copy*.

NEAR-POINT COPYING. Copying with constant access to a model placed close at hand (for example, copying from a textbook). Requires visual perception in association with a

kinesthetic-motor response. Usually an easier task than *far-point copying.* Contrast with *far-point copying.*
VISUAL-MOTOR INTEGRATION. The ability to associate visual stimuli with motor responses. Coordinating vision with the movements of the body or parts of the body.
VISUAL PERCEPTION. Ability to identify, organize, and understand sensory stimuli received through the eye.

ORAL LANGUAGE AND AUDITORY PROCESSING

AUDITORY PERCEPTION. Ability to identify, organize, and understand external auditory stimuli, such as environmental sounds, music, or speech.
DISTINCTIVE FEATURE. A distinguishing acoustic or articulatory feature of a *phoneme,* such as voicing, stop, nasality, or place of articulation.
DYSPHASIA. Impairment of the ability to acquire symbols for a language system. The partial or complete loss of ability to comprehend spoken words (receptive dysphasia) or to speak words (expressive dysphasia). Associated with injury, disease, or abnormality of the speech centers.
ECHOLALIA. The parrotlike, senseless repetition of sounds, words, phrases, or sentences spoken by another person, without understanding the meaning of the language.
EXPRESSIVE LANGUAGE. The ability to produce language for communication purposes. Speaking and writing are the expressive language skills.
GRAMMAR. The study of word classes, their inflections, and their functions and relationship in sentences. A part of *syntax.*
HEARING VOCABULARY. Recognition vocabulary, generally measured through a picture vocabulary test. More heavily weighted with *receptive language* than with *expressive language.* Provides a rough estimate of verbal *intelligence.*
LANGUAGE. A conventionalized system of audible and visible signs (symbols) by which thoughts are conveyed.
LINGUISTICS. The scientific study of the form and function of *language.*
MORPHEME. The smallest unit of speech that is meaningful. For example, *farm,* the *er* in *farmer,* and the *ing* in *farming* are all morphemes.
MORPHOLOGY. The aspect of *linguistics* that deals with the study of and the rules for the formation of words in any particular language (for example, the formation of plurals, possessives, and compounds).
PHONEME. The smallest unit of sound in a language. Each phoneme is made up of a set of *distinctive features.* Each individual letter sound or blend, such as /p/ or /ch/, are phonemes.
PHONOLOGY. The study of the linguistic system of speech sounds in any language.
PRAGMATICS. Rules governing the use of language in context; that is, language as communication. Such features as conversational turn-taking and topic maintenance are examples of pragmatic skills.
PSYCHOLINGUISTICS. The study of the psychological and linguistic aspects of the language process.
RECEPTIVE LANGUAGE. The ability to comprehend the spoken or written word. Listening and reading are the receptive language skills.
SEMANTICS. The study of meaning in language, including the relationship among language, thought, and behavior.
SYNTAX. The study and science of the grammar system of a language. The linguistic rules of word order and the function of words in a sentence (sentence structure).

FINE AND GROSS MOTOR SKILLS

BILATERAL INTEGRATION. Integration of the sensorimotor function of the two sides of the body, including such factors as the ability to smoothly coordinate the two hands (or two legs) in bilateral (two-sided) motor activities. The tendency to cross the midline of the body, and the ability to distinguish the right side of the body from the left.
BODY IMAGE. The concept and awareness of one's own body. Includes the impressions one receives from internal data as well as feedback resulting from contact with others.
FINE MOTOR SKILL. The development of small muscle skills (for example, the use of eye-hand coordination in cutting, writing, tying shoes, and other tasks).
GROSS MOTOR SKILL. The development of large muscle skills (for example, walking, running, climbing, throwing, and other activities).
KINESTHESIA. Movement sense. Perception of position, direction, and speed of movement of the body or part of the body. Principal receptors are in the joints, ligaments, and inner ear.
MOTOR PLANNING. See *praxis.*
POSTURAL MECHANISMS. Motor responses, generally automatic, that allow an individual to maintain a desired position in relation to gravity and the earth's surface. An example is the shifting of body weight necessary to maintain sitting balance on a moving object.
PRAXIS (Motor planning). The ability to plan and to execute unfamiliar skilled motor tasks.
SENSORY INTEGRATION. The organization of incoming sensory information by the brain. Also a specific type of perceptual-motor training.
TACTILE PERCEPTION. The ability to recognize and give meaning to sensory stimuli that are received through the sense of touch.
VESTIBULAR SYSTEM. Detects sensations related to equilibrium and position. Sensitive to both movement (linear, angular, and rotational, acceleration and deceleration) and position of the head in relation to the pull of gravity.

References

Anastasiow, Nicholas J. et al. 1973. *Educational Psychology: A Contemporary View.* Del Mar, Calif.: CRM Books.

Armstrong, Robert J., and Jensen, John A. 1981. *Slosson Intelligence Test, 1981 Norms Tables: Application and Development.* East Aurora, N.Y.: Metrics Press.

Arter, J. A., and Jenkins, J. R. 1978. Differential Diagnosis—Prescriptive Teaching: A Critical Appraisal. Center for the Study of Reading, University of Illinois: Technical Report no. 80.

Ayres, A. Jean. 1973. *Sensory Integration and Learning Disorders.* 2nd ed. Los Angeles: Western Psychological Services.

Bannatyne, Alex. 1968. Diagnosing Learning Disabilities and Writing Remedial Prescriptions. *Journal of Learning Disabilities* vol. 1.

———. 1974. Diagnosis: A Note on the Recategorization of the WISC Scaled Scores. *Journal of Learning Disabilities* vol. 7.

Bateman, Barbara. 1963. *Reading and Psycholinguistic Processes of Partially Sighted Children.* Council for Exceptional Children Monograph Series A, no. 5.

Bayley, Nancy. 1969. *Bayley Scales of Infant Development.* New York: The Psychological Corporation.

Betts, Emmett A. 1946. *Foundations of Reading Instruction.* New York: American Book Co.

Blank, Marion. 1968. Cognitive Processes in Auditory Discrimination in Normal and Retarded Readers. *Child Development* vol. 39.

Bliesmer, Emery P. 1962. Evaluating Progress in Remedial Reading Programs. *The Reading Teacher* vol. 15.

Brill, F.A. 1979. Uses and Misuses of the WRAT, Wide Range Achievement Test. Comments to National Association of School Psychologists, San Diego, California.

Brown, Roger. 1973. *A First Language: The Early Stages.* Cambridge, Mass.: Harvard University Press.

Brown, Virginia L.; Hammill, Donald D.; and Wiederholt, J. Lee. 1978. *Test of Reading Comprehension Examiner's Manual.* Austin, Texas: Pro-Ed.

Burgemeister, B.B.; Blum, L.H.; and Lorge, I. 1972. *Columbia Mental Maturity Scale* (3rd ed.). New York: Harcourt Brace Jovanovich.

Burt, Marina K.; Dulay, Heidi C.; and Chávez, Eduardo Hernández. 1975. *Rationale and Technical Report.* New York: The Psychological Corporation.

Ceci, Stephen J.; Ringstorm, Maureen; and Lea, Stephen E. G. 1981. Do Language-Learning Disabled Children (L/LD's) Have Impaired Memories? In Search of Underlying Processes. *Journal of Learning Disabilities* vol. 14, no. 3.

Chomsky, Noam. 1957. *Syntactic Structures.* The Hague: Mouton.

———. 1965. *Aspects of the Theory of Syntax.* Cambridge, Mass.: MIT Press.

Compton, C. L.: Bisagno, J.; and Tretten, S. 1979. Written Language: A Comparison of Learning Disabled and Nonlearning Disabled Children in Third, Fifth, and Seventh Grades. Presentation at the Association for Children with Learning Disabilities. San Francisco, California.

Cratty, Bryant J. 1970. *Perceptual and Motor Development in Infants and Children.* New York: Macmillan.

Curr, W., and Gorlay, N. 1960. The Effects of Practice and Performance in Scholastic Tests. *British Journal of Educational Psychology* vol. 30.

DeAvila, Edward A., and Duncan, Sharon E. 1981. *A Convergent Approach to Language Assessment: Theoretical and Technical Specifications on the Language Assessment Scales.* San Rafael, Calif.: Linguametrics Group.

de Hirsch, Katrina; Jansky, Jeanette J.; and Langford, William S. 1966. *Predicting Reading Failure.* New York: Harper & Row.

Dembinski, Raymond J., and Mauser, August J. 1977. What Parents of the Learning Disabled Really Want from Professionals. *Journal of Learning Disabilities* vol. 10.

DeRenzi, E., and Vignolo, L. 1962. The Token Test: A Sensitive Test to Detect Receptive Disturbance in Aphasics. *Brain* vol. 85.

Elkins, J. 1972. Some Psycholinguistic Aspects of the Differential Diagnosis of Reading Disability in Grades I and II. Ph.D. dissertation, University of Queensland.

Evans, Patricia R., and Peham, Mary Ann Sachs. 1981. Testing and Measurement in Occupational Therapy: A Review of Current Practice with Special Emphasis on The Southern California Sensory Integration Tests. Monograph No. 15. University of Minnesota: Institute for Research Learning Disabilities.

Farr, Roger. 1969. *Reading: What Can Be Measured?* Newark, Del.: International Reading Association Research Fund.

Ferrier, E. E. 1966. An Investigation of the ITPA Performance of Children with Functional Defects of Articulation. *Exceptional Children* vol. 32.

Fillmore, Charles. 1968. The Case for Case. In *Universals in Linguistic Theory,* edited by Emmon Bach and Robert T. Harms. New York: Holt, Rinehart and Winston.

Foster, S. 1963. Language Skills for Children with Persistent Articulation Disorders. Ph.D. dissertation, Texas Women's University.

References

Gaines, R. 1972. Review of Southern California Figure-Ground Visual Perception Test. In *Buros' Seventh Mental Measurements Yearbook*, edited by Oscar K. Buros. Highland Park, N.J.: Gryphon Press.

Gesell, Arnold, and Amatruda, Catherine S. 1949. *Gesell Developmental Schedules*. New York: The Psychological Corporation.

Gillingham, Anna, and Stillman, Bessie W. 1960. *Remedial Training for Children with Specific Language Disability in Reading, Spelling, and Penmanship*. 6th ed. Cambridge, Mass.: Educators Publishing Service.

Hallahan, Daniel P., and Cruickshank, William M. 1973. *Psychoeducational Foundations of Learning Disabilities*. Englewood Cliffs, N.J.: Prentice-Hall.

Hammill, Donald D., and Weiderholt, J. L. 1972. Review of the Frostig Visual Perception Test and the Related Training Program. In *The First Review of Special Education* vol. 1, edited by L. Mann and D. Sabatino. Philadelphia: JSE Press, Grune & Stratton.

Harris, Dale B. 1963. *Children's Drawings as Measures of Intellectual Maturity*. New York: Harcourt Brace Jovanovich.

Hessler, Gary. 1982. *Use and Interpretation of the Woodcock-Johnson Psycho-Educational Battery*. Hingham, Mass.: Teaching Resources.

Horstmeier, DeAnna S., and MacDonald, James D. 1978. *Ready, Set, Go: Talk to Me*. Columbus, Ohio: Charles E. Merrill.

Johnson, Wendell; Darley, Frederic L.; and Spriestersbach, D. C. 1963. *Diagnostic Methods in Speech Pathology*. New York: Harper & Row.

Karlin, Robert, and Jolly, Hayden. 1965. The Use of Alternate Forms of Standardized Reading Tests. *The Reading Teacher* vol. 19.

Kaufman, Nadeen L., and Kaufman, Alan S. 1974. Comparison of Normal and Minimally Brain-Dysfunctioned Children on the McCarthy Scales of Children's Abilities. *Journal of Clinical Psychology* vol. 30.

———. 1977. *Clinical Evaluation of Young Children with the McCarthy Scales*. New York: Grune & Stratton.

Keogh, Barbara, and Becker, Laurence D. 1973. Early Detection of Learning Problems: Questions, Cautions and Guidelines. *Exceptional Children* vol. 40.

Kephart, Newell C. 1960. *The Slow Learner in the Classroom*. Columbus, Ohio: Charles E. Merrill.

Kirk, Samuel A., and Kirk, Winifred D. 1971. *Psycholinguistic Learning Disabilities*. Urbana: University of Illinois Press.

———. 1978. Uses and Abuses of the ITPA. *Journal of Speech and Hearing Disorders* vol. 43.

Koppitz, Elizabeth M. 1963. *The Bender-Gestalt Test for Young Children* vol. 1. New York: Grune & Stratton.

———. 1975. *The Bender-Gestalt Test for Young Children* vol. 2. New York: Grune & Stratton.

Landis, D. 1972. Review of Southern California Perceptual Motor Tests. In *Buros' Seventh Mental Measurements Yearbook*, edited by Oscar K. Buros. Highland Park, N.J.: Gryphon Press.

Lau vs Nichols. 1975. Washington, D.C.: Department of Health, Education, and Welfare, Office for Civil Rights.

Lee, Laura, and Koenigsknecht, Roy A. 1974. *Developmental Sentence Analysis*. Evanston, Ill.: Northwestern University Press.

Lindquist, E. F., and Hieronymus, A. N. 1956. *Iowa Test of Basic Skills*. Boston: Houghton Mifflin.

Lorge-Thorndike Teacher's Word Book of 30,000 Words. 1944. New York: Teacher's College of Columbia University.

MacDonald, J. D.; Blott, J. P.; Gordon, K.; Spiegel, G.; and Hartmann, M. C. 1974. An Experimental Parent-Assisted Treatment Program for Preschool Language-Delayed Children. *Journal of Speech and Hearing Disorders* vol. 39.

Marston, D., and Ysseldyke, James. 1980. *Derived Subtest Scores from the Woodcock-Johnson Psycho-Educational Battery*. Hingham, Mass.: Teaching Resources Corporation.

Meeker, M. 1969. *The Structure of Intellect*. Columbus, Ohio: Charles E. Merrill.

Moriarity, Alice E. 1972. Denver Developmental Screening Test. In *Buros' Seventh Mental Measurements Yearbook*, edited by Oscar K. Buros. Highland Park, N.J.: Gryphon Press.

Morrissey, Patricia. 1979. Pre-Academic Predictors of Success in a Multisensory Reading Program. Ed.D. dissertation, University of San Francisco.

Myers, P. I., and Hammill, D. D. 1976. *Methods for Learning Disorders*. New York: Wiley.

Myklebust, Helmer R. 1973. *Development and Disorders of Written Language, Volume Two: Studies of Normal and Exceptional Children*. New York: Grune & Stratton.

Noll, J. D. November, 1970. The Use of the Token Test with Children. Paper presented at the Annual Convention of the Speech and Hearing Association. New York.

Osgood, Charles E. 1957. A Behavioristic Analysis. In *Contemporary Approaches to Cognition*. Cambridge, Mass.: Harvard University Press.

Osgood, Charles E., and Sebeok, T. A., eds. 1965. *Psycholinguistics*. Bloomington: Indiana University Press.

Paraskevopoulos, John, and Kirk, Samuel. 1969. *The Development and Psychometric Characteristics of the Revised Illinois Test of Psycholinguistic Abilities*. Urbana: University of Illinois Press.

Pintner, Rudolf; Cunningham, Bess V.; and Durost, Walter N. 1966. *Pintner-Cunningham Primary Test*. New York: Harcourt Brace Jovanovich.

Ratusnik, Daniel L., and Koenigsknecht, Roy A. 1975. Internal Consistency of the Northwestern Syntax Screening Test. *Journal of Speech and Hearing Disorders* vol. 40.

Reed, H. B. C. 1978. Review of Southern California Sensory Integration Tests. In *Buros' Seventh Mental Measurements Yearbook*, edited by Oscar K. Buros. Highland Park, N.J.: Gryphon Press.

Rockowitz, Ruth J., and Davidson, Phillip W. 1979. Discussing Diagnostic Findings with Parents. *Journal of Learning Disabilities* vol. 12.

Salvia, John, and Ysseldyke, James E. 1978. *Assessment in Special and Remedial Education*. Boston: Houghton Mifflin.

Salvia, John; Ysseldyke, James E.; and Lee, M. 1975. 1972 Revision of the Stanford-Binet Intelligence Scale: A Farewell to the Mental Age. *Psychology in the Schools* vol. 76.

Sattler, J. M. 1965. Analysis of Functions of the 1960 Stanford-Binet Intelligence Scale, Form L–M. *Journal of Clinical Psychology* vol. 21.

Satz, Paul; Friel, Janette; and Goebel, Ron A. 1975. Some Predictive Antecedents of Specific Reading Disability: A Three Year Follow-Up. *Bulletin of the Orton Society* vol. 25.

Sequential Tests of Basic Skills. 1958. Palo Alto, Calif.: Educational Testing Service.

Smith, Judith M.; Smith, Donald E.; and Brink, James R. 1977. *A Technology of Reading and Writing* vol. 2. New York: Academic Press.

State of California. *Assessing Pupils Suspected of Having a Specific Learning Disability*. 1982. State of California Education Code Sections 56320–56329.

Tiegs, E. W., and Clark, W. W. 1970. *California Achievement Tests*. New York: CTB/McGraw-Hill.

Toronto, Allen. 1972. A Developmental Spanish Language Analysis Procedure for Spanish-speaking Children. Ph.D. dissertation, Northwestern University.

Valett, Robert E. 1964. A Clinical Profile for the Stanford-Binet. *Journal of School Psychology* vol. 2.

Wallace, Gerald, and Larsen, Stephen C. 1978. *Educational Assessment of Learning Problems: Testing for Teaching*. Boston: Allyn and Bacon, Inc.

Wechsler, David. 1947. *Wechsler-Bellevue Intelligence Scale*. New York: The Psychological Corporation.

———. 1951. *Escala de Intelligencia Wechsler Para Niños*. New York: The Psychological Corporation.

Wepman, Joseph, and Morency, Anne. 1973a. *Auditory Memory Span Test*. Los Angeles: Western Psychological Services.

———. 1973b. *Auditory Sequential Memory Test*. Los Angeles: Western Psychological Services.

Wiig, E. H., and Semel-Mintz, E. M. 1974. Logico-Grammatical Sentence Comprehension by Learning-Disabled Adolescents. *Perceptual and Motor Skills* vol. 38.

———. 1975. Productive Language Abilities in Learning-Disabled Adolescents. *Journal of Learning Disabilities* vol. 8.

———. 1976. *Language Disabilities in Children and Adolescents*. Columbus, Ohio: Charles E. Merrill.

———. 1980. *Language Assessment and Intervention for the Learning Disabled*. Columbus, Ohio: Charles E. Merrill.

Woodcock, Richard. 1975. *Development and Standardization of the Woodcock-Johnson Psycho-Educational Battery*. Hingham, Mass.: Teaching Resources Corporation.

Index

A

A. P. Watt and Son, 286
Academic Therapy Publications, 71, 125, 182, 205
Adaptive Behavior Inventory for Children, 304, 306, 307
American Guidance Service, Inc., 22, 53, 81, 112, 155, 220, 300
American Orthopsychiatric Association, Inc., The, 130
Anastasiow, Nicholas J., 2, 7
Arena, John, 71
Armstrong, Robert J., 280, 281
Arter, A. J., 5
Arthur, Grace, 282
Assessment of Basic Skills Spanish Edition, 32
Assessment of Children's Language Comprehension, 157-158, 316, 317, 318, 328, 329
Auditory Memory Span Test, 111
Auditory Sequential Memory Span Test, 111
Ayers, A. Jean, 219, 223

B

Baker, Harry J., 93
Bannatyne, Alex, 270
Barnell Loft, Ltd., 66
Barrett, Mark, 184
Basic Achievement Skills Individual Screener, 26-28, 315, 316, 318, 320, 324
Basic School Skills Inventory, 248-250, 329
Bateman, Barbara, 144
Bayley, Nancy, 236
Bayley Infant Scales, Revised, 236, 277
Becker, Laurence D., 231
Beery, Keith E., 134
Beery-Buktenica Developmental Test of Visual-Motor Integration, 134-137, 318, 329
Bender, Lauretta, 130
Bender Visual Motor Gestalt Test, The, 6, 130-133, 137, 304, 305, 318, 320
Beringer, Marjorie L., 203
Ber-Sil Company, The, 203
Ber-Sil Spanish Test, 203-204, 329
Betts, Emmett A., 12
Bijou, S. W., 19
Bilingual Syntax Measure, 209-211, 213
Bisagno, J., 72
Blank, Marion, 111
Bliesmer, Emery P., 11
Blott, J. P., 178
Blum, L. H., 183

Boehm, Ann E., 162
Boehm Test of Basic Concepts, 162-164, 317, 318, 328, 329
Brigance, Albert H., 29, 237
Brigance Diagnostic Inventories, 8, 29-32, 315, 316, 318, 324, 328
Brigance Diagnostic Inventory of Early Development, 237-240, 329
Brigance® K and I Screen, 240
Brill, F. A., 8
Brink, James R., 4
Brown, Roger, 173
Brown, Virginia L., 8, 59, 191
Bruininks, Robert H., 220
Bruininks-Oseretsky Test of Motor Proficiency, 220-222, 329
Buktenica, Norman, 134
Burgemeister, B. B., 183
Burt, Marina K., 209, 210

C

C. H. Stoelting Company, 282
California Achievement Tests, 1
Carrow, Elizabeth, 159
Catterson, Jane H., 42
Ceci, Stephen J., 4
Charles E. Merrill Publishing Company, 148, 176, 180, 251
Chávez, Eduardo Hernández, 209, 210
Chomsky, Noam, 173
Clark, W. W., 1
Clinical Evaluation of Language Functions, 148-154, 317, 318
Colarusso, Ronald P., 125
Coloured Progressive Matrices, 286-289, 318
Compton, C. L., 72
Connolly, Austin J., 81
Consulting Psychologists Press, Inc., 118, 157
Cratty, Bryant J., 219
Crippled Children and Adults of Rhode Island, Inc., 244
Critchlow, Donald C., 205
Cruickshank, William M., 219
Curr, W., 9
Curriculum Associates, Inc., 29, 86, 237

D

Darley, Frederic L., 170
Davidson, Phillip W., 14
DeAvila, Edward A., 212, 213
de Hirsch, Katrina, 231
Del Rio Language Screening Test, 207-208, 329

Dembinski, Raymond J., 14
Denver Developmental Screening Test, 170, 233-236, 240, 281, 329
DeRenzi, E., 166
Detroit Tests of Learning Aptitude, 93-101, 188, 318
Developmental Sentence Scoring, 172-175, 317, 318, 329
Diagnostic Achievement Test in Spelling, 66-68, 316
Diagnostic Analysis of Reading Errors, 69-70, 316, 318
Diagnostic Spelling Potential Test, 71-72, 315, 316, 318
DiSimoni, Frank, 165
Dodds, Josiah, 233
Dos Amigos Verbal Language Scales, 205-206, 213
Dulay, Heidi C., 209, 210
Duncan, Sharon E., 212, 213
Dunn, Leota M., 155
Dunn, Lloyd M., 22, 155
Durrell, Donald D., 42
Durrell Analysis of Reading Difficulty, 42-45, 315, 316, 317, 324

E

Educators Publishing Service, Inc., 49, 102, 106, 257
Elkins, J., 147
Enright, Brian E., 86
Enright™ Diagnostic Inventory of Basic Arithmetic Skills, 86-90, 316
Environmental Language Inventory, 176-179, 317, 318, 329
Escala de Intelligencia Wechsler Para Niños, 267
Evans, Patricia R., 224
Expressive One-Word Picture Vocabulary Test, 182-183, 317, 318, 329

F

Farr, Roger, 11
Ferrier, E. E., 145
Fillmore, Charles, 173
Fisher-Logemann Test of Articulation Competence, The, 325, 326
Follett Publishing Company, 134
Foster, R., 157
Foster, S., 145
Foundation for Knowledge in Development, The, 241
Frankenburg, William, 233
Fristoe, M., 112
Frostig, Marianne, 118

G

Gaines, R., 224
Gardner, Morrison F., 182
Gates, Arthur, 46, 56
Gates-MacGinitie Silent Reading Tests, 9, 10, 55, 56-58, 315, 324
Gates-McKillop-Horowitz Reading Diagnostic Tests, 3, 46-48, 58, 315, 316, 324
Gesell, Arnold, 280
Gidden, J., 157
Gillespie, Jacquelyn, 69
Gillingham, Anna, 261
Gilmore, Eunice C., 36
Gilmore, John V., 36
Gilmore Oral Reading Test, 36-38, 47, 315, 320, 324
Goldman, R., 112
Goldman-Fristoe Test of Articulation, The, 325, 326
Goldman-Fristoe-Woodcock Test of Auditory Discrimination, 112-113, 116, 318
Goldsworthy, Candace, 180
Goodenough, Florence, 311
Goodenough-Harris Drawing Test, 311-313, 329
Gordon, K., 178
Gorlay, N., 9
Gray, William S., 34
Gray Oral Reading Tests, 34-35, 47, 315, 324
Grune & Stratton, Inc., 73

H

Hainsworth, Peter K., 244
Hallahan, Daniel P., 219
Hammill, Donald D., 5, 8, 59, 63, 77, 123, 125, 187, 191, 248
Hanna, C., 207
Harcourt Brace Jovanovich, Inc., 36, 42, 209, 311
Harris, Dale B., 311, 313
Hartmann, M. C., 178
Hedrick, E. Prather, 169
Hessler, Gary, 299
Hieronymus, A. N., 1
Horowitz, Elizabeth, 46
Horstmeier, DeAnna S., 177
Houghton Mifflin Company, 276
Huisingh, Rosemary, 184

I

Illinois Test of Psycholinguistic Abilities, 103, 116, 141-147, 170, 188, 199, 200, 201, 202, 317, 318, 329
Iowa Test of Basic Skills, 1

J

Jansky, Jeanette, 231
Jastak, J. F., 19
Jastak, S. R., 19
Jastak Associates, Inc., 19, 69
Jenkins, J. R., 5
Jensen, John A., 280, 281
Johnson, M. Bonner, 293
Johnson, Wendell, 170
Jolly, Hayden, 9
Jorgensen, Carol, 184

K

Karlin, Robert, 9
Kaufman, Alan S., 291, 300
Kaufman, Nadeen L., 291, 300
Kaufman Assessment Battery for Children, 300-302, 318, 329
Keogh, Barbara, 231
Kephard, Newell C., 219
KeyMath Diagnostic Arithmetic Test, 8, 81-85, 316, 322
Kirk, S. A., 141, 143, 145, 147
Kirk, W. D., 141, 142, 145, 147, 198
Koenigsknecht, Roy A., 168, 172, 173, 175, 208
Koppitz, Elizabeth M., 131, 132, 305
Koppitz Developmental Scoring System, 130, 132
Kraner, Robert E., 254
Kraner Preschool Math Inventory, 254-256, 329

L

Ladoca Project and Publishing Foundation, Inc., 233
Landis, D., 224
Langford, William S., 231
Language Assessment Scales, 212-214
Language Research Associates, 110
Larsen, Stephen C., 2, 5, 63, 77, 191, 236
Larsen-Hammill Test of Written Spelling, 25, 63-65, 78, 316
Lau vs Nichols, 210
Lea, Stephen E. G., 4
Learning Concepts, Inc., 159, 254
Lee, Laura, 167, 172, 173, 175, 208
Lee, M., 277
Lefever, Welty, 118
Leigh, James E., 248
Leiter, Russell, 282
Leiter International Performance Scale and the Arthur Adaptation, 204, 282-285, 329
Leland, Bernice, 93
Leverman, D., 207
Lewis, June F., 303

Lincoln-Oseretsky Development Scale, 221
Lindamood, Charles, 114
Lindamood, Patricia, 114
Lindamood Auditory Conceptualization Test, 114-116, 318
Lindquist, E. F., 1
Linguametrics Group, 212
Linguisystems, Inc., 184
Lorge, I., 183

M

McCarthy, Dorothea, 290
McCarthy, J. J., 141, 145
McCarthy, William G., 49
McCarthy Individualized Diagnostic Reading Inventory, 49-52, 315, 324
McCarthy Scales of Children's Abilities, 290-292, 329
MacDonald, James D., 176, 177, 178
MacGinitie, Walter, 56
McKillop, Anne, 46
Malcomesius, Neva, 106
Malcomesius Specific Language Disability Test, 106-108, 316, 318
Maldonado, A., 207
Marianne Frostig Developmental Test of Visual Perception, 3, 118-124, 318, 329
Markwardt, Frederick C., Jr., 22
Marston, D., 299
Meeker, M., 277
Meeting Street School Screening Test, The, 244-247, 329
Mercer, Jane R., 303
Merrill, Maud A., 276
Merrill Publishing Company, Charles E., 148, 176, 180, 251
Miller, Lucy J., 241
Miller Assessment for Preschoolers, 241-243, 329
Morency, Anne, 111
Moriarity, Alice E., 236
Morrissey, Patricia, 231
Motor-Free Visual Perception Test, 125-129, 318, 329
Multilevel Informal Language Inventory, 180-181, 317, 318, 329
Myers, P. I., 5
Myklebust, Helmer R., 73, 75
Myklebust Picture Story Language Test, 73-76, 78, 79, 316, 318

N

Nachtman, William, 81
National Educational Laboratory Publishers, Inc., 207
Newcomer, Phyllis L., 187
Noll, J. D., 166

Index

Northwestern Syntax Screening Test, 167-168, 197, 317, 318, 329
Northwestern University Press, 167, 172, 196

O

Osgood, Charles E., 142, 146

P

Paraskevopoulos, John, 147
Pascal and Suttell Scoring System, 130, 132
Peabody Individual Achievement Test, 22-25, 315, 316, 324
Peabody Picture Vocabulary Test—Revised, 155-156, 175, 185, 188, 192, 204, 316, 318, 329
Peham, Mary Ann Sachs, 224
Pintner-Cunningham Primary Test, 261
Pond, R. E., 251
Preschool Language Scale, 251-253, 328, 329
Pritchett, E. Milo, 81
Pro-Ed, 34, 59, 63, 77, 93, 187, 191, 248
Prueba Illinois de Habilidades Psicolinguisticas, 198-202
Psychological Corporation, The, 26, 36, 42, 162, 209, 265, 286, 290, 303, 311

R

Ratusnik, Daniel L., 168
Raven, J. C., 286
Reed, H. B. C., 225
Revised Bayley Infant Scales, 236, 277
Ringstorm, Maureen, 4
Riverside Publishing Company, The, 56
Rockowitz, Ruth J., 14
Rosenzweig, P., 207

S

Salvia, John, 2, 3, 123, 124, 147, 277
Sattler, J. M., 277
Satz, Paul, 231
Screening Test of Spanish Grammar, 175, 196-197, 329
Sebeok, T. A., 146
Semel-Mintz, Eleanor M., 148, 149, 151, 152, 153
Sequenced Inventory of Communication Development, 169-171, 317, 318, 329
Sequential Tests of Basic Skills, 1
Shohet, Jacqueline, 69
Siqueland, Marian L., 244
Slingerland, Beth, 102, 257

Slingerland Pre-Reading Screening Procedures, 103, 257-261, 329
Slingerland Screening Tests for Identifying Children with Specific Language Disability, 10, 102-105, 107, 260, 316, 318,
Slosson, Richard L., 279
Slosson Educational Publications, Inc., 279
Slosson Intelligence Test for Children and Adults, 279-281, 329
Smith, Donald E., 4
Smith, Judith M., 4
Southern California Sensory Integration Tests, 223-230, 243, 318, 329
Spache, George D., 39
Spache Diagnostic Reading Scales, 39-41, 47, 58, 315, 317, 324
Spiegel, G., 178
Spriestersbach, D. C., 170
Stanford-Binet Intelligence Scale, 204, 236, 267, 276-278, 280, 281, 284, 291, 329
Stark, J., 157
State of California, 5
Steiner, V. G., 251
Stillman, Bessie W., 261
Stoelting Company, C. H., 282
System of Multicultural Pluristic Assessment, 303-310

T

Teachers College Press, 46, 56
Teaching Resources Corporation, 114, 165, 215, 293
Templin-Darley Tests of Articulation, The, 188, 325, 327
Terman, Lewis M., 276
Test for Auditory Comprehension of Language, 159-161, 188, 317, 318, 328, 329
Test of Adolescent Language, 79, 191-194, 315, 317, 318
Test of Language Development, 79, 187-190, 192, 193, 315, 316, 317, 318
Test of Reading Comprehension, 59-61, 79, 192, 193, 315, 324
Test of Written Language, 77-79, 316, 318
Tiegs, E. W., 1
Tobin, A., 169
Token Test for Children, 165-166, 317, 318, 329
Toronto, Allen S., 175, 196, 207, 208
Tretten, S., 72

U

University of Arizona, 198
University of Illinois Press, 141
University of Washington Press, 169

V

Valett, Robert E., 277
Vignolo, L., 166
von Isser, Aldine, 198

W

Wallace, Gerald, 2, 5, 236
Watt and Son, A. P., 286
Wechsler, David, 265
Wechsler Adult Intelligence Scale, 70, 267, 275, 277
Wechsler-Bellevue Intelligence Scale, 272
Wechsler Intelligence Scale for Children—Revised, 70, 188, 204, 265-275, 277, 281, 284, 304, 305, 328
Wechsler Preschool and Primary Scale of Intelligence, 267, 275, 277, 291, 329
Wepman, Joseph M., 110, 111
Wepman Auditory Discrimination Test, 110-111, 116, 153, 188, 318
Western Psychological Services, 223
Whittlessey, John R. B., 118
Wide Range Achievement Test, 3, 8, 9, 10, 19-21, 25, 28, 72, 315, 316, 320, 324
Wiederholt, J. Lee, 8, 59, 123, 191
Wiig, Elisabeth H., 148, 149, 151, 152, 153
Wittenberg, William, 66
Woodcock, Richard W., 53, 112, 215, 293, 299
Woodcock-Johnson Psycho-Educational Battery, 216, 293-299, 302, 315, 316, 317, 318, 320, 328, 329
Woodcock Language Proficiency Battery—Spanish, 215-217
Woodcock Reading Mastery Tests, 4, 53-55, 216, 299, 315, 322, 324
Word Test, The, 184-186, 317, 318

Y

Ysseldyke, James E., 2, 3, 123, 124, 147, 277, 299

Z

Zachman, Linda, 184
Zimmerman, I. L., 251

Ministry of Education & Training
MET Library
13th Floor, Mowat Block, Queen's Park
Toronto   M7A 1L2